Mobile Cloud Visual Media Computing

Gang Hua · Xian-Sheng Hua
Editors

Mobile Cloud Visual Media Computing

From Interaction to Service

 Springer

Editors
Gang Hua
Visual Computing Group
Microsoft Research Asia
Beijing
China

Xian-Sheng Hua
Alibaba Group
Hangzhou
China

ISBN 978-3-319-34490-4   ISBN 978-3-319-24702-1 (eBook)
DOI 10.1007/978-3-319-24702-1

Springer International Publishing AG Switzerland is part of Springer Science+Business Media
(www.springer.com)

Preface

Laptop computers have become smaller and smaller, whilst smart mobile phones have been made bigger and bigger, becoming an essential part of people's daily activities. These sensor-rich devices deal with all kinds of media data, including texts, images, videos, audio, and geo-data, among others. Collectively, they form an ecosystem for multimedia acquisition, processing, communication, and presentation, which provides a lot of opportunities for new multimedia applications.

However, when developing new mobile multimedia applications, an inevitable issue is the limited capacity a smart phone can provide in terms of computing, storage, and battery life. Thanks to the great data transmission capacity and the rapid development of cloud computing technologies, it is natural to think about migrating majority of the media processing and storage to the cloud. It is this marriage of the mobile and cloud ecosystems which has provided us with such tremendous opportunities for new multimedia applications.

In 2010, observing this trend, we organized a workshop on mobile cloud media computing in conjunction with ACM Multimedia 2010. We have also led the organization of workshops on mobile vision in conjunction with CVPR and ICCV, and special issues on similar topics in International Journal of Computer Vision, and IEEE Trans. on Circuits and Systems for Video Technologies. These experiences are what motivated us to edit this book, which is intended to capture a snapshot of the state-of-the-art of this emerging field of research.

Although we intended to cover a broader set of topics, we are inevitably constrained by the limited time and availability of contributing authors. In the end, we have only covered a subset of the topics, revealing just the tip of iceberg of this active research area. In particular, this book includes work on mobile computational photography, mobile augmented reality, mobile visual search and recognition, cloud visual computing and mobile applications, and mobile multi-sensor fusion, with a wide variety of applications covering mobile assistance for the visually impaired and mobile experience sharing.

This area of research and development is fast evolving, especially considering that mobile and cloud computing and services have now become the first priority of many leading technology companies such as Microsoft, Amazon, Apple, Google, Facebook, IBM, Alibaba, Baidu, and Tencent. Therefore, it is likely that there have been many more new technologies, applications, and services developed and built upon during the publication of this book. Nevertheless, we would like the reader to use this book as a source of inspiration for new research and development, instead of just using it as a reference to the "state-of-the-art."

Last but not least, we would like to thank our families for their support in the process of putting this book together. Gang Hua especially would like to dedicate this book to his wife, Yan Gao, and daughter, Kayla Hua. The book would not have been possible without their support. We hope you enjoy this book, and of course, we welcome your feedback/suggestions/comments!

Seattle, WA, USA   Gang Hua
September 2015   Xian-Sheng Hua

Contents

Contributors

Harsh Agrawal Virginia Tech, Blacksburg, VA, USA

Prakriti Banik Virginia Tech, Blacksburg, VA, USA

Dhruv Batra Virginia Tech, Blacksburg, VA, USA

Neelima Chavali Virginia Tech, Blacksburg, VA, USA

K.T. Tim Cheng Department of Electrical and Computer Engineering, University of California, Santa Barbara, CA, USA

Victor Fragoso West Virginia University, Morgantown, USA

Yash Goyal Virginia Tech, Blacksburg, VA, USA

Kristen Grauman University of Texas at Austin, Austin, TX, USA

Christopher Ham Robotics Institute, Carnegie Mellon University, Pittsburgh, PA, USA

Xian-Sheng Hua Alibaba Group, Hangzhou, Zhejiang Province, China

Hongrui Jiang University of Wisconsin, Engineering Hall, Madison, WI, USA

Ayman Kaheel Yahoo Inc., Sunnyvale, CA

Hongzhi Li Deptartment of Computer Science, Columbia University, New York, NY, USA

Jia Li Department of Statistics, The Pennsylvania State University, University Park, PA, USA

Jin Li Microsoft Research, Redmond, WA, USA

Zhu Li Samsung Research America, Richardson, TX, USA

Jie Liu Microsoft Research, Redmond, WA, USA

Simon Lucey Robotics Institute, Carnegie Mellon University, Pittsburgh, PA, USA

Clint Solomon Mathialagan Virginia Tech, Blacksburg, VA, USA

Akrit Mohapatra Virginia Tech, Blacksburg, VA, USA

Abhishek Nagar Samsung Research America, Richardson, TX, USA

Ahmed Osman Imperial College London, London, UK

Travis Portz Amazon.com, Seattle, WA, USA

Motaz El Saban Microsoft Technology & Research, Advanced Technology Lab, Cairo, Egypt

Mohammed Shoaib Microsoft Research, Redmond, WA, USA

Surya Singh Robotics Design Lab, University of Queensland, Brisbane, QLD, Australia

Brandon M. Smith Computer Sciences Department, University of Wisconsin, Madison, WI, USA

Yingli Tian The City College of New York, New York, NY, USA

Matthew Turk University of California, Santa Barbara, USA

Swagath Venkataramani School of ECE, Purdue University, West Lafayette, IN, USA

James Z. Wang College of Information Sciences andTechnology, The Pennsylvania State University, University Park, PA, USA

Bo Xiong University of Texas at Austin, Austin, TX, USA

Xin Yang Department of Electronics and Information Engineering, Huazhong University of Science and Technology, Wuhan, Hubei, China

Lei Yao Houzz Inc., Palo Alto, CA, USA

Chucai Yi The City College of New York, New York, NY, USA

Junsong Yuan School of Electrical and Electronic Engineering, Nanyang Technological University, Singapore, Singapore

Li Zhang Google, Seattle, WA, USA

Gangqiang Zhao School of Electrical and Electronic Engineering, Nanyang Technological University, Singapore, Singapore

Zejia Zheng Michigan State University, East Lansing, MI, USA

Shengqi Zhu Google, Mountain View, CA, USA

Part I
Mobile Augmented Reality

Chapter 1
Computer Vision for Mobile Augmented Reality

Matthew Turk and Victor Fragoso

Abstract Mobile augmented reality (AR) employs computer vision capabilities in order to properly integrate the real and the virtual, whether that integration involves the user's location, object-based interaction, 2D or 3D annotations, or precise alignment of image overlays. Real-time vision technologies vital for the AR context include tracking, object and scene recognition, localization, and scene model construction. For mobile AR, which has limited computational resources compared with static computing environments, efficient processing is critical, as are consideration of power consumption (i.e., battery life), processing and memory limitations, lag, and the processing and display requirements of the foreground application. On the other hand, additional sensors (such as gyroscopes, accelerometers, and magnetometers) are typically available in the mobile context, and, unlike many traditional computer vision applications, user interaction is often available for user feedback and disambiguation. In this chapter, we discuss the use of computer vision for mobile augmented reality and present work on a vision-based AR application (mobile sign detection and translation), a vision-supplied AR resource (indoor localization and post estimation), and a low-level correspondence tracking and model estimation approach to increase accuracy and efficiency of computer vision methods in augmented reality.

1.1 Introduction

Augmented reality (AR) provides a live experience of the physical world with computer-generated augmentation appropriate to the location and particular task at hand. The augmentation is often specific textual information (e.g., the name of a nearby person or the date of a building's construction), location or geometric information (e.g., outlining or marking the destination building or door), or a virtual entity

M. Turk (✉)
University of California, Santa Barbara, USA
e-mail: mturk@cs.ucsb.edu

V. Fragoso
West Virginia University, Morgantown, USA
e-mail: victor.fragoso@mail.wvu.edu

© Springer International Publishing Switzerland 2015
G. Hua and X.-S. Hua (eds.), *Mobile Cloud Visual Media Computing*,
DOI 10.1007/978-3-319-24702-1_1

(e.g., an animated character or an advertisement placed appropriately in the scene). This information may be delivered by several different modalities or channels, such as audio (speech or sound directed individually to the user), video (through a display screen or another way of projecting imagery to the user), haptics (touch-based interaction), or other means. While AR may include a wide range of technologies, modalities and devices, the most typical AR systems aim to provide visual information through a transparent (optical see-through) or video see-through display—perhaps delivered via a smartphone or a head-mounted device.

In order to properly deliver spatial information, an AR system needs to know the location of the user and device either coarsely or precisely, depending on the application and the type of augmentation. In Sect. 1.3, we present research in pose estimation and localization for indoor environments. Many AR systems have used easily recognizable visual markers placed in the scene to aid tracking and localization (e.g., [25, 49]). However, this limits AR to structured environments, and most recent work in the field has sought to avoid this restriction. In the most demanding case, the precise position of the camera sensor is required, along with an accurate geometric and photometric model of the user's environment, in order to deliver artifact-free annotations that appear well integrated with the visual scene. Real-time, artifact-free mobile augmented reality with nontrivial models for augmentation is still a significant research challenge. Small errors can easily translate to significant misalignments, which are especially noticeable over time as a graphical overlay jitters with respect to the underlying scene. In some AR applications, apparent jitter can be reduced by using thick lines, temporal filtering, good annotation design, and other mechanisms, but misalignment remains a limiting factor in most augmented reality systems.

Markerless AR systems rely on low-level tracking and modeling techniques [20] to build 3D models and compute the camera position and orientation with respect to a known coordinate system. Typical approaches start with feature detection and description, then match features from frame to frame, using known geometric constraints to build a (often sparse) model comprising 3D locations of keypoints and the pose of the camera with respect to the model. While these are all areas that have been long studied in the computer vision field, augmented reality brings a different set of constraints and demands to the problem, which has led to practical solutions that are well-matched to the AR context (e.g., [26, 50]). In Sect. 1.4, we present work on keypoint correspondences and model estimation that aims to improve the accuracy, speed, and robustness of vision-based tracking and modeling.

To create a model of a full workspace or large area, low-level tracking and modeling techniques must handle issues that arise when synthesizing multiple portions of a scene, when combining rotational motion with more general (rotational + translational) motion, when closing the loop on a scene (returning to a portion previously modeled), and other challenging issues. In recent years, much progress has been made in systems that provide SLAM (simultaneous localization and mapping) capabilities for mobile robots, micro aerial vehicles, and AR applications. While beyond the scope of this chapter, our work in live tracking and mapping for both rotation-only and general motion [21] may be helpful in merging models and avoiding undesired calibration procedures in consumer AR applications.

Some augmented reality applications focus on objects in the camera's field of view than on (or in addition to) general scene geometry, providing information about objects of interest or giving a user the ability to interact with a virtual representation of the object. For example, someone playing an augmented game may indicate an object for the virtual character to go to, or a consumer may select an object to get additional information (such as vendor and price) that may float above the object in the AR display. In Sect. 1.2, we describe a system for automatic sign translation, which augments the scene by replacing the text of a sign by its translation, while displaying the appropriate sign geometry and background colors.

Given the impressive advances in recent years in mobile computing hardware and devices and in computer vision algorithms for tracking, modeling, and recognition, in addition to the rapid maturity of mobile computing ecosystems and a tremendous consumer demand for mobile devices and applications—not to mention the captivating futuristic portrayals in film and television—the field of mobile augmented reality has captured the imagination of many and is poised to become a mainstream technology for entertainment, productivity, learning, and other important areas. However, much progress is still needed in order to deliver the high-quality experience that is envisioned. This chapter describes a few efforts toward this goal of improved vision-based AR technologies to support compelling user experiences.

1.2 Sign Translation

One compelling augmented reality application is the translation of text in natural scenes (or sign translation) using a mobile device; see Fig. 1.1 for an illustration. This application, besides being useful when traveling abroad, imposes interesting and challenging mobile computer vision problems: text detection, visual tracking, and character recognition, among others. To guarantee a satisfactory user experience, the application must solve these problems as efficiently and quickly as possible.

With these constraints in mind, we developed TranstlatAR [17], a translation system that uses the camera and the touchscreen of a mobile device. The system identifies the words of interest from the live camera stream and presents the translation as an AR overlay which seamlessly replaces the original text in the live camera stream, matching background and foreground colors estimated from the source images. In the following sections, we describe the translation system as well as an automatic text detector tailored for this system.

1.2.1 Overview of the System

TranslatAR's architecture, shown in Fig. 1.2, was designed such that all the expensive operations run in the background thread, while the system maintains interactive frame rates for tracking and augmentation. In the following sections, we describe several

Fig. 1.1 *Top row* TranslatAR in operation. The user detects the text he or she wishes to translate and taps on it (*top left*). The system automatically detects the extent of the text, extracts the letters via OCR, and produces a translation, which is then presented as a live augmented reality (AR) overlay (*top right*). *Bottom row* TranslatAR used in two other situations

components in the system, such as the text detection algorithm, text extraction and recognition, the translation, the visual tracking, and the translation overlay process.

1.2.2 Text Detection

The goal of the text detection component is to compute an accurate bounding box enclosing the sign to translate. This computed bounding box is important to initialize the visual tracker as well as to extract the text via OCR.

The original text detection algorithm implemented in the system required the user to tap on the text of interest; the user's input enabled the text detection process to be efficient given the computational resources of a mobile device. Thus, given a point c onto which the user tapped, the system first finds the bounding box around the text, then the exact location and orientation of the text within. This process is illustrated in Fig. 1.3 and is explained in the following sections.

Bounding box. To find approximate upper and lower text boundaries, first the image gradients I_x and I_y are computed. A short horizontal line segment s_h around the input point c is then moved vertically upward and downward, respectively, until the following criterion is met (for δ_y consecutive scanlines):

$$\max_{(x,y)\in s_h} |I_x(x, y)| < \varepsilon, \tag{1.1}$$

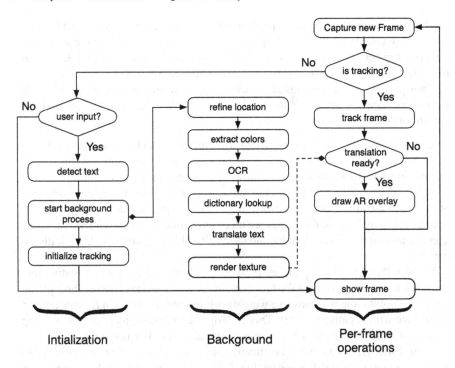

Fig. 1.2 Architecture of TranslatAR: Initialization and per-frame operations run in the main thread, while the rest of the operations are executed in the background

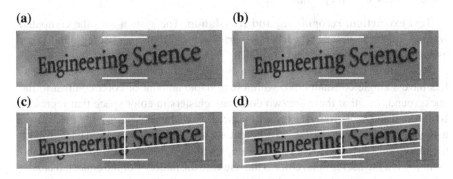

Fig. 1.3 Text detection in operation after the user's tap. First, the vertical extent of the text is determined (**a**). Subsequently, using the assumed text height, the horizontal extent is estimated (**b**). A constrained and modified Hough transform is used to estimate the baseline and orientation (**c**), and finally, the area is expanded to account for ascenders and descenders (**d**)

that is, until the segment s_h does not cross any vertical edges. The example in Fig. 1.3a shows the final upper and lower location of s_h. The same process is applied to compute the left and right boundaries, sweeping a vertical line segment s_v over I_y. The algorithm uses knowledge obtained in the first step by making the length of

s_v relative to the distance between upper and lower s_h (i.e., the estimated text height). Here, the required width of the "gap" δ_x is set slightly larger so that the algorithm does not stop between letters. The result of this process is shown in Fig. 1.3b. Values for ε, δ_x, δ_y, and the lengths of s_h and s_v were obtained experimentally.

Though fast and simple, this approach is able to detect an approximate bounding box in many conditions. However, it is susceptible to fail for very nonuniform backgrounds.

Location and orientation refinement. To detect the exact location and orientation of the upper and lower "baselines" of the text, the algorithm applies a constrained and modified Hough transform as follows: First, only pixels within the bounding box are considered, and only lines that cross the vertical line through c at an angle of $\pm 15°$ are taken into account. This reduces the computational cost considerably, ensures that only "reasonable" lines are taken as candidates for baselines, and leverages the assumption/limitation that the user will hold the phone roughly parallel to the text.

Second, the algorithm optimizes the voting scheme for the task of finding text baselines as follows: horizontal edges (i.e., in I_y) vote for lines passing through the respective point (vote with positive weight), while vertical edges (in I_x) vote against them (vote with negative weight). This is designed so that the ideal line goes along horizontal edges while cutting few or no vertical edges. The result can be seen in Fig. 1.3c. Finally, lines are moved vertically until no edge intersections are detected to account for ascenders and descenders (Fig. 1.3d). The resulting quadrilateral region of interest is warped into a rectangle, correcting any perspective distortion and showing the text as if seen orthogonally.

Text extraction, recognition, and translation. The system uses the computed warped image as described earlier to perform background and foreground color estimation and to "read" the text via OCR.

We begin describing the color estimation. The algorithm assumes that the letters have a single constant color with a reasonable amount of color contrast to the background, i.e., that there are two dominant clusters in color space that represent foreground and background. They are extracted from the subsampled rectified image using K-Means [1] with $k = 2$. To differentiate between foreground and background, the algorithm retrieves a few labeled samples along the left and right borders and assumes that the background color is the one with the majority of the collected labels; this is justified as the detection algorithm automatically includes a small margin.

This approach estimates both colors very accurately and fast when the assumptions are met. It can fail for very nonuniform backgrounds when there are significant specularities on the letters. However, in such cases, one of the other components (detection, OCR) is likely to fail, and though improving the user experience, the color estimation is not crucial to the operation.

The system relies on a standard OCR system for extraction and recognition of the letters and uses the warped image containing the word of interest for this task. The system used Tesseract [45], as it is freely available and was easy to integrate. As bad text detection frequently causes the OCR to return spurious, non-alphanumeric characters (such as punctuation marks), the system computes the ratio of alphanumeric characters to all characters in the string as a rough indicator of successful extraction.

The following (optional) step was motivated by preliminary tests with the OCR which showed that single letters were frequently misrecognized. With a string returned from the OCR, the system searches through a dictionary of valid words to identify the nearest neighbor with respect to the Levenshtein distance [32]. The Levenshtein distance to the found string is computed for each dictionary word within ±2 of the length of the found string, and the word with the smallest distance is taken as replacement for the original string returned by the OCR. This implementation clearly docs not scale to large dictionaries and is only meant as proof-of-concept add-on.

With the extracted string, the system uses Google Translate API,[1] an existing free online translation service, to do the actual text-to-text translation. The input language is detected automatically by Google Translate, and the desired output language can be selected by the user in our GUI.

1.2.3 Visual Tracking and AR Overlay

Visual tracking enables the system to keep track of the word of interest in the live video stream and to present the translation in a live AR-style overlay. Fortunately, several circumstances make tracking in our application easier than in the general case: (1) it can be assumed that the text is displayed on a near-to-planar surface, (2) as the region of interest consists of text, it is automatically well-textured and contains features with high contrast, which is important for tracking, (3) the system is only required to track over short periods of time (as long as it takes the system to obtain the translation and the user to read it), (4) the system assumes a "cooperative" user who will not move the phone jerkily.

The application implemented a tracking system based on ESM [4], in which an image region is tracked by iteratively minimizing the difference between a reference frame (the template) and the current frame over a warp transformation. In other words, the tracker computes a warp that aligns the template image onto the current frame. Though costly for large intra-frame movements and/or large image templates, in our case (due to the above constraints), it provides sufficiently fast and robust tracking even for a relatively small template.

Based on the transformation computed by the tracker, a graphical augmentation is rendered onto the live video screen; first the bounding box is displayed while the text is being translated, and then, as soon as it becomes available, the translation itself is seamlessly augmented in the live stream.

---

[1]https://developers.google.com/translate/.

1.2.4 Implementation Details

The system was implemented on the Nokia N900 smartphone, which is based on a TI OMAP 3430 SoC with a 600 MHz ARM Cortex A8 CPU and runs the Linux-based operating system Maemo. The application was developed in C++, using OpenCV and libCVD for computer vision tasks (processing frames of size 320 × 240), GStreamer for frame capture, and Qt for the GUI, which consists of a large viewfinder and a few buttons for configuration (e.g., language selection).

The ESM tracker was implemented from scratch using libCVD. It uses a down-sampled grayscale version of the warped rectangular text bounding box as a template and the respective previous frames homography as initial estimate for the 8-degree-of-freedom alignment. The graphical augmentation was implemented in OpenGL ES 2, leveraging the device's GPU; the translated text is rendered with OpenCV and then passed to the vertex shader along with the transformation estimated by the tracker, and finally the fragment shader renders the texture onto the current frame. HTTP requests to and responses from Google's online translation service are handled with the curl library,[2] a library for transferring data using various protocols.

1.2.5 Evaluation

Runtime. Table 1.1 presents an overview of the execution times of the main system components on the N900. As the expensive steps are offloaded into a background thread, the system maintains interactive frame rates for tracking and live feedback throughout the computation. The application achieved a frame rate of about 26 fps.

Text detection. To evaluate the text localization method [17], we used the ICDAR 2003 detection dataset. This dataset contains 251 images of varying size with at least one word in each image. Ground truth is provided in the form of a horizontal bounding box for each word.

As the algorithm was designed to work with video frames of a fixed size, the images were resized to 320 × 240 pixels. To conduct automated evaluation, the experiment simulated the required user input: the starting point c. This point was calculated/simulated as the center of the rectangle provided by the dataset, and it was adjusted properly to the new dimensions. As the dataset only provides an enclosing horizontal rectangle, and since the algorithm computes the (more accurate) quadrilateral, we calculated the minimal enclosing horizontal rectangle to be able to compare against the provided ground truth.

The performance measures proposed by Lucas [35] are based on a matching score m_p between two text area rectangles, which is defined as the area of the intersection divided by the area of the minimum bounding box containing both rectangles. m_p is 1 for two identical rectangles and 0 for nonintersecting pairs.

---

[2]Libcurl is available at http://curl.haxx.se/.

Table 1.1 Average execution times on the Nokia N900 for the main steps of the processing pipeline in TranslatAR

Component	Time (ms)
Initialization upon input	
Find text bounding box	71.0
Initialize tracker	5.0
Background thread	
Text location refinement	414
Extract colors	10
OCR	630
Render translation texture	10
Per-frame operations	
Capture and preprocess frame	21.9
Tracking	8.5
Render AR overlay and display frame	7.7
Total per-frame	38.1

With the expensive steps offloaded into a background thread, the system maintains a frame rate of about 26 fps

For automatic detectors, there will not be a unique 1:1 matching between detected and ground truth areas, hence the respective best m_p for each detected and ground truth area is taken and subsequently averaged to yield precision and recall, respectively. Different values for precision and recall thus result from detecting too many or too few areas, but no distinction is made between too large and too small areas. However, due to the manual "seeding" of the algorithm, there is guaranteed to be a 1:1 matching, and therefore the ICDAR definition of precision and recall both default to the average m_p for our algorithm. For further analysis, we also calculated pixel-wise precision and recall (e.g., as used by Park and Jung [39]), i.e., the ratio of pixels correctly labeled as text versus all pixels labeled as text, and the ratio of pixels correctly labeled as text versus all text pixels.

To optimize the parameters of the algorithm, we used the training part of the ICDAR set, then evaluated the metrics on the test part. The obtained are pixel-wise precision and recall of 31 and 68 %, respectively, and an average $m_p =$ ICDAR precision of 41 %. This falls within the middle range of values published by Lucas [35], but cannot compete with the best scoring algorithms described by Lucas [35] and Epshtein et al. [14], which achieve precision and recall values of 60–70 %. It should be noted that the described algorithm requires a single point as input, while the other algorithms are fully automatic, but also that the described algorithm runs in less than 0.5 s on a mobile device and is hence one to two orders of magnitude faster than the aforementioned algorithms (see timings in [14, 35]).

A few examples of good and bad detection are shown in Fig. 1.4. The algorithm is prone to "overshoot" all the way to the borders of the image for nonuniform backgrounds, but it rarely cuts off letters. Note that the latter error is more fatal in our application than the former (in which case the OCR still has a chance to ignore the extra parts).

Fig. 1.4 Examples of good (*top* and *mid rows*) and bad (*bottom row*) text localization on the ICDAR 2003 dataset. The *blue point* in each quadrilateral represents the (simulated) input of the user. TranslatAR's algorithm was able to very accurately detect the text at different scales and under perspective distortion. The failure cases are mostly due to very nonuniform background and/or lighting effects (first two). For very large letters, the expansion algorithm used to detect the texts bounding box can stop inside one of the letters (*bottom right*)

Table 1.2 Reasons of failure of the detection-extraction-translation process on a set of 30 video clips

Component	No. of words	% of failures	% of all
Detector failed	7	16.3	8.9
Color est. failed	6	14.0	7.6
OCR	26	60.8	32.9
Translation	4	9.3	5.1
Correct result	36 of 79	–	45.6

If one component fails, the later components are not evaluated—e.g., the OCR failed 26 times, although detector and color estimation delivered a good result

Component test. We used our own set of 30 video clips of various outdoor signs, each containing several words, to further test the system as a whole and determine which components cause failures. Here, both providing the user input as well as evaluating the result was done manually. The results are listed in Table 1.2. As emerges from the table, the OCR is the most common cause of failure, while the detector works correctly in 72 out of 79 cases.

1.2.6 Automatic Text Detection

To enhance the user experience in the mobile AR translation systems, we developed an automatic text detection algorithm (see Petter et al. [41] for full details). In order to offer a fast automatic text detector, we focused in finding a single letter. The algorithm was designed on the following premise: detecting one letter provides useful information that is processed with efficient rules to quickly find the reminder of a word. This approach allows for detecting all the contiguous text regions in an image quickly. Moreover, the algorithm presented a method that exploits the redundancy of the information contained in the video stream to remove false alarms; see Fig. 1.5 for an illustration of this automatic text detection algorithm.

The general structure of the algorithm is shown in Fig. 1.6. The algorithm works on a grayscale image and can be overall described into three main steps: (1) Localize a first potential letter (zone of interest); (2) Verify that a letter was found; (3) Find the rest of the word based on the found letter.

Step 1: Finding a Zone of Interest

The aim of this step is to find a zone of interest that may contain a letter. The approach is based on existing methods [19, 33, 51] because of their efficiency and good performance. These methods leverage the high rate of edges contained in text

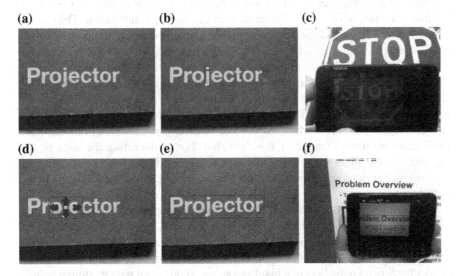

Fig. 1.5 Automatic text detection for TranslatAR. The algorithm scans the input image (**a**) until it finds a zone of interest that contains text (**b**). Subsequently, the algorithm expands the zone of interest with efficient rules (**d**), and finally, our method produces the final bounding box (**e**). Final bounding box with real examples (*right-most column*)

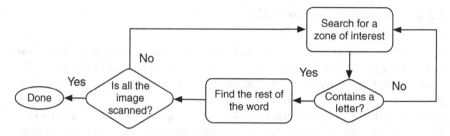

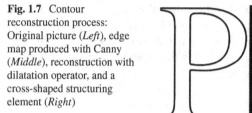

Fig. 1.6 Overview of the automatic text detection

Fig. 1.7 Contour
reconstruction process:
Original picture (*Left*), edge
map produced with Canny
(*Middle*), reconstruction with
dilatation operator, and a
cross-shaped structuring
element (*Right*)

areas. Therefore, a potential letter can be found on an edge map by building objects composed of closed contours that later can be categorized as letter or non-letter. In the following paragraphs, we explain in more detail the building blocks of this step.

Prior to detecting edges, a Gaussian smoothing filter of size 5×5 pixels is applied to reduce noise that could cause errors in further computation. The Canny edge detector [8] is used for producing a binary map indicating the presence per-pixel of every edge. This edge detector is efficient and provides accurate results which makes it suitable for our purpose.

The original image is sometimes too blurry for edges to be detected. Thus, some shapes, including letters, could be overlooked by the edge detection and not appear in the edge map (see Fig. 1.7). To ensure the continuity of the contour, a preprocessing step is necessary before starting the contour building step. Avoiding this step can produce an incorrect contour by the algorithm. For reconnecting the edge pixels together, we use dilation, a binary morphological tool. For our implementation, a cross-shaped structuring element of pixel size 3 worked the best for filling the holes in the contours.

The algorithm starts scanning from left to right and top to bottom to find an edge pixel in the binary map. When an edge pixel is found, the contour of the object containing this pixel is built with an 8-connectivity connected component algorithm. The 8-connectivity algorithm [10] is a region-based segmentation algorithm which checks the 8-pixel neighbors of a pixel and connects this pixel with its similar neighbors. Information about the bounding box containing the computed contour, such as height, width, position of the centroid, etc., is available as an outcome of this step.

Step 2: Determining if a Letter Was Found

The main intention of this step is to verify whether or not the zone of interest actually contains a character. This task is not straightforward, as the words contained on billboards, road signs, or books have different sizes or fonts which make learning precise shapes of letters a challenging task. However, since signs are typically meant to be easily readable, discriminating text regions from non-text regions with geometric information should be possible.

A Support Vector Machine (SVM) and a set of image features are adopted to accomplish the discriminating task. SVMs are widely used in the literature (e.g., [28, 52]) and are quite useful for binary categorization tasks. SVMs have a strong mathematical foundation and provide a simple geometric explanation of their classification.

In order to select the best features to address this discrimination task, experiments were conducted for evaluating several combinations of image features. The most effective features found were the First-Order Moments (FOM)

$$FOM_1 = \sum_x \sum_y xI(x, y) \tag{1.2}$$

$$FOM_2 = \sum_x \sum_y yI(x, y), \tag{1.3}$$

and Second-Order Moments (SOM) normalized with the number of pixels on the contour (NB),

$$SOM_1 = \frac{\sum_x \sum_y x^2 I(x, y)}{NB} \tag{1.4}$$

$$SOM_2 = \frac{\sum_x \sum_y y^2 I(x, y)}{NB}, \tag{1.5}$$

where x, y are the coordinates of the pixel in the clipped zone of interest and $I(x, y)$ denotes the intensity of the pixel.

Step 3: Finding the Rest of the Word

In order to robustly find the rest of the word given the position of the first letter, we combined two features that provide information about the surrounding characters: image intensities and the edge map. These features determine when to stop scanning in the surrounding areas, and therefore, to determine the spatial extent of the bounding box.

Given the first letter of the word or phrase to be detected, the background and foreground intensities in the grayscale domain can be extracted. We can safely assume in most cases that each word is contained in a homogeneous colored background and the letters have approximately the same intensity; we can then infer the intensity and find the remaining letters. The K-Means algorithm with k $= 2$ is used to find the two intensities. In order to know which intensity corresponds to the letter, we create a second bounding box with the same center as the first bounding box of the zone of interest. The width and height of the new bounding box are computed as follows: width$_2 =$ width $+ \delta w$ and height$_2 =$ height $+ \delta h$, where $\delta h = \delta w = 2$ pixels (see Fig. 1.8). The pixels on the perimeter of that new box are likely to be background elements, and therefore, the closest intensity to the mean of those perimeter pixels is chosen to be the intensity of the background. Consequently, the remaining intensity is attributed to the letter.

Edge pixels around the found letter are likely to be part of the rest of the word because text regions present a high edge density. Useful information to estimate the position of the remaining letters is extracted from the adjacent edge pixels of the zone of interest.

In order to speed up the full word bounding box computation, the algorithm scans the image horizontally with three line segments. A single line segment is positioned on top, middle, and bottom of the found characters bounding box. Each segment is then scanned on the left and right side of the zone of interest considering a gap of size s on every side. The algorithm looks for pixels with intensities similar to the letters intensity along the segment. Edge pixels that are present in the analyzed gap are considered simultaneously. In this manner we guarantee that in fact we are likely to see pixels representing letters on the image. The size of the gap used in our algorithm is calculated as follows: $s = 1.1 \times H$, where H is the height of the found letter. The size as a function of the height allows us to consider the breach that exists between two adjacent characters in a word. However, when such breach is less than $1.1 \times H$, the algorithm considers both adjacent words as a single word. The procedure is applied until no edge pixels are detected or no similar intensity is found in the analyzed gap of every line segment. As an outcome of this procedure we obtain the width of the bounding box.

To find the height boundaries, the algorithm scans pixels along horizontal line segments with lengths equals to the computed bounding box widths described earlier (see Fig. 1.9a). The algorithm scans these lines following the same pixel criteria of intensities and edges used earlier. The algorithm moves the lines up and down until this criteria is fulfilled.

The combination of these two procedures computes a rectangular bounding box that encloses the letters of a certain text in the analyzed image (see Fig. 1.9b). Scanning with three horizontal parallel line segments tolerates a certain perspective

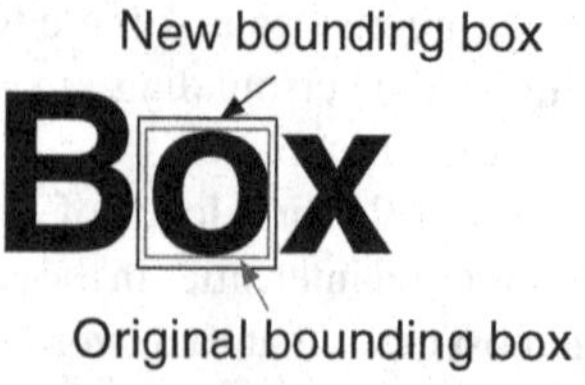

Fig. 1.8 Method to find the intensity of the background. A second box is created and the mean of the intensity of the pixels on the perimeter of the new box is associated to the background

New bounding box

Original bounding box

(a)   **(b)**

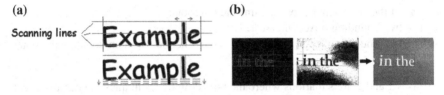

Fig. 1.9 *Left* Horizontal and vertical scanning to find letter pixels (intensity or edge pixels). Gaps of size *s* are analyzed between the letters during the procedure. *Right* Considering only information from edges (*left*) or intensity (*middle*) can determine an incorrect bounding box. Combining both features produces a better bounding box (*right*). **a** Scanning lines. **b** Bounding box computation

distortion of the letters that compose the word. However, the produced bounding box computed with these procedures may be slightly larger or smaller than the minimum bounding box due to noise present in the image.

Once a word is found, the search for additional words in the image continues until every pixel of the image not part of a word bounding box has been scanned.

Filtering False Alarms by Leveraging Temporal Information from Video Stream

An additional step is applied when the algorithm is used on a video stream, which is the case in an augmented reality translation system. In order to keep track of stable text regions and remove false alarms as much as possible, the algorithm leverages the temporal information that we can obtain from the video stream. We are interested in tracking these stable text regions. Since the scene does not change much from frame to frame, assuming that the frames on the video stream are generated at a high frame rate, the stable regions repeat and the position and area of the true positives detected bounding boxes does not vary much; therefore, false alarms will behave more unstably in this sense. The stability of these correct bounding boxes allows the algorithm to remove a fair amount of false positives.

The algorithm retains the center position and the area of the detected bounding boxes on the first frame. On subsequent frames, the system redetects the bounding boxes and matches them with the previously seen boxes based on areas and centroids. For every retained bounding box we increment a counter c if the bounding box matches a previously seen region, and decremented if it is not seen. A bounding box is considered to be stable if $c > 1$.

There are three different cases for matching that occur when comparing two bounding boxes (see Fig. 1.10):

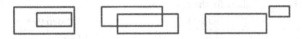

Fig. 1.10 Considered cases when comparing bounding boxes: Inclusion (*left*), Intersection (*middle*), and Disjunction (*right*)

1. One of the bounding boxes contains the other one.
2. The two bounding boxes intersect.
3. The two bounding boxes do not intersect and neither of them contains the other one.

Cases 1 and 2 are situations where the bounding boxes in question can represent the same word. In order to know which case correspond to two bounding boxes, the positions of their upper left and lower right corners are compared. Once two bounding boxes are considered to be potentially the same word, further aspects are analyzed in order to determine a match.

To determine a match for the first case 1 the algorithm evaluates the ratio r between the smallest area and the biggest area. A match is determined if $r > 0.7$. For the second case, the algorithm evaluates the absolute value of the displacement of the centers $c_1 = (x_1, y_1)$ and $c_2 = (x_2, y_2)$, i.e., $\delta x = |x_1 - x_2|$ and $\delta y = |y_1 - y_2|$, as well as the ratio of the areas used in the first case. The method declares a match considering the following criteria: $\delta x < \varepsilon_x$, $\delta y < \varepsilon_y$, and $r > 0.7$, where $\varepsilon_x = 0.35 \times$ width, $\varepsilon_y = 0.35 \times$ height (the height and width correspond to the smallest bounding box). Subsequently, the algorithm averages the centroids and areas of the matching bounding boxes in order to keep track of the box on the remaining frames.

Evaluation

We carried out a series of experiments in order to thoroughly evaluate the text detection algorithm and the integration of this method with TranslatAR.

We created our own dataset to test the algorithm in a more realistic context, i.e., low-resolution, mobile camera, and others. This dataset comprises 400 images, each containing a single word from natural scene which follow the assumptions made for this project (see Sect. 1.2.6), and 400 non-text images.

In order to evaluate the performance of the proposed method, we evaluated every outcome manually, and the outcome was labeled as successful if all the letters of the word were contained in the bounding box. The results of this experiment are reported in Table 1.3.

Table 1.3 Accuracy of the automatic text detector

True positives (%)	False positives (%)	Precision (%)	Recall (%)	f-score (%)
87	41	68	87	76

Table 1.4 Distribution of failure for the missed words

1st step (%)	2nd step (%)	3rd step (%)
4.57	81.04	14.39

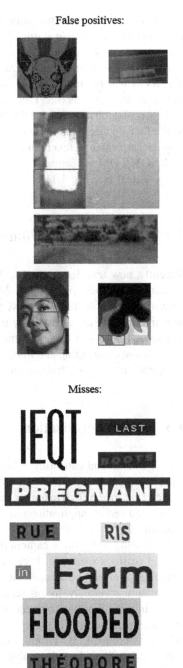

Fig. 1.11 Words correctly detected (*left*) and failures (*right*)

The algorithm found the majority of the words; however, it is also susceptible to a substantial rate of false alarms. By analyzing the failures, both missing words and false alarms, we concluded that the main problem occurs when verifying the zone of interest (i.e., the second step, see Sect. "Step 2: Determining if a Letter Was Found"). The SVM was the most common source of failure for the case of false negatives, failing to detect words (see Table 1.4).

It was also observed that false alarms arise in images with high edge densities, as the first step declares those regions as zones of interest and therefore the second step declares them as text regions. Moreover, another observation was that the SVM with SOM/FOM as features tends to declare any symmetrical non-text region in an image as text (see Fig. 1.11).

1.2.7   Discussion and Future Work

Recently, new text detection [24, 37, 38] and extraction [5, 29] in natural scenes algorithms and new powerful mobile devices have become available. Thus, these algorithms can potentially improve the performance of the text detection and extraction significantly as long as they run efficiently on a mobile device. As shown in this section, the OCR (or text extraction system) and the text detection components are the most challenging and important pieces in this application, as they enable the computation of a good translation.

1.3   Indoor Localization

The computational capability of mobile phones has been rapidly increasing to the point where augmented reality has become feasible on such devices. In this section, we describe an approach to indoor localization and pose estimation in order to support augmented reality applications in an indoor environment and on a mobile phone platform.

Estimating an accurate camera pose is crucial for delivering a high-quality augmented reality experience, because the application needs to understand how the camera is oriented and located with respect to the scene in order to augment virtual information accurately. In this section, we describe a system [40] that localizes the device in a familiar environment and determines its position and orientation using the camera and sensors in the mobile device. Once the 6 degrees-of-freedom (DOF) pose is determined, 3D virtual objects from a database can be projected onto the image and displayed for the mobile user.

The application has two main phases: an offline data acquisition and an online pose estimation. The offline data acquisition phase consists of building a database by acquiring images at different locations in the environment, while the online pose estimation computes the position and orientation of the device by matching features

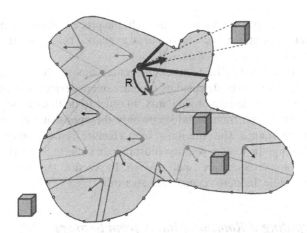

Fig. 1.12 Indoor localization application overview. The database contains several images taken at different locations (the *green dots*) in the indoor environment (*blue blob*). The arrows are the optical axes and the angles represent fields of view. The pose (translation T and rotation R) between the cell phone image (*bold blue lines*) and a database image is computed by image matching. Then the 3D virtual objects (represented by *yellow cubes*) are projected onto the mobile device image. Here, only one virtual object is seen by the mobile device

between the device image and an image from the database; the pose estimation also uses information from the sensors (accelerometer and magnetometer) for the computation as we discuss later in this section. In Fig. 1.12 we show an overview of the application.

The application enables the user both to visualize virtual objects in the camera image and to localize the user in a familiar environment. We describe in detail the process of building the database and the pose estimation algorithm used on the mobile phone. We discuss the performance evaluation of the proposed algorithm as well as its accuracy in terms of re-projection error of the 3D virtual objects onto the cell phone image.

1.3.1 Building the Environment Database

The first step in the application is to acquire data in advance about the environment; e.g., to go through a museum and create an image database that will be used subsequently by AR applications in the building. This involves carrying a camera rig through the space and preprocessing this data on a host computer. For each image, the acquisition process stores the pose of the camera (its absolute rotation and position) and its intrinsic parameters. Then the process extracts SURF features [2] in each of the images and stores their positions in the image as well as their descriptors. The goal of the mobile application is to localize the user metrically. Therefore, the process uses a stereo camera for building the image database and to estimate the depth for every pixel of each captured image. As a result, the process stores the 3D position of the features in each image. For a reason to be explained below, the 3D position of the center of the images are stored as well.

Among all the detected SURF features, the system chooses the most robust ones; i.e., those that are likely to be detected by mobile camera device and be close to the new feature in terms of descriptor similarity. In order to do that, the system tracks each feature over several frames and keeps only the ones that were successfully tracked over all the frames. The criterion to keep a feature from one frame to the next one is the following: the feature position must remain close to its previous position and their descriptor distances are small enough. In practice, the system tracks the SURF features, while the stereo camera remains still.

1.3.2 Computing a Rotation Matrix from Sensors

Once the database has been collected and processed, the indoor environment is ready to support location-based AR on the mobile phone. As it is described later, having a coarse estimate of the pose makes the image retrieval step easier and accelerates the pose estimation algorithm. For this work, we used the N97 phone from Nokia. The device has several sensors, such as GPS, an accelerometer, a magnetometer, and a rotation sensor, that can help the application in estimating the pose.

As the first part of the pose estimation step, a "world" coordinate system is defined. As a right-handed Cartesian coordinate system, the application used the system (E, g, N), where E is the unit vector representing east, g is the unit vector representing the gravity force, and N is the unit vector representing north. In this section, we describe how the system obtains the rotation matrix of the camera pose from sensor measurements.

The accelerometer senses the second derivative of the position. Assuming the measurements are noise free, it is thus theoretically feasible to obtain the position by double integrating the accelerometer data. However, experiments showed that the data produced by this sensor is too noisy to get a reliable estimation of the position. Figure 1.13 shows the results of an experiment comparing the ground truth 2D trajectory and the trajectory estimated with the accelerometer data, while the user walked holding the phone upright. The graph shows a bird's-eye view, with an equal number of points in both curves. An accurate trajectory estimate would overlap the rectangular ground truth; in contrast, the accelerometer-based position estimate was wildly off.

Another solution to estimate the position is to use the GPS data which gives the location of the user with a few meters of error. Depending on the application that can be adequate. However, if the system is used indoors there is usually no GPS signal available, so the position cannot be estimated with the cell phone's GPS sensor. Therefore, if there is no GPS signal available, the system uses the last computed

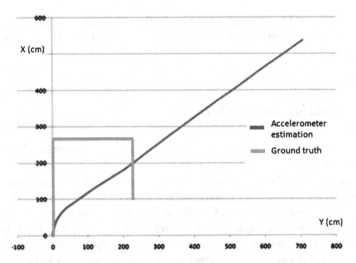

Fig. 1.13 Accelerometer accuracy for trajectory estimation. The 2D position (*top-down view*) of a walking user holding the cell phone is estimated using the accelerometer data (*blue line*) and compared to ground truth (*green line*). The accelerator-only estimate is not useful

user location (i.e., the position computed for the previous frame). Moreover, the application assumes that the user does not walk more than two meters between two frames, so that the previous estimated position can be reused to estimate a new one.

The accelerometer sensor outputs three channels that represent the acceleration along the three cell phone axes. Besides measuring acceleration due to the user, the accelerometer measures the gravity acceleration. Thus if the user is not moving, the three gravity components projected in the cell phone reference system can be measured by the sensor. This enabled the system to obtain the tilt of the phone, that is, two parameters out of three of the cell phone rotation matrix. The same information can also be obtained from the rotation sensor. This sensor gives three angles that represent the amount of rotation around the three cell phone axes. These angles can be used to retrieve the three components of the gravity vector in the cell phone reference frame. The advantage of using this rotation sensor rather than the accelerometer is that the outputs of this sensor are not sensitive to user movements. However, the sensor is less precise than the accelerometer because the angles are quantized to 15°.

The last parameter to compute is the amount of rotation around a vertical axis. To fully determine the rotation, the system needs additional information from the magnetometer. The 2D magnetometer (or digital compass) outputs the angle from the projection of the North vector onto the cell phone plane and one cell phone axis. This angle gives the system one parameter, which is enough to compute the full orientation of the mobile device because the system already has two parameters given by the accelerometer/rotation sensor. By expressing the components of all three cell phone axes from the gravity components and the magnetometer angle, the application can obtain the full cell phone rotation matrix. In the subsequent paragraphs, we will describe how the system estimates the camera pose leveraging this rotation matrix computation.

1.3.3 Localizing the Mobile Device

Once the augmented reality application captures an image, it searches the database for the most relevant stored image to fully estimate the device's pose. The database can contain an arbitrarily large number of images and searching among all the images is not feasible, since the feature matching process is a time-expensive step on the mobile device. Fortunately, most of the database images do not need to be searched because the portion of the environment they represent is not even visible to the user. We describe how the camera pose can be obtained from the mobile device's sensors and use it so that the system can discard images that are not likely to being seen by the user; for example, images that represent a scene behind the user.

The system uses two criteria to select only the relevant images. First, the system checks that the database image centers are visible by the mobile phone camera. This is computed using the stored 3D points representing the database image centers. For this criterion, the system assumes two premises: (1) the overlapping region (if there is some) between two images (the database image and the mobile camera image) is not large enough for estimating the pose accurately when a center is not inside the cameras field of view; and (2) the user moves smoothly so that user's location is continuous. Due to the uncertainty on the estimated phone orientation from sensors, the system extends the field of view to search for 3D points. The system increases the number of images to be searched as a function of the uncertainty, i.e., the more uncertainty the more images to search. Second, the system discards images whose orientation differ significantly from the camera's orientation to prevent bad image matching configurations. Thanks to these assumptions, the image search is restricted and the search process is more efficient.

For every database image, the system loads in memory its 3D center point and the absolute pose of the stereo camera that captured the image; this information is about 36 bytes for each image. The system loads feature descriptors on demand for each image as well.

Among the images that have been selected to be searched, the system selects the best matching candidate by using a classic nearest-neighbor feature matching approach. The SURF features are detected in the cell phone image and the descriptors are computed at each of these points. Then for every image of the database found as a result of the search process aforementioned, the features from the cell phone image are matched to the ones from the database image. For each feature of the cell phone image, the nearest neighbor in the database image features set is searched. Subsequently, the system keeps only good matches, that is, matches that have a low enough distance between each other, and also the ones for which the ratio between the second best distance and the best distance is high enough; note that this is the inverse of the Lowe's ratio [34]. As an outcome of this method, the system obtains sets of good matches between the cell phone image and each of the possible database images. Subsequently, the system selects the image from the database that has the highest number of good matches with the cell phone image, as it is used to compute the pose.

The nearest-neighbor (NN) search of descriptors for feature matching is performed using a KD-Tree structure. The system computes and stores a KD-Tree for every image during the preprocessing step. The NN search is implemented using the best-bin-first technique [3], a technique which is about 90 % as accurate as linear search but 100 times faster.

Once the selected database image has been matched with the cell phone image, the system obtains a set of candidate matches, from which incorrect matches need to be removed. The system estimates first a homography via the least median of square algorithm [43], and keeps only points that roughly satisfy the planar criterion checked via the estimated homography. The system uses a high threshold so that depth changes are allowed. Subsequently, a fundamental matrix is computed exploiting the matches supporting the previously computed homography within a RANSAC [15] scheme using the 8-point algorithm [23].

At this point the system has a set of putative correct matches between the cell phone and the database images, which enable the application to compute the pose. From these matches, the system then computes a set of 2D-3D matches by associating the 2D feature detected on the device with the 3D point corresponding to the 2D feature on the database image. Then, given these 2D-3D matches, the system solves for the translation and rotation of the device with respect to the world. To explain this in detail, let c_i be 2D point in the cell phone image, X_i be a 3D point in the database coordinate system, and K_c be the calibration matrix of the cell phone. The algorithm minimizes the reprojection error over the mobile device's extrinsic parameters (rotation matrix R and translation vector T), i.e.,

$$\underset{R,T}{\text{minimize}} \sum_i \left\| \frac{K_c(RX_i + T)}{\alpha} - \begin{bmatrix} c_i \\ 1 \end{bmatrix} \right\|_2^2, \tag{1.6}$$

where $\alpha = (K_c(RX_i + T))_3$ is the third vector entry. This measure is minimized as the system's goal is to align the virtual with the real world as accurately as possible. To this end, the reprojection error (Eq. 1.6) is in the form of a least-squares problem which can be solved via the Levenberg–Marquardt [31] (LM) method. However, to use the LM solver an initial solution must be computed first. We describe a method to initialize this solver in the following paragraphs.

The initialization method assumes that the rotation matrix $\hat{R}$ can be estimated via sensor measurements. Then the method focuses on finding a good initial translation vector T. To this end, the method obtains the translation vector by solving the following problem:

$$\underset{T}{\text{minimize}} \quad \sum_i \left\| K_c(\hat{R}X_i + T) - \alpha \begin{bmatrix} c_i \\ 1 \end{bmatrix} \right\|_2^2. \tag{1.7}$$

Equation (1.7) uses the estimated rotation matrix $\hat{R}$ from the sensor measurements and the problem ends up being a linear unconstrained least-squares problem, which can be solved for T efficiently using linear algebra methods.

After solving the problem described in Eq. (1.6) over the rotation matrix R and a translation vector T, which are the parameters describing how the camera is oriented and positioned with respect to the scene, the system is now able to display AR augmentations onto the device's image.

1.3.4 Evaluation

To evaluate the approach, we built a database of an environment and used planar objects in the scene for visual assessment. The evaluation consisted in estimating the camera pose and drawing a quadrangle enclosing planar objects that were recognized and depicted by the mobile device. In Fig. 1.14 we show an augmentation of planar objects in the scene and confirm that minimizing the reprojection error finds a good camera pose estimate that can be useful for an AR application. In Fig. 1.15a, we show quadrangle augmentations of three different recognized planar objects in the scene.

It is possible to use the estimates in order to localize the user within an environment; the translation vector T is the parameter that reveals the location of the user with respect to the scene. A visualization of these localizations are shown in Fig. 1.15b. From this experiment, the observed estimated user's location error was about 10–15 cm.

The implementation was done in Symbian C++ and Open C/C++ on a Nokia N97 cell phone. It is equipped with a single-core ARM 434 MHz processor with

Fig. 1.14 Augmented images with (*left*) and without (*right*) the reprojection error minimization. The *green quadrangle* is the augmented virtual information onto the real scene

(a)   **(b)**

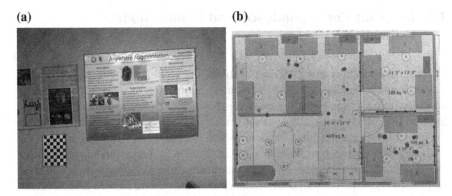

Fig. 1.15 *Left* Quadrangle augmentation of planar objects after estimating the mobile camera pose. *Right* Localization of the user within an environment by using the camera pose estimates. *Green points* are ground truth positions and *red points* are the estimated ones. One can notice a *single green point* alone in the middle of the floor plan. The matching process failed here because the cell phone image quality was inadequate. **a** Augmentation of 3 objects. **b** Estimated users' position

128Mb of RAM. The most expensive step in this application is the SURF detection an description algorithm, which takes more than 8 s to run on a 640 × 480 image. This is mostly due to the fact that Symbian only emulates the floating point precision because it does not natively support it; the used SURF implementation uses floating point numbers. This could be reduced by using a fixed-precision version of the SURF algorithm (or using a mobile platform with floating point computation, which are now common). For comparison, the algorithm runs at 10 fps for 640 × 480 images on a 1.73 GHz computer. The second most expensive computation is feature matching, which took about 1.1 s. The pose estimation took about one third of a second; the pose refinement algorithms used double precision numbers, which increased execution times.

1.3.5 Discussion and Future Work

The approach presented in this section was tailored for mobile phones that did not have powerful computational resources. However, this has changed recently and now we can find powerful mobile devices containing floating point units, multi-core and fast processors, and more RAM. Fortunately, algorithms solving for the camera pose from 2D to 3D correspondences, also known as the perspective-n-point (PnP) problem, have become more efficient and mobile device friendly, e.g., [27, 30, 46]. As potential future directions, these PnP can be used to directly estimate camera poses. Moreover, inertial measurements can be leveraged and used in combination with the aforementioned algorithms to quickly and accurately compute a camera pose estimate.

1.4 Keypoint Correspondences and Robust Model Estimation

In many augmented reality (AR) applications, the accuracy of the camera pose is a critical component to ensure a high-quality augmentation. This is because it is necessary to understand how the camera is positioned and oriented with respect to the world in order to accurately augment virtual objects onto images; see for instance the indoor localization application described in Sect. 1.3.

A common approach to estimate camera poses is by understanding the relative motion of the cameras depicting a scene; this process is a crucial part in structure from motion (SfM) [13]. To get an understanding of all the relative camera motions given a collection of images, a set of keypoint correspondences between image pairs must be computed first. Subsequently, different models, such as homographies, essential matrices, and fundamental matrices, are computed from these correspondences and are used later to extract valuable camera pose information.

In general, we wish to compute these models as quickly as possible. This is very important in particular to mobile augmented reality applications because they need to perform the augmentations as fast as possible. Nevertheless, several nuisances make this estimation process nontrivial; for instance, a critical nuisance is the presence of incorrect keypoint correspondences between image pairs. These incorrect correspondences, the "outliers," have to be filtered in order to compute accurate models.

In this section, we present two approaches that speed up the process of robustly estimating models from contaminated keypoint correspondences with outliers. We describe two different methods to estimate the correctness of the correspondences leveraging information from the matching distances using the statistical theory of extreme values [9, 12].

1.4.1 Computing Keypoint Correspondences

To compute keypoint correspondences between a reference image and a query image, we first need to detect features or keypoints on both images. Subsequently, for every keypoint a descriptor is computed, e.g., SIFT [34] or SURF [2]. These descriptors, which are a representation for every detected keypoint, are used to establish the keypoint correspondences following the nearest-neighbor (NN) rule: the jth query keypoint is assigned to the $i^\star$th reference keypoint such that

$$i^\star = \arg\min_i \left\{ \|\mathbf{q}_j - \mathbf{r}_i\| \right\}_{i=1}^n, \tag{1.8}$$

where $\mathbf{r}_i$ and $\mathbf{q}_j$ are the reference and query descriptors, respectively. In other words, the NN rule computes the least dissimilar reference keypoint given a query keypoint.

1.4.2 Predicting Correctness for Keypoint Correspondences

Incorrect correspondences, or outliers, occur when the truth reference keypoint is not the least dissimilar, or when the truth reference keypoint was not detected in the query image. To detect these outliers produced by the NN rule (see Eq. 1.8), we proposed a predictor based on the statistical theory of extreme values [16]. The predictor, which is called MRRayleigh, computes a correctness probability which later is used to label the correspondences as correct or incorrect and to speed up a robust estimation process.

The main premise of the predictor, which was inspired by the work of Scheirer et al. [44], is that computing a statistical model for the minimum distances generated from the incorrect correspondences is possible by exploiting the statistical theory of extreme values. Thus, checking if a minimum distance used in the NN rule is likely to be a sample generated from this model or not allows us to estimate the correctness of the correspondence.

More formally, we consider the descriptor distance $d_{ij} = \|\mathbf{q}_j - \mathbf{r}_i\|$ to be a continuous random variable following a distribution F. We know that some distances correspond to correct correspondences and others to incorrect ones. Thus, there are two underlying random processes generating distances for correct and incorrect correspondences, which we call F_c and $F_{\bar{c}}$, respectively. The NN matching process then takes a decision by observing several distances samples from these distributions. Because we are matching 2D features corresponding to actual 3D points, there must be a single correct answer and thus a single distance corresponding to a correct match. However, we can also have the case that there is no correct answer at all because a reference keypoint was not detected in the query image. Therefore, we can expect that there is at most a distance corresponding to a correct match among all the distances computed when using the NN matcher for a query $\mathbf{q}_j$. In other words, we have at most a single sample drawn from F_c and many samples from $F_{\bar{c}}$.

In order to compute a model that explains the behavior of the minimum distance that the $F_{\bar{c}}$ process can generate, we use the distributions suggested from the statistical theory of extreme values. In Fig. 1.16 we provide an illustration of the densities involved for this processing. Next, we review the main theorem used in our approach.

Review of the Fisher–Tippet–Gnedenko Theorem

The Fisher–Tippet–Gnedenko Theorem, also known as the block maxima theorem, provides a family of distributions to model the maximum or minimum values that a random process can generate:

Theorem 1 *Let X_i be a sequence of i.i.d. random variables and let*

$$M_n = \max \{X_1, \ldots, X_n\}$$

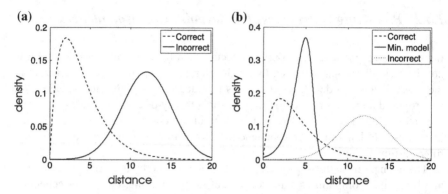

Fig. 1.16 *Left* The two underlying random processes' densities involved in the generation of the distances, correct match distances density (*dashed curve*) and incorrect match distances density (*continuous curve*). *Right* The minimum distance that the random process for incorrect matches can generate is a random variable, thus a density describing it can be obtained (*continuous curve*); the underlying two random processes: correct (*dashed curve*) and incorrect (*dotted curve*) processes. **a** Random processes. **b** The minimum model

denote the maximum. If there exist sequences of normalizing constants $a_n > 0$, $b_n \in \mathbb{R}$, and a nondegenerate probability distribution function G, such that

$$\mathbb{P}(a_n^{-1}(M_n - b_n) \leq z) \to G(z) \; as \; n \to \infty \tag{1.9}$$

then G(z) is of the same type as one of the three extremal-type distributions: Gumbel, Fréchet, and Weibull.

In other words, the block maxima theorem states that the rescaled sample maximum $\left(a_n^{-1}(M_n - b_n)\right)$ converges in distribution to a variable having an extremal-type distribution. We refer the reader to [9, 12] for the proof of this theorem. Although Theorem 1 considers maximum values, we can still use it to model sampled minima using one of the three extremal-type distributions. To do so, we must first apply a simple transformation: $X' = -X \Rightarrow \max\{X'\} = -\min\{X\}$.

To determine exactly which of the three extremal-type distribution to use for modeling the maxima/minima, we need the domain of attraction tests [9, 12]. However, the generalized extreme value distribution (GEV),

$$G(z; \mu, \sigma, \xi) = \begin{cases} \exp\left\{-\left[1 + \xi\left(\frac{z-\mu}{\sigma}\right)\right]^{-\frac{1}{\xi}}\right\} & \text{if} \;\; \xi \neq 0 \\ \exp\left\{-\exp\left[-\frac{z-\mu}{\sigma}\right]\right\} & \text{if} \;\; \xi = 0 \end{cases}, \tag{1.10}$$

subsumes the three extremal-type distributions. Thus, we can use the GEV to model maxima or minima from a random process, avoiding the domain of attraction tests. The GEV distribution has three parameters: location μ, scale σ, and shape ξ.

MRRayleigh: The Predictor

To estimate the correctness of a correspondence, we calculate a confidence or belief given their distances used in the NN matching process. To do so, we proposed the MRRayleigh predictor [16], shown in Algorithm 1.

Algorithm 1 MRRayleigh

Require: $\{d_{1:n}\}$, k, and $\delta \in (0, 1)$
Ensure: $v \in \{1, 0\}$ and p
1: $D_k \leftarrow$ Get the smallest k samples from $\{d_{1:n}\}$
2: $d^* \leftarrow \min D_k$
3: $\sigma \leftarrow$ Fit Rayleigh distribution to $D_k \setminus d^*$
4: $p \leftarrow \mathbb{P}(C = \text{correct}|d^*, D_k) = 1 - \text{RayleighCDF}(d^*; \sigma)$
5: **if** $p > \delta$ **then**
6:    Predict correspondence as correct: $v = 1$
7: **else**
8:    Predict correspondence as incorrect: $v = 0$
9: **end if**

This predictor requires the distances $\{d_{1:n}\}$ obtained by comparing a given query descriptor $\mathbf{q}$ with the set of reference descriptors $\{\mathbf{r}_i\}_{i=1}^n$; k, a number of samples that define the left tail of $F_{\bar{c}}$; and a threshold δ, which is used to decide if a correspondence is correct or incorrect. The predictor computes a correctness confidence or belief p and returns $v = 1$ when the correspondence is likely to be correct, and $v = 0$ otherwise.

The idea of the predictor is to compute a model for the minimum distance that the process $F_{\bar{c}}$ can generate using the distributions stated in Theorem 1, and use it to verify if the minimum sample used in the NN matcher is a sample that is likely to be generated from the computed model. To compute this model, the algorithm selects the k lowest distances, which are samples from the tail of $F_{\bar{c}}$ (Step 1). Subsequently, the algorithm fits a Rayleigh distribution, which is a special case of the Weibull distribution, to the k samples discarding the minimum (Steps 2–3). Next, the algorithm computes the confidence by evaluating the Rayleigh's inverse cumulative distribution function (cdf) at the minimum distance (Step 4). Finally, the algorithm decides given this confidence and a threshold if the correspondence is likely to be correct or incorrect (Steps 5–9).

In Fig. 1.17, we present the prediction performance using two different descriptors, SIFT and SURF, for computing correspondences on the publicly available affine covariant features dataset [36]. This dataset contains eight sub-datasets, each with systematic variations of a single imaging condition: viewpoint, scale, image blur, illumination, or jpeg compression. Every sub-dataset contains six images: a reference image and five query images of the same scene varying a single imaging condition. In addition, every sub-dataset provides five homographies that relate the reference image with each of the query images in the sub-dataset. These homographies were

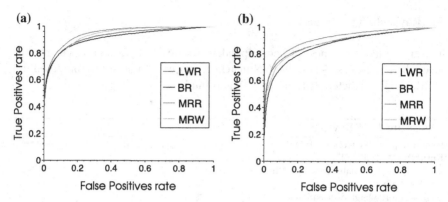

Fig. 1.17 ROC curves for correctness correspondence prediction. The experiment compares Lowe's ratio [34] (LWR), Brown's ratio [7] (BR), Meta-Recognition [44] (MRW), and MRRayleigh [16] (MRR) on the Oxford dataset [36]. MRRayleigh outperforms the other predictors. *Left* Prediction performance for SIFT matches. *Right* Prediction performance for SURF matches. **a** SIFT matches. **b** SURF matches

used to compute the ground truth for correct correspondences for SIFT and SURF matches. To obtain the receiver operating characteristic (ROC) curves, the threshold δ was varied from 0 to 1, and $k = 0.5\%n$, where n is the number of reference features. We can see in Fig. 1.17 that the proposed MRRayleigh (MRR) outperforms the other methods, Lowe's ratio [34] (LWR), Brown's ratio [7] (BR), and Meta-Recognition [44] which uses Weibull distribution for prediction, regardless of the descriptor.

1.4.3 Nonuniform Sampling Strategies for Robust Model Estimation

Because the MRRayleigh algorithm provides a confidence on the correctness of a NN matching decision, it is possible to create a nonuniform sampling strategy for robustly estimating a model leveraging the computed confidences. The classical method to estimate these models robustly in the presence of outliers is RANSAC [15]. This method samples the data uniformly to generate hypotheses or models, which later are checked against all the data to assess their quality. The hypothesis that explains most of the data is the solution that this method returns. To speed up the convergence of this method, nonuniform sampling strategies can be devised (e.g., [11, 16, 18, 42]).

SWIGS: A Nonuniform Sampling Strategy from MRRayleigh Predictions

We describe two approaches leveraging the benefits of extreme value theory (EVT). The first method, SWIGS [16], uses the confidence computed by MRRayleigh to compute a nonuniform sampling strategy. The strategy is obtained by computing a weight for every correspondence, i.e.,

$$w_i = \frac{p_i}{\sum_{i=1}^{n} p_i},$$ (1.11)

where p_i is the confidence for the ith correspondence. These weights form a discrete probability mass function over the correspondences, which is used as the nonuniform sampling strategy.

To evaluate the performance of SWIGS (the nonuniform sampling strategy), we presented an experiment on homography estimation in a dense matching scenario [16] using the affine covariant features dataset [36]. The nonuniform sampling strategy was combined with MLESAC [48], a variant of RANSAC whose purpose is to calculate a hypothesis or model that maximizes a likelihood function instead of maximizing the support of the model.

The experiment compared SWIGS with other nonuniform sampling methods combined with MLESAC: BEEM [22]; a Guided-Sampling [47] with a general distribution considering all the imaging conditions (GEN); a Guided-Sampling [47] that considers only the distribution for a specific imaging condition (SPEC); BLOGS [6] where $m_l = d_1^{-1}$, and $m_{lr} = m_{lc} = d_2^{-1}$ as our approach considers a different matching procedure; and a classical random sampling (uniform distribution) for a baseline.

The results of this experiment are shown in Fig. 1.18, where the first two rows show the results obtained for SIFT, and the rest for SURF matches. The percentage of correct matches or correspondences are presented in the first and third rows, while the iterations are in the second and fourth rows. The x-axis indicates the index of the images contained in the considered sub-datasets (omitting the reference image, which is index 1); an increasing index represents a larger variation with respect to the reference image. Each column presents the results for a different sub-dataset: bikes, boat, graf, trees and wall, from left to right.

We can observe that SWIGS tends to require in general fewer iterations than the other methods (second and fourth rows) to find models that consider a comparable or higher percentage of correct matches within the allowed number of iterations (first and third row). We note that SWIGS, SPEC, and BEEM tend to find models that consider approximately the same number of matches. The GEN method struggles more to find models that consider a high percentage of correct matches in scenes with repetitive textures, e.g., wall, and trees sub-datasets; repetitive textures can cause a considerable overlap between correct and incorrect matching scores distributions. BLOGS and a random sampling (Uniform) method perform similarly in finding models that consider a high portion of the correct matches.

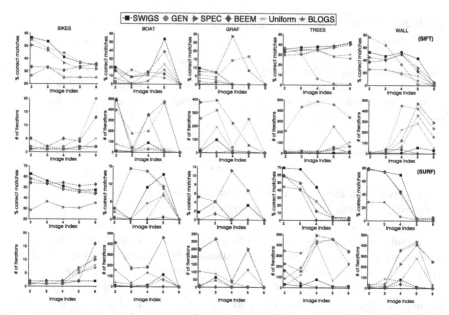

Fig. 1.18 Performance evaluation across several sub-datasets (bikes, boat, graf, trees, wall from *left* to *right*). Of all the 5000 repetitions of the experiment, the *first* and *third rows* present the median of the percentage of correct matches found by the best computed models within the allowed number of iterations, while the *second* and *fourth rows* present the median number of iterations at which the best model was found. The *first* and *second rows* present the results for SIFT, and the *third* and *fourth* for SURF

The experimental results presented in this section demonstrate that SWIGS can perform similarly or better in finding models that consider a good portion of correct matches in a dense matching scenario. The experiments also show that SWIGS tends to require fewer iterations than the other guiding sampling methods without sacrificing the number of correct matches found. Moreover, this confirms that MRRayleigh confidences tend to identify good matches, and these confidences yield an efficient and accurate nonuniform sampling strategy.

EVSAC: A Nonuniform Sampling Strategy for Low Inlier Ratio Cases

The second method that leverages extreme value theory (EVT), EVSAC [18], estimates the correctness belief p_i differently. The main premise of EVSAC is that there is a single pair of distributions F_c and $F_{\bar{c}}$ when matching two images. In contrast, MRRayleigh assumes there exist a pair of distributions F_c and $F_{\bar{c}}$ for every query feature, i.e., for every NN search for the query feature. Given this new assumption, the task is to find the parameters for F_c and $F_{\bar{c}}$ as well as the mixture parameter ε to compute a model for the minimum distances used by the NN matcher. These minimum distances can be considered as samples drawn from a distribution $F = \varepsilon F_c + (1 - \varepsilon)F_{\bar{c}}$.

Algorithm 2 EVSAC

Require: $\{d_{i,1:k}\}_{i=1}^n$
Ensure: $\{w_i\}_{i=1}^n$ and $\{p_i\}_{i=1}^n$
1: $\mathbf{v} \leftarrow \text{Predict}(\{d_{i,1:k}\}_{i=1}^n)$
2: $(\alpha, \beta) \leftarrow \text{FitGamma}(\{d_{i,(1)} \text{ such that } v_i = 1\})$
3: $(\mu, \sigma, \xi) \leftarrow \text{FitGEV}(\{d_{i,(2)}\})$
4: Calculate the empirical cdf using $d_{i,j}$.
5: Find ε by solving (1.12)
6: Calculate posterior weights p_i using Eq. (1.13)
7: Calculate weights w_i using Eq. (1.14)
8: Use the weights w_i for generating hypotheses

EVSAC's algorithm (shown in Algorithm 2) computes these parameters as well as the new nonuniform sampling strategy. EVSAC requires the k smallest distances $\{d_{i,1:k}\}_{i=1}^n$ for every ith correspondence, and computes the weights w_i as well as the correctness confidence p_i. The first step in this algorithm is to label each correspondence as correct or incorrect (Step 1); for this step, EVSAC uses the MRRayleigh predictor algorithm. Subsequently, the algorithm fits a gamma distribution to the distances of those correspondences labeled as correct, i.e., $v_i = 1$, in step 2. Then, the algorithm fits a generalized extreme value distribution (GEV) to the second smallest distances in step 3.

EVSAC uses the GEV distribution to model the underlying distribution that the minimum distances from the incorrect correspondences follow; this is because now we have several minimum distances sampled from a single distribution $F_{\bar{c}}$. This implies that the mixture model explaining the minimum distances in the matching process becomes $F = \varepsilon F_c + (1 - \varepsilon)G_{\bar{c}}$, where $G_{\bar{c}}$ is the GEV distribution. Theorem 1 applies only for modeling the minimum distances sampled from $F_{\bar{c}}$ because we have several samples from this distribution, i.e., we have more incorrect correspondences assuming that there is at most a single correct correspondence. On the other hand, this Theorem does not apply to F_c because we sample a single sample at most when we match a query feature; recall that Theorem 1 requires a sufficiently large number of samples taken from the underlying distribution.

After estimating the parameters of the distributions, EVSAC estimates the mixture model parameter ε in steps 4 and 5. To do so, EVSAC solves the following constrained least-squares problem:

$$\begin{aligned} \underset{\mathbf{y}}{\text{minimize}} \quad & \frac{1}{2}\|A\mathbf{y} - \mathbf{b}\|_2^2 \\ \text{subject to} \quad & \mathbf{1}^T\mathbf{y} = 1 \\ & \mathbf{0} \preceq \mathbf{y} \preceq \mathbf{u}, \end{aligned} \tag{1.12}$$

where the symbol $\preceq$ indicates entrywise comparison, and

$$A = \begin{bmatrix} F_c(d_1) & G_{\bar{c}}(d_1) \\ \vdots & \vdots \\ F_c(d_n) & G_{\bar{c}}(d_n) \end{bmatrix}, \quad \mathbf{b} = \begin{bmatrix} F(d_1) \\ \vdots \\ F(d_n) \end{bmatrix}, \mathbf{y} = \begin{bmatrix} \varepsilon \\ \varepsilon' \end{bmatrix}, \text{ and } \mathbf{u} = \begin{bmatrix} \tau \\ 1 \end{bmatrix}.$$

The matrix $A \in \mathbb{R}^{n \times 2}$ is formed by evaluating all the n minimum distances on the cumulative distributions functions. The vector $\mathbf{b} \in \mathbb{R}^n$ is formed by evaluating the empirical cumulative distribution function on all the minimum distances. EVSAC imposes the constraint $\varepsilon \leq \tau$, as this improves the quality of the estimation of the mixing parameter. τ is computed as the ratio of the number of correspondences labeled as correct and n.

EVSAC computes in step 6 the correctness believes $p_i = \mathbb{P}(C = \text{correct}|d)$ for every correspondence using the Bayes' rule:

$$\mathbb{P}(C = \text{correct}|d) = \frac{\varepsilon f_c(d)}{\varepsilon f_c(d) + (1 - \varepsilon)g_{\bar{c}}(d)}, \tag{1.13}$$

where C is a discrete random variable indicating correctness, d is a minimum distance, and f_c and $g_{\bar{c}}$ are the probability density functions for F_c and $G_{\bar{c}}$, respectively. Subsequently, EVSAC calculates the weights w_i for every correspondence as follows:

$$w_i = \frac{p_i v_i}{\sum_{i=1}^{n} p_i v_i}, \tag{1.14}$$

where v_i is the binary value returned by the predictor in step 1. These weights w_i again describe a probability mass function over the correspondences which is used as the nonuniform sampling strategy.

We now present an evaluation of the performance of EVSAC to find the parameters of our probabilistic framework: ε, and the distribution parameters using the MRRayleigh predictor [16] only as the predictor in step 1. We compared the estimated parameters against the parameters obtained assuming that we had a perfect correct match detector.

We first examine the accuracy of the estimation of ε in Table 1.5. The estimate of ε using the upper bound in vector $\mathbf{u}$ used in (1.12), $\hat{\varepsilon}$, tends to be closer to the real value, while the estimate without the upper bound ($\tilde{\varepsilon}$) can overshoot sometimes.

Next, we examine the quality of the estimation of the different probability densities and the posterior used to compute the weights w_i. In the first column of Fig. 1.19, we can observe that EVSAC (continuous curves) is able to approximate with a good accuracy the mixture of densities obtained with the ground truth data (dashed curves). In the second column, we present the posterior probabilities computed from the estimated model (continuous curves) and the posterior obtained from the ground truth (dashed curves). This means that EVSAC estimates an accurate posterior that essentially maximizes the information in the matching distances when computing a confidence value.

Table 1.5 Estimation of ε comparison: $\hat{\varepsilon}$ is the estimation with τ set as an upper bound (see Eq. 1.12), and $\tilde{\varepsilon}$ is without

Image pairs	ε	$\hat{\varepsilon}$	$\tilde{\varepsilon}$
Oxford-Bark (1–4 SURF)	0.0131	0.0141	0.1870
Oxford-Boat (1–6 SURF)	0.0257	0.0270	0.1429
Oxford-Bark (1–3 SIFT)	0.0479	0.0438	0.1291
Oxford-Trees (1–6 SIFT)	0.1028	0.1119	0.2467
Strecha-Brussel (2–3 SIFT)	0.1855	0.2067	0.2263
Strecha-Brussel (1–2 SURF)	0.2964	0.3115	0.3632

The upper bounded estimate tends to provide more accurate estimations

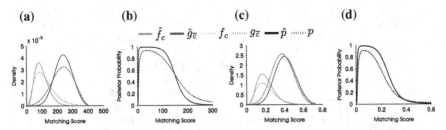

Fig. 1.19 Comparison of the mixture of densities and posterior probability computed using EVSAC against the ground truth for a pair of images with SIFT matches (**a–b**) and SURF matches (**c–d**). In both experiments the matching score metric is the Euclidean distance. The density estimations $\hat{f}_c$ and $\hat{g}_{\bar{c}}$ are close to the densities f_c and $g_{\bar{c}}$ computed with an oracle. In the second column, we compare the estimated posterior probability $\hat{p}$ with the posterior p computed with the oracle

To evaluate the nonuniform sampling strategy that EVSAC computes, a homography experiment is presented. EVSAC is compared against the following nonuniform sampling algorithms: Guided-MLESAC [47], BEEM's prior estimation step [22], BLOGS' global search mechanism [6], and PROSAC [11]. All these sampling algorithms were included in a classical hypothesis-test loop, where the support was always being maximized, and a solution was considered "good" if it satisfied the maximality constraint, i.e., the constraint that a good hypothesis was generated within a certain number of iterations (see [11] for more details on this constraint). The homography was computed using the OpenCV findHomography() function without the RANSAC option. An inlier (or correct correspondence) was considered if the reprojection error of the homography was less than 5 pixels. The algorithms were allowed to run until a maximum number of iterations (hypothesis test loops) calculated adaptively is reached, and the algorithm converged when 90 % of the inliers (correct matches) were detected. The found hypothesis was refined afterwards using a nonlinear method.

The results of this experiment are summarized in Table 1.6. The affine covariant features dataset [36] used for the experiment presented very challenging scenarios, where the inlier ratios ε ranged from 1–10 % for SIFT and SURF matches. The experiments were run 300 times. We present the average number of inliers detected (I); the average RMS reprojection error (E) in pixels w.r.t.to the error achieved by

Table 1.6 Homography estimation results for SIFT and SURF matches

		BEEM	BLOGS	PROSAC	GMLESAC	EVSAC
A: SURF	I	14 ± 0	14 ± 0	14 ± 0	14 ± 0	14 ± 0
	E	0 ± 0	0 ± 0	0 ± 0	0 ± 0	0 ± 0
	M	1443	2524	4	1521	11
	T	563.1	1008.3	2	511	4.2
	F	0	0	0	0	0
$\varepsilon = 0.01, n = 992$	R	100%	96%	0.33%	0.33%	100%
B: SIFT	I	12 ± 3	12 ± 2	10 ± 2	11 ± 3	12 ± 2
	E	0.1 ± 0.02	0.1 ± 0.04	0.37 ± 0.03	0.24 ± 0.04	0.16 ± 0.03
	M	41	17	2752900	10044	10
	T	13.3	5.3	375482	1446.4	3.3
	F	6.6	10.7	136.7	37.8	12.1
$\varepsilon = 0.02, n = 992$	R	100%	100%	100%	100%	100%
C: SURF	I	24 ± 2	22 ± 4	27 ± 4	29 ± 2	24 ± 2
	E	0.1 ± 0.01	0.1 ± 0.01	0.1 ± 0.02	0.03 ± 0.05	0.2 ± 0.1
	M	3741	4072	1458250	209963	1965
	T	1172.3	1509.5	284838	28092.1	572.3
	F	2	9	3.2	2.9	4.2
$\varepsilon = 0.035, n = 992$	R	100%	99%	100%	100%	100%
D: SURF	I	39 ± 2	39 ± 2	38 ± 6	38 ± 9	39 ± 2
	E	0.04 ± 0.02	0.01 ± 0.001	0.02 ± 0.1	0.01 ± 0.2	0.02 ± 0.01
	M	39	82	655073	4151	4
	T	10.9	21.5	145207	838.4	1.3
	F	0	0.1	1.3	3.9	0.1
$\varepsilon = 0.04, n = 981$	R	100%	100%	98%	99%	100%
E: SURF	I	40 ± 2	40 ± 2	38 ± 6	33 ± 9	40 ± 2
	E	0.04 ± 0.03	0.002 ± 0.001	0.45 ± 0.53	0.02 ± 0.13	0.02 ± 0.01
	M	149	355	321952	4713	92
	T	42.9	98.5	56176.5	2111.9	26.3
	F	0.3	0.2	0.6	35.7	0.8
$\varepsilon = 0.05, n = 807$	R	100%	100%	100%	100%	100%
F: SIFT	I	41 ± 3	41 ± 4	36 ± 6	41 ± 3	41 ± 3
	E	0.08 ± 0.02	0.002 ± 0.01	0.17 ± 0.04	0.05 ± 0.02	0.04 ± 0.02
	M	71	14	218811	341	22
	T	15.7	3.5	40750.7	67.5	5.4
	F	1.7	0.7	8.4	1.1	0.1
$\varepsilon = 0.05, n = 807$	R	100%	100%	100%	100%	100%
G: SURF	I	81 ± 8	81 ± 9	60 ± 23	81 ± 8	82 ± 7
	E	0.02 ± 0.01	0.03 ± 0.009	0.02 ± 0.06	0.02 ± 0.006	0.03 ± 0.004
	M	177	193	4507	918	73
	T	49.6	53.6	1616.2	226.5	21.9
	F	0.8	0.7	13.3	0.6	0.4
$\varepsilon = 0.10, n = 992$	R	100%	100%	100%	100%	100%
H: SIFT	I	82 ± 9	82 ± 9	69 ± 16	80 ± 8	82 ± 8
	E	0.02 ± 0.016	0.05 ± 0.008	0.09 ± 0.04	0.03 ± 0.003	0.03 ± 0.003
	M	72	26	3649	773	8
	T	13.9	5.5	834	120.1	4.1
	F	0.7	1.1	4.5	1	0.8
$\varepsilon = 0.103, n = 992$	R	100%	100%	100%	100%	100%

The results are sorted by inlier ratio (ε) in ascending order. EVSAC performed well when the inlier ratio is low, and performed equivalently when the inlier ratio increased

the ground truth data; the average number of models/hypotheses generated (M); the average time in milliseconds (T); the average Frobenius norm of the error between estimated homography and the computed homography with the ground truth (F); and the percentage of "good" runs where each algorithm converged (R). The results are sorted in ascending order by the inlier ratio. We can observe that EVSAC tends to perform overall faster when the inlier ratio is very low (see rows **A**, **B**, **C**, **D**, and **E**), and performs equivalent or faster than BEEM and BLOGS as soon as the inlier ratio increased (see rows **F**, **G**, **H**). PROSAC and GMLESAC struggled to converge fast when the inlier ratio was very low ($\varepsilon < 11\%$).

1.4.4 Discussion and Future Work

We have presented two different nonuniform sampling strategies that can help in estimating models, such as homographies, essential matrices, and fundamental matrices, robustly in the presence of outliers. The two methods leverage the correctness confidences that the statistical theory of extreme values allows us to compute. These nonuniform sampling methods can help in speeding up various processes, such as structure-from-motion and feature-based tracking, for use in mobile applications. A natural extension of these nonuniform sampling algorithms is to modify them so that they can work for estimations of camera poses from 2D to 3D correspondences, which is an important step for augmented reality applications as shown in Sect. 1.3.

1.5 Summary

In this chapter, we have provided insight into some of the problems, constraints, and opportunities that arise in the domain of computer vision for mobile augmented reality applications. Mobile AR requires robust, real-time computer vision methods for tracking, modeling, localization, and other tasks, executing on a mobile device with a foreground process that may require significant resources, and with additional sensors that may aid the visual processing. As these devices become even more ubiquitous, powerful, and integrated into people's daily lives, the opportunities for mobile computer vision will continue to grow rapidly.

The TranslatAR sign translation system described in Sect. 1.2 provides an example of a full application using computer vision and augmented reality in a mobile environment. The indoor localization capability of Sect. 1.3 gives insight into a vision-based resource that may be used by AR or other kinds of mobile applications that require spatial information (i.e., camera pose). Advances in fast, robust keypoint correspondences and model estimation (Sect. 1.4) indicate how efficient low-level choices, informed by theory, can provide tracking and modeling that is well suited to the mobile domain with its limited resources.

With recent advances in all areas of mobile AR, there is now great enthusiasm for real-world applications on mobile devices—an increasingly important domain for the computer vision field.

Acknowledgments We wish to acknowledge our colleagues who were involved in various aspects of the research reported on in this chapter: Steffen Gauglitz, Shane Zamora, Jim Kleban, Marc Petter, Charles Baur, Pradeep Sen, Sergio Rodriguez. This work was partially supported by UC MEXUS-CONACYT (Fellowship 212913) and NSF award 1219261. Parts of this chapter present research originally published in references [16–18, 40, 41].

References

1. Arthur, D., Vassilvitskii, S.: K-means++: the advantages of careful seeding. In: Proceedings of the Eighteenth Annual ACM-SIAM Symposium on Discrete Algorithms, SODA'07, pp. 1027–1035. Society for Industrial and Applied Mathematics, New Orleans, Louisiana (2007)
2. Bay, H., Ess, A., Tuytelaars, T., Van Gool, L.: Speeded-up robust features (SURF). Comput. Vis. Image Underst. **110**(3), 346–359 (2008)
3. Beis, J.S., Lowe, D.G.: Shape indexing using approximate nearest-neighbour search in high-dimensional spaces. In: Proceedings of the IEEE Conference on Computer Vision and Pattern Recognition (CVPR) (1997)
4. Benhimane, S., Malis, E.: Real-time image-based tracking of planes using efficient second-order minimization. Proc. IEEE Int. Conf. Intell. Robot. Syst. (IROS 2004) **1**, 943–948 (2004)
5. Bissacco, A., Cummins, M., Netzer, Y., Neven, H.: Photoocr: reading text in uncontrolled conditions. In: Proceedings of the IEEE International Conference on Computer Vision (ICCV) (2013)
6. Brahmachari, A.S., Sarkar, S.: Blogs: balanced local and global search for non-degenerate two view epipolar geometry. In: Proceedings of the IEEE International Conference on Computer Vision, pp. 1685–1692 (2009)
7. Brown, M., Winder, S., Szeliski, R.: In: Proceedings of the IEEE Conference on Computer Vision and Pattern Recognition (2005)
8. Canny, J.: A computational approach to edge detection. IEEE Trans. Pattern Anal. Mach. Intell. **8**(6), 679–698 (1986)
9. Castillo, E., Hadi, A.S., Balakrishnan, N., Sarabia, J.M.: Extreme Value and Related Models with Applications in Engineering and Science. Wiley, Hoboken (2005)
10. Cheng, C.-C., Peng, G.-J., Hwang, W.-L.: Subband weighting with pixel connectivity for 3-d wavelet coding. IEEE Trans. Image Process. **18**(1), 52–62 (2009)
11. Chum, O., Matas, J.: Matching with prosac—progressive sample consensus. In: Proceedings of the IEEE Conference on Computer Vision and Pattern Recognition (2005)
12. Coles, S.: An Introduction to Statistical Modeling of Extreme Values. Springer, Berlin (2001)
13. Crandall, D., Owens, A., Snavely, N., Huttenlocher, D.: SfM with MRFs: discrete-continuous optimization for large-scale reconstruction. IEEE Trans. Pattern Anal. Mach. Intell. **35**(12), 12 (2013)
14. Epshtein, B., Ofek, E., Wexler, Y.: Detecting text in natural scenes with stroke width transform. In: Proceedings of IEEE Conference on Computer Vision and Pattern Recognition (CVPR) (2010)
15. Fischler, M.A., Bolles, R.C.: Random sample consensus: a paradigm for model fitting with applications to image analysis and automated cartography. Commun. ACM **24**(6), 381–395 (1981)
16. Fragoso, V., Turk, M.: SWIGS: a swift guided sampling method. In: Proceedings of the IEEE Conference on Computer Vision and Pattern Recognition (CVPR) (2013)

17. Fragoso, V., Gauglitz, S., Zamora, S., Kleban, J., Turk, M.: TranslatAR: a mobile augmented reality translator. In: Proceedings of the IEEE Workshop on Applications of Computer Vision (WACV'11) (2011)
18. Fragoso, V., Sen, P., Rodriguez, S., Turk, M.: EVSAC: accelerating hypotheses generation by modeling matching scores with extreme value theory. In: Proceedings of IEEE International Conference on Computer Vision (ICCV) (2013)
19. Gao, J., Yang, J.: An adaptive algorithm for text detection from natural scenes. In: Proceedings of the IEEE Conference on Computer Vision and Pattern Recognition (CVPR) (2001)
20. Gauglitz, S., Höllerer, T., Turk, M.: Evaluation of interest point detectors and feature descriptors for visual tracking. Int. J. Comput. Vis. **94**(3), 335–360 (2011)
21. Gauglitz, S., Sweeney, C., Ventura, J., Turk, M., Höllerer, T.: Live tracking and mapping from both general and rotation-only camera motion. In: Proceedings of the 11th IEEE International Symposium on Mixed and Augmented Reality (ISMAR'12), pp. 13–22. Atlanta, Georgia (2012)
22. Goshen, L., Shimshoni, I.: Balanced exploration and exploitation model search for efficient epipolar geometry estimation. IEEE Trans. Pattern Anal. Mach. Intell. **30**(7), 1230–1242 (2008)
23. Hartley, R.I., Zisserman, A.: Multiple View Geometry in Computer Vision. Cambridge University Press, Cambridge (2000). ISBN 0521623049
24. Jaderberg, M., Vedaldi, A., Zisserman, A.: Deep features for text spotting. In: Computer Vision ECCV 2014. Lecture Notes in Computer Science, vol. 8692, pp. 512–528. Springer International Publishing, Berlin (2014)
25. Kato, H., Billinghurst, M.: Marker tracking and hmd calibration for a video-based augmented reality conferencing system. In: Proceedings of the 2nd IEEE and ACM International Workshop on Augmented Reality, 1999 (IWAR'99), pp. 85–94 (1999)
26. Klein, G., Murray, D.: Parallel tracking and mapping for small AR workspaces. In: Proceedings of the Sixth IEEE and ACM International Symposium on Mixed and Augmented Reality (ISMAR'07), Nara, Japan (2007)
27. Kneip, L., Li, H., Seo, Y.: UPnP: an optimal O(n) solution to the absolute pose problem with universal applicability. In: Computer Vision ECCV 2014. Lecture Notes in Computer Science, vol. 8689, pp. 127–142. Springer International Publishing, Berlin (2014)
28. Lee, C.W., Jung, K., Kim, H.J.: Automatic text detection and removal in video sequences. Pattern Recognit. Lett. **24**(15), 2607–2623 (2003)
29. Lee, C.-Y., Bhardwaj, A., Di, W., Jagadeesh, V., Piramuthu, R.: Region-based discriminative feature pooling for scene text recognition. In: Proceedings of the IEEE Conference on Computer Vision and Pattern Recognition (CVPR) (2014)
30. Lepetit, V., Moreno-Noguer, F., Fua, P.: EPnP: an accurate O(n) solution to the PnP problem. Int. J. Comput. Vis. **81**(2), 155–166 (2009)
31. Levenberg, K.: A method for the solution of certain non-linear problems in least squares. Q. J. Appl. Math. **II**(2), 164–168 (1944)
32. Levenshtein, I.V.: Binary codes capable of correcting deletions, insertions, and reversals. Cybern. Control Theory **10**(8), 707–710 (1966)
33. Liu, Y., Goto, S., Ikenaga, T.: A contour-based robust algorithm for text detection in color images. IEICE—Trans. Inf. Syst. **E89–D**(3), 1221–1230 (2006)
34. Lowe, D.G.: Distinctive image features from scale-invariant keypoints. Int. J. Comput. Vis. **60**(2), 91–110 (2004)
35. Lucas, S.M.: LCDAR 2005 text locating competition results. Proc. IEEE Conf. Doc. Anal. Recognit. **1**, 80–84 (2005)
36. Mikolajczyk, K., Schmid, C.: A performance evaluation of local descriptors. IEEE Trans. Pattern Anal. Mach. Intell. **27**(10), 1615–1630 (2005)
37. Neumann, L., Matas, J.: Real-time scene text localization and recognition. In: Proceedings of the IEEE Conference on Computer Vision and Pattern Recognition (CVPR) (2012)
38. Neumann, L., Matas, J.: Scene text localization and recognition with oriented stroke detection. In: Proceedings of the IEEE International Conference on Computer Vision (ICCV) (2013)

39. Park, A., Jung, K.: Automatic word detection system for document image using mobile devices. In: Human-Computer Interaction. Interaction Platforms and Techniques. Lecture Notes in Computer Science, vol. 4551, pp. 438–444. Springer, Berlin (2007)

40. Paucher, P., Turk, M.: Location-based augmented reality on mobile phones. In: Proceedings of IEEE Conference on Computer Vision and Pattern Recognition Workshops (CVPR Workshops) (2010)

41. Petter, M., Fragoso, V., Turk, M., Baur, C.: Automatic text detection for mobile augmented reality translation. In: Proceedings of IEEE International Conference on Computer Vision Workshops (ICCV Workshops) (2011)

42. Raguram, R., Frahm, J.-M., Pollefeys, M.: A comparative analysis of ransac techniques leading to adaptive real-time random sample consensus. In: Computer Vision ECCV 2008. Springer, Berlin (2008)

43. Rousseeuw, P.J.: Least median of squares regression. J. Am. Stat. Assoc. **79**(388), 871–880 (1984)

44. Scheirer, W.J., Rocha, A., Micheals, R.J., Boult, T.E.: Meta-eecognition: the theory and practice of recognition score analysis. IEEE Trans. Pattern Anal. Mach. Intell. **33**(8), 1689–1695 (2011)

45. Smith, R.: An overview of the tesseract ocr engine. In: Proceedings of the Ninth International Conference on Document Analysis and Recognition, ICDAR'07, vol. 02, pp. 629–633. IEEE Computer Society (2007)

46. Sweeney, C., Fragoso, V., Hllerer, T., Turk, M.: gDLS: a scalable solution to the generalized pose and scale problem. In: Computer Vision ECCV 2014. Lecture Notes in Computer Science, vol. 8692, pp. 16–31. Springer International Publishing, Berlin (2014)

47. Tordoff, B.J., Murray, D.W.: Guided-MLESAC: faster image transform estimation by using matching priors. IEEE Trans. Pattern Anal. Mach. Intell. **27**(10), 1523–1535 (2005)

48. Torr, P.H.S., Zisserman, A.: MLESAC: a new robust estimator with application to estimating image geometry. Comput. Vis. Image Underst. **78**(1), 138–156 (2000)

49. Wagner, D., Schmalstieg, D.: Artoolkitplus for pose tracking on mobile devices. In: Proceedings of the 12th Computer Vision Winter Workshop (CVWW'07), pp. 139–146 (2007)

50. Wagner, D., Mulloni, A., Langlotz, T., Schmalstieg, D.: Real-time panoramic mapping and tracking on mobile phones. In: IEEE Virtual Reality Conference (VR). IEEE, pp. 211–218 (2010)

51. Ye, Q., Gao, W., Wang, W., Zeng, W.: A robust text detection algorithm in images and video frames. Proc. IEEE Int. Conf. Inf. Commun. Signal Process. **2**, 802–806 (2003)

52. Ye, Q., Huang, Q., Gao, W., Zhao, D.: Fast and robust text detection in images and video frames. Image Vis. Comput. **23**(6), 565–576 (2005)

Part II
Mobile Computational Photography

Chapter 2
High-Quality Video Denoising for Motion-Based Exposure Control

Li Zhang, Travis Portz and Hongrui Jiang

Abstract New digital cameras, such as Canon SD1100 and Nikon COOLPIX S8100, have an autoexposure (AE) function that is based on motion estimation. The motion estimation helps to set short exposure and high ISO for frames with fast motion, thereby minimizing most motion blur in recorded videos. This AE function largely turns video enhancement into a denoising problem. This paper studies the problem of how to achieve high-quality video denoising in the context of motion-based exposure control. Unlike previous denoising works which either avoid using motion estimation, such as BM3D Dabov et al. TIP 16:2007, [1], or assume reliable motion estimation as input, such as Liu, ECCV, 2010, [2], our method evaluates the reliability of flow at each pixel and uses the "lifespan" of reliable flow trajectories as a weight to integrate spatial denoising and temporal denoising. This weighted combination scheme makes our method robust to optical flow failure over regions with repetitive texture or uniform color and combines the advantages of both spatial and temporal denoising. Our method also exploits high-quality frames in a sequence to effectively enhance noisier frames. In experiments using both synthetic and real videos, our method outperforms the state-of-the art Dabov et al. TIP 16:2007, Liu, ECCV, 2010, [1, 2].

L. Zhang (✉)
Google, 651 North 34th Street, Seattle, WA 98103, USA
e-mail: zhl@google.com

T. Portz
Amazon.com, Seattle, WA, USA
e-mail: travis@travisportz.com

H. Jiang
University of Wisconsin, Engineering Hall, 1415 Engineering Drive,
Madison, WI 53706, USA
e-mail: hongrui@engr.wisc.edu

© Springer International Publishing Switzerland 2015
G. Hua and X.-S. Hua (eds.), *Mobile Cloud Visual Media Computing*,
DOI 10.1007/978-3-319-24702-1_2

2.1 Introduction

In most automated vision systems and consumer cameras, it is desirable to automatically determine an appropriate exposure time based on the scene; this function is known as autoexposure (AE). Traditionally, AE is mainly determined by environment *brightness*: bright scenes lead to short exposure time. This control scheme is simple to implement and has been widely adopted. However, when the brightness level of a scene remains constant, this scheme does not consider camera motion or subject motion and therefore often leads to motion blur.

As more computing power is put in digital cameras, new cameras, such as Canon SD1100 and Nikon COOLPIX S8100, have an AE function that is based on motion estimation. In a nutshell, the apparent motion estimated from two consecutive frames is used to guide the exposure time and ISO setting for the next frame, so that blur is minimized. In the captured video, most frames do not have blur, but those with short exposure time will be noisy due to the high ISO setting. This AE function largely turns video enhancement into a denoising problem.

This chapter presents a research work on the problem of how to achieve high-quality video denoising in the context of motion-based exposure control. This problem is pertinent as motion deblurring in general is a challenging problem; achieving high-quality denoising in this context may greatly *reduce*, although not eliminate, the need of motion deblurring for video enhancement. This problem is promising as Fig. 2.1 shows; it is also difficult in its own ways.

- Within a sequence captured using motion-based AE, there are often high-quality frames, which correspond to the frames with little apparent motion and captured with relatively long exposure and low ISO.[1] Ideally, we would want to use the high-quality frames to better enhance the noisier frames; at the same time, we would not want the noisy frames to compromise the high-quality frames during the denoising process.

- Noisy frames are captured with high ISO and short exposure because of fast motion. To exploit high-quality frames to enhance noisy frames, we would need robust motion estimation that can handle large displacement. In our experiments, we commonly found displacement of 70 or more, which confound even top-performing optical flow methods that have been adopted in state-of-the-art video denoising.

In this chapter, we present a high-quality video denoising method in the context of motion-based exposure control, by combining spatial denoising and temporal denoising in a novel way. Our combination is based on an intuitive observation. Specifically, spatial methods like BM3D [1] perform well if the image has abundant locally similar structure. Its performance starts to degrade when the local structure is unique. Motion-compensated filtering on the other hand works best when local patches are unique, because the optical flow can be reliably estimated. Therefore,

---

[1]For example, although it is hard to hold a camera perfectly still for a long period, it is also rare that our hands would continuously shake a camera; shaky intervals are always intermingled with steady moments.

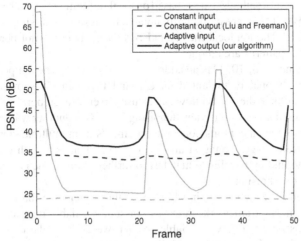

Fig. 2.1 The benefit of denoising videos captured with motion-based exposure control. *Top*: A panoramic image from which we generate a synthetic video whose viewport (*red box*) moves along the red zigzag curve with varying speed. *Bottom*: If a constant short exposure is applied to each frame to minimize blur, the captured video has constant low PSNR (*dashed red curve*), and a state-of-the-art video denoising [2] improves its PSNR to about 34dB (*dashed black curve*). If exposure time is set *adaptively* based on motion estimation, the input video has higher PSNR (*solid red curve*), and our denoising algorithm produces a much higher quality video with a total PSNR of 39 dB (*solid black curve*). Best viewed electronically in color

our idea is to detect the length of reliable flow trajectories for each pixel and use the length as a weight to combine the results of BM3D and motion-compensated filtering.

Unlike previous denoising works which either avoid using motion estimation, such as BM3D [1], or assume reliable motion estimation as input, such as [2], our method selectively operates in whichever regime works best. As a result, our algorithm performs better than both VBM3D [3] and the latest video denoising algorithm [2].

Our flow reliability evaluation is based on a forward—backward consistency check, which is a widely used technique in stereo and motion estimation. However, this reliability measure of motion estimation has not been exploited for improving video denoising performance in the literature, to the best of our knowledge.

2.2 Related Work

Our work is most related to image and video denoising and enhancement.

Denoising

Image denoising has been studied for several decades. A complete review is beyond the scope of this paper. We refer the readers to the previous work sections in [1, 4] for excellent reviews of the literature. An incomplete list of recent works includes [1, 4–9]. In particular, the methods that are based on local self-similarity, such as nonlocal means [4] and BM3D [1], are particularly notable because of their simple ideas and impressive results. The nonlocal means and BM3D methods do not perform well when local image patterns are unique.

Video denoising [2, 3, 10, 11] can address this limitation as the temporal dimension provides additional redundant data. Liu and Freeman [2] showed that the spatial regularization in the optical flow can be used to ensure temporal coherence in removing structured noise. Multi-view denoising [12–14] is another way of addressing this limitation, which exploits noisy measurements from multiple viewpoints to reconstruct a clean image. Zhang et al. [14] observed that 3D depth can be used as a constraint to find more reliable matches to further improve the performance of multi-view image denoising.

Our work is most related to [2], in which the authors integrate robust optical flow into a nonlocal means framework; their work assumes reliable flow as input. Our work does not assume the flow is reliable. Rather, we evaluate the flow trajectory reliability for each pixel and use the reliability measure as a weight to combine spatial denoising and temporal denoising results.

Video Enhancement using Stills

Our work is also related to works that use high-quality digital photos to enhance low-resolution videos. For example, Bhat et al. [15] and Schubert et al. [16] proposed an approach to enhance low-resolution videos of a static scene using multi-view stereo to compute correspondences between low-resolution video and high-resolution images; Gupta et al. [17] use optical flow to compute correspondences and can therefore handle dynamic scenes as well. Watanabe et al. [18] propagate high-frequency information in high-resolution frames to low-resolution frames using motion compensation. Nagahara et al. [19] take a similar approach but use morphing based on feature matching instead of motion compensation. In our work, the frame resolution is the same; what differs is the noise level. We do not assume reliable flow as input; instead, we use the lifespan of reliable flow trajectory to combine spatial denoising and temporal denoising.

2.3 Denoising Algorithm

Our denoising algorithm is based on the following intuition. If an image region has *unique* texture patterns, we would prefer to use temporal denoising, because optical flow can be estimated reliably and spatial denoising usually does not work well. On the other hand, if an image region has repetitive texture or uniform color, we would prefer to use spatial denoising because optical flow is unreliable and self-similarity makes spatial denoising work effectively. We do not judge the flow reliability using a binary decision. Instead, we softly combine the spatial and temporal denoising result using our reliability measure as weight. Next we explain our algorithm in detail.

Spatial Denoising

We use the single-image denoising method CBM3D [1] to perform our spatial denoising:

$$\hat{I}_S(\mathbf{z}) = \text{CBM3D}(I, \mathbf{z}), \tag{2.1}$$

where I is the input image and $\mathbf{z}$ is pixel location. We apply this single denoising method to each frame using the corresponding frame noise variance as parameter. We do not use CVBM3D, the video version of CBM3D, because CVMB3D only handles constant noise variance across the whole video volume, which would compromise the high-quality frames in the captured video. We choose CBM3D due to its performance, efficiency, and public availability; other spatial denoising methods, such as nonlocal means [4], can also be used instead.

Temporal Denoising Along Reliable Flow

Let I_t be the frame we are currently denoising. We compute the optical flow over a temporal window of $\pm H$ frames, where we use $H = 5$ as in [2]. The flow may not be reliable for every pixel and every frame in the temporal window. We use the forward–backward consistency as a measure of flow reliability. If the flow vector from a pixel in frame i to a pixel in frame j is denoted $\mathbf{v}_{ij}$, then the flow consistency error is $\|\mathbf{v}_{ij} + \mathbf{v}_{ji}\|^2$. We consider the flow to be consistent if the error is below some threshold (1 and 3 are used in our synthetic and real experiments, respectively).

For each pixel in frame I_t, we determine the number of frames of consistent forward flow up to at most frame $t + H$, and backward flow down to at most $t - H$. If the per pixel flow is not consistent at frame $t + 1$, we do not consider frame $t + 2$ for that pixel. The number of consistent frames in the forward and backward directions are denoted H_f and H_b, respectively. H_f and H_b are functions of the pixel under consideration; however, we omit the function notation for simplicity.

Once we have determined the "lifespan" $[t - H_b, t + H_f]$ of a reliable flow, the temporal pixel estimate is computed by filtering along the optical flow:

$$\hat{I}_T(\mathbf{z}) = \frac{1}{Z} \sum_{i=t-H_b}^{t+H_f} W(\mathbf{z}_i) \cdot I_i(\mathbf{z}_i), \tag{2.2}$$

where Z is a normalization factor and $W(\mathbf{z}_i)$ is given by:

$$W(\mathbf{z}_i) = \left(\beta_i^2 + \beta_t^2\right)^{-\frac{3}{2}} \exp\left\{-\frac{\|P(\mathbf{z}) - P(\mathbf{z}_i)\|^2}{\beta_i^2 + \beta_t^2}\right\}, \qquad (2.3)$$

where $\beta_i = g_i \cdot \beta_0$ with g_i being the gain used to capture frame i and β_0 being proportional to the base noise level of the camera. In Eq. (2.3), we note

- The first term assigns larger weight to pixels from cleaner frames. This weighting scheme facilitates using the high-quality frames to better enhance the noisier frames; at the same time, it discourages using the noisy frames to compromise the high-quality frames during the denoising process.
- The exponential term assigns smaller weight to pixels that came from optical flows with poorer block matches. The distance between two patches is computed using a weighted SSD as in [2].

In addition to having the exponential term based on the patch distance, we use a threshold,

$$\tau_t = m \cdot \beta_t + \tau_0, \qquad (2.4)$$

to reject pixels with large patch distances. The linear form and parameters for τ_t were determined empirically by maximizing the PSNR of a simulated video sequence. With pixel intensities in the range [0,1], we used $m = 0.40$ and $\tau_0 = -5.3 \cdot 10^{-4}$.

Combining Spatial and Temporal Denoising

To combine the spatial and temporal denoising results, we linearly interpolate using the number of consecutive frames of flow consistency $H_b + H_f$ as the weight:

$$\hat{I}(\mathbf{z}) = \frac{H_f + H_b}{2H} \hat{I}_T(\mathbf{z}) + \left(1 - \frac{H_f + H_b}{2H}\right) \hat{I}_S(\mathbf{z}). \qquad (2.5)$$

When a pixel does not have any consistent flows, we rely purely on the CBM3D estimate. When a pixel has perfectly consistent flows (within the temporal window), we rely purely on the temporal estimate.

2.3.1 Efficient Flow for Large Motion

Now we describe how we compute optical flow for denoising in our experiments. Optical flow is not our technical contribution; we describe it so that our paper is reproducible.

In real videos, we found that flow vectors can easily be 70 pixels or more. This large motion easily confounds many top-performing flow algorithms evaluated in [20], which typically handle flow magnitudes of 10 or fewer pixels. For example, we tried the flow algorithm [21] used in [2] as input for video denoising. The algorithm does

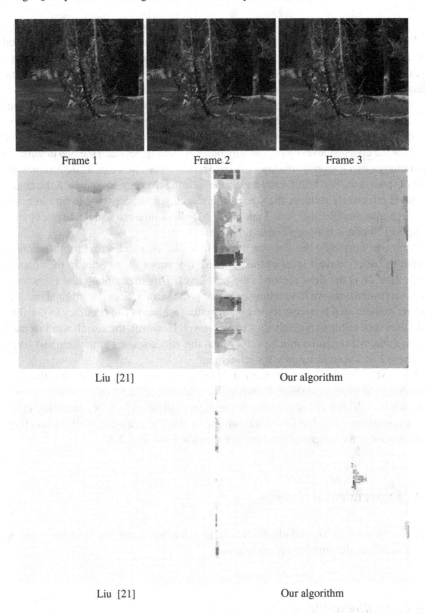

Frame 1   Frame 2   Frame 3

Liu [21]   Our algorithm

Liu [21]   Our algorithm

Fig. 2.2 Optical flow results for three consecutive frames in the *mountain* scene. *Top*: The displacement between frames 1 and 2 is large, whereas the displacement between frames 2 and 3 is small. *Middle*: Our optical flow outperforms the optical flow in [21] for large displacements. The left to right motion causes the pixels on the left edge of frame 1 to be invisible in frame 2, which is why our flow is inaccurate on that edge. *Bottom*: The optical flow in [21] outperforms our method for small displacements by producing a smoother flow. Best viewed electronically in color

not produce correct flow for a typical pair of frames with large motion as shown in Fig. 2.2. We believe this is because most flow algorithms use derivative-based continuous optimization which is easily trapped in local minima, even if an image pyramid is used. To handle large motions in our video, we fall back to a traditional hierarchical block matching technique to compute our optical flow.

Suppose we are computing the optical flow from frame i to j. We start by constructing image pyramids of downsampled versions of I_i and I_j with L levels, where the coarsest level has been downsample by a factor of 2^{L-1}. We then compute a flow field for the coarsest level by performing block matching between the two downsampled images using search windows of size $M \times M$. The choice of M determines the size of motion the algorithm can handle. Performing the primary search at the coarsest level effectively reduces the size of the search space necessary to find matches for large motions. We use $L = 3$ and $M = 61$, allowing us to handle displacements of up to 120 pixels between consecutive frames.

Next, we upsample the flow field by a factor of two and refine it by searching within the next coarsest level of the pyramid. If $\mathbf{v}$ was a flow vector in the coarsest level, then $2\mathbf{v}$ is the flow vector in the next level. This upsampling and refinement step is repeated until we have a flow field that is the same size as our original images. The refinement step is necessary to obtain better resolution and accuracy in our flow field than is possible using only the coarsest level. However, the search window used during refinement can be much smaller than the window used at the coarsest level; we use a 7×7 search window for refinement.

We first compute flow between neighboring frames, then concatenate the flow to initialize motion estimation between the reference frame t to any other frame i between $[t - H, t + H]$, and finally refine the initialization by block matching in the finest resolution only. We found this simple method works quite well for handling large motion; an example of the flow result is shown in Fig. 2.2.

2.4 Experimental Results

Our results are best viewed electronically in color. More results, including videos, are available in the supplementary material.

2.4.1 Synthetic Video

We first test our system on three different synthetic video sequences. Each sequence is generated by moving a 512×512 window around a large panoramic image as shown in Fig. 2.3. The motion of the windows have speeds ranging from 0 to 750 pixels per second and undergo two changes of direction. Motion-based exposure control is simulated on the sequences to determine the optimal exposure time T for

City scene   Mountain scene

Fig. 2.3 Our synthetic video sequences are generated from panoramic images. A 512×512 pixel window follows the trajectory shown in red. The motion in each sequence has variable speed and undergoes multiple direction changes. Best viewed electronically in color

each frame. If d is the displacement between the previous two frames and f is the frame rate, then

$$T = \frac{1}{d \cdot f}. \tag{2.6}$$

This results in one pixel of motion during the camera's exposure time. The actual exposure time is clamped between 1 ms and $1/f$, where we use $f = 7.5$ frames per second. Once the exposure time has been set, we set the gain to:

$$g = \frac{T_{\max}}{T} \tag{2.7}$$

such that the video sequence maintains a constant brightness level. We then add white Gaussian noise to the current frame with $\sigma = g \cdot \sigma_0$ where σ_0 is chosen such that $\sigma = 25$ (out of 255) for the shortest exposure time. We also generate videos with constant short and long exposure times for comparison.

We run the input sequences through CBM3D and Liu and Freeman [2] using the known σ parameters for each frame. For our algorithm, we use $\beta_0 = 0.1$ in Eq. (2.3) (with pixel intensities in the range $[0,1]$) and specify the gain values for the individual frames. The value for β_0 was found empirically to provide full denoising power without sacrificing texture preservation.

The per frame PSNRs can be seen in Fig. 2.4 for the *city* and *mountain* sequences and in Fig. 2.1 for the *station* sequence. Our algorithm provides higher PSNR than the state-of-the-art algorithms for all of the frames containing significant noise levels. Our results do have lower PSNR for frames that were very clean to begin with. However, the difference is imperceptible with our results having a mean square error of only about 10^{-3} of an intensity level in the cleaner frames.

The improvements in our results over CBM3D are primarily made in the regions with unique texture and structure, as can be seen in Figs. 2.5 and 2.6. In these regions, the optical flow is reliable, thus temporal denoising is effective. The weights between the temporal and spatial estimates are shown in Fig. 2.7. In smooth regions where our optical flow is unreliable, our denoising algorithm falls back on CBM3D which performs well on smooth regions.

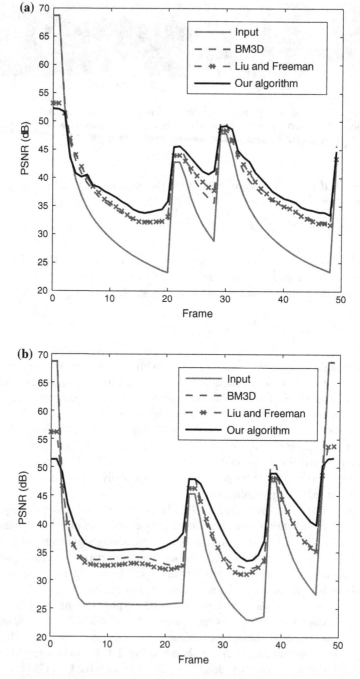

Fig. 2.4 PSNR results for the synthetic video sequences. In frames with significant noise levels, our algorithm outperforms other state-of-the-art denoising algorithms. Best viewed electronically in color. **a** City scene. **b** Mountain scene

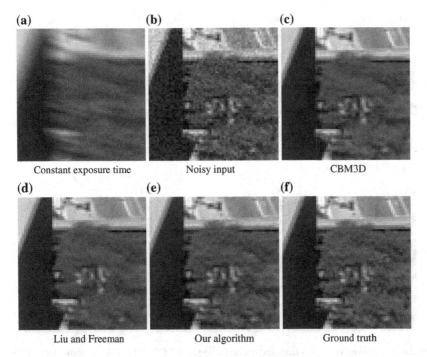

Fig. 2.5 A close-up of results from the *city* sequence. The motion-based AE provides a sharp but noisy image, shown in (**b**), as opposed to the blurry image captured with a constant exposure time, shown in (**a**). Our denoising algorithm outperforms CBM3D [1] (applied to each individual frame using corresponding frame noise variance) and Liu and Freeman [2] (using the known noise variance for each individual frame). More detail is preserved in the tree while the building is still properly smoothed. Best viewed electronically in color

2.4.2 Real Video

To test our system on a real video sequence, we first needed motion-based exposure control. We implemented the motion estimation portion of the exposure control algorithm using a standard hierarchical image registration technique. The remainder of the exposure control algorithm works just as described for the synthetic video. Since the image registration only tracks global translational motion, we designed our real experiment to have primarily translational motion. We set up two cameras facing out the side window of an automobile. We used one camera, a Canon EOS 7D, to capture a video sequence with a constant exposure time of $1/30$ s and the other camera, a Point Grey Grasshopper, to capture a video sequence with motion-based exposure control. As shown in Fig. 2.8, our algorithm preserves detail better than [2], because optical flow is hard to be estimated reliably in the presence of large motion, multiple depth layers, and thin structure. Our method measures flow reliability and is robust to inaccurate flow input.

More results are available in the supplementary material.

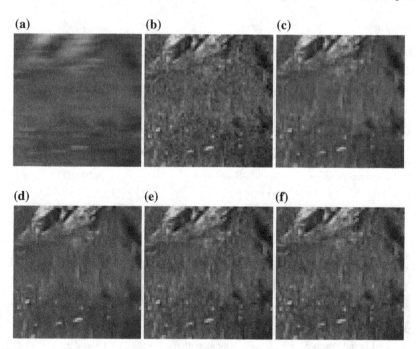

Fig. 2.6 A close-up of results from the *mountain* sequence. CBM3D [1] loses some detail in the yellow flowers, while [2] over-smooths the grass. Our algorithm performs better at denoising both the flowers and the grass. Best viewed electronically in color. **a** Constant exposure time. **b** Noisy input. **c** CBM3D. **d** Liu and Freeman. **e** Our algorithm. **f** Ground truth

Denoised frame   Weight map   Denoised frame   Weight map

Fig. 2.7 Two weight maps from the synthetic sequences. Lighter colors denote pixels that rely more on temporal denoising than spatial denoising. The darker regions in the weight maps correspond to smooth regions of the image where optical flow trajectory is less reliable. The horizontal motion in the video sequences causes the sides of the image to be invisible in neighboring frames, which is why we see the vertical bands of constant weight. Best viewed electronically in color

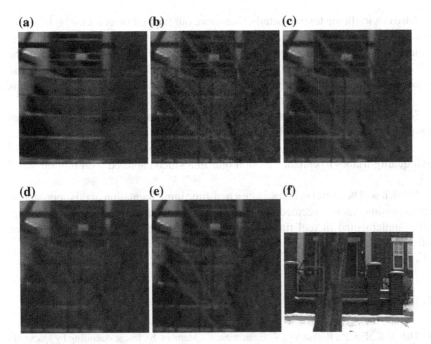

Fig. 2.8 Results from the driving sequence. Our results are comparable to CBM3D [1], which preserves the detail of the tree reasonably well. The tree branches and some of the other fine details were over-smoothed by Liu and Freeman [2] due to inaccurate flow in the presence of large motion, multiple depth layers, and thin structure. Best viewed electronically in color. **a** Constant exposure time. **b** Noisy input. **c** CBM3D. **d** Liu and Freeman. **e** Our algorithm. **f** Full denoised frame

2.5 Conclusion

In this chapter, we have proposed a high-quality video denoising algorithm in the context of motion-based exposure control. Unlike previous denoising works which either avoid using motion estimation, such as BM3D [1], or assume reliable motion estimation as input, such as [2], our method uses the "lifespan" of reliable flow trajectory as a weight to integrate spatial denoising and temporal denoising. This weighted combination scheme (1) makes our method robust to optical flow failures over regions with repetitive texture or uniform color, (2) combines the advantages of both spatial and temporal denoising, and (3) outperform the state-of-the art. There are several avenues for future research.

First, we would like to investigate better weighting schemes. In the current formulation, when the lifespan of a reliable flow is zero, the algorithm resorts to CBM3D; in this case, temporal coherence is not enforced. This differs from [2], which uses smooth optical flow to obtain temporal consistency in the presence of structural noise. However, as Figs. 2.5, 2.6, and 2.8 show, this temporal consistency is obtained at the expense of sacrificing texture details. Therefore our method is suited for higher quality cameras with little compression artifact, while [2] is more suited for low-quality cameras with strong structured noise and compression artifacts. Furthermore, the lack of temporal consistency in our results is not as noticeable since the motion-based exposure control only produces noisy frames when there is large motion. Nevertheless, a better weighting scheme would address this limitation.

Second, although motion-based AE reduces motion blur significantly, it does not completely eliminate motion blur because exposure is set based on the motion of previous frames; there is always a delay. It is desirable to use the noisy frames and/or high-quality frames to enhance motion blur in a video captured with motion-based AE.

Third, it will be useful to investigate a real-time implementation of this approach so that denoising can be executed before compression. Our approach has the potential to be implemented in real time as all components are block based; no complex optimization, such as conjugate gradient, is involved in the optical flow estimation.

References

1. Dabov, K., Foi, R., Katkovnik, V., Egiazarian, K., Member, S.: Image denoising by sparse 3D transform-domain collaborative filtering. TIP **16**, 1395–1411 (2007)
2. Liu, C., Freeman, W.T.: A high-quality video denoising algorithm based on reliable motion estimation. In: Proceedings of the 11th European conference on computer vision conference on Computer vision: Part III (ECCV). Springer, Berlin (2010). http://portal.acm.org/citation.cfm?id=1927006.1927061
3. Dabov, K., Foi, A., Egiazarian, K.: Video denoising by sparse 3D transform-domain collaborative filtering. In: Proceedings of the 15th European Signal Processing Conference (2007)
4. Buades, A., Coll, B., Morel, J.M.: A review of image denoising algorithms, with a new one. Simulation **4**, 490–530 (2005)
5. Roth, S., Black, M.J.: Fields of Experts: A framework for learning image priors. CVPR **2**, 860–867 (2005)
6. Elad, M., Aharon, M.: Image Denoising Via Learned Dictionaries and Sparse representation. CVPR pp. 895–900 (2006)
7. Lyu, S., Simoncelli, E.P.: Statistical modeling of images with fields of gaussian scale mixtures. NIPS (2006)
8. Tappen, M.F., Liu, C., Adelson, E.H., Freeman, W.T.: Learning gaussian conditional random fields for low-level vision. CVPR, pp. 1–8. IEEE Computer Society, CA, USA (2007). http://doi.ieeecomputersociety.org/10.1109/CVPR.2007.382979
9. Foi, A., Katkovnik, V., Egiazarian, K.: Pointwise shape-adaptive DCT for high-quality denoising and deblocking of grayscale and color images. TIP **16**(8), 2080–2095 (2007)
10. Bennett, E.P., McMillan, L.: Video enhancement using per-pixel virtual exposures. SIGGRAPH pp. 845–852. ACM, California, New York (2005). http://doi.acm.org/10.1145/1186822.1073272
11. Chen, J., Tang, C.K.: Spatio-temporal markov random field for video denoising. CVPR (2007)
12. Vaish, V., Levoy, M., Szeliski, R., Zitnick, C.L., Kang, S.B.: Reconstructing occluded surfaces using synthetic apertures: stereo, focus and robust measures. CVPR **2**, 1063–6919. IEEE Computer Society, CA, USA (2006). http://doi.ieeecomputersociety.org/10.1109/CVPR.2006.244

13. Heo, Y.S., Lee, K.M., Lee, S.U.: Simultaneous depth reconstruction and restoration of noisy stereo images using Non-local pixel distribution. CVPR pp. 1–8. IEEE Computer Society, CA, USA (2007)
14. Zhang, L., Vaddadi, S., Jin, H., Nayar, S.: Multiple view image denoising. CVPR, IEEE Computer Society, CA, USA (2009). http://doi.ieeecomputersociety.org/10.1109/CVPRW.2009.5206836
15. Bhat, P., Zitnick, C.L., Snavely, N., Agarwala, A., Agrawala, M., Curless, B., Cohen, M., Kang, S.B.: Using photographs to enhance videos of a static scene. In: Kautz J., Pattanaik S. (eds.) Proceedings of the Eurographics Symposium on Rendering (2007). http://www.cs.washington.edu/homes/pro/papers/videoEnhancement/videoEnhancement.htm
16. Schubert, F., Mikolajczyk, K.: Combining high-resolution images with low-quality videos. BMVC08 pp. 1–10 (2008) http://www.visionbib.com/bibliography/match-pl503.html#TT48849
17. Gupta, A., Bhat, P., Dontcheva, M., Curless, B., Deussen, O., Cohen, M.: Enhancing and experiencing spacetime resolution with videos and stills. In: International Conference on Computational Photography (2009) http://grail.cs.washington.edu/projects/enhancing-spacetime/
18. Watanabe, K., Iwai, Y., Nagahara, H., Yachida, M., Suzuki, T.: Video synthesis with high spatio-temporal resolution using motion compensation and spectral fusion. IEICE—Trans. Inf. Syst. **E89-D**, pp. 2186–2196, Oxford University Press, Oxford, UK (2006). http://portal.acm.org/citation.cfm?id=1184860.1185056
19. Nagaharaf, H., Matsunobuf, T., Iwaif, Y., Yachidaf, M., Suzuki, T.: High-resolution video generation using morphing. ICPR **4**, 338–341 (2006) doi:10.1109/ICPR.2006.626
20. Baker, S., Scharstein, D., Lewis, J., Roth, S., Black, M.J., Szeliski, R.: A database and evaluation methodology for optical flow. ICCV (2007)
21. Liu, C.: Beyond pixels: Exploring new representations and applications for motion analysis. Dissertation, Massachusetts Institute of Technology, Cambridge (2009)

Chapter 3
Panoramic Video Construction from Mobile Video Streams

Motaz El Saban and Ayman Kaheel

Abstract Constructing a panoramic video out of multiple incoming live mobile video streams is a challenging problem with many applications in consumer, education, and security domains. This problem involves multiple users live streaming the same scene from different points of view, using their mobile phones, with the objective of constructing a panoramic video of the scene. The main challenge in this problem is the lack of coordination between the streaming users, resulting in too much, too little, or no overlap between incoming streams. To add to the challenge, the streaming users are generally free to move, which means that the amounts of overlap between the different streams are dynamically changing. In this chapter, we propose a method for automatically coordinating between streaming users, such that the quality of the resulting panoramic video is enhanced. The method works by analyzing incoming video streams, and automatically providing active feedback to the streaming users. We investigate different methods for generating and presenting the active feedback to the streaming users resulting in an improved panoramic video output compared to the case where no feedback is utilized.

3.1 Introduction

Today, smartphones are more ubiquitous than ever. The overwhelming majority of these phones have video capturing, network connection, and different sensors capabilities. The rapid increase in the number of mobile phones and their capabilities has led to the emergence of many new scenarios and applications. One very common consumer application is live video streaming, which leads to the continuous rise of online services addressing this application [1, 2]. These online services allow users to capture and stream live video to a website where other users/friends can watch

M.E. Saban (✉)
Microsoft Technology & Research, Advanced Technology Lab, Cairo, Egypt
e-mail: motazel@microsoft.com

A. Kaheel
Yahoo Inc., Sunnyvale, CA
e-mail: aymank@yahoo-inc.com

© Springer International Publishing Switzerland 2015
G. Hua and X.-S. Hua (eds.), *Mobile Cloud Visual Media Computing*,
DOI 10.1007/978-3-319-24702-1_3

the video at the same time it is being captured. Considerable research work has been carried out to build services on top of the mobile live video streaming; such as stitching in real-time incoming streams [3] and real-time augmentation in the viewfinder to automatically equip the user with useful information on the scene content while shooting [4, 5]. In this chapter, we focus on panoramic video construction, the goal is to produce a panoramic video stream out of the multiple video streams captured at the same location using mobile devices. The promise of such a stitching service is hindered by the fact that users, without coordination among themselves, can produce streams that are either unstitchable or stitchable with large amount of overlap between the captured video streams; hence, the benefit out of combining multiple streams is diminished. The underlying assumption here is that every user is capturing the scene with little information about other users viewing volumes. In this chapter, we introduce the concept of Active Feedback which utilizes network connection capabilities of mobile phones for providing hinting information for the capturing users. The main objective of the feedback information is to maximize the probability of a successful panoramic video result. The intention here is to provide a per-user feedback to guide that particular user. Toward that end, the system receives the incoming user stream along with other streams, analyzes them, generates the feedback, and send the feedback to the streaming user in real-time to help him improve the live generated video. It is worth noting here that for the feedback to be useful, there is a real-time constraint on analyzing the incoming streams. To the best of our knowledge, the proposed approach for improving panoramic video quality through user interaction has not been attempted before in the literature. The key technical contributions in this work are:

- Constructing a real-time feedback system for enhancing panoramic video construction quality.
- Investigating different methods for triggering, computing, and presenting the feedback
- Conducting a user study to evaluate different feedback aspects and show the gains achieved by utilizing interaction

The rest of this chapter is organized as follows. Section 3.2 reviews related work. Section 3.3 presents an overview of the proposed active feedback stitching system. Section 3.4 describes details of the proposed implementation of the stitching and active feedback methods. Section 3.5 describes the experimental setup, the datasets used for evaluation and the results. Finally, Sect. 3.6 draws some conclusions and proposes directions for future work.

3.2 Related Work

We review related work relevant to this chapter along two main areas: (a) video stitching and (b) providing feedback for users while shooting videos. In the area of video stitching, a number of research publications have addressed the problem of creating a panoramic image out of a single video [6–8]. The main idea is to stitch together video frames from a single video feed to generate one wide panoramic image. In this chapter, we deal with creating a panoramic video out of multiple videos such as in [9, 10]. In most of the previous work on video stitching, the techniques are based on image stitching which is a very well researched area [11, 12]. However, there are main difference between image stitching and video stitching as the latter has unique features that can be used for the stitching process, such as audio and the temporal information. Besides, video faces more challenges like moving cameras, lack of consistency in terms of stitching individual frames or dropping some of them. On the evaluation side of stitching algorithms, there are two main types of evaluation used in the literature: (a) subjective, by using human judges to evaluate the presentation of example images or videos and (b) objective, by using synthetically distorted images using known transformation matrices as in [13]. In [13], the authors estimate the transformation matrices, and compare it with the original one for measuring the error. The obvious drawback of evaluation using synthetic datasets is that they do not model in full the real-case scenario when videos are captured.

The second area of related work is on providing feedback to users while they are shooting a video, such as the interesting work in [6, 14]. However, [6, 14] focused on generating a panoramic image using videos. The work here focuses on generating panoramic video using videos. Another interesting work is presented in [15] where the authors generate a wide video texture output from a single panning video with minimal user interaction. Though, there are some similarities with this work, the end goal is the not same and the work in [15] does not consider any user feedback while generating the actual stitched output. An alternative form of feedback commonly available nowadays is in digital cameras offering a panoramic picture mode. These devices help the shooter in capturing successive pictures to produce a wider scene by giving suggestions on where to snap the next picture. Nevertheless, the type of feedback provided in these digital cameras is still quite primitive compared to the ones explored in the presented work and there is no published work evaluating the generated feedback.

3.3 System Overview

In Fig. 3.1, the architecture of an end-to-end generic mobile video streaming system is shown augmented with real-time stitching of incoming video streams and active feedback information to streamers. The server receives all streamed videos, stitches them together and provides the output panoramic video. We briefly describe the utilized video stitching method as the focus of this chapter is not on how to generate the stitched video output, rather on how to utilize user feedback to generate a better quality stitching. This concept can be applied to any stitching method such as the work in [6, 7, 12]. In this work, we propose stitching timely synchronized videos

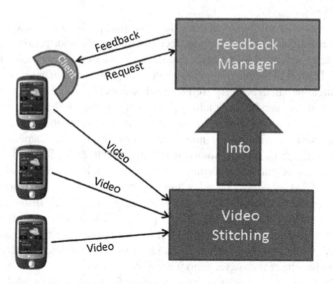

Fig. 3.1 System Architecture with the active feedback part colored in *red*

using a frame-by-frame basis as in [3][1] and briefly summarized in Sect. 3.7.1. For each time synchronized pair of frames, the stitching algorithm implements the two main steps, alignment, and compositing. The purpose of alignment is to estimate a geometric transformation matrix relating the frame pair. It involves extracting interest point features from both images, and matching them together.

Various forms of visual features have been used in the literature including points, edges, regions, and contours [17–19] for tasks such as stitching, category, and instance recognition. In this work we concentrate on point features, as they are the most commonly used owing to their general nature. The main stages in a typical feature-based image matching pipeline are feature detection, feature description, and feature correspondence. In the feature detection stage, each image is searched for local features, often called interest points, with the desirable properties to be invariant under a class of image transforms as well as being distinctive. The feature description stage involves describing each interest point in terms of the surrounding patch of pixels, either using a single value or a distribution involving raw, moments, or gradient components [20–25]. Then, the interest point descriptor is represented as a feature vector and feature correspondence is established using a distance metric on that vector.

Most modern day interest-point detectors are able to deal with in-plane image rotation. The state-of-the-art method to achieve rotational invariance is to estimate a dominant orientation at each detected interest point. Once the local orientation of an interest point has been estimated, an oriented patch around the detected point can be extracted and used to form a feature descriptor. The simplest possible orientation

---

[1] Temporal information can be easily integrated to avoid frame-by-frame stitching as proposed in [9, 16].

estimate is the average gradient within a region around the interest point. SIFT uses a better technique, it looks at the histogram of orientations computed around the interest point. SURF, on the other hand, uses the responses to Haar wavelets for orientation assignment. A number of fully affine invariant detectors and descriptors have been proposed in the literature [24, 26–29]; two detectors are considered to be the state of the art, maximally stable extremal region (MSER) [25] and Affine SIFT (ASIFT) [30]. MSER works by thresholding the image at all possible gray levels. Regions whose rate of change of area w.r.t. threshold is minimal are defined as maximally stable and are returned as detected regions. This results in regions that are invariant to affine geometric transformations. ASIFT follows a different approach; it simulates all image views obtainable by varying the two camera axis orientation parameters, namely, the latitude and the longitude angles. Then, it deals with scale, translation, and in-plane rotation by using the SIFT method itself. It is worth noting that the full affine invariant descriptors are considerably more computational expensive than the rotational invariant descriptors. For the sake of achieving a real-time performance without much sacrifice to effectiveness we chose Shi-Tomasi's detector [31] with a feathering scheme for composition [32], though are more elaborate methods for interest point extraction and composition such as [33, 34].

On top of this generic video streaming and stitching architecture, we are proposing the use of a feedback channel that can improve the resulting panoramic video. In Fig. 3.1, the proposed contributions are colored in red and are composed of two main parts, the mobile client and the feedback manager.

Mobile client A new mobile component is added to the mobile client and has two main responsibilities: (a) pool the server frequently, asking for feedback, and (b) retrieve the feedback signal from the server, and present it to the user. We have investigated different rates for feedback generation as well as different presentation schemes.

Feedback Manager The feedback manager component is the main part responsible for generating the feedback. It receives video streams and other information from the video stitching component, and generates suitable feedback for each user.

3.4 Active Feedback

Active feedback is the concept of providing in real-time feedback information to the video shooter in order to improve the quality of the final stitched video. We investigate the concept of active feedback for improved video panorama along a number of dimensions: (a) goals for providing feedback, (b) different scenarios for video shooting, (c) feedback triggers, (d) feedback implementation, and (e) feedback presentation. For simplicity, we first consider, the base case when only two users are using the system. Scaling to more than two users is addressed next.

3.4.1 Goals

The goal of Active Feedback is to provide a better viewing experience to the end user watching the stitched video. More specifically, we define a better viewing experience as either an increase in the width of the stitched videos by minimizing the amount of overlap in case of stitchable pairs or a guidance given to users to render the videos stitchable in case of non-stitchable videos. In the latter case, feedback would be useful if the streams used to be stitchable at some previous time point.

3.4.2 Video Shooting Scenarios

The most important video shooting cases where feedback could be applied are:

- Two users are shooting two views of the same scene that have an amount of overlap and the two views are stitchable. We call this case "stitchable".
- Two users are shooting two views of the same scene that had an amount of overlap between them and the two videos used to be stitchable. Then one of the users moved his mobile away from the overlapped area and the videos became non stitchable. We call this case "used to be stitchable".
- Two users are shooting two views of the same scene with no overlap between them. We call this case "never stitched before".

We note that in the above cases, feedback is not necessarily generated; rather these are plausible situations for feedback. Generating feedback will depend on triggers discussed next.

3.4.3 Triggers

There are many possible events that could trigger the feedback manager to create and send feedback to clients. In our investigation, we have experimented with a number of trigger variants with each one experimentally evaluated on a collected real-dataset.

OverlapRatio: The amount of overlap between two videos exceeds 30% of one of the videos. The percentage 30% was experimentally validated to be the minimum required overlap to perform successful video stitching [3].
IPLocation: One, or more, of the interest point used in stitching previous frames is about to get out of the overlapped area.
MotionTracking: The videos became not stitchable because one of the users has moved his camera away.
Initial Condition: If there is no stitching happening and we know that users are located within proximity.

In our experiments, we will have two set of triggers evaluated. The first set is a combination of triggers 1, 3, and 4 referenced as *OverlapRatioSet*. The other set is a combination of triggers 2, 3, and 4 and referenced as *IPLocationSet*.

3.4.4 Implementation

The instantiation of the Active Feedback concept involves two main aspects. The first aspect involves how the feedback is being generated. The second describes how the feedback is being delivered from the server to the mobile clients. In all feedback cases, the feedback manager generates feedback signals and instructions at the server side while the mobile clients pull the server on a regular basis for feedback. We use a pull mode for communication instead of a push mode as this mode allows the clients to have more control over the feedback rate according to their own capabilities [35].

Active Feedback Triggers

OverlapRatio: Using the transformation matrix between two videos, we calculate the amount of overlap between both videos. If the amount of overlap is less than or equal 30%, we send instructions to the video shooters to increase the overlap. We perform that by requesting the user on the right to move the camera to the left and the user on the left to move the camera to the right. It is worth noting that we could generate feedback to one user only, but for simplicity we issued it for both users leaving selection of which user to send feedback to for future work. In the implementation, the clients use the HTTP protocol for retrieving the feedback. We have implemented an ASP.NET HTTP module as a disk-based approach wouldn't be able to handle the reader/writer synchronization problem between the feedback manager writing the feedback, and the mobile clients reading it.

IPLocation: We keep track of matched interest points in the area of overlap and caused the generation of the transformation matrix between the two videos. We track the motion of these interest points using Luca Kanade optical flow [36] and verify if any of them moved out of the overlap area due to camera movement. In such a case, we send feedback to the users asking them to move in a direction opposite to their last motion. It is worth noting that there has been a significant body of work on optical flow methods with [37] and [38] providing good survey and comparative evaluation of existing methods. For our purpose, Luca Kanade provided sufficiently acceptable results.

MotionTracking: we keep track of camera motion using also Luca Kanade optical flow. If the videos cease to be stitchable, we retrieve the positions of both cameras right before stitching was unsuccessful and give feedback to users requesting them to return to the last known stitchable position.

Fig. 3.2 Feedback method
using arrows pointing to
suggest motion direction

InitialCondition: Initially, if the two videos are not stitchable, we send back a composite image of the two streamed frames and put them side-by-side as a feedback for the users. This gives the users a chance to know where other users are located within proximity.

Feedback Presentation

An important aspect of the active feedback concept is the way the feedback will be presented to the end user on his device. There are a number of alternatives for presentation including: (a) suggested movement direction arrows, (b) a feedback image, and (c) a combination of both. As shown in Fig. 3.2, a set of arrows advise the user to move left, right, rotate clockwise, or anti-clockwise.[2] Use of a feedback image is also illustrated in Fig. 3.3 where a snapshot of the user's video and the other user's video is shown. In this particular case, the two videos can not be stitched together.

3.4.5 Scalability

To extend Active Feedback to more than two videos, we estimate a global alignment to understand the initial position of all videos. The global alignment determines the order of the videos (right to left in our case as we assume a $1D$ camera arrangement). We then run the feedback generation algorithm on the mobiles in pairs and propagate the feedback to other mobiles. For example, consider L mobiles with order

---

[2]we assume that the captured scene is at a large enough distance such that in-plane camera motion would be sufficient. If the assumption is violated, motion parallax problems will arise. Dealing with these issues are left for future work.

Fig. 3.3 Feedback method using a feedback image with a snapshot of both users frames

$n_1, n_2, \ldots, n_L$. n_1 is being the leftmost mobile and n_L is being the rightmost mobile. We apply the Active Feedback techniques on the pair (n_1, n_2). If the feedback manager decides that n_2 should move a distance $t_{x_{21}}$ (this is the distance in x axis that mobile phone number 2 should move with respect to mobile 1). Then, we apply the Active Feedback techniques on the pair (n_2, n_3). If the Feedback Manager decides that n_3 should move a distance $t_{x_{32}}$, then the total amount of movement for n_3 will be $(t_{x_{21}} + t_{x_{32}})$. Note that t_x could be positive or negative. Clearly, the computational complexity of the feedback generation process is much lower compared to the video stitching pipeline itself. Hence, the proposed scalability algorithm could scale up to the maximum number of streams supported by the stitching algorithm which presents the computational bottleneck in this case.

3.5 Experimental Results

The reported experiments aimed at answering three main question categories.[3] The first category is related to the amount of improvement gained by introducing the Active Feedback concept to the process of live mobile video stitching. More specifically, we want to answer the questions: (a) does stitching recall and precision increase after using feedback, (b) is the video generated wider, (c) which set of triggers is preferred, and (d) how does feedback affect stitching consistency.

The second category of questions is related to the way the Active Feedback is presented to the user, specifically how useful are the arrows and the feedback images with bounding boxes. The last category is related to the evaluation of the quality of

---

[3] We provide in the supplementary material with this submission the set of frames that were used in the human evaluation study to aid in understanding what the human judges were asked to evaluate.

the feedback itself. Specifically, we want to investigate a suitable rate for the feedback generation and how useful is the feedback. In other words, should the user follow it or not.

3.5.1 Datasets

For the purpose of evaluating the stitching output, a number of authors have proposed to use synthetically distorted images with known transformation matrices as in [13]. The obvious drawback of evaluation using synthetic datasets is that they do not model in full the real-case scenario when videos are captured. For that reason and due to the lack of publicly available datasets for evaluating the proposed active feedback concept, there is a need for collecting our own dataset. In the collected set, special care has been taken to cover different capturing conditions such as day and night and textured and structured scenes. Table 3.1 gives a description of each video set and its total number of frames. Fig. 3.4 shows sample images from this dataset.

For each scene, two users were standing in front of the view, holding their mobile phones, and shooting the videos. The users were instructed to focus on the same scene (example the small green park in the first video see (a). Nevertheless, we gave them the freedom to horizontally and/or rotate the mobile phones (in-plane only) as they deem suitable. For the each scene, we ran the experiment three times,

Table 3.1 Dataset description

Title	Description	Number of frames
LoungeArea	Indoor, close scene, light	396
ParkAtCity1	Daylight, distant scene, slow motion	568
ParkAtCity2	In shade, distant scene	592
NileRoad1	Daylight, slow motion, distant scene	357
NileRoad2	In shade, moving cars and people, distance scene	647

Fig. 3.4 Sample stitched results from the dataset

once without using Active Feedback, and twice with Active Feedback but with two different implementations (*OverlapRatioSet* vs. *IPLocationSet*). For the runs that contain the feedback, we instructed the users to try to follow the feedback as much as possible. We saved the resulting video files and carried a number of analyses as detailed next.

3.5.2 Performance Gains by Active Feedback

The goal of these set of experiments is to evaluate the different set of proposed triggers for active feedback. We compared *OverlapRatioSet* to *IPLocationSet* schemes using the measures: (a) precision, recall and $F1$ measures of the stitched frames, (b) output video size (and overlap area), and (d) video stitching consistency.

Percentage of Correctly Stitched Frames

We compared the average percentage of correctly stitched frames versus non-stitched frames in the whole video dataset using feedback and without using it. The average percentage was calculated as follows:

$$R = \frac{N_S}{N} * 100\,\% \tag{3.1}$$

where R is the percentage of the stitched frames, N_s is the number of the stitched frames and N is the total number of frames. Without using Active Feedback, the ratio was 49.9 %, while with using Active Feedback with RatioOverlapSet the ratio was 65.2 and 69.3 % with *IPLocationSet*.

Stitching Precision and Recall

We estimated the stitching precision, recall, and $F1$ measures on the data set. The precision (Pr) is calculated as the ratio of the number of correctly stitched pairs by the algorithm to the total number of claimed-to-be stitched, while the recall is calculated as the ratio of correctly stitched pairs to the total number of frames that can be stitched by a human judge. Finally, $F1$ measure summarizes performance into a single metric as $\frac{2PR}{P+R}$.

Video Output Size and Overlap Area

We have calculated the average width of output videos in both cases where feedback is utilized and not utilized. While the width of a single video stream is 240 pixels, the average of the stitched video streams is 339 pixels using Active Feedback with *OverlapRatioSet*, 301 pixels using active feedback with *OverlapRatioSet* and 295 pixels without using Active Feedback. This means that Active Feedback increases the width of the final video by 15 %. As width in terms of pixels is an absolute measure, we sought a relative measure to normalize for the initial video size. We have experimented with the normalized average area of overlap (percentage wise) in both cases. It was calculated as follows:

$$O = \frac{O_p}{w_1 * h_1 * w_2 * h_2} * 100\%$$ (3.2)

where O is the overlap percentage, O_p is the number of pixels that are in the overlap area, w_1 and h_1 and w_2 and h_2 are the width and the height of the first and second videos respectively. The smaller the percentage overlap the larger is the resulting output video. Using Active Feedback the overlap ratio was found to be 58.8 and 72.8 % with *OverlapRatioSet* and *IPLocationSet*, respectively, while with no active feedback, it was found to be 73.5 %. This indicates a 20 % decrease in overlap in the the output video.

Video Stitching Consistency

Another method for evaluating video output quality is to measure how consistent video stitching is generated. To elaborate more, Fig. 3.5 shows two graphs. The horizontal axis is time while the vertical one represents whether the frames are stitchable or not, with value 1 meaning frames were stitchable at time t while value 0 means frames were not stitchable. In theory, both graphs have the same percentage of the stitched frames. However, s_2 is more convenient, because the switching frequency between stitching and non-stitching states is less than s_1 and hence less annoying or confusing to a watching user. Hence, it is important to measure if Active Feedback decreases video stitching consistency. We propose to use a total variation (TV) like measure for a video V having N frames to capture the notion of consistency in a video using:

$$TV(V) = \frac{\sum_{t=1}^{N} |s(t) - s(t-1)|}{N} * 100\%$$ (3.3)

where $s(t)$ equals 1 it frames at time t were stitchable, and 0 otherwise and N is the total number of the frames.

Fig. 3.5 Stitching consistency example. The vertical axis is a binary measure of whether stitching was produced or not for a given time point

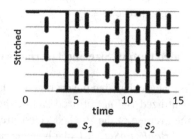

Table 3.2 Stitching results summary comparing different active feedback methods to the case where there is no feedback

	Pr	Re	F_1	Width	Overlap
NoFeedback	0.95	0.49	0.65	295	73.48
OverlapRatioSet	**0.97**	0.65	0.78	**338**	**58.847**
IPLocationSet	0.96	**0.69**	**0.80**	301	72.75

The results in Table 3.2 summarize the performance of the different suggested active feedback methods against the case where there is no feedback. A clear difference is visible across all metrics with the *OverlapRatioSet* being the best according to the amount of overlap in the output frames and a very close second in $F1$ measure. The improvement in $F1$ is almost 20% compared to the baseline of no feedback. It is worth pointing out that a possible explanation to why *IPLocationSet* is better than *OverlapRatioSet* in terms of recall is that *IPLocationSet* tries to keep all interest points found in the overlapped area. If there is an interest point on the leftmost part of both videos, it will always try to include this point. This will definitely increase the number of stitched frames. As for the stitched output consistency, using Active Feedback, the average *TV* is found to be 17 and 14% using *OverlapRatioSet* and *IPLocationSet* respectively, as compared to 15% when Active Feedback is not used. These results indicate that Active Feedback does not hurt consistency of the stitched videos. Table 3.2 summarizes all results using the metrics discussed in this section.

3.5.3 Feedback Assessment

We conducted a user study on the quality of the feedback itself. We randomly selected 408 stitched frames with their feedback and showed them to nine judges (eight males and a female in their 20's), and asked them to evaluate the feedback that was automatically generated. We instructed them that the feedback goal is to decrease output video overlap, but not too much to the case that the overlap is not enough to stitch the two videos. Then, for every feedback frame, they needed to assess whether there was a need for feedback or not and in case the feedback was given if it was right or not.

Out of the whole sample, the users judged that in 40.14% of the frames provided feedback was valuable (true positive), 37.4% of the frames didn't have feedback and that was the right system decision (true negative). These numbers add up to 77.5% constituting success cases. On the other hand, in 18.8% of the frames, the system has not provided feedback while the users judged it would have been beneficial (false negative). Finally, a small percentage (3.6%) of the frames, the system provided feedback that was not necessary (false positive). We have investigated the reason behind high percentage (18.8%) of false negatives and found out that this is due to a single user who judged the false negative at 60%, a value considered as an outlier with respect to other users. Finally, it is worth noting that given the observed high inter judge agreement, it was deemed enough to have only nine judges.

3.5.4 Feedback Presentation

Our final experiment aimed at assessing feedback presentation and rate of generation, albeit on a small scale. We requested from three users (two males and one female in their 20's) who have tested the active feedback concept to evaluate the way the feedback was conveyed, whether through arrows, images, or a combination of both. While one of the users reported that the use of arrows was quite intuitive, two of them were complaining that arrows were sometimes confusing because they did not know how much they should move. On the other hand combining arrows with a feedback image was judged as a very useful presentation methodology, since the feedback images were helpful in understanding what the other user is shooting, and what is the best way to collaborate with him.

As for evaluating different rates for feedback generation, we have run experiments with three different rates (1 feedback/ 0.5 s, 1 feedback/ 1 s and 1 feedback/ 3 s). The users who participated in this experiment judged that a feedback rate of once a second seems reasonable, while having it every 0.5 s is confusing and every 3 s is too slow.

3.6 Conclusion

In this chapter, we introduced the concept of Active Feedback which provides guiding information for capturing users to maximize the probability of a successful panoramic video result. The system receives incoming user streams, analyzes them, generates the feedback, and sends it back to the shooting user in real-time to help him improving the live generated video. We discussed different cases where feedback can be provided along with triggers and presentation methods. For all of these aspects, we have conducted a user study aiming at making an intelligent choice for the design alternatives. Results show that adding the feedback component enhances the overall viewing experience measured by a number of different measures such as stitching precision and recall and output video size. As far as the future work is concerned, there are a number of areas worth investigating. First, providing feedback in a 3D manner (in all directions) can open new possibilities and obviously will face extra challenges such as accurate and fast 3D motion estimation. Second, it is worth investigating in how to maintain a video size that is somehow stable across frames and does not change abruptly as this was one of the desired behaviors gathered by the user study. Finally, it would be interesting to devise a scheme that can adaptively change the feedback rate based on device capabilities and network conditions.

3.7 Appendix

3.7.1 Leveraging Frame Correlation in Stitching

In this section, we investigate three approaches for enhancing the efficiency of the video stitching process using time information from video frames with little or no effect on effectiveness:

- Exploit the area of overlap from previous frame
- Use motion vectors for transformation calculation
- Track interest points (IPs) from previous frames

We started this investigation by a study of the time spent in the various stitching steps to identify the most time-consuming steps to target during algorithm development. Based on conducted experiments, it was found that IP detection and descriptor computation (for SURF) takes more than 80 % of the time in stitching two frames. Hence, most of the investigated approaches in this paper are aiming at minimizing the time spent in IP detection and description. In the subsequent discussion, frames at the current time step will be referenced as frames (n) and frames from the previous time step will be referenced as frames $(n - 1)$.

Area of Overlap from Previous Frames

The premise in this approach is that knowledge of the area of overlap (in case that the video stitching algorithm declares frames as stitchable) from frames $(n - 1)$ can potentially limit the search space for IPs in frames (n). The stitching algorithm performs the same steps as in the case of the first frame pairs but instead of trying to detect IPs in the new whole frame, they are detected in the area of overlap found in frames $(n - 1)$ only, plus some buffer region in the frames (n) (best value experimentally determined to be a 20 pixel band). The efficiency of the buffer-based approach performance is inversely proportional to the size of the overlap area between frames $(n - 1)$ and (n).

Using Motion Vectors for Speed up

This approach was discussed earlier in [10]. The basic idea in this approach is to use global motion estimates of IPs between frames (through motion vector estimation) to avoid recomputation of the new transformation matrix. Some improvements are applied to the original algorithm in [10] including motion vectors estimation using SURF descriptors matching. Our conducted experiments have shown that it is better to use the first frame in computing motion vectors for other frames. Besides, we introduce another improvement by limiting the number of created descriptors to speed up the stitching process by generating descriptors one-by-one and matching them until we get certain number of matches between current frame and first frame. The found matches are used to calculate motion vectors. Finally, as in [10], the geometric transformation matrix in frame (n), R_n, is updated using the transformation matrix at first frame, R_1 and global motion estimates, V_A and V_B, in both pair of video frames at the current frame: $R_n = V_A R_1 (V_B)^{-1}$

Using Optical Flow for Tracking IPs

The main idea behind this approach is to avoid recomputation of the expensive stages of IP detection and descriptors in the alignment process between incoming frames. For that purpose, we track IPs from frames $n - 1$ to find their 2D locations in frames (n) using Lucas–Kanade optical flow [39]. Once we find the new location of IPs in frames (n), their descriptors are obtained from frames $(n - 1)$ in order to avoid recomputation. Tracked IPs are filtered by discarding foreground moving objects, which leads to a more stable stitching using background IPs. IP filtering is based on finding the 2D global motion (d_x, d_y) of all IPs by averaging 2D motion parameters of all IPs and then removing IPs falling outside the 2σ range from the mean value in either d_x, or d_y. It is worth noting that beyond IP filtering process, the estimated global motion is not used in the stitching process itself in frames (n). Using IP descriptors from previous frames is not perfect as it neglects illumination and 3D viewpoint variations and may lead to error accumulation over time. Hence, a criterion is used to signal when we require to do an image-based stitching for a given frame pair (without usage of previous frames information). The suggested criterion is based on the number of IPs that can be successfully matched between the frame pairs of frames (n).

Data Set and Evaluation Results

Since there are no existing suitable data sets for testing our proposed techniques, we have resorted to collecting our own dataset using commonly available mobile phones with video capturing capabilities. Human data collectors were asked to capture time-stamped videos simultaneously at multiple locations, at different time of the day and while performing various camera motions to enable a general assessment, for varying video content, shooting distance, lighting condition, and camera motion. It is worth noting also that instructions were given to the shooters to try to shoot for a common object so as to maximize chance of overlap. Videos were captured using mobile phone cameras with a CIF video resolution (352×288) and with an average frame rate of 11 frames/s.

Upon data collection, a human judge was asked to manually label a sample of 1275 pairs of frames. The human labeler was asked to mark the corresponding video frames as correctly stitched by the algorithm or not (both alignment and blending); and whether they could be stitched by a human or not. Although the output of our system is a stitched video and not frames, we opted to label individual frame pairs to get an upper bound on stitching errors, since a human can miss small stitching issues if watching an output video compared to the case of watching a single video frame. The evaluation aims at measuring precision/recall values for stitching frame pairs as well as stitching time for various descriptors and time information usage methodologies. Note that we are not evaluating the matching capability of the different descriptors (that has been already extensively studied in [40] among other works). Experiments were conducted on an Intel Core™2 Duo CPU E8400 @ 3.00GHZ, with 4.0 GB RAM. In the dataset used, the total number of possibly stitched frame pairs is 892 pairs leaving a relatively small percentage of non-stitchable pairs, as the experiments have shown that a negligible fraction (<5%) of the non-stitchable frames were judged, erroneously, as stitchable by the algorithm.

From our results SIFT has the best recall compared to all other techniques, but the required time is much more than all others. Our aim here is to find a good compromise between accuracy and execution time. Hence, we choose the SURF descriptor as our baseline for the experiments as it is shows experimentally comparable precision/recall values as the SIFT with almost 40 % of the execution time. From our experimental results, SURF and optical flow method performed the best achieving 37 % relative execution time reduction compared to our baseline with comparable accuracy. It is worth noting that we may need to do a pure image-based stitching on some frames, in case time information is not useful. The image-based stitching is invoked when the previous frames cannot be stitched or when the current frame inliers number is less than six (experimentally determined). On average, the image-based stitching algorithm was performed every 15 frames.

3.8 Appendix

3.8.1 Leveraging Device Sensor Information in Geometric Alignment

A related problem space to the stitching problem is the simultaneous localization and mapping (SLAM) [41]. The SLAM problem asks if it is possible for a mobile robot to be placed at an unknown location in an unknown environment and for the robot to incrementally build a consistent map of this environment while simultaneously determining its location within this map. One class of approaches attempts to solve this problem using mainly visual information (VSLAM) [41–43]. In VSLAM, the mobile robots are equipped with a 3-cameras stereo vision system and uses feature descriptors such as SIFT for extracting landmark candidates. The candidates then are matched between cameras to determine the 3D position. The interesting aspect in this problem is that the robots are in many cases equipped with accelerometers for determining the speed of the robot. This inspired our work to leverage accelerometer and sensor data while performing geometric alignment between video frames.

Calculating Rotational Angles from 3D Accelerometer Information

A 3-D accelerometer is an electromechanical device that can measure the 3D acceleration forces a_x, a_y, a_z along the x, y, and z axes. For convenience, the three axes are chosen aligned with the capturing device axes. When the device is steady, these values correspond to components of gravitational acceleration along the different axes. Each value theoretically ranges from 0 to 9.80665 m^2/sec. The remaining of the discussion of this section will use mobile phone as an example for the capturing device.

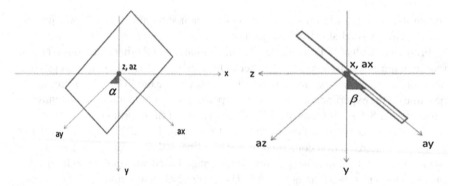

Fig. 3.6 Device coordinates front view (*right*) and side view (*left*)

The three acceleration values can be embedded in the image header, according to any information embedding standard, similar to the Information Interchange Model (IIM) [44]. Alternatively, this information can be stored in a separate metadata file. Such as metadata information was used in Seon et al. work [45] for instance to guide search within video archives. The accelerometer returns the a_x, a_y, a_z values along the axes that are shown in Fig. 3.6. In case the device is held upright, a_y would have a value of 9.80665 with a_x and a_z equal to zero.

In other positions, the gravitational force would have components in the x, z directions as well. In order to calculate the rotation angle in the (x, y) plane and the rotation angle in the (z, y) plane, denoted by α in Fig. 3.6 (left) and β in Fig. 3.6 (right) respectively, we need to calculate the 3D rotational transformation between the vector representing the gravitational acceleration $(0, |Y|, 0)$ and the vector generated by the accelerometer (a_x, a_y, a_z). The value of $|Y|$ is theoretically 9.80665, however because of the imperfections of the 3D accelerometer the value need to be calculated as $|Y| = \sqrt{a_x^2 + a_y^2 + a_z^2}$.

The 3D transformation relating the mobile device coordinates and the world coordinates is described using the Eq. 3.4.

$$\begin{pmatrix} a_x \\ a_y \\ a_z \end{pmatrix} = \begin{pmatrix} \cos\alpha & \sin\alpha\,\cos\beta & -\sin\alpha\,\sin\beta \\ -\sin\alpha & \cos\alpha\,\cos\beta & -\cos\alpha\,\sin\beta \\ 0 & \sin\beta & \cos\beta \end{pmatrix} \begin{pmatrix} 0 \\ |Y| \\ 0 \end{pmatrix} \tag{3.4}$$

3.8.2 Fusion of Feature-Based Descriptors with Accelerometer Readings

As mentioned earlier, descriptors such as SIFT and SURF are in-plane rotation invariant, i.e., rotation in the vertical (x, y) plane. This invariance is achieved by estimating a reproducible orientation for each interest point, and the interest point descrip-

tor is always represented with respect to this orientation. The exact method of the
point orientation estimation depends of the particular descriptor used. In this paper,
we propose to depend on the angles calculated from the accelerometer readings,
instead of estimating the orientation at each interest point, to provide in-plane and tilt
rotational invariance. The proposed approach proceeds as follows; perform the feature detection step, then correct globally for both the in-plane and tilt rotational
angles, and thereafter apply the feature description step. In essence, this approach
can be used to augment any state-of-the-art descriptor, however, in this paper, we concentrate on SIFT and SURF. It is important to note here that the proposed approach
is designed to compensate for camera rotation; however, it would not provide the
desired invariance in cases where the image contents are rotated. Correcting for the
in-plane rotation angle α calculated from Eq. 3.4 would alleviate the need for estimating the orientation values associated with different interest points in both SIFT
and SURF. We correct for the angle α by using the rotational transformation matrix
in Eq. 3.5.

$$\begin{pmatrix} x' \\ y' \end{pmatrix} = \begin{pmatrix} cos\theta & -sin\theta \\ sin\theta & cos\theta \end{pmatrix} \begin{pmatrix} x \\ y \end{pmatrix} \tag{3.5}$$

With respect to the second angle, let us recall that the SIFT and SURF descriptors
are not designed to deal with affine deformations, instead, they are assumed to be
second-order effects that are covered to some degree by the overall robustness of the
descriptor. In addition, Lowe [46] has claimed that the additional complexity of full
affine invariant features often negatively impact their robustness and does not pay
off, except in cases of large viewpoint differences. In our approach, we compensate
for the tilt rotation angle β before applying the SIFT and SURF descriptors. This
will enable the descriptors to respond consistently across affine deformations, such
as (local) perspective foreshortening, without any additional computational cost. We
will show empirically that this method indeed improves the results of the descriptors.

Experimental Setup

We conducted a number of experiments aiming at testing the hypothesis that compensating for in-plane and tilt angles computed from accelerometer readings can
improve matching accuracy as well as processing times of interest point descriptors.
We evaluate the proposed approach when applied to two state-of-the art interest point
descriptors namely SIFT and SURF.

Datasets

Since datasets previously used in the literature for comparing interest point descriptors do not have accelerometer readings associated, we resorted to collecting our own
dataset using mobile phones aiming at a balanced collection between textured and
structured scenes and a variation in both in-plane and out-of plane (tilt) rotations. We
call this dataset "real dataset," for which sample images are illustrated in Fig. 3.7.

In order to remove any selection bias from our end in the data collection process,
we have also used a set of standard images from the dataset used in [40], then we

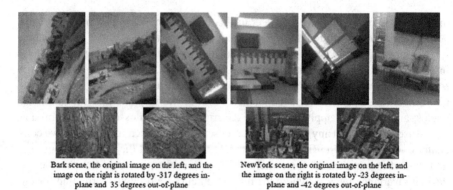

Bark scene, the original image on the left, and the
image on the right is rotated by -317 degrees in-
plane and 35 degrees out-of-plane

NewYork scene, the original image on the left, and
the image on the right is rotated by -23 degrees in-
plane and -42 degrees out-of-plane

Fig. 3.7 *Above* samples from the real dataset including structured and textured scenes. *Below* samples from the synthetically generated dataset where various amounts of in-plane and out-of-plane rotation are introduced

have subjected these images to artificial geometric transformations and measured the matching performance. We have selected a total of 14 images from the images in [40]. For each selected image we have generated 30 images by introducing random in-plane rotations from 0 to 360 degree and tilt rotation (around x-axis) from −45 to 45 degrees. Figure 3.7 shows sample images from this dataset. Results reported in the remaining of this section are average over all the images corresponding to a scene.

Evaluation Criteria

We have adopted three main measures for testing the matching capability of the proposed fusion of interest point-based scheme and accelerometer readings. These measures are the standard precision and recall, and computation time. It is worth mentioning that using accelerometer readings for compensating for rotation angle of the capturing device does not directly change the way interest points are detected or described in SIFT or SURF. However, by compensating for in-plane and tilt rotation angles before interest point description, we are able to show that one can expect a boost in performance as the job of detection and description becomes easier. In the following, we use SIFT+ to signify the case when SIFT is augmented with the rotational angles calculated from the accelerometer readings, and likewise, we use SURF+ to indicate the usage of the augmented SURF.

Recall and $(1 - precision)$ values are used to measure the quality of image descriptors as previously suggested in descriptors comparisons [40]. These measures are based on computing the total number of correspondences (ground truth) and the ones correctly and incorrectly computed.

Another important aspect in our comparisons is the computational time savings. The time savings come from the fact that we do not have to estimate the orientation of interest points patches as this is compensated for globally using accelerometer readings. Furthermore, employing the tilt angle from the accelerometer alleviate the need for the complex calculations associated with fully affine transforms.

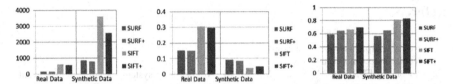

Fig. 3.8 Experiemental results for the four schemes for the real and synthetic datasets. *Left* Computation time, middle: (1 − *precison*) and *right* recall

Results and Analysis

The first comparison on real and synthetically generated datasets concerns the computation time and the savings achieved when utilizing accelerometer readings for compensating for rotational angles. This eliminates the need for any expensive calculation of rotation angles based on image content and replaces it with few inexpensive calculations. The running times of SIFT, SURF, SIFT+, and SURF+ are shown with in Fig. 3.8 (left) for the synthetic and real datasets, respectively, using a 3GHz Intel Core™2 Duo CPU with 4.00 GB of RAM and running a 32-bit operating system (Windows 7 Enterprise). Results show savings in computation time in most of the cases. The savings over SIFT are more pronounced, since SURF is a speeded up version of SIFT. The computation time comparison shows a larger improvement in the case of synthetic data. This is in part attributed to the smaller resolution of images taken by mobile phones (320 × 240) in the real dataset, rendering the compensation for global rotation angles more expensive than estimating angles on an interest point level, because of the small number of interest points detected on average.

In the descriptor evaluation, the overlap error threshold is fixed to 50 % for the computation of correspondences. Hence, for each image pair, we have a single precision/recall value pair rather than a full graph. Figure 3.8 (right) shows recall values for the synthetic and real datasets respectively with an overall improvement noticeable especially for the case of comparing with SIFT. These results also show that the relative improvement when using SURF+ compared to SURF alone is considerably higher than in the case of using SIFT+ compared to SIFT alone. This is because of the fact that SURF is an approximation of SIFT, and thus less accurate. On the other hand, precision values do not enjoy the same level of improvement as the recall values. Figure 3.8 (middle) shows that the results with and without the accelerometer information are very comparable.

Acknowledgments The authors would like to thank Ahmad Abd El Hamid, Mostafa Izz, and Mahmoud Refaat for contributing to this chapter's content.

References

1. Live cast. http://www.periscopeapp.co
2. Meerkat. http://meerkatapp.co/
3. Kaheel, A., El-Saban, M., Refaat, M., Izz, M.: Mobicast—a system for collaborative event casting using mobile phones ACM Mobile and Ubiquitous Multimedia—MUM (2009)
4. El-Saban, M., Wang, X.-J., Hasan, N., Bassiouny, M., Refaat, M.: Seamless annotation and enrichment of mobile captured video streams in real-time. In: ICME, IEEE International Conference on Multimedia & Expo (ICME) (2011)
5. Bassiouny, M., El Saban, M.: Object matching using feature aggregation over a frame sequence. In: WACV. IEEE (2011)
6. Agarwala, A., Agrawala, M., Cohen, M., Salesin, D., Szeliski, R.: Photographing long scenes with multi-viewpoint panoramas. In Proceeding of the SIGGRAPH, vol. 25, pp. 853–861 (2006)
7. Sorek, N., Bregman-Amitai, O.: Method for constructing a composite image, Samsung Electronics patent, Jan. 2009
8. Hannuksela, J., Sangi, P., Heikkila, J., Liu, X., Doermann, D.: Document image mosaicing with mobile phones. In: ICIAP (2007)
9. El-Saban, M., Refaat, M., Kaheel, A., Hamid, A.: Stitching videos streamed by mobile phones in real-time. In: ACM MM (2009)
10. Shimizu, T., Yoneyama, A., Takishima, Y.: A fast video stitching method for motion-compensated frames in compressed video streams. In: International Conference on Consumer Electronics (2006)
11. Kopf, J., Uyttendale, M., Deussen, O., Cohen, M.: Capturing and viewing gigapixel images. In: SIGGRAPH (2007)
12. Brown, M., Lowe, D.: Automatic panoramic image stitching using invariant features. In: ICCV (2007)
13. Boutellier, J., Silvn, O., Tico, M., Korhonen, L.: Objective evaluation of image mosaics. In: International Conference VISIGRAPH (2007)
14. Baudisch, P., et al.: Panoramic viewfinder: providing a realtime preview to help users avoid flaws in panoramic pictures. In: OZCHI (2005)
15. Agarwala, A., Zheng, C., Pal, C., Agrawala, M., Cohen, M., Curless, B., Salesin, D., Szeliski, R., Panoramic video textures. In: Proceeding of the SIGGRAPH, vol. 24, pp. 821–827 (2005)
16. El-Saban, M., Izz, M., Kaheel, A: Fast stitching of videos captured from freely moving devices by exploiting temporal redundancy, In: ICIP. IEEE (2010)
17. Martin, D., Fowlkes, C., Malik, J.: Learning to detect natural image boundaries using local brightness, color, and texture cues. IEEE Trans. Pattern Anal. Mach. Intell. 26(5), 530–549 (2004)
18. Gevers, T., van de Weijer, J., Stokman, H.: In: Lukac, R., Plataniotis, K.N. (eds.) Color Image Processing: Methods and Applications. Color feature detection. CRC Press, Boca Raton (2006)
19. Mortensen, E.N.: Vision-assisted image editing. Comput. Gr. 33(4), 55–57 (1999)
20. Shi, J,. Tomasi, C.: Good features to track. In: IEEE Computer Society Conference on Computer Vision and Pattern Recognition (CVPR 94) pp. 593–600 (1994)
21. Zhang, Z., et al.: A robust technique for matching two uncalibrated images through the recovery of the unknown epipolar geometry. Artif. Intell. 78, 87–119 (1995)
22. Florack, L.M.J., Haar Romeny, BMt, Koenderink, J.J., Viergever, M.A.: General intensity transformations and differential invariants. JMIV 4, 171–187 (1994)
23. Mindru, F., Tuytelaars, T., Van Gool, L., Moons, T.: Moment invariants for recognition under changing viewpoint and illumination. CVIU 94, 3–27 (2004)
24. Baumberg, A.: Reliable feature matching across widely separated views. In: IEEE Computer Society Conference on Computer Vision and Pattern Recognition (CVPR 2000), pp. 774–781 (2000)
25. Matas, J., et al.: Robust wide baseline stereo from maximally stable extremal regions. Image Vis. Comput. 22(10), 761–767 (2004)

26. Lindeberg, T., Garding, J.: Shape-adapted smoothing in estimation of 3-D shape cues from affine deformations of local 2-D brightness structure. Image Vis. Comput. **15**(6), 415–434 (1997)
27. Mikolajczyk, K., Schmid, C.: Scale & affine invariant interest point detectors. Int. J. Comput. Vis. **60**(1), 63–86 (2004)
28. Mikolajczyk, K., et al.: A comparison of affine region detectors. Int. J. Comput. Vis. **65**(1–2), 43–72 (2003)
29. Tuytelaars, T., Mikolajczyk, K.: Local invariant feature detectors. Found. Trends Comput. Gr. Comput. Vis. **3**(1) (2007)
30. Morel, J.M., Yu, G.S.: ASIFT: a new framework for fully affine invariant image comparison. SIAM J. Imaging Sci. **2**, 438–469 (2009)
31. Shi, J., Tomasi, C.: Good features to track. In: Proceeding of the CVPR (1994)
32. Szeliski, R.: Image alignment and stitching: a tutorial, Microsoft Research. Technical report, MSR-TR-2004-92 (2006)
33. Zomet, A., Levin, A., Peleg, S.: Seamless image stitching by minimizing false edges. IEEE Trans. Image Process. (2006)
34. Agarwala, A.: Efficient gradient-domain compositing using quadtrees. ACM Trans. Gr. (2007)
35. Duan, Z., Gopalan, K., Dong, Y.: Push versus pull: Implications of protocol design on controlling unwanted traffic. In: Proceeding of the USENIX SRUTI (2005)
36. Bouguet, J.: Pyramidal implementation of the Lucas–Kanade feature tracker: description of the algorithm, Intel Research Labs. Technical report, OpenCV Document (2000)
37. Aggarwal, J.K., Nandhakumar, N.: On the computation of motion from sequences of images-a review, In: IEEE, vol. 76, pp. 917–935 (1988)
38. Baker, S., Scharstein, D., Lewis, J.P., Roth, S., Black, M., Szeliski, R.: A database and evaluation methodology for optical flow. In: ICCV (2007)
39. Lucas. B.D. Kanade, T.: An iterative image registration technique with an application to stereo vision. In: Proceedings of Imaging understanding workshop (1981)
40. Mikolajczyk, K., Schmid, C.: A performance evaluation of local descriptors. In: TPAMI (2005)
41. Davison, A.J., Murray D.W.: Simultaneous localization and map-building using active vision. In: IEEE Transactions on Pattern Analysis and Machine Intelligence (2002)
42. Gil, A., Reinoso, O., Burgard, W., Stachniss,C., Martnez Mozos, O.: Improving data association in rao-blackwellized visual SLAM. In: IEEE/RSJ International Conference on Intelligent Robots & Systems (2006)
43. Little, J., Se, S., Lowe D.G.: Global localization using distinctive visual features. In: IEEE/RSJ International Conference on Intelligent Robots & Systems (2002)
44. IPTC (1999). IPTC-NAA Information Interchange Model Version 4.1. Retrieved April 4, 2010, from http://www.iptc.org/std/IIM/4.1/specification/IIMV4.1.pdf
45. Seon H.K., Sakire A.A., Byunggu Y., Roger Z.: Vector model in support of versatile georeferenced video search. In: MMSys '10 Proceedings of the First Annual ACM SIGMM Conference on Multimedia systems
46. Lowe, D.G.: Distinctive image features from scale-invariant keypoints. Int. J. Comput. Vis. **60**(2), 91–110 (2004)

Chapter 4
Intentional Photos from an Unintentional Photographer: Detecting Snap Points in Egocentric Video with a Web Photo Prior

Bo Xiong and Kristen Grauman

Abstract Wearable cameras capture a first-person view of the world, and offer a hands-free way to record daily experiences or special events. Yet, not every frame is worthy of being captured and stored. We propose to automatically predict *"snap points"* in unedited egocentric video—that is, those frames that look like they could have been intentionally taken photos. We develop a generative model for snap points that relies on a Web photo prior together with domain-adapted features. Critically, our approach avoids strong assumptions about the particular *content* of snap points, focusing instead on their *composition*. Using 17 h of egocentric video from both human and mobile robot camera wearers, we show that the approach accurately isolates those frames that human judges would believe to be intentionally snapped photos. In addition, we demonstrate the utility of snap point detection for improving object detection and keyframe selection in egocentric video.

4.1 Introduction

Photo overload is already well known to most computer users. With cameras on mobile devices, it is all too easy to snap images and videos spontaneously, yet it remains much less easy to organize or search through that content later. This is already the case when the user actively decides which images are worth taking. *What happens when that user's camera is always on, worn at eye-level, and has the potential to capture everything he sees throughout the day?* With increasingly portable wearable computing platforms (like Google Glass, Looxcie, etc.), the photo overload problem is only intensifying.

Of course, not everything observed in an egocentric video stream is worthy of being captured and stored. Egocentric videos contain substantial motion and are often boring to watch. Even though the camera follows the wearer's activity and

B. Xiong (✉) · K. Grauman
University of Texas at Austin, 2317 Speedway, Austin, TX 78712, USA
e-mail: bxiong@cs.utexas.edu

K. Grauman
e-mail: grauman@cs.utexas.edu

© Springer International Publishing Switzerland 2015
G. Hua and X.-S. Hua (eds.), *Mobile Cloud Visual Media Computing*,
DOI 10.1007/978-3-319-24702-1_4

Fig. 4.1 Can you tell which row of photos came from an egocentric camera?

approximate gaze, relatively few moments actually result in snapshots the user would have intentionally decided to take, where he actively manipulating the camera. Many frames will be blurry, contain poorly composed shots, and/or simply have uninteresting content. This prompts the key question we study in this work: can a vision system predict *"snap points"* **in unedited egocentric video—that is, those frames that look like intentionally taken photos?**

To get some intuition for the task, consider the images in Fig. 4.1. Can you guess which row of photos was sampled from a wearable camera, and which was sampled from photos posted on Flickr? Note that subject matter itself is not always the telling cue; in fact, there is some overlap in content between the top and the bottom rows. Nonetheless, we suspect it is easy for the reader to detect that a head-mounted camera grabbed the shots in the first row, whereas a human photographer purposefully composed the shots in the second row. These distinctions suggest that it may be possible to learn the generic properties of an image that indicate it is well composed, independent of the literal content.

While this anecdotal sample suggests that detecting snap points may be feasible, there are several challenges. First, egocentric video contains a wide variety of scene types, activities, and actors. This is certainly true for human camera wearers going about daily life activities, and it will be increasingly true for mobile robots that freely explore novel environments. Accordingly, a snap point detector needs to be largely domain invariant and generalize across varied subject matter. Secondly, an optimal snap point is likely to differ in subtle ways from its less-good temporal neighbors, i.e., two frames may be similar in content but distinct in terms of snap point quality. That means that cues beyond the standard texture and color favorites may be necessary. Finally, and most importantly, while it would be convenient to think of the problem in discriminative terms (e.g., training a snap point versus non-snap point classifier), it is burdensome to obtain adequate and unbiased labeled data. Namely, we would need people to manually mark frames that appear intentional, and to do so at a scale to accommodate arbitrary environments.

We introduce an approach to detect snap points from egocentric video that requires no human annotations. The main idea is to construct a generative model of what human-taken photos look like by sampling images posted on the Web. Snapshots that people upload to share publicly online may vary vastly in their content, yet all share the key facet that they were intentional snap point moments. This makes them an ideal source of positive exemplars for our target learning problem. Furthermore, with such

Fig. 4.2 Understandably, while effective for human-taken photos (*left*), today's best object detectors break down when applied to egocentric video data (*right*). Each image displays the person detections by the DPM [9] object detector

a Web photo prior, we sidestep the issue of gathering negatively labeled instances to train a discriminative model, which could be susceptible to bias and difficult to scale. In addition to this prior, our approach incorporates domain adaptation to account for the distribution mismatch between Web photos and egocentric video frames. Finally, we designate features suited to capturing the framing effects in snap points.

We propose two applications of snap point prediction. For the first, we show how snap points can improve object detection reliability for egocentric cameras. It is striking how today's best object detectors fail when applied to arbitrary egocentric data (see Fig. 4.2). Unsurprisingly, their accuracy drops because detectors trained with human-taken photos (e.g., the Flickr images gathered for the PASCAL VOC benchmark) do not generalize well to the arbitrary views seen by an ego camera. We show how snap point prediction can improve the precision of an off-the-shelf detector, essentially by predicting those frames where the detector is most trustworthy. For the second application, we use snap points to select keyframes for egocentric video summaries.

We apply our method to 17.5 h of videos from both human-worn and robot-worn egocentric cameras. We demonstrate the absolute accuracy of snap point prediction compared to a number of viable baselines and existing metrics. Furthermore, we show its potential for object detection and keyframe selection applications. The results are a promising step toward filtering the imminent deluge of wearable camera video streams.

4.2 Related Work

We next summarize how our idea relates to existing work in analyzing egocentric video, predicting high-level image properties, and using Web image priors.

Egocentric video analysis: Egocentric video analysis, pioneered in the 90s [35, 44], is experiencing a surge of research activity, thanks to today's portable devices. The primary focus is on object [29, 38] or activity recognition [6, 8, 24, 29, 37, 39, 43]. Compared with well-posed photographs, egocentric videos contain more uninformative frames, which are often poorly composed and illuminated [11]. Motion cues [38] in egocentric video are useful to segment foreground objects and therefore improve object recognition. Gaze information [29] can also improve both object and activity recognition. No prior work explores snap point detection.

We consider object detection and keyframe selection as applications of snap points for unconstrained wearable camera data. In contrast, prior work for detection in ego-centric video focuses on controlled environments (e.g., a kitchen) and hand-held objects (e.g., the mixing bowl) [6, 8, 29, 38, 43]. Nearly, all prior keyframe selection work assumes third-person static cameras (e.g., [31, 32]), where all frames are already intentionally composed, and the goal is to determine which are the representative for the entire video. In contrast, snap points aim to discover intentional-looking frames, not maximize diversity or representativeness. Some video summarization work tackles dynamic egocentric video [27, 34]. Such methods could exploit snap points as a filter to limit the frames they consider for summaries. Our main contribution is to detect human-taken photos, not a novel summarization algorithm.

We are not aware of any prior work using purely visual input to automatically trigger a wearable camera, as we propose. Methods in ubiquitous computing use manual intervention [35] or external nonvisual sensors [15, 16] (e.g., skin conductivity or audio) to trigger the camera. Our image-based approach is complementary; true snap points are likely a superset of those moments where abrupt physiological or audio changes occur.

Predicting high-level image properties: A series of interesting works predict properties from images like saliency [33], professional photo quality [20], memorability [18], aesthetics, interestingness [4, 13], or suitability as a candid portrait [10]. These methods train a discriminative model using various image descriptors, and then apply it to label human-taken photos. In contrast, we develop a generative approach with (unlabeled) Web photos, and apply it to *find* human-taken photos. Critically, a snap point need not be beautiful, memorable, etc., and it could even contain mundane content. Snap points are thus a broader class of photos. This is exactly what makes them relevant for the proposed object detection application. In contrast, an excellent aesthetics detector (for example) would fire on a narrower set of photos, eliminating non-aesthetic photos that could nonetheless be amenable to off-the-shelf object detectors.

Web image priors: The Web is a compelling resource for data-driven vision methods. Both the volume of images as well as the accompanying noisy meta-data open up many possibilities. Most relevant to our work are methods that exploit the biases of human photographers. This includes work on discovering iconic images of landmarks [28, 42, 47] (e.g., the Statue of Liberty) or other tourist favorites [1, 14, 19, 22] by exploiting the fact that people tend to take similar photos of popular sites. Similarly, the photos users upload when trying to sell a particular object (e.g., a used car) reveal that object's canonical viewpoints, which can help select keyframes to summarize short videos of the same object [21]. Event video summarization [23] can also benefit from Web image collections of the same event. Our method also learns about human framing or composition biases, but, critically, in a manner that transcends the specific content of the scene. That is, rather than learn when a popular landmark or object is in view, we want to know when a well-composed photo of *any* scene is in view. Our Web photo prior represents the photos humans intentionally take, independent of subject matter.

Our approach[1] uses a nonparametric representation of snap points, as captured by a large collection of Web photos. At a high level, this relates to work in vision exploiting big data and neighbor-based learning. This includes person detection [46], scene parsing with dense correspondences [30], geographic localization [14], action recognition [5], and pose estimation [40]. Beyond the fact that our task is unique and novel, all these methods assume labels on the training data, whereas our method relies on the distribution of photos themselves.

4.3 Approach

Our goal is to detect snap points, which are those frames within a continuous egocentric video that appear as if they were composed with intention, as opposed to merely observed by the person wearing the camera. In traditional camera-user relationships, this "trigger" is left entirely to the human user. In the wearable camera-user relationship, however, the beauty of being hands-free and always-on should be that the user no longer has to interrupt the flow of his activity to snap a photo. Notably, whether a moment in time is photoworthy is only partially driven by the subject matter in view. The way the photo is composed is similarly important, as is well understood by professional photographers and intuitively known by everyday camera users.

We take a nonparametric, data-driven approach to learn what snap points look like. First, we gather unlabeled Web photos to build the prior (Sect. 4.3.1), and extract image descriptors that capture cues for composition and intention (Sect. 4.3.2). Then, we estimate a domain-invariant feature space connecting the Web and ego sources (Sect. 4.3.3). Finally, given a novel egocentric video frame, we predict how well it agrees with the prior in the adapted feature space (Sect. 4.3.4). Figure 4.3 shows the overview of our approach. To illustrate the utility of snap points, we also explore applications for object detection and keyframe selection (Sect. 4.3.5).

Section 4.4 will discuss how we systematically gather ground truth labels for snap points using human judgments, which is necessary to evaluate our method, but, critically, is *not* used to train it.

4.3.1 Building the Web Photo Prior

Faced with the task of predicting whether a video frame is a snap point or not, an appealing solution might be to train a discriminative classifier using manually labeled exemplars. Such an approach has proven successful for learning other high-level image properties, like aesthetics and interestingness [4, 13], quality [20], canonical views [21], or memorability [18]. This is thanks in part to the availability of relevant meta-data for such problems: users on community photo albums manually score

---

[1]This chapter expands upon our work as first presented at ECCV 2014 [50].

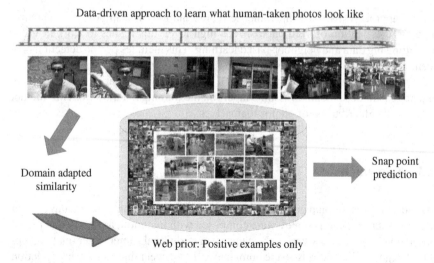

Fig. 4.3 Overview of our approach. Our method takes an unedited egocentric video as input, and predicts how well it agrees with the Web photo prior in a domain-adapted feature space. We leverage the fact that Internet photos are "free" positives of intentional photos, and so our method does not require any explicitly labeled data

images for visual appeal [4, 20], and users uploading ads online manually tag the object of interest [21].

However, this familiar paradigm is problematic for snap points. Photos that appear human-taken exhibit vast variations in appearance, since they may have almost arbitrary content. This suggests that large-scale annotations would be necessary to cover the space. Furthermore, snap points must be isolated within ongoing egocentric video. This means that labeling *negatives* is tedious—each frame must be viewed and judged in order to obtain clean labels.

Instead, we devise an approach that leverages *unlabeled* images to learn snap points. The idea is to build a prior distribution using a large-scale repository of Web photos uploaded by human photographers. Such photos are by definition human-taken, span a variety of contexts, and (by virtue of being chosen for upload) have an enhanced element of *intention*. We use these photos as a generative model of snap points.

We select the Scene UNderstanding (SUN) database as our Web photo source [48], which originates from Internet search for hundreds of scene category names. Our choice is motivated by two main factors. First, the diversity of photos is high— 899 categories in all drawn from 70 K WordNet terms—and there are many of them (130 K). Second, its scope is fairly well matched with wearable camera data. Human- or robot-worn cameras observe a variety of dailylife scenes and activities, as well as interactions with other people. SUN covers not just locations, but settings that satisfy "I am in a *place*, let's go to a *place*" [48], which includes many scene-specific interactions, such as shopping at a pawnshop, visiting an optician, driving in a car, etc. See Fig. 4.4.

Fig. 4.4 Example images from the SUN dataset [48]. It contains a diverse category of scene types and a wide range of objects

4.3.2 Image Descriptors for Intentional Cues

To represent each image, we designate descriptors to capture intentional composition effects.

Motion: Non-snap points will often occur when a camera wearer is moving quickly, or turning his head abruptly. We therefore extract a descriptor to summarize *motion blur*, using the blurriness estimate of [2]. We also explored flow-based motion features, but found their information to be subsumed by blur features computable from individual frames.

Composition: Snap points also reflect intentional framing effects by the human photographer. This leads to spatial regularity in the main line structures in the image— e.g., the horizon in an outdoor photo, buildings in a city scene, the table surface in a restaurant—which will tend to align with the image axes. Thus, we extract a *line alignment* feature: we detect line segments using the method in [25], and then record a histogram of their orientations with 32 uniformly spaced bins. To capture framing via the 3D structure layout, we employ the geometric class probability map [17]. We

Fig. 4.5 Illustration of HOG, blurriness, and line alignment features on a short sequence of ego-centric video frames. Each frame shows a *bar* in *bottom right* indicating how much each descriptor agrees with the Web prior. Here, each frame with the highest bar in each mini-sequence would rate highest as a snap point (if using each feature alone). The line alignment feature helps to find snap points that correspond to the moment when the camera wearer looks straight at the scene. The blurriness feature helps to find clear frames, and the HOG composition feature helps to find semantically meaningful frames

also extract GIST [36], HOG [3], self-similarity (SSIM) [41], and dense SIFT [26], all of which capture alignment of interior textures, beyond the strong line segments. An accelerometer, when available, could also help gage coarse alignment; however, these descriptors offer a fine-grained visual measure helpful for subtle snap point distinctions. See Fig. 4.5.

Feature combination: For all features but line alignment, we use code and default parameters provided by [48]. We reduce the dimensionality of each feature using principal component analysis (PCA) to compactly capture 90 % of its total variance. We then standardize each dimension to ($\mu = 0$, $\sigma = 1$) and concatenate the reduced descriptors to form a single vector feature space X, which we use in what follows.

4.3.3 Adapting from the Web to the Egocentric Domain

While we expect egocentric video snap points to agree with the Web photo prior along many of these factors, there is also an inherent mismatch between the statistics of the two domains. Egocentric video is typically captured at low resolution with modest quality lenses, while online photos (e.g., on Flickr) are often uploaded at high resolution from high-quality cameras. Egocentric videos often contain frames that are blurry or badly composed. Figure 4.6 shows some typical egocentric frames and images from SUN dataset, both from shopping malls. The examples show that despite some partial overlap in content, there is also a clear domain shift between the two sources of images.

Ego–Shopping Mall   Sun–Shopping Mall

Fig. 4.6 Comparison of shopping mall frames from egocentric video and shopping mall images from SUN dataset

Therefore, we establish a domain-invariant feature space connecting the two sources. Given unlabeled Web photos and egocentric frames, we first compute a subspace for each using PCA. Then, we recover a series of intermediate subspaces that gradually transit from the "source" Web subspace to the "target" egocentric subspace. We use the geodesic flow kernel (GFK) algorithm of [12], an unsupervised domain adaptation method which requires no labeled target data and is kernel-based. The algorithm computes a geodesic flow kernel which can be used to measure similarity in feature space. Since we assume no labels on the target domain and use a kernel-based classifier, this makes GFK a good fit. In contrast, supervised domain adaptation algorithms, which require labels on the target domain, would not be applicable.

Let $x_i, x_j \in X$ denote image descriptors for a Web image i and egocentric frame j. The idea is to compute the projections of an input x_i on a subspace $\phi(t)$, for all $t \in [0, 1]$ along the geodesic path connecting the source and target subspaces in a Grassmann manifold. Values of t closer to 0 correspond to subspaces closer to the Web photo prior; values of t closer to 1 correspond to those more similar to egocentric video frames. The infinite set of projections is achieved implicitly via the geodesic flow kernel [12] (GFK):

$$K_{GFK}(x_i, x_j) = \langle z_i^\infty, z_j^\infty \rangle = \int_0^1 (\phi(t)^T x_i)^T (\phi(t)^T x_j) dt, \qquad (4.1)$$

where z_i^∞ and z_j^∞ denote the infinite-dimensional features concatenating all projections of x_i and x_j along the geodesic path.

Intuitively, this representation lets the two slightly mismatched domains (Web and ego) "meet in the middle" in a common feature space, letting us measure similarity between both kinds of data without being overly influenced by their superficial resolution/sensor differences.

4.3.4 Predicting Snap Points

With the Web prior, image features, and similarity measure in hand, we can now estimate how well a novel egocentric video frame agrees with our prior. We take a simple data-driven approach. We treat the pool of Web photos as a nonparametric distribution, and then estimate the likelihood of the novel ego frame under that distribution based on its nearest neighbors' distances.

Let $W = \{x_1^w, \ldots, x_N^w\}$ denote the N Web photo descriptors, and let x^e denote a novel egocentric video frame's descriptor. We retrieve the k nearest examples $\{x_{n_1}^w, \ldots, x_{n_k}^w\} \subset W$, i.e., those k photos that have the highest GFK kernel values when compared to x^e.[2] Then we predict the snap point confidence for x^e:

$$S(x^e) = \sum_{j=1}^{k} K_{GFK}\left(x^e, x_{n_j}^w\right), \tag{4.2}$$

where higher values of $S(x^e)$ indicate that the test frame is more likely to be human-taken. For our dataset of $N = 130\,K$ images, similarity search is fairly speedy (0.01 s per test case in Matlab), and could easily be scaled for much larger N using hashing or kd-tree techniques.

This model follows in the spirit of prior data-driven methods for alternative tasks, e.g., [14, 30, 40, 46], the premise being to keep the learning simple and let the data speak for itself. However, our approach is label-free, as all training examples are (implicitly) positives, whereas the past methods assume at least weak meta-data annotations.

While simple, our strategy is very effective in practice. In fact, we explored a number of more complex alternatives—one-class SVMs, Gaussian mixture models, nonlinear manifold embeddings—but found them to be similar or inferior to the neighbor-based approach. The relatively lightweight computation is a virtue given our eventual goal to make snap point decisions onboard a wearable device.

4.3.5 Leveraging Snap Points for Egocentric Video Analysis

Filtering egocentric video down to a small number of probable snap points has many potential applications. We are especially interested in how they can bolster object detection and keyframe selection. We next devise strategies for each task that leverage the above predictions $S(x^e)$.

---

[2]We use $k = 60$ based on preliminary visual inspection, and found that results were similar for other k values of similar order ($k \in [30, 120]$).

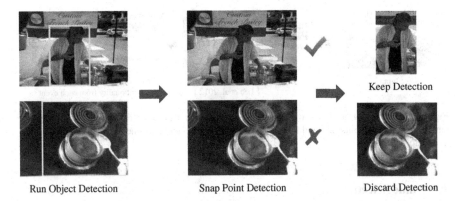

Run Object Detection   Snap Point Detection   Discard Detection

Fig. 4.7 Overview of our approach to improve object detection. We first run a deformable parts object detector trained with intentional (Flickr) photos. Then we run our snap point detection to determine whether we want to trust the object detection results. If the frame does not appear to be a snap point, we will discount the object detector's outputs

Object Detection

In the object recognition literature, it is already disheartening that how poorly detectors trained on one dataset tend to generalize to another [45]. Unfortunately, things are only worse if one attempts to apply those same detectors on egocentric video (recall Fig. 4.2). Why is there such a gap? Precisely because today's very best object detectors are learned from human-taken photos, whereas egocentric data on wearable cameras—or mobile robots—consist of very few frames that match those statistics. For example, a winning person detector on PASCAL VOC trained with Flickr photos, like the deformable parts model (DPM) [9], expects to see people in similarly composed photos, but only a fraction of egocentric video frames will be consistent and thus detectable.

Our idea is to use snap points to predict those frames where a standard object detector (trained on human-taken images) will be most trustworthy. This way, we can improve precision; the detector will avoid being misled by incidental patterns in non-snap point frames. See Fig. 4.7 for an overview of our approach. We implement the idea as follows, using the DPM as an off-the-shelf detector.[3] We score each test ego frame by $S(x^e)$, and then keep all object detections in those frames scoring above a threshold τ. We set τ as 30 % of the average distance between the Web prior images and egocentric snap points. For the remaining frames, we eliminate any detections (i.e., flatten the DPM confidence to 0) that fall below the confidence threshold in the standard DPM pipeline [9]. In effect, we turn the object detector "on" only when it has high chance of success.

---

[3]http://www.cs.berkeley.edu/~rbg/latent/.

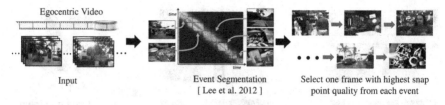

Fig. 4.8 Overview of our keyframe selection method. Given an egocentric video, we first identify temporal event segments [27] and for each such event, we select the frame most confidently scored as a snap point

Keyframe Selection

As a second application, we use snap points to create keyframe summaries of egocentric video. The goal is to take hours of wearable data and automatically generate a visual storyboard that captures key events. We implement a simple selection strategy. First, we identify temporal event segments using the color- and time-based grouping method described in [27], which finds chunks of frames likely to belong to the same physical location or scene. This is done by performing complete-link agglomerative clustering on both global appearance and temporal nearness of all frames of egocentric video. Then, for each such event, we select the frame most confidently scored as a snap point. See Fig. 4.8 for an illustration.

Our intent is to see if snap points, by identifying frames that look intentional, can help distil the main events in hours of uncontrolled wearable camera data. Our implementation is a proof of concept to demonstrate snap points' utility. We are not claiming a new keyframe selection strategy, a problem studied in depth in prior work [27, 31, 32, 34].

4.4 Datasets and Collecting Ground Truth Snap Points

Datasets: We use two egocentric datasets. The first is the publicly available UT Egocentric Dataset (**Ego**),[4] which consists of four videos of 3–5 h each, captured with a head-mounted camera by four people doing unscripted daily life activities (eating, working, shopping, driving, etc.). The second is a mobile robot dataset (**Robot**) newly collected for this project. We used a wheeled robot to take a 25 min video both indoors and outdoors on campus (coffee shops, buildings, streets, pedestrians, etc.). The camera is a FireFly USB 2.0 camera, connected to the robot with a pan-tilt unit. The camera on the robot moves constantly from left to right, pauses, and then rotates back in order to cover a wide range of viewpoints. Our robot was able to take pictures from different viewpoints even when physically located at the same place.

---

[4]http://vision.cs.utexas.edu/projects/egocentric_data.

Both the human and robot datasets represent incidentally captured video from always-on, dynamic cameras, and unscripted activity. We found other existing ego collections less suited to our goals, either due to their focus on a controlled environment with limited activity (e.g., making food in a kitchen [8, 29]) or their use of chest-mounted or fisheye lens cameras [7, 37], which do not share the point of view of intentional hand-held photos.

Ground truth: Our method requires no labeled data for learning: it needs only to populate the Web prior with human-taken photos. However, to *evaluate* our method, it is necessary to have ground truth human judgments about which ego frames are snap points. The following describes our crowdsourced annotation strategy to get reliable ground truth.

We created a "magic camera" scenario to help MTurk annotators understand the definition of snap points. Their instructions were as follows: *Suppose you are creating a visual diary out of photos. You have a portable camera that you carry all day long, in order to capture everyday moments of your daily life. For instance, you would like to capture scenes such as a dining place where you have dinner with friends, a dog you stopped to pet, children you saw playing in a park, the cashier at the check-out counter, a peaceful street where you took a walk at sunset, or a small but elegant shop that you visited. Unfortunately, your magic camera can also trigger itself from time to time to take random pictures, even while you are holding the camera. At the end of the day, all pictures, both the ones you took intentionally and the ones accidentally taken by the camera, are mixed together. **Your task is to distinguish the pictures that you took intentionally from the rest of pictures that were accidentally taken by your camera.***

In Fig. 4.9, we show the instructions that were used on Amazon Mechanical Turk to collect annotations. Workers were required to rate each image into one of the four categories: (a) very confidently intentional, (b) somewhat confident intentional, (c) somewhat confident accidental, and (d) very confident accidental. Since the task can be ambiguous and subjective, we issued each image to 5 distinct workers. We obtained labels for 10,000 frames in the ego data and 2,000 frames in the Robot data, sampled at random.

We devised a scoring system to obtain reliable fine-grained ground truth. Every time a frame receives a rating of category (a), (b), (c), or (d) from any of the 5 workers, it receives 5, 2, -1, -2 points, respectively. Most workers assign category (b) or (c) to the frames and rarely assign category (a), unless they certainly believe that the image is taken intentionally. As a result, if a frame receives a rating of category (a), we reward the frame 5 points. On the other hand, since there are many more negative frames than positive frames, if a frame receives a rating of category (d), it does not get penalized as much (-2). This lets us rank all ground truth examples by their true snap point strength.

To alternatively map these total scores across all 5 annotations to binary ground truth, we threshold a frame's total score: strictly more than 10 points is deemed intentional. This means a frame must receive at least one vote on category (a) in order to be considered an intentional frame (5 votes on category (b) means all workers had some doubt if the frame was intentional; it will receive a total of 10 points but not more than 10 points). If one outlier worker assigns an intentional frame a rating of category (d), as long as the frame receives at least two ratings of category (a) and

Fig. 4.9 Instructions used on Amazon Mechanical Turk to collect annotations

two ratings of category (b) from the other four different workers, the frame will still be an intentional frame.

Annotators found 14 % of the ego frames and 23 % of the robot frames to be snap points, respectively. The robot data contain more snap points because the robot we used to collect data had less motion compared with human. Out of the 10,000 labeled frames in the ego data, there are 998 frames that all five workers reach consensus on the category, 1748 frames that four workers reach consensus on, and 3871 frames that three workers reach consensus. Out of the 2,000 labeled frames in the robot data, there are 213 frames that all five workers reach consensus on the category, 306 frames that four workers reach consensus on, and 691 frames that three workers reach consensus on. The total MTurk cost was about $500.

Our dataset and software are available online.[5]

4.5 Results

We experiment on the two datasets described above, ego and robot, which together comprise 17.5 h of video. Since no existing methods perform snap point detection, we define several **baselines** for comparison:

- **Saliency** [33]: uses the CRF-based saliency method of [33] to score an image. This baseline reflects that people tend to compose images with a salient object in the center. We use the implementation of [4], and use the CRF's log probability output as the snap point confidence.
- **Blurriness** [2]: uses the blur estimates of [2] to score an image. It reflects that intentionally taken images tend to lack motion blur. Note that blur is also used as a feature by our method; here we isolate how much it would solve the task if used on its own, with no Web prior.
- **People likelihood**: uses a person detector to rank each frame by how likely it is to contain one or more people. We use the max output of the DPM [9] detector. The intuition is people tend to take images of their family and friends to capture meaningful moments, and as a result, many human-taken images contain people. In fact, this baseline also implicitly captures how well-composed the image is, since the DPM is biased to trigger when people are clear and unoccluded in a frame (recall Fig. 4.2).
- **Discriminative SVM**: uses a RBF kernel SVM trained with the ground truth snap points/non-snap points in the ego data. We run it with a leave-one-camera-wearer-out protocol, training on 3 of the ego videos and testing on the 4th. This baseline lets us analyze the power of the unlabeled Web prior compared to a standard discriminative method. Note, it requires substantially more training effort than our approach.

---

[5]http://vision.cs.utexas.edu/projects/ego_snappoints.

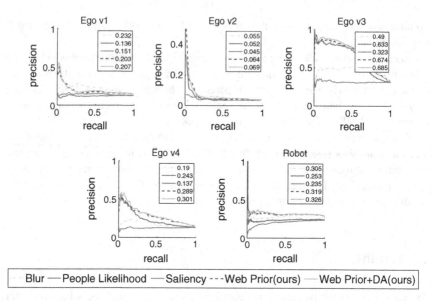

Fig. 4.10 Snap point detection precision/recall on the four ego videos (*top row* and *bottom left*) and the robot video (*bottom right*). Numbers in legend denote mAP. Best viewed in color (color figure online)

4.5.1 Snap Point Accuracy

First, we quantify how accurately our method predicts snap points. Figure 4.10 shows the precision–recall curves for our method and the three unsupervised baselines (saliency, blurriness, people likelihood). Table 4.1 shows the accuracy in terms of two standard rank quality metrics, Spearman's correlation ρ and Kendall's τ. While the precision–recall plots compare predictions against the binarized ground truth, these metrics compare the full orderings of the confidence-valued predictions against the raw MTurk annotators' ground truth scores (cf. Sect. 4.4). They capture that even for two positive intentional images, one might look better than the other to human judges. We show results for our method with and without the domain adaptation (DA) step.

Overall, our method outperforms the baselines. Notably, the same prior succeeds for both the human-worn and robot-worn cameras. Using both the Web prior and DA gives best results, indicating the value of establishing a domain-invariant feature space to connect the Web and ego data.

On ego video 4 (v4), our method is especially strong, about a factor of 2 better than the nearest competing baseline (Blur). On v2, mAP is very low for all methods, since v2 has very few true positives (only 3 % of its frames, compared to 14 % on average for Ego). Still, we see stronger ranking accuracy with our Web prior and DA. On v3, people likelihood fares much better than it does on all other videos, likely because v3 happens to contain many frames with nice portraits. On the robot data,

Table 4.1 Snap point ranking accuracy (higher rank correlations are better)

Methods	Ego v1		Ego v2		Ego v3		Ego v4		Robot	
	ρ	τ	ρ	τ	ρ	τ	ρ	τ	ρ	τ
Rank coefficient										
Blurriness	**0.347**	**0.249**	0.136	0.094	0.479	0.334	0.2342	0.162	0.508	0.352
People likelihood	0.002	0	−0.015	−0.011	0.409	0.289	0.190	0.131	0.198	0.134
Saliency	0.027	0.019	0.008	0.005	0.016	0.011	−0.021	−0.014	−0.086	−0.058
Web prior (Ours)	0.321	0.223	0.144	0.100	**0.504**	**0.355**	**0.452**	0.317	0.530	0.373
Web prior+DA (Ours)	0.343	0.239	**0.179**	**0.124**	0.501	0.353	**0.452**	**0.318**	**0.537**	**0.379**

however, it breaks down, likely because of the increased viewpoint irregularity and infrequency of people.

While our method is nearly always better than the baselines, on v1 Blur is similar in ranking metrics and achieves higher precision for higher recall rates. This is likely due to v1's emphasis on scenes with one big object, like a bowl or tablet, as the camera wearer shops and cooks. The SUN Web prior has less close-up object-centric images; this suggests that we could improve our prior by increasing the coverage of object-centric photos, e.g., with ImageNet-style photos.

Figure 4.11 shows examples of images among those our method ranks most confidently (top) and least confidently (bottom) as snap points, for both datasets. We see that its predictions capture the desired effects. Snap points, regardless of their content, do appear intentional, whereas non-snap points look accidental. Please see our project webpage for more extensive video results.

Figure 4.12 examines the effectiveness of each feature we employ, were we to take them individually. We see that each one has something to contribute, though they are best in combination (Fig. 4.10). HOG on ego is exceptionally strong. This is in spite of the fact that the exact locations visited by the ego camera wearers are almost certainly disjoint from those that happen to be in the Web prior. This indicates that the prior is broad enough to capture the diversity in appearance of everyday environments.

All baselines so far required no labeled images, same as our approach. Next we compare to a discriminative approach that uses manually labeled frames to train a snap point classifier. Figure 4.13 shows the results, as a function of the amount of labeled data. We give the SVM-labeled frames from the held-out ego videos. (We do not run it for the robot data, since the only available labels are scene-specific; it is not possible to run the leave-one-camera-wearer-out protocol.) *Despite learning without any explicit labels*, our method generally outperforms the discriminative SVM. The discriminative approach requires thousands of hand-labeled frames to come close to our method's accuracy in most cases. This is a good sign: while expanding the Web prior is nearly free, expanding the labeled data is expensive and tedious. In fact, if anything, Fig. 4.13 is an optimistic portrayal of the SVM baseline. That is because both the training and testing data are captured on the very same camera; in general scenarios, one would not be able to count on this benefit.

The results above are essential to validate our main idea of snap point detection with a Web prior. Next we provide proof of concept results to illustrate the utility of snap points for practical applications.

4.5.2 Object Detection Application

Today's best object detection systems are trained thoroughly on human-taken images—for example, using labeled data from PASCAL VOC or ImageNet. This naturally makes them best suited to run on human-taken images at test time. Our data statistics suggest only 10–15 % of egocentric frames may fit this bill. Thus,

Fig. 4.11 Frames our method rates as likely (*top*) or unlikely (*bottom*) snap points. Our predictions capture the desired effects: snap points appear intentional while non-snap points look accidental

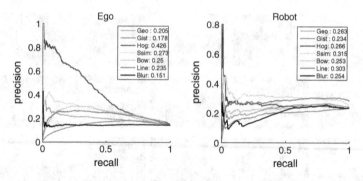

Fig. 4.12 Accuracy per feature if used in isolation. Performance is best when using all features

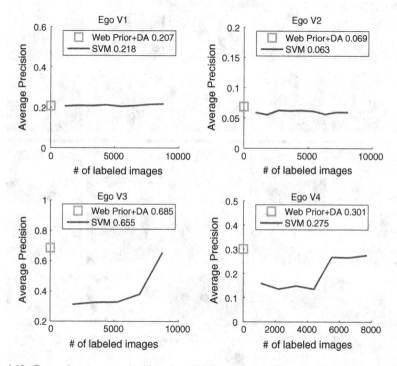

Fig. 4.13 Comparison to supervised baseline. SVM's mAP (legend) uses *all* labeled data

using the method defined in Sect. 4.3.5, we aim to use snap points to boost object detection precision.

We collected ground truth person and car bounding boxes for the ego data via DrawMe [49]. Since we could not afford to have all 17.5 h of video labeled, we sampled the labeled set to cover 50–50 % snap points and non-snap points. We obtained labels for 1000 and 200 frames for people and cars, respectively (cars are more rare in the videos).

Figure 4.14 shows the results, using the PASCAL detection criterion. We see that snap points improve the precision of the standard DPM detector, since they let us ignore frames where the detector is not trustworthy. Of course, this comes at the cost of some recall at the tails. This seems like a good trade-off for detection in video, particularly, since one could anchor object tracks using these confident predictions, and then iteratively refine less confident predictions with object tracks, in order to make up the recall.

Figure 4.15 shows some eliminated person detections of both success and failure cases. While many false positive detections were eliminated, a few true positive detections from non-snap points frames were also eliminated. In these cases, where the detector is robust to the poorly composed frames, our approach can reduce recall.

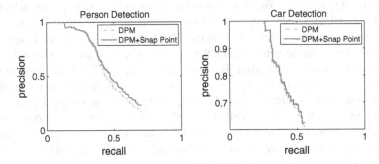

Fig. 4.14 Snap points boost precision for an off-the-shelf object detector by focusing on frames that look human-taken

Fig. 4.15 Examples of person detections that are eliminated by our method. The three frames in the *top row* are false detections that are properly eliminated by snap point detection. We also include three failure cases in the *bottom row*, where true positive detections on non-snap point frames are eliminated

4.5.3 Keyframe Selection Application

Keyframe or "storyboard" summaries are an appealing way to peruse long egocentric video, to quickly get the gist of what was seen. Such summaries enable noveleak interfaces to let a user "zoom-in" on time intervals that appear most relevant. As a final proof of concept result, we apply snap points for keyframe selection, using the method defined in Sect. 4.3.5.

Figures 4.16 and 4.17 show example results on the ego data, where the average event length is 30 min, and Fig. 4.18 shows results on the robot data. Keyframe selection requires subjective evaluation; we have no ground truth for quantitative evaluation. We present our results alongside a baseline that uses the exact same event segmentation as [27] (cf. Sect. 4.3.5), but selects each event's frame at random instead of prioritizing snap points. We also show the result of an existing keyframe selection method [32], which selects a sequence of keyframes that maximize diversity.

We see that the snap point-based summaries contain well-composed images for each event. The baseline, while seeing the same events, often uses haphazard shots that do not look intentionally taken. The method of Liu et al. [32] maximizes diversity in the low-level image feature space and often selects semantically uninformative frames that do not look intentionally taken, suggesting it is not a good fit for keyframe selection on egocentric video. While our method generally appears to outperform the baselines, it can make mistakes as well. For example, our method picks a frame of a shopping mall in the first event of the second video (see the first frame in the seventh row in Fig. 4.16), when it would be preferable to pick a frame when a friend was eating as done by the baseline (see the first frame in the ninth row in Fig. 4.16) since the main event was having lunch with a friend. This suggests that our method can be improved by reasoning about importance or human attention, so that it could better select keyframes from important time intervals or when the camera wearer was paying attention.

4.6 Conclusions and Future Work

An onslaught of lengthy egocentric videos is imminent, making automated methods for intelligently filtering the data of great interest. Whether for easing the transfer of existing visual recognition methods to the ego domain, or for helping users filter content to photoworthy moments, snap point detection is a promising direction. Our data-driven solution uses purely visual information and requires no manual labeling. Our results on over 17 h of video show that it outperforms a variety of alternative approaches.

Ultimately, we envision snap point detection being run online with streaming egocentric video, thereby saving power and storage for an always-on wearable device. Currently, a bottleneck is feature extraction. In future work, we will consider ways to triage feature extraction for snap points, and augment the generative model with

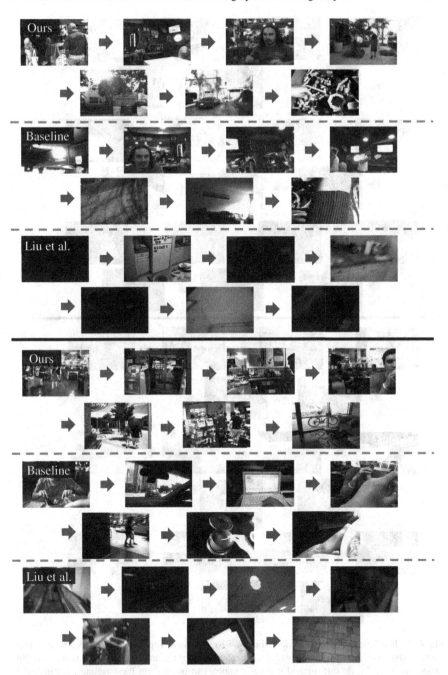

Fig. 4.16 Example keyframe selections for two 4-h ego videos. Top result is produced by our snap point method, middle result is the event segmentation baseline, and bottom result is the existing method of [32]. Our method was able to produce a sequence of informative and well-composed photos. In the first video, we can see that the camera wearer went to a market, had lunch, took a walk, and then went back home to play lego. The other two summaries are less informative

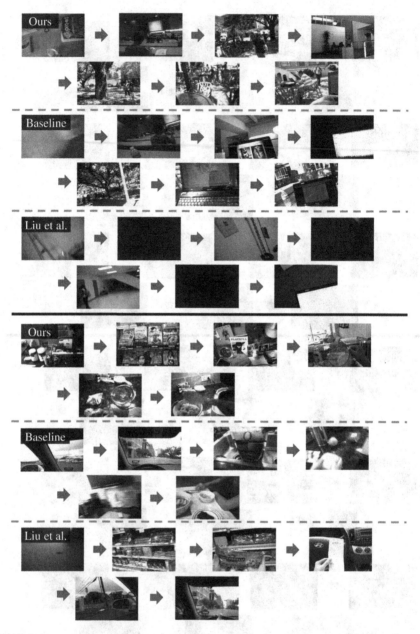

Fig. 4.17 Example keyframe selections for two 4-h ego videos. Top result is produced by our snap point method, middle result is the event segmentation baseline, and bottom result is the existing method of [32]. While our method generally appears to outperform the baselines, it can make mistakes as well. Our method picks a frame of a bunch of books on a bookshelf in the second event of the second video (see the *second frame* in the *seventh row*), when it would be preferable to pick a frame of groceries as done by the method of [32] (see the *second frame* in the *second last row*) since the main event was groceries shopping

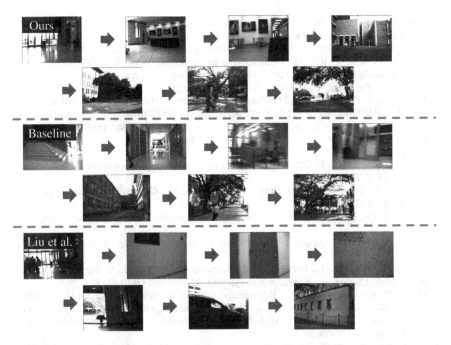

Fig. 4.18 Example keyframe selections for the robot video. Top result is produced by our snap point method, middle result is the event segmentation baseline, and bottom result is the existing method of [32]. We see that our snap point-based method was able to pick a representative frame for each location that the robot visited. The other two summaries contain blurry or uninformative frames

user-labeled frames to learn a personalized model of snap points. While we are especially interested in wearable data, our methods may also be applicable to related sources, such as bursts of consumer photos or videos captured on mobile phones.

Acknowledgments This research is sponsored in part by ONR YIP and gifts from Intel and Google. We thank Piyush Khandelwal, Jacob Menashe, and Peter Stone for helping us collect the Robot video. We also thank Yong Jae Lee for helpful discussions and for kindly providing code to generate baseline results.

References

1. Chen, C.Y., Grauman, K.: Clues from the beaten path: location estimation with bursty sequences of tourist photos. In: CVPR (2011)
2. Crete-Roffet, F., Dolmiere, T., Ladret, P., Nicolas, M.: The blur effect: perception and estimation with a new no-reference perceptual blur metric. In: SPIE (2007)
3. Dalal, N., Triggs, B.: Histograms of oriented gradients for human detection. In: IEEE Computer Society Conference on Computer Vision and Pattern Recognition, CVPR 2005, vol. 1, pp. 886–893. IEEE (2005)

4. Dhar, S., Ordonez, V., Berg, T.L.: High level describable attributes for predicting aesthetics and interestingness. In: CVPR (2011)
5. Efros, A., Berg, A., Mori, G., Malik, J.: Recognizing action at a distance. In: ICCV (2003)
6. Fathi, A., Farhadi, A., Rehg, J.: Understanding egocentric activities. In: ICCV (2011)
7. Fathi, A., Hodgins, J., Rehg, J.: Social interactions: a first-person perspective. In: CVPR (2012)
8. Fathi, A., Rehg, J.: Modeling actions through state changes. In: CVPR (2013)
9. Felzenszwalb, P., Girshick, R., McAllester, D., Ramanan, D.: Object detection with discriminatively trained part based models. PAMI **32**(9), 1627–1645 (2010)
10. Fiss, J., Agarwala, A., Curless, B.: Candid portrait selection from video. In: TOG (2011)
11. Flint, A., Reid, I., Murray, D.: Learning texton models for real-time scene context. In: CVPR Workshops (2009)
12. Gong, B., Shi, Y., Sha, F., Grauman, K.: Geodesic flow kernel for unsupervised domain adaptation. In: CVPR (2012)
13. Gygli, M., Grabner, H., Riemenschneider, H., Nater, F., Van Gool, L.: The interestingness of images. In: ICCV (2013)
14. Hays, J., Efros, A.: im2gps: estimating geographic information from a single image. In: CVPR (2008)
15. Healey, J., Picard, R.: Startlecam: a cybernetic wearable camera. In: Wearable Computers (1998)
16. Hodges, S., Williams, L., Berry, E., Izadi, S., Srinivasan, J., Butler, A., Smyth, G., Kapur, N., Wood, K.: SenseCam: a retrospective memory aid. In: UBICOMP (2006)
17. Hoiem, D., Efros, A., Hebert, M.: Recovering surface layout from an image. In: IJCV (2007)
18. Isola, P., Xiao, J., Torralba, A., Oliva, A.: What makes an image memorable? In: CVPR (2011)
19. Kalogerakis, E., Vesselova, O., Hays, J., Efros, A., Hertzmann, A.: Image sequence geolocation with human travel priors. In: ICCV (2009)
20. Ke, Y., Tang, X., Jing, F.: The design of high-level features for photo quality assessment. In: CVPR (2006)
21. Khosla, A., Hamid, R., Lin, C.J., Sundaresan, N.: Large-scale video summarization using web-image priors. In: CVPR (2013)
22. Kim, G., Xing, E.: Jointly aligning and segmenting multiple web photo streams for the inference of collective photo storylines. In: CVPR (2013)
23. Kim, G., Sigal, L., Xing, E.P.: Joint summarization of large-scale collections of web images and videos for storyline reconstruction. In: CVPR (2014)
24. Kitani, K., Okabe, T., Sato, Y., Sugimoto, A.: Fast unsupervised ego-action learning for first-person sports videos. In: CVPR (2011)
25. Kosecka, J., Zhang, W.: Video compass. In: ECCV (2002)
26. Lazebnik, S., Schmid, C., Ponce, J.: Beyond bags of features: spatial pyramid matching for recognizing natural scene categories. In: CVPR (2006)
27. Lee, Y.J., Ghosh, J., Grauman, K.: Discovering important people and objects for egocentric video summarization. In: CVPR (2012)
28. Li, X., Wu, C., Zach, C., Lazebnik, S., Frahm, J.M.: Modeling and recognition of landmark image collections using iconic scene graphs. In: ECCV (2008)
29. Li, Y., Fathi, A., Rehg, J.M.: Learning to predict gaze in egocentric video. In: ICCV (2013)
30. Liu, C., Yuen, J., Torralba, A.: Nonparametric scene parsing: label transfer via dense scene alignment. In: CVPR (2009)
31. Liu, D., Hua, G., Chen, T.: A hierarchical visual model for video object summarization. PAMI **32**(12), 2178–2190 (2010)
32. Liu, T., Kender, J.: Optimization algorithms for the selection of key frame sequences of variable length. In: ECCV (2002)
33. Liu, T., Sun, J., Zheng, N., Tang, X., Shum, H.: Learning to detect a salient object. In: CVPR (2007)
34. Lu, Z., Grauman, K.: Story-driven summarization for egocentric video. In: CVPR (2013)
35. Mann, S.: Wearcam (the wearable camera): personal imaging systems for long term use in wearable tetherless computer mediated reality and personal photo/videographic memory prosthesis. In: Wearable Computers (1998)

36. Oliva, A., Torralba, A.: Modeling the shape of the scene: a holistic representation of the spatial envelope. In: IJCV (2001)
37. Pirsiavash, H., Ramanan, D.: Detecting activities of daily living in first-person camera views. In: CVPR (2012)
38. Ren, X., Gu, C.: Figure-ground segmentation improves handled object recognition in egocentric video. In: CVPR (2010)
39. Ryoo, M., Matthies, L.: First-person activity recognition: what are they doing to me? In: CVPR (2013)
40. Shakhnarovich, G., Viola, P., Darrell, T.: Fast pose estimation with parameter-sensitive hashing. In: ICCV (2003)
41. Shechtman, E., Irani, M.: Matching local self-similarities across images and videos. In: IEEE Conference on Computer Vision and Pattern Recognition, 2007. CVPR'07, pp. 1–8. IEEE (2007)
42. Simon, I., Seitz, S.: Scene segmentation using the wisdom of crowds. In: ECCV (2008)
43. Spriggs, E., la Torre, F.D., Hebert, M.: Temporal segmentation and activity classification from first-person sensing. In: Workshop on Egocentric Vision, CVPR (2009)
44. Starner, T., Schiele, B., Pentland, A.: Visual contextual awareness in wearable computing. In: International Symposium on Wearable Computers (1998)
45. Torralba, A., Efros, A.: Unbiased look at dataset bias. In: CVPR (2011)
46. Torralba, A., Fergus, R., Freeman, W.T.: 80 million tiny images: a large dataset for non-parametric object and scene recognition. PAMI **30**(11), 1958–1970 (2008)
47. Weyand, T., Leibe, B.: Discovering favorite views of popular places with iconoid shift. In: ICCV (2011)
48. Xiao, J., Hays, J., Ehinger, K., Oliva, A., Torralba, A.: SUN database: large-scale scene recognition from abbey to zoo. In: CVPR (2010)
49. Xiao, J.: Princeton vision toolkit (2013). http://vision.princeton.edu/code.html
50. Xiong, B., Grauman, K.: Detecting snap points in egocentric video with a web photo prior. In: ECCV (2014)

Chapter 5
Photo Composition Feedback and Enhancement

Exploiting Spatial Design Categories and the Notan Dark-Light Principle

Jia Li, Lei Yao and James Z. Wang

Abstract In this chapter, we present techniques to provide composition feedback and enhancement for photographs. In order to suit mobile applications, we have designed systems requiring minimal input from the users. The essence of composition is to create unity in a picture, which includes the balance of visual elements from many aspects. We hereby explore several fundamental concepts in composition and develop our new methods accordingly. Albeit much exploited by artists, these concepts have barely crossed over to multimedia or computer vision research. First, we have developed a tool to categorize images by spatial design into diagonal, horizontal, vertical, and centered composition types. Composition in this regard is known to be well associated with aesthetics and emotional response. For instance, placing visual elements diagonally creates a sense of movement; and horizontal placement tends to convey tranquility. This composition analysis tool enables the retrieval of highly aesthetic exemplar images from the corpus which are similar in content and composition to the snapshot. Second, the arrangement of dark and light masses in a picture, referred to as Notan in visual art, is a crucial factor in composition. We propose an approach to adjust the tonal values in an image, targeting directly at achieving an aesthetically more appealing Notan. This method addresses

Lei Yao done this work when she was with College of Information Sciences and Technology, The Pennsylvania State University, University Park, Pennsylvania, USA.

J. Li
Department of Statistics, The Pennsylvania State University, University Park, PA, USA
e-mail: jiali@psu.edu

L. Yao
Houzz Inc., Palo Alto, CA, USA
e-mail: simplely@gmail.com

J.Z. Wang (✉)
College of Information Sciences and Technology, The Pennsylvania State University, University Park, PA, USA
e-mail: jwang@psu.edu

© Springer International Publishing Switzerland 2015
G. Hua and X.-S. Hua (eds.), *Mobile Cloud Visual Media Computing*,
DOI 10.1007/978-3-319-24702-1_5

113

composition enhancement from a high level of spatial arrangement, a remarkable difference from improving relatively low-level characteristics such as contrast and dynamic ranges.

5.1 Introduction

Cameras on mobile phones are becoming the primary means of photo creation for common people. Because of the convenience of mobile phones, it is effortless to take snapshots and share with others. As a result, pictures are being created at a much faster pace. It is estimated that as many as one trillion photos will be taken in the year of 2015. Software tools that make it easier for average photographers to improve photo taking will likely have broad acceptance. Understanding visual aesthetics [6] can aid various applications including summarization of photo collections [19], selection of high-quality images for display [10], and extraction of aesthetically pleasing images for retrieval [18]. It can also be used to render feedback to the photographer on the aesthetics of his/her photographs.

In order to make image aesthetic quality assessment more dynamic and to reach out to the general public with a practical perspective, we conducted research to develop new technologies that can provide on-site feedback to the photographers [41]. We focused on feedback from a high-level composition perspective. *Composition* is the art of putting components together with conscious thoughts. In photography, it concerns the arrangement of various visual elements, such as line, color, texture, tone, and space. Composition is closely related to the aesthetic qualities of photographs. Partly because the problem is not well defined, insufficient research efforts have been placed on photographic composition within technical fields such as image processing and computer vision. We studied photographic composition from the perspective of spatial design, i.e., how visual elements are geometrically arranged in a picture.

Providing instant feedback on the composition style can help photographers reframe the subject leading to an aesthetically composed image. We recognized that the abstraction of composition can be done by analyzing the arrangement of the objects in the image. This led us to identify five different forms of compositions, namely, textured images, and diagonally, vertically, horizontally, and center composed images. In our work, these composition types are recognized by three classifiers, i.e., the "textured" versus "non-textured" classifier, the diagonal element detector, and the k-NN classifier for "horizontal", "vertical", and "centered" composition categories. Understanding the composition layout of the query image facilitates the retrieval of images that are similar in composition and content.

Many other applications have been built around suggesting improvizations to the image composition [3, 16] through image retargeting, and color harmony [5] to enhance aesthetics. These applications are more offline in nature. Although they are able to provide useful feedback, it is not on the spot, and requires considerable input from the user. On-site professional feedback that we propose can accomplish image improvements that are impossible once the photographer moves away from the photo-taking location.

Building upon our feedback framework, we developed a new method to provide tonal adjustment function based on exemplar pictures chosen by the user. The retrieved images provided by the composition feedback serve as candidates for the exemplar. With a simple click, even on a mobile device a user can pick an exemplar from a short list of images. Particularly in the current work, we make use of an important composition or design concept of dark and light arrangement of masses, sometimes referred to as *"Notan"* by artists. The Notan is fundamental to a composition that artists are advised to examine the Notan of a painting before heading out to paint [27].

In the tonal adjustment, we try to reach a chosen Notan design by transforming the tonal values. This is in some measure like the dodging and burning operations performed in the darkroom by analog photographers. In dodging and burning, the photographer chooses an area to darken or brighten so that details in such areas can be brought out to enhance the overall composition. In our work, for the consideration of both the limitation of the mobile device and the fact that general users are not necessarily knowledgeable in photography, the computer system automatically determines the areas that should be brightened or darkened, as well as the level of adjustment. The decision is guided by a Notan design, which can be either automatically suggested by the computer or selected by the user from a number of candidates. The involvement of the user is minimal. While tonal adjustment has been a common image processing technique, our approach offers a new perspective because it is based on high-level composition concept of Notan rather than low-level features such as contrast and dynamic range.

Future generations of digital cameras are expected to have access to the high-speed mobile network and possess substantial internal computational power, the same way as today's smart phones. Camera phones can already send photos to a remote server on the Internet and receive feedback from the server [30]. As a photographer composes, the photos in a lower resolution are streamed via the network to a cloud server. Our software system on the server analyzes the photos and sends on-site feedback to the photographer so that immediate recomposition can be possible. We propose a system comprising of the modules described below.

Given an input image, the **composition analyzer** evaluates its composition properties from different perspectives. For example, visual elements with great compositional potential, such as diagonals and curves, are detected. Photographs are categorized by high-level composition properties. Composition-related qualities, e.g., visual balance and simplicity of background, are also evaluated. Images similar in composition as well as content can be retrieved from a database of photos with high aesthetic ratings so that the photographer can learn through examples.

In the **retrieval module**, a ranking scheme is designed to integrate the composition properties into a content-based retrieval system. In our experiments, we used SIMPLIcity, an image retrieval system based on color, texture, and shape features [35]. Images with high aesthetic ratings, as well as similar composition properties and visual features, are retrieved. An effective way to learn photography as a beginner is often through observing master works and imitating. Practicing good composition in the field helps develop creative sensibility and even unique styling. Especially for amateur photographers, well-composed photographs can be valuable learning resources. By retrieving high-quality similarly composed photographs, our approach can provide users with practical assistance in improving photography composition.

In the **enhancement module**, tonal adjustment can be made to achieve better composition. We explore the concept of Notan, a crucial factor in composition regarding the arrangement of dark and light masses in an image. A new tonal transformation method is developed to achieve the desired Notan design with minimal required user interactions.

The rest of the chapter is organized as follows. The categorization of spatial design is presented in Sect. 5.2, with corresponding evaluation results in Sect. 5.3. We describe our Notan-guided tonal transform in Sect. 5.4. Experiments on the tonal transform method are provided in Sect. 5.5. We summarize in Sect. 5.6.

5.2 Spatial Design Categorization

After studying many guiding principles in photography, we find that there are several typical spatial designs. Our goal is to automatically classify major types of spatial designs. In our work, we consider the following typical composition categories: horizontal, vertical, centered, diagonal, and textured.

According to long-existing photography principles, lines formed by linear elements are important because they lead the eye through the image and contribute to the mood of the photograph. Horizontal, vertical, and diagonal lines are associated with serenity, strength, and dynamism respectively [11]. We thus include horizontal, vertical, and diagonal in the composition categories. Photographs with a centered main subject and a clear background fall into the category called centered. The photos in the textured category appear like a patch of texture or a relatively homogeneous pattern, for example, a brick wall.

The five categories of composition are not mutually exclusive. We apply several classifiers sequentially to an image: textured versus non-textured, diagonal versus non-diagonal, and finally a possibly overlapping classification of horizontal, vertical, and centered compositions. For example, an image can be classified as non-textured, diagonal, and horizontal. We use a method in [35] to classify textured images. It has been demonstrated that retrieval performance can be improved for both textured and non-textured images by first classifying them [35]. The last two classifiers are developed in the current work, with details to be presented later.

A conventional image retrieval system returns images according to visual similarity. However, photographers often need to search for pictures based on composition rather than visual details. To accommodate this, we integrate composition classification with the SIMPLIcity image retrieval system [35]. Furthermore, we provide the option to rank retrieved images by their aesthetic ratings so that the user can focus on highly rated photos.

5.2.1   The Dataset

The spatial composition classification method is tested on a dataset crawled from photo.net, a photography community where peers can share, rate, and critique photos. These photographs are mostly general-purpose pictures and have a wide range of aesthetic quality. Among the crawled photos, a large proportion have frames which can distort the visual content in image processing and impact analysis results. We remove frames from the original images in a semi-automatic fashion. The images containing frames are picked manually and a program is used to remove simple frames with flat tones. Frames embedded with pattern or text usually cannot be correctly removed. These photos are simply removed from the dataset when we recheck the cropped images in order to make sure the program has correctly removed the frames from images. We construct a dataset with $13,302$ unframed pictures. Those pictures are then rescaled so that the long side of the image has at most 256 pixels. We manually labeled 222 photos, among which 50 are horizontally composed, 51 are vertically composed, 50 are centered, and 71 are diagonally composed. Our classification algorithms are developed and evaluated based on this manually labeled dataset. The entire dataset are used in system performance evaluation.

5.2.2   Textured Versus Non-textured Classifier

We use the textured versus non-textured classifier in SIMPLIcity to separate textured images from the rest. The algorithm is motivated by the observation that if pixels in a textured area are clustered using local features, each cluster of pixels yielded are scattered across the area due to the homogeneity appearance of texture. For non-textured images, on the other hand, the clusters tend to be clumped. An image is divided evenly into $4 \times 4 = 16$ large blocks. The algorithm thus calculates the proportion of pixels in each cluster that belong to any of the 16 blocks. If the cluster of pixels is scattered over the whole image, the proportions over the 16 blocks are expected to be roughly uniform. For each cluster, the χ^2 statistic is computed to measure the disparity between the proportions and the uniform distribution over the 16 blocks. The average value of the χ^2 statistics for all the clusters is then thresholded to determine whether an image is textured or not.

5.2.3   Diagonal Design Element Detection

Diagonal elements are strong compositional constituents. The diagonal rule in photography states that a picture appears more dynamic if the objects fall or follow a diagonal line. Photographers often use diagonal elements as the visual path to draw viewers' eyes through the image.[1] The visual path is the path of eye movement when viewing a photograph [36]. When such a visual path stands out in the picture, it also has the effect of uniting individual parts in a picture. The power of the diagonal lines in composition was exploited very early on by artists. For instance, Speed [31] discussed in great details how Velazquez used the diagonal lines to unite a picture in his painting "The Surrender of Breda."

Because of the importance of diagonal visual paths for composition, we create a spatial composition category for diagonally composed pictures. More specifically, there are two subcategories, diagonal from upper left to bottom right (\) and from upper right to bottom left (/). We declare the composition of a photo as diagonal if diagonal visual paths can be detected.

Detecting the exact diagonal visual paths is challenging. Typically, segmented regions or edges provided by image processing techniques can only be viewed as *ingredients*, aka local patterns, either because of the nature of the picture or the limitation of the processing algorithms. In contrast, an *element* refers to a global pattern, e.g., a broken curve (multiple detectable edges) that is present in a large area of the image plane.

There has been literature on the general principles regarding visual elements to be briefly described below. We designed our algorithm for detecting diagonal visual paths according to these principles. While we present these principles using the diagonal category as an example, they apply in a similar way to other directional visual paths.

1. *Principle of multiple visual types*: Lines are effective design elements in creating compositions, but perfectly straight lines rarely exist in the natural world. Lines we perceive in photographs usually belong to one of these types: outlines of forms, narrow forms, lines of arrangement, and lines of motion or force [8]. We do not restrict diagonal elements to actual diagonal lines of an image plane. They can be the boundary of a region, a linear object, or even an imaginary line along which different objects align. Linear objects, such as pathways, waterways, and the contour of a building, can all create visual paths in photographs. When placed diagonally, they are generally perceived as more dynamic and interesting than other compositions. Figure 5.1 shows examples of using diagonal compositions in photography.

Fig. 5.1 Photographs of diagonal composition

---

2. *Principle of wholes or Gestalt Law*: Gestalt psychologists studied early on the phenomenon of human eyes perceiving visual components as organized patterns or wholes, known as the Gestalt law of organization. According to the Gestalt law, the factors that aid in human visual perception of forms include proximity, similarity, continuity, closure, and symmetry [32].

3. *Principle of tolerance*: Putting details along diagonals creates more interesting compositions. Visual elements such as lines and regions slightly off the ideal diagonal direction can still be perceived as diagonal and are usually more natural and interesting.[2]

4. *Principle of prominence*: A photograph can contain many lines, but dominant lines are the most important in regard to the effect of the picture [9].[3] Visual elements need sufficient span along the diagonal direction in order to strike a clear impression.

Following the above principles, we first find diagonal ingredients from low-level visual cues using both regions obtained by segmentation and connected lines obtained by edge detection. Then, we apply the Gestalt law to merge the ingredients into elements, i.e., more global patterns. The prominence of each merged entity is then assessed. We now describe the algorithms for detecting diagonal visual paths using segmented regions and edges, respectively.

Diagonal Segment Detection: Image segmentation is often used to simplify the image representation. It can generate semantically meaningful regions that are easier for analysis. We describe below our approach to detecting diagonal visual paths based on segmented regions. We use a recent image segmentation algorithm [14] because it achieves state-of-the-art accuracy at a speed sufficiently fast for real-time applications. The algorithm also ensures that the segmented regions are spatially connected, a desirable trait many algorithms do not possess.

After image segmentation, we find the orientation of each segment, defined as the orientation of the moment axis of the segment. The moment axis is the direction along which the spatial locations of the pixels in the segment have maximum variation. It is the first principal component direction for the set of pixel coordinates. For instance, if the segment is an ellipse (possibly tilted), the moment axis is simply the long axis of the ellipse. The orientation of the moment axis of a segmented region measured in degrees is computed according to Russ [29].

Next, we apply the Gestalt Law to merge certain segmented regions in order to form visual elements. Currently, we only deal with a simple case of disconnected visual path, where the orientations of all the disconnected segments are diagonal.

Let us introduce a few notations before describing the rules for merging. We denote the normalized column vector of the diagonal direction by $\mathbf{v}_d$ and that of its orthogonal direction by $\mathbf{v}_d^c$. We denote a segmented region by S, which is a set of pixel coordinates $\mathbf{x} = (x_h, x_v)^t$. The projection of a pixel with coordinate $\mathbf{x}$ onto any direction characterized by its normalized vector $\mathbf{v}$ is the inner product $\mathbf{x} \cdot \mathbf{v}$.

---

[2]http://www.picture-thoughts.com/photography/compos-ition/angle/.

[3]http://www.great-landscape-photography.com/photography-composition.html.

The projection of S onto $\mathbf{v}$, denoted by $\mathscr{P}(S, \mathbf{v})$, is a set containing the projected coordinates of all the pixels in S. That is, $\mathscr{P}(S, \mathbf{v}) = \{\mathbf{x} \cdot \mathbf{v} : \mathbf{x} \in S\}$. The length (also called spread) of the projection $|\mathscr{P}(S, \mathbf{v})| = \max_{\mathbf{x}_i, \mathbf{x}_j \in S} |\mathbf{x}_i \cdot \mathbf{v} - \mathbf{x}_j \cdot \mathbf{v}|$ is the range of values in the projected set.

The rules for merging, i.e., similarity, proximity, and continuity, are listed below. Two segments satisfying all of the rules are merged.

- *Similarity*: Two segments S_i, $i = 1, 2$, with orientations e_i, $i = 1, 2$, are similar if the following criteria are satisfied:

1. Let $[\check{\varphi}, \hat{\varphi}]$ be the range for nearly diagonal orientations. $\check{\varphi} \leq e_i \leq \hat{\varphi}$, $i = 1, 2$. That is, both S_1 and S_2 are nearly diagonal.
2. The orientations of S_i, $i = 1, 2$, are close:

$$|e_1 - e_2| \leq \beta \text{ , where } \beta \text{ is a predefined threshold.}$$

3. The lengths of $\mathscr{P}(S_i, \mathbf{v}_d)$, $i = 1, 2$, are close:

$$r = \frac{|\mathscr{P}(S_1, \mathbf{v}_d)|}{|\mathscr{P}(S_2, \mathbf{v}_d)|} \text{ , } r_1 \leq r \leq r_2 \text{ ,}$$

where $r_1 < 1$ and $r_2 > 1$ are predefined thresholds.

- *Proximity*: Segments S_i, $i = 1, 2$, are proximate if their projections on the diagonal direction, $\mathscr{P}(S_i, \mathbf{v}_d)$, $i = 1, 2$, are separated by less than p, and the overlap of their projections is less than q.
- *Continuity*: Segments S_i, $i = 1, 2$, are continuous if their projections on the direction orthogonal to the diagonal, $\mathscr{P}(S_i, \mathbf{v}_d^c)$, $i = 1, 2$, are overlapped.

We select the thresholds according to the following:

1. $\beta = 10°$.
2. $r_1 = 0.8$, $r_2 = 1.25$.
3. The values of p and q are decided adaptively according to the sizes of S_i, $i = 1, 2$. Let the spread of S_i along the diagonal line be $\lambda_i = |\mathscr{P}(S_i, \mathbf{v}_d)|$. Then $p = k_p \min(\lambda_1, \lambda_2)$ and $q = k_q \min(\lambda_1, \lambda_2)$, where $k_p = 0.5$ and $k_q = 0.8$.
   The value of p determines the maximum gap allowed between two disconnected segments to continue a visual path. The wider the segments spread over the diagonal line, the more continuity they present to the viewer. Therefore, heuristically, a larger gap is allowed, which is why p increases with the spreads of the segments. On the other hand, q determines the extent of overlap allowed for the two projections. By a similar rationale, q also increases with the spreads. If the projections of the two segments overlap too much, the segments are not merged because the combined spread of the two differs little from the individual spreads.
4. The angular range $[\check{\varphi}, \hat{\varphi}]$ for nearly diagonal orientations is determined adaptively according to the geometry of the rectangle bounding the image.

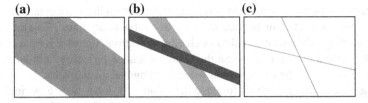

Fig. 5.2 Diagonal orientation bounding conditions. **a** Single stripe. **b** $\frac{1}{6} \to \frac{1}{3}$ stripes. **c** Angular range (color figure online)

As stated in [12], one practical extension of the diagonal rule is to have the objects fall within two boundary lines parallel to the diagonal. These boundary lines are one-third of the perpendicular distance from the diagonal to the opposite vertex of the rectangular photograph. This diagonal stripe area is shown in Fig. 5.2a. A similar suggestion is made in an online article (see footnote 2), where boundary lines are drawn using the so-called sixth points on the borders of the image plane. A sixth point along the horizontal border from the upper left corner locates on the upper border and is away from the corner by one-sixth of the image width. Similarly, we can find other sixth (or third) points from any corner and either horizontally or vertically.

Suppose we look for an approximate range for the diagonal direction going from the upper left corner to the bottom right. The sixth and third points with respect to the two corners are found. As shown in Fig. 5.2b, these special points are used to create two stripes marked by lime and blue colors respectively. Let the orientations of the lime stripe and the blue stripe in Fig. 5.2b be φ_1 and φ_2. Then we set $\check{\varphi} = \min(\varphi_1, \varphi_2)$, and $\hat{\varphi} = \max(\varphi_1, \varphi_2)$. A direction $\mathbf{v} \in [\check{\varphi}, \hat{\varphi}]$ is claimed nearly diagonal. Similarly, we can obtain the angular range for the diagonal direction from the upper right corner to the bottom left. The orientations of the stripes is used, instead of nearly diagonal bounding lines, because when the width and the height of an image are not equal, the orientation of a stripe twists toward the elongated side to some extent.

From now on, a "segment" can be a merged entity of several segments originally provided by the segmentation algorithm. For brevity, we still call the merged entity a segment. Applying the principle of tolerance, we filter out a segment from diagonal if its orientation is outside the range $[\check{\varphi}, \hat{\varphi}]$, the same rule that was applied to the smaller segments before merging.

After removing non-diagonal segments, at last, we apply the principle of prominence to retain only segments with a significant spread along the diagonal direction. For segment S, if $|\mathscr{P}(S, \mathbf{v}_d)| \geq k_l \times l$, where l is the length of the diagonal line and $k_l = \frac{2}{3}$ is a threshold, the segment is declared a diagonal visual path. It is observed that a diagonal visual path is often a merged entity of several small and non-prominent individual segments originally produced by the segmentation algorithm.

Diagonal Edge Detection: According to the principle of multiple visual types, besides segmented regions, lines and edges can also form visual paths. Moreover, segmentation can be unreliable sometimes because oversegmentation and under-segmentation often cause diagonal elements to be missed. We observe that among photographs showing diagonal composition, many contain linear diagonal elements. Those linear diagonal elements usually have salient boundary lines along the diagonal direction, which can be found through edge detection. Therefore, we use edges as another visual cue, and combine the results obtained based on both edges and segments to increase the sensitivity of detecting diagonal visual paths.

We use the Edison algorithm for edge detection [17]. It has been experimentally demonstrated that the edge detection can generate cleaner edge maps than many other methods. We examine all the edges to find those oriented diagonally and significant enough to be a visual path.

Based on the same set of principles, the whole process of finding diagonal visual paths based on edges is similar to the detection of diagonal segments. The major steps are described below. We denote an edge by E, which is a set of coordinates of pixels located on the edge. As with segments, we use the notation $\mathscr{P}(E, \mathbf{v})$ for the projection of E on a direction $\mathbf{v}$.

1. *Remove non-diagonal edges*: First, edges outside the diagonal stripe area, as shown in Fig. 5.2a, are excluded. Second, for every edge E, compute the spread of the projections $s_d = |\mathscr{P}(E, \mathbf{v}_d)|$ and $s_o = |\mathscr{P}(E, \mathbf{v}_d^c)|$. Recall that $\mathbf{v}_d$ is the diagonal direction and $\mathbf{v}_d^c$ is its orthogonal direction. Based on the ratio s_d/s_o, we compute an approximation for the orientation of edge E. Edges well aligned with the diagonal line yield a large value of s_d/s_o, while edges well off the diagonal line have a small value. We filter out non-diagonal edges by requiring $s_d/s_o \geq \zeta$. The choice of ζ will be discussed later.
2. *Merge edges*: After removing non-diagonal edges, short edges along the diagonal direction are merged into longer edges. The merging criterion is similar to the proximity rule used for diagonal segments. Two edges are merged if their projections onto the diagonal line are close to each other but not excessively overlapped.
3. *Examine prominence*: For edges formed after the merging step, we check their spread along the diagonal direction. An edge E is taken as a diagonal visual element if $|\mathscr{P}(E, \mathbf{v}_d)| \geq \xi$, where ξ is a threshold to be described next.

The values of thresholds ζ and ξ are determined by the size of a given image. ζ is used to filter out edges whose orientations are not quite diagonal, and ξ is used to select edges that spread widely along the diagonal line. We use the third points on the borders of the image plane to set bounding conditions. Figure 5.2c shows two lines marking the angular range allowed for a nearly diagonal direction from the upper left corner to the lower right corner. Both lines in the figure are off the ideal diagonal direction to some extent. Let ζ_1 and ζ_2 be their ratios of s_d to s_o, and ξ_1 and ξ_2 be their spreads over the diagonal line. The width and height of the image are denoted by w and h. By basic geometry, we can calculate ζ_i and ξ_i, $i = 1, 2$, using the formulas:

$$\zeta_1 = \frac{h^2 + 3w^2}{2hw}, \quad \zeta_2 = \frac{3h^2 + w^2}{2hw}, \quad \xi_1 = \frac{h^2 + 3w^2}{3\sqrt{h^2 + w^2}}, \quad \xi_2 = \frac{3h^2 + w^2}{3\sqrt{h^2 + w^2}}.$$

The thresholds are then set by $\zeta = \min(\zeta_1, \zeta_2)$ and $\xi = \min(\xi_1, \xi_2)$.

5.2.4   Horizontal, Vertical, and Centered Compositions

Now we present our method for differentiating the remaining three composition categories: horizontal, vertical, and centered. Photographs belonging to each of these categories have distinctive spatial layouts. For instance, a landscape with blue sky at the top and a grass field at the bottom conveys a strong impression of horizontal layout. Images from a particular category usually have some segments that are characteristic of that category, e.g., a segment lying laterally right to left for horizontal photographs, and a homogeneous background for centered photographs.

In order to quantitatively characterize spatial layout, we define the *spatial relational vector* (SRV) of a region to specify the geometric relationship between the region and the rest of the image. The spatial layout of the entire image is then represented by the set of SRVs of all the segmented regions. The dissimilarity between spatial layouts of images is computed by the IRM distance [15]. Ideally, we want to describe the spatial relationship between each semantically meaningful object and its surrounding space. However, object extraction is inefficient and extremely difficult for photographs in general domain, regions obtained by image segmentation algorithms are used instead as a reasonable approximation.

The SRV is proposed to characterize the geometric position and the peripheral information about a pixel or a region in the image plane. It is defined at both the pixel level and the region level. When computing the pixel-level SRV, the pixel is regarded as the reference point, and all the other pixels are divided into eight zones by their relative positions to the reference point. If the region that contains the pixel is taken into consideration, SRV is further differentiated into two modified forms, inner SRV and outer SRV. The region-level inner (outer) SRV is obtained by averaging pixel-level inner (outer) SRVs over the region. Details about SRV implementation are given below. SRV is scale-invariant, and depends on the spatial position and the shape of the segment.

At a pixel with coordinates (x, y), four lines passing through it are drawn. As shown in Fig. 5.3a, the angles between adjacent lines are equal and stride symmetrically over the vertical, horizontal, 45° and 135° lines. We call the eight angular areas of the plane upper, upper-left, left, bottom-left, bottom, bottom-right, right, and upper-left zones. The SRV of the pixel (x, y) summarizes the angular positions of all the other pixels with respect to (x, y). Specifically, we calculate the area percentage v_i of each

Fig. 5.3 Division of the image into eight angular areas with respect to a reference pixel

(a)   **(b)**

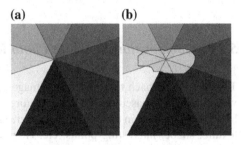

zone, $i = 0, \ldots, 7$, with respect to the whole image and construct the pixel-level SRV $V_{x,y}$ by $V_{x,y} = (v_0, v_1, \ldots, v_7)^t$.

The region-level SRV is defined in two forms, called inner SRV, denoted by V', and outer SRV, denoted by V'', respectively. At any pixel in a region, we can divide the image plane into eight zones by the above scheme. As shown in Fig. 5.3b, for each of the eight zones, some pixels are inside the region and some are outside. Depending on whether a pixel belongs to the region, the eight zones are further divided into 16 zones. We call those zones within the region as inner pieces and those outside as outer pieces. Area percentages of the inner (or outer) pieces with respect to the area inside (or outside) the region form the inner SRV $V'_{x,y}$ (or outer SRV $V''_{x,y}$) for pixel (x, y).

The region-level SRV is defined as the average of pixel-level SRVs for pixels in that region. The outer SRV V_R'' of a region R is $V_R'' = \sum_{(x,y) \in R} V_{x,y}''/m$, where m is the number of pixels in region R. In practice, to speed up the calculation, we may subsample the pixels (x, y) in R and compute V_R'' by averaging over only the sampled pixels. If a region is too small to occupy at least one sampled pixel according to a fixed sampling rate, we compute V_R'' using the pixel at the center of the region.

We use the outer SRV to characterize the spatial relationship of a region with respect to the rest of the image. Then an image with N segments $R_i, i = 1, \ldots, N$, can be described by N region-level outer SRVs, $V_{R_i}'', i = 1, \ldots, N$, together with the area percentages of R_i, denoted by w_i. In summary, an image-level SRV descriptor is a set of weighted SRVs: $\{(V_{R_i}'', w_i), i = 1, \ldots, N\}$. We call this descriptor the *spatial layout signature*.

We use k-NN to classify the three composition categories: horizontal, vertical, and centered. Inputs to the k-NN algorithm are the spatial layout signatures of images. The training dataset includes equal number of manually labeled examples in each category. In our experiment, the sample size for each category is 30. The distance between the spatial layout signatures of two images is computed using the IRM distance. The IRM distance is a weighted average of the distances between any pair of SRVs, one in each signature. The weights are assigned in a greedy fashion so that the final weighted average is minimal. Details about IRM are referred to [15, 35].

We conducted our experiments on a single compute node with two quad-core Intel processors running at 2.66 GHz and 24 GB of RAM. For the composition analysis process, the average time to process a 256×256 image is 3 s, including image segmentation [14], edge detection [17], and the composition classification as described.

5.2.5 Composition-Sensitive Photo Retrieval

The classic approach taken by many image retrieval systems [7] is to measure the visual similarity based on low-level features. A large family of visual descriptors have been proposed in the past to characterize images from the perspectives of color, texture, shape, interesting points, etc. However, due to the fact that many visual descriptors are generated by local feature extraction processes, the overall spatial composition of the image is usually lost. In semantic content oriented applications, spatial layout information of an image may not be critical. But for photography applications, the overall spatial composition can be a critical factor affecting how an image is perceived. For photographers, it is often more interesting to search for photos with similar composition or design style rather than visual details. As described above, our algorithms capture strong compositional elements in photos and classify them into six composition categories, with five main categories named textured, horizontal, vertical, centered and diagonal, and the diagonal category is further divided into two categories diagonal$_{ulbr}$ (upper left to bottom right) and diagonal$_{urbl}$ (upper right to bottom left). The composition classification is used in the retrieval system to return images with similar composition.

We use the SIMPLIcity system to retrieve images with similar visual content, and then re-rank the top K images by considering their spatial composition and aesthetic ratings. SIMPLIcity is a semantic-sensitive region-based image retrieval system. IRM is used to measure visual similarity between images. For a thorough description of algorithms used in SIMPLIcity, readers are referred to the original publication [35]. In our system, the rank of an image is determined by three factors: its visual similarity to the query, the spatial composition categorization, and the aesthetic rating. Since these factors are of different modality, we use a ranking scheme rather than a complicated scoring equation.

Given a query, we first retrieve K images through SIMPLIcity, which gives us an initial ranking. When composition is taken into consideration, images with the same composition categorization as the query are moved to the top of the ranking list.

The composition classification is nonexclusive in the context of image retrieval. For instance, a textured image can be classified concurrently into horizontal, vertical, or centered categories. We code the classification results obtained from the classifiers by a six-dimensional vector c, corresponding to six categories (recall that the diagonal category has two subcategories diagonal$_{ulrb}$ and diagonal$_{urbl}$). Each dimension records whether the image belongs to a particular category, with 1 being yes and 0 no. Note that an image can belong to multiple classes generated by different classifiers. The image can also be assigned to one or more categories among horizontal, vertical, and centered, if neighbors belonging to the category found by k-NN reach a substantial number (in our experiments $k/3$ is used). Nonexclusive classification is more robust than exclusive classification in practice because a photograph may be reasonably assigned to more than one composition category. Nonexclusive classification can also reduce the negative effect of misclassification into one class. Figure 5.4 shows example pictures that are classified as more than one category.

The compositional similarity between the query image and another image can be defined as

$$s_i = \sum_{k=0}^{3} I(c_{q_k} = c_{ik} \text{ and } c_{q_k} = 1) + 2\sum_{k=4}^{5} I(c_{q_k} = c_{ik} \text{ and } c_{q_k} = 1),$$

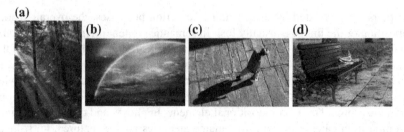

Fig. 5.4 Photographs classified into multiple categories. Categories are shown with symbols. **a** | and \. **b** − and /. **c** | and /. **d** | and /

where c_q and c_i are categorization vectors for the query image and the other image, and I is the indicator function returning 1 when the input condition is true, 0 otherwise. The last two dimensions of the categorization vector correspond to the two diagonal categories. We multiply the matching function by 2 to encourage matching of diagonal categories in practice. Note that the value of s_i is between 0 and 6, because one image can at most be classified into five categories, which are textured, diagonal$_{ulbr}$, diagonal$_{urbl}$, and two of the other three. Therefore by adding composition classification results, we divide the K images into 8 groups corresponding to compositional similarity from 0 to 7. The original ranking based on visual similarity remains within each group. Although the composition analysis is performed on the results returned by SIMPLIcity, we can modify the influence of this component in the retrieval process by adjusting the number of images K returned by SIMPLIcity. The larger K is, the stronger factor composition is to overall retrieval.

5.3 Evaluation Results on Composition Feedback

The spatial design categorization process was incorporated as a component into our OSCAR (On-Site Composition and Aesthetics feedback through exemplars) system [41]. User evaluation was conducted on composition layout classification, similarity and aesthetics quality of retrieved images, and the helpfulness of the feedback for improving photography. We only present results for the study on composition classification here. Interested readers are referred to that paper for comprehensive evaluation results. Professional photographers or enthusiasts would have been ideal subjects for such studies. However, due to time constraints, we were unable to recruit professionals. Instead, we recruited around 30 students, most of whom were graduate students at Penn State with practical knowledge of digital images and photography. All photos used in these studies are from photo.net.

A collection of around 1,000 images were randomly picked to form the dataset for the study on composition. Each participant is provided with a set of 160 randomly chosen images and is asked to describe the composition layout of each image. At an online site, the participants can view pages of test images, next to each of which are

Table 5.1 Distribution of the entropy for the votes of users

	[0,0.5]	(0.5,1.0]	(1.0,1.5]	(1.5,2.0]	(2.0, 2.5]
h	36.12	29.96	17.18	15.42	1.32
v	12.98	45.67	19.71	20.19	1.44
c	25.36	45.48	13.12	14.87	1.17
ulbr	12.99	44.16	19.48	19.48	3.90
urbl	16.87	43.37	18.07	20.48	1.20
t	10.77	36.92	10.77	36.92	4.62
none	6.59	39.56	17.58	34.07	2.20

For each composition category, the percentage of photos yielding a value of entropy in any bin is shown. h: horizontal, v: vertical, c: centered, ulbr: diagonal (upper left, bottom right), urbl: diagonal (upper right, bottom left), t: textured, none: none of the above

seven selection buttons: "Horizontal", "Vertical", "Centered", "Diagonal (upper left, bottom right)", "Diagonal (upper right, bottom left)", "Patterned", and "None of the above". Multiple choices are allowed. We used "Patterned" for the class of photos with homogeneous texture (or the textured class in our earlier description). We added the "none of the above" choice to allow more flexibility for the user's perception. A total of 924 images were voted each by three or more users.

In order to understand compositional clarity, we examine the variation in users' votes on composition layout. We quantify the ambiguity in the choices of composition layout using entropy. The larger the entropy in the votes, the higher the ambiguity is in the composition layout of the image. The entropy is calculated by the formula $\sum p_i \log 1/p_i$, where p_i, $i = 0, \ldots, 6$, is the percentage of votes for each category. The entropy was calculated for all 924 photos and its value was found to range between 0 and 2.5. We divided the range of entropy into five bins. The photos are divided into seven groups according to the composition category receiving the most votes. In each category, we compute the proportion of photos yielding a value of entropy belonging to any of the five bins. These proportions are reported in Table 5.1. We observe that among the seven categories, horizontal and centered categories have the strongest consensus among users, while "none of the above" is the most ambiguous category.

We evaluate our composition classification method in the case of both exclusive classification and nonexclusive classification. The users' votes on composition are used to form the ground truth, with specifics to be explained shortly. We consider only six categories, i.e., horizontal, vertical, centered, diagonal$_{ulbr}$, diagonal$_{urbl}$, and textured for this analysis. The "none of the above" category was excluded for the following reasons:

- The "none of the above" category is of great ambiguity among users, as shown by the above analysis.
- Only a very small portion of images is predominantly labeled as "none of the above." Among the 924 photos, 17 have three or more votes for "none of the above."

Table 5.2 The confusion matrix for exclusive classification of 494 images into six composition categories

	h	v	c	ulbr	urbl	t
h	107	0	20	3	8	4
v	1	32	39	3	2	10
c	10	7	132	8	11	12
ulbr	4	0	5	18	0	2
urbl	2	1	13	0	22	1
t	0	2	6	0	0	9

Each row corresponds to a ground truth class. h: horizontal, v: vertical, c: centered, ulbr: diagonal (upper left, bottom right), urbl: diagonal (upper right, bottom left), t: textured, none: none of the above

- We notice that these 17 "none of the above" photos vary greatly in visual appearance; and hence it is not meaningful to treat such a category as a compositionally coherent group. It is difficult to define such a category. A portion of images in this category shows noisy or complex scenes without clear centers of attention. This can be a separate category for consideration in future work.

We conducted exclusive classification only on photos of little ambiguity according to users' choices of composition. The number of votes a category can receive ranges from zero to five. To be included in this analysis, a photo has to receive three or more votes for one category (that is, the ground-truth category) and no more than one vote for any other category. With this constraint, 494 out of the 924 images were selected. Table 5.2 is the confusion matrix based on this set of photos.

We see that the most confusing category pairs are vertical versus centered and diagonal$_{urbl}$ versus centered. Figure 5.5a shows some examples labeled as vertical

Fig. 5.5 Photo examples mistakenly classified as centered by our algorithm. **a** Photos labeled as vertical by users. **b** Photos labeled diagonal$_{urbl}$ by users

by users, while classified as centered by our algorithm. We observe that the mis-classification is mainly caused by the following: (1) vertical images in the training dataset cannot sufficiently represent this category; (2) users are prone to label images with vertically elongated objects as vertical, although such images may be classified as centered in the training data; and (3) the vertical elements fail to be captured by image segmentation. Figure 5.5b gives diagonal$_{urbl}$ examples mistakenly classified as centered. The failure to detect diagonal elements results mainly from: (1) diagonal elements located beyond the diagonal tolerance set by our algorithm; and (2) imaginary diagonal visual paths, e.g., the direction of an object's movement.

In nonexclusive classification, the criterion for a photo being assigned to one category is less strict than in the exclusive case. A photo is labeled as a particular category if it gets two or more votes on that category. In total there are 849 out of the 924 photos with at least one category voted twice or more. The results reported below is based on these 849 photos.

The composition categorization of a photo is represented by a six-dimensional binary vector, with 1 indicating the presence of a composition type, and 0 the absence. Let $M = (m_0, \ldots, m_5)$ and $U = (u_0, \ldots, u_5)$ denote the categorization vector generated by our algorithm and by users respectively. The value m_0 is set to 1 if and only if there are 10 or more nearest neighbors (among 30) labeled as horizontal. The values of m_1 and m_2, corresponding to the vertical and centered categories are set similarly. For the diagonal categories, m_i, where $i = 3, 4$, is set to 1 if any diagonal element is detected by our algorithm. Finally, m_5 is set to 1 if the textured versus non-textured classifier labels the image as textured. Three ratios are computed to assess the accuracy of the nonexclusive classification.

- Ratio of partial detection r_1: the percentage of photos for which at least one of the user labeled categories is declared by the algorithm. Based on the 849 photos, $r_1 = 80.31\%$.
- Detection ratio r_2: the percentage of photos for which all the user labeled categories are captured by the algorithm. Define $M \succ U$ if $m_j \geq u_j$ for any $j \in [0, 5]$. So r_2 is the percentage of images for which $M \succ U$. We have $r_2 = 66.00\%$.
- Ratio of perfect match r_3: the percentage of photos for which $M = U$. We have $r_3 = 33.11\%$.

5.4 Notan-Guided Tonal Transform

The tonal value, i.e., the luminance, in a picture is a major factor for the visual impression conveyed by the picture. In art, the luminance at a location is simply called the value. Artists have remarked on the prominent role of values even for color paintings. [31] wrote:

> By drawing is here meant the expression of form upon a plane surface. Art probably owes more to form for its range of expression than to color. Many of the noblest things it is capable of conveying are expressed by form more directly than by anything else. And it is interesting

to notice how some of the world's greatest artists have been very restricted in their use of color, preferring to depend on form for their chief appeal.

While recognizing the importance of color, Payne [23] remarked "Perhaps color might be called a nonessential factor in composition, since unity may be created without it." Regarding values, Payne [23] wrote:

Dark and light usually refers to the range of values in the entire design while light and shade generally denote the lighted and shaded parts of single items. Both light and dark and light and shade are active factors in composition.

The use of light and shade to create the sense of solidity or relief on a plane surface, a technique called *chiaroscuro*, is an invention in the West. The giants in art, Leonardo Da Vinci, Raphael, Michelangelo, and Titian, are masters of this technique. The art of the East has a very different tradition, emphasizing the arrangement of dark and light in the overall design. Speed [31] called this approach of the East *mass drawing*. Again quoting from [31],

The reducing of a complicated appearance to a few simple masses is the first necessity of the painter. . . . The art of China and Japan appears to have been more influenced by this view of natural appearances than that of the West has been, until quite lately. . . . Light and shade, which suggest solidity, are never used, a wide light where there is no shadow pervades everything, their drawing being done with the brush in masses. (referring to the East art)

Until fairly modern time, Chinese paintings were mostly done in black ink, and even the colored ones have very limited range in chroma. In Chinese ink painting, a graceful juxtaposition of dark and light is a preeminent principle for aesthetics, called *Nong-Dan*. "Nong" literally means high concentration in liquid solution, while "Dan" means thin concentration. For ink, Nong-Dan refers to the concentration of black pigment. Hence, "Nong" leads to dark, and "Dan" leads to light. The same concept is used in Japanese painting and the Japanese imported directly the two Chinese characters in Kanji. The English translation from Kanji is *Notan*.

Relatively recently, Notan has been used in the West as a compact word meaning the overall design in black and white, or a small number of tonal scales. Mass Notan study focuses on the organization of simplified tonal structure rather than details. For example, a scene is reduced to an arrangement of major shapes (mass) with different levels of tonal values. The goal of a mass Notan study is to create a harmonious and balanced design (or "big picture"). [27] recommends strongly the practice of mass Notan study as an initial step in painting to secure balanced and pleasing composition.

The essence of Notan is also well recognized in photography. Due to the difficulty in controlling light, especially in outdoor environments, photographers use dodging and burning techniques to achieve desired exposures for regions that cannot be reached by a single shot. Traditionally, dodging and burning are darkroom techniques applied during the film-to-paper printing process to alter the exposure of certain areas without affecting the rest of the photo. Specifically, dodging brightens an area, and burning darkens. Ansel Adams extensively used dodging and burning techniques in developing many of his famous prints. He mentioned in his book *The Print* [2] that most of his prints are not the reproduction of the scenes but instead his visualization of the scenes. As Ansel Adams put it, "dodging and burning are steps to take care of mistakes God made in establishing tonal relationships."

In the digital era, to realize one's personal visualization, a photographer can modify the tonal structure using photo editing software. However, applying dodging and burning digitally can be time-consuming and requires a considerable level of mastery in photography, both technically and artistically.

In our work, we aim at developing a system that performs dodging and burning kind of adjustments on the tonal values of photographs with minimum user involvement. This is motivated by the need to enhance photos on mobile devices and to reach a broader set of users. The restrictive interface of the mobile device prohibits extensive manual photo editing. Moreover, an average user may not have sufficient art understanding and professional patience to improve the composition effectively, as the process can be much more sophisticated than a mere change of dynamic range or contrast. Although most people are clear about whether they find a photo aesthetically pleasing, it is a different matter when it comes to creating an aesthetically pleasing picture. This is the gap between an amateur and an artist.

Our system, targeting an average user, makes photo composition editing nearly automatic. In fact, the only involvement of a user is to input his/her judgment on whether a picture or a design is appealing or desired. It is a small step to turn the system fully automatic, but we feel that it is actually beneficial to inject some personal taste as allowed by the amount of interaction on the mobile device. Specifically, two strategies are exploited. First, to enhance a picture, a collection of Notan structures are created based on the original picture. A user can select a favorite Notan or the system chooses one closest to the Notan structure of an exemplar picture. This helps the user pinpoint easily a favored design. Second, in order to make the altered picture convey such a design, tonal transform is applied. This step is automatic by matching the tonal value distributions with those of the exemplar picture. The differences between our system and some existing tonal transform methods will be discussed at a more technical level in a short moment. In the current work, we assume a given exemplar picture. As an extension to the work, we can invoke a search engine using text and/or images to suggest exemplar pictures. A plethora of highly aesthetic online photo collections exist.

Prior research most relevant to ours includes style transfer and tone reproduction. As a particular type of style, color transfer studies the problem of applying the color palette of a target image to a source image, essentially reshaping the color distribution of the source image to accord with the target at some cost. The histogram matching algorithm derives a tone-mapping function from the cumulative density functions of the source and the target. Various techniques have been developed [1, 21, 24–26, 28, 39, 40]. These methods process the color distribution globally and do not consider spatial information. Pixels of the same color are subject to the same transformation regardless of whether they are in dark or light regions. Artifacts can be easily brought in when the source histogram is very different from the target. [37] conducted color transfer between corresponding regions chosen by the user in the source image and the target image. [33] formed correspondence between segmented regions in the source image and the target before color transfer.

5.4.1 Method Overview

Let us first define a few terminologies. *Source image* is the image to be altered, while the *exemplar image* serves as a good example for the luminance distribution and possibly the Notan as well. The Notan we intended to obtain for the source image is *source Notan*, while the Notan of the exemplar image is called *exemplar Notan*. The tonal value or luminance will also be referred to as intensity in the sequel.

The outline of the Notan-guided tonal transform is as follows:

- Identify the source Notan and exemplar Notan.
- Perform Notan-guided region-wise histogram matching between the source image and the exemplar image.
- Postprocess the transformed image to remove possible artifacts at region boundaries.

The source and exemplar images are subject to segmentation by the algorithm in [14]. The average luminance of each segment is computed. To obtain the exemplar Notan, we first obtain a binarization threshold for the luminance using Otsu's method [20] which assumes a bimodal distribution and calculates the optimum threshold such that the two classes separated by the threshold have minimal intra-class variance. This threshold decides whether any segmented region in the exemplar image is either dark (below threshold) or light (above). The source Notan can be obtained by different schemes. When the luminance threshold slides from small to large, more segmented regions in the source image are marked as dark. Because there are only finitely many segments, there are only finitely many possible Notans by thresholding at different values. With n segments, there are at most $n + 1$ Notans. We can either let the algorithm choose a Notan automatically for the source image or let the user select his favorite Notan from the candidates. In the fully automatic setting, we have tested two schemes. We can either use Otsu's method to decide the threshold between dark and light (Automatic Scheme 1) or choose the source Notan with the proportion of dark area closest to that of the exemplar Notan (Automatic Scheme 2).

The algorithm for Notan-guided region-wise histogram matching will be presented later. The proposed approach differs from existing work in several ways. Instead of deriving a global tone-mapping function from two intensity distributions, a mapping function is obtained for each region in the source image. The mapping function is parameterized by the generalized logistic function. Although the regions are subject to different transforms, the parameters in the region-wise mapping functions are optimized simultaneously to minimize an overall matching criterion between the source and the exemplar images. The approach does not require a correspondence established between regions in the two images. Furthermore, as elaborated in the next subsection, the spatial arrangement of dark and light, as embedded in Notan, plays an important role in determining the transform. In another word, the tonal transform is not just for matching two intensity histograms, but also an attempt to reach certain spatial patterns of dark and light.

Compared with traditional histogram manipulation algorithms, one advantage of applying transformation functions in a region-wise fashion is to avoid noisy artifacts within regions. However, its performance depends on region segmentation to some extent. If the same object is mistakenly segmented into several regions, different transformation functions applied on its parts may cause artifacts. In real dodging and burning practice, a similar situation can be remedied by careful localized motion of the covering material during the darkroom exposure development or applying a subtle dodging/burning brush over a large area in digital photo editing software. We use fuzzy region maps to cope with this problem. Bilateral filter is employed to generate fuzzy maps for regions. Bilateral filter is well known for its edge-preserving property. It considers both spatial adjacency and intensity similarity. We use the fast implementation in [22].

5.4.2 Region-Wise Histogram Matching

The intensity histogram records the proportion of pixels at a series of tonal scales, but not where the tonal values locate in the image. In this subsection, we describe the method for region-wise histogram matching between the source and exemplar images. A certain level of spatial coherence is obtained by the region-wise approach in comparison to the existing methods of global histogram matching. In the next subsection, we will revise the histogram matching criterion to take into account Notan, thereby attempting directly to achieve a favored spatial design.

A *sub-histogram* is defined as the intensity histogram of a region. The image segmentation algorithm in [14] is used to divide an image into semantically meaningful regions. The image is converted into the CIELab color space and the luminance channel is extracted to build the per region sub-histogram. The range of the intensity values is $[0, 1]$. In the discussion below, the histogram is in fact a probability density function. We use the terminology "histogram" loosely here to be consistent with the often used term "histogram matching."

Let $H_i(x)$, $x \in [0, 1]$ be the sub-histogram for the ith region and n be the number of regions. Let $H(x)$ be the histogram for the entire image. We parameterize $H_i(x)$ by a single Gaussian or a two component Gaussian mixture. The main reason to use a Gaussian mixture instead of the usual histogram obtained by discretization is to ensure smoothness of H, a necessity for applying an optimization software package used in the region-wise histogram matching algorithm. Although $H_i(x)$ should have finite support, we ignore the tail of the Gaussian distribution because the variance of X is usually small in a single region obtained by similarity-based segmentation. The two-component option is provided to accommodate intensity distributions of clearly textured regions. Suppose the number of components for $H_i(x)$ is $K_i \in \{1, 2\}$. We have

$$H(x) = \sum_{i=1}^{n} H_i(x) = \sum_{i=1}^{n} \sum_{j=1}^{K_i} p_{ij} \frac{1}{\sqrt{2\pi}\sigma_{ij}} \exp{-\frac{(x - u_{ij})^2}{2\sigma_{ij}^2}}.$$

We use an unsupervised clustering algorithm [4] to estimate K_i and the mean μ_{ij} and the variance σ_{ij} of each component. Similarly, the intensity distribution of the exemplar image $\tilde{H}$ is also approximated by GMM. Instead of summing over sub-histograms, a single GMM with $\tilde{K}$ components is used to represent the entire image. $\tilde{K}$ is also estimated by the algorithm in [4].

To measure the distance between two distributions with support on [0, 1], we use the integrated difference between their cumulative density functions [38]:

$$D(H, \tilde{H}) = \int_0^1 \left(\int_0^\lambda H(x)dx - \int_0^\lambda \tilde{H}(x)dx \right)^2 d\lambda. \tag{5.1}$$

We adopt a special case of the generalized logistic function as the tone-mapping function. The generalized logistic function is defined as

$$Y(x) = A + \frac{K - A}{(1 + Qe^{-B(x-M)})^{1/v}}.$$

The general expression above provides a high degree of flexibility. We retain only two parameters b and m to allow changes in curvature and translation of the inflection point [34].

$$Y(x) = \frac{1}{1 + e^{-b(x-m)}}. \tag{5.2}$$

The reason for choosing the above function is that it can accomplish different types of tonal adjustment by setting different parameters, allowing a unified expression for the transformation functions. Moreover, the logistic curve tends to preserve contrast. Figure 5.6 illustrates some tone-mapping curves generated by (5.2) with different values of b and m.

Fig. 5.6 Tone-mapping curves with various parameters

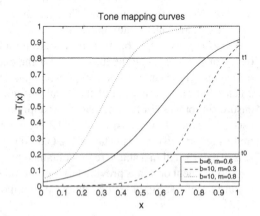

We constrain the parameter space of b and m such that $Y(x)$ in Eq. (5.2) is monotonically increasing and the intensity range after transformation is not compressed too much. The first condition can be met provided $b > 0$. For the second condition, we set two thresholds t_0 and t_1 such that:

$$Y(0) = \frac{1}{1 + e^{bm}} \le t_0, \quad Y(1) = \frac{1}{1 + e^{-b(1-m)}} \ge t_1. \tag{5.3}$$

A right (left) translation of the inflection point, i.e., $m \gg 0.5$ ($m \ll 0.5$), will darken (brighten) the region, causing a burning (dodging) effect.

Let the parameters of the transform $Y(x)$ for the ith region be b_i and m_i. For the overall image, the tonal transformation is then parameterized by $T = \{m_1, b_1, \ldots, m_n, b_n\}$. After we apply the transformation functions on individual regions, the intensity distribution of the modified image becomes

$$H(y; T) = \sum_{i=1}^{n} \frac{dX_i(y)}{dy} H_i(X_i(y); T),$$
$$\text{where } X_i(y) = Y_i^{-1}(y). \tag{5.4}$$

We cast region-wise histogram matching as an optimization problem. The objective function $F(T)$ measures the distance between the intensity distributions of the transformed source image and the exemplar image. Suppose the source image contains n regions with average intensities $\mu_i, i = 1, \ldots, n$, and the average intensities of the regions after tone mapping become $\mu_i', i = 1, \ldots, n$. The optimization problem for the region-wise histogram matching is:

$$F(T) = \min_{T} D(H(y; T), \tilde{H}(y)),$$
$$\text{s.t. } (\mu_i - \mu_j)(\mu_i' - \mu_j') \ge 0,$$
$$\forall 1 \le i \le n, \; 1 \le j \le n. \tag{5.5}$$

Recall D is the distance defined in (5.1). The optimization is constrained so that the original order of region intensities is retained (the relative brightness of the regions will not be reversed). We use the package called CFSQP developed at the University of Maryland [13] to solve the optimization.

The major problem with the global tone-mapping function is the complete loss of the spatial information. The approach of transferring color between matched regions is intuitive but requires correspondence between regions, which is only meaningful for images very similar in content. For example, Fig. 5.7a shows a pair of images taken as the source image and the exemplar image. Their intensity distributions are very different from each other. Figure 5.7 compares two global approaches, global histogram matching and color normalization [28], with the proposed region-wise approach. When the source image is low-keyed and the exemplar is high-keyed, a global mapping function tends to remove too many details in the dark areas and

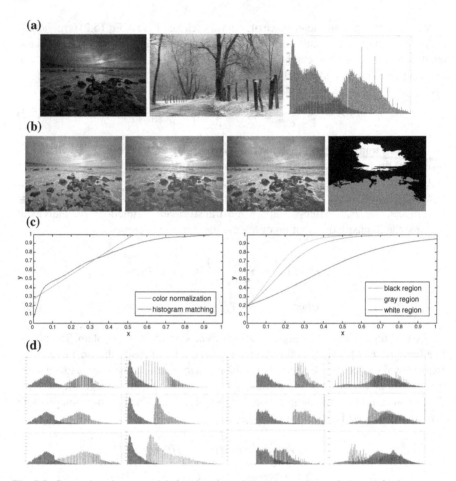

Fig. 5.7 Comparison between global and region-wise tone mapping. **a** *Left to right* the source image, the exemplar image, the intensity histograms (*gray* for the source image and *blue* for the exemplar). **b** First three images from *left to right* the modified image by histogram matching, by color normalization, and by region-wise adjustment. Last image: the segmented regions. **c** Tone-mapping curves. *Left* histogram matching (*blue*) and color normalization (*red*). *Right* Transformation functions for different regions (*red curve* for *black region*; *green* for *gray region*; and *blue* for *white region*). **d** *Left to right* histograms for the segmented region shown in *black*, region in *gray*, region in *white*, and the entire image before and after matching. The histograms in *gray* are for the original image before matching; *red* for the modified image; and *blue* for the exemplar image. *Row 1* results for global histogram matching. *Row 2* color normalization. *Row 3* region-wise histogram matching (color figure online)

overexpose the light areas. With region-wise adjustments, however, each transformation function contributes to the overall histogram matching while its transformed range is not severely constrained by other regions. For example, the tone-mapping curve of a dark region can have a higher growth rate than light regions (Fig. 5.7b).

5.4.3 *Notan-Guided Matching*

The objective function for region-wise histogram matching provided in (5.5) ignores the spatial arrangement of dark and light. We thus introduce a new objective function dependent on the Notan. Consequently, the revised image tends to yield a Notan appearance close to the specified source Notan. Let H_{dark} and H_{light} be the intensity distributions for the dark and light areas of the source image respectively, where the dark and light areas are decided by the source Notan. Similarly, let $\tilde{H}_{dark}$ and $\tilde{H}_{light}$ be the intensity distributions for the dark and light areas of the exemplar image respectively. The new optimization problem is

$$F_n(T) = \min_T \left(D(H_{dark}(y; T), \tilde{H}_{dark}(y)) + D(H_{light}(y; T), \tilde{H}_{light}(y)) \right),$$

$$\text{s.t. } (\mu_i - \mu_j)(\mu_i' - \mu_j') \geq 0, \text{ for any } 1 \leq i \leq n, 1 \leq j \leq n. \tag{5.6}$$

Comparing optimization (5.6) with (5.5), we see that the new objective function is the sum of two separate distribution distances, one involving only the dark areas in the two images and the other only the light areas. However, because of the constraints to retain the intensity ordering of the regions, the optimization problem cannot be decoupled into one for the dark areas and one for the light areas.

Figure 5.8 illustrates the impact of the chosen source Notan on the modified image under the same exemplar image and exemplar Notan. Two different Notans are shown for each source image in Fig. 5.8. The Notans are accompanied by their corresponding modified images. By imposing different Notans, the modified images generated by optimization (5.6) present quite different dark-light compositions. On a mobile device, we can potentially show users a few options of source Notans and let them pick what they find most appealing.

A side benefit of Notan-guided matching is to better keep contrast. When the proportions of dark and light areas differ substantially between the source image and the exemplar, matching without Notan often results in over reduced contrast (an overall whitened or blackened look). The effect of large disparity in dark-light proportion is mitigated by the Notan, which enforces matching the dark areas and light areas separately. For example, the exemplar image in Fig. 5.9b has a proportionally small dark area (rocks) which contrasts with a large light area, while the source image has a relatively large dark area. In this example, we used the threshold given by Otsu's method to generate the source Notan. The modified image obtained by region-wise histogram matching without Notan (optimization 5.5), shown in Fig. 5.9d, seems to be overexposed with much reduced contrast. This issue is more serious with modified images obtained by global histogram matching in (e) and color normalization in (f). The result of Notan guided matching in (c) keeps the best contrast.

Considering the stringent interface on a mobile device, we explore a scenario when an exemplar image is not available. Interestingly, we may enhance the composition of an image by just specifying a desired Notan. In Fig. 5.10, the source image itself serves as the exemplar image. The exemplar Notan is obtained using the threshold

(a)

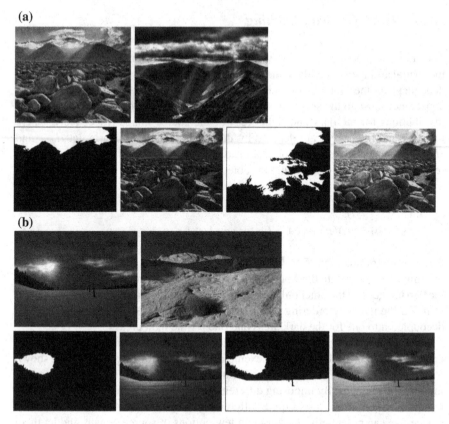

(b)

Fig. 5.8 Modification by different Notan patterns for two example images. *Top row* in each example: the source image (*left*) and the exemplar image (*right*). *Bottom row* in each example: two source Notan patterns and the modified images (on the right of the corresponding Notan). **a** Example 1. **b** Example 2

of Otsu's method. The source Notan is manually chosen, supposedly more appealing than the automatically picked Notan. The results demonstrate that the modified images indeed seem better composed. This self-boosting method may seem surprising at first glance. To better understand this, note that the exemplar Notan will have a more contrasted dark and light because of the way the threshold is chosen. It should also be closer to what the Notan of the source image without modification appears to be. However, the spatial arrangement of the dark and light is not as pleasant as what is specified by the manually chosen Notan. What is essentially done by our algorithm is to make the manually set dark and light areas appear better divided and hence more obvious to the eye. This is achieved by histogram matching with the exemplar dark and light areas, which by set up are well contrasted.

This experiment of self-boosting composition enhancement hints that choosing a source Notan is more important than an exemplar image. Here, we used the source

(a)   (b)   (c)

(d)   (e)   (f)

Fig. 5.9 Contrast comparison. **a** Source image. **b** Exemplar image. **c** Notan-guided region-wise histogram matching (optimization 5.6). **d** Modified image generated by region-wise histogram matching (optimization 5.5). **e** Global histogram matching. **f** Color normalization

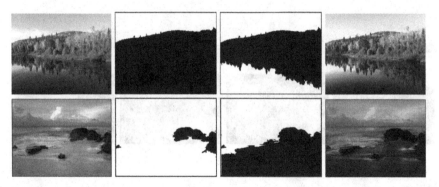

Fig. 5.10 Modifying images by choosing a favored Notan without using an exemplar image. *Left to right* original image (serving as both source and exemplar), exemplar Notan, source Notan (manually selected), modified image

image as the exemplar image. We may also generate artificial intensity distributions for dark and light and plug them into optimization (5.6), thereby bypassing completely exemplar image and exemplar Notan. This can be interesting to investigate.

As explained in Sect. 5.4.1, we allow a fully automatic setting where the Notan of the source image is chosen among a set of possible Notans generated by different thresholds between dark and light. This is motivated by the need of mobile devices where minimal user interaction is desired. In this setting, we exploit the exemplar image not only for histogram matching but also for selecting a source Notan. The underlying assumption is that the exemplar image is well composed in the two tonal scales of dark and light. The source Notan closest to the exemplar Notan in terms of dark and light proportions is used. This is no doubt a rather simple similarity

(a)   **(b)**   **(c)**   **(d)**

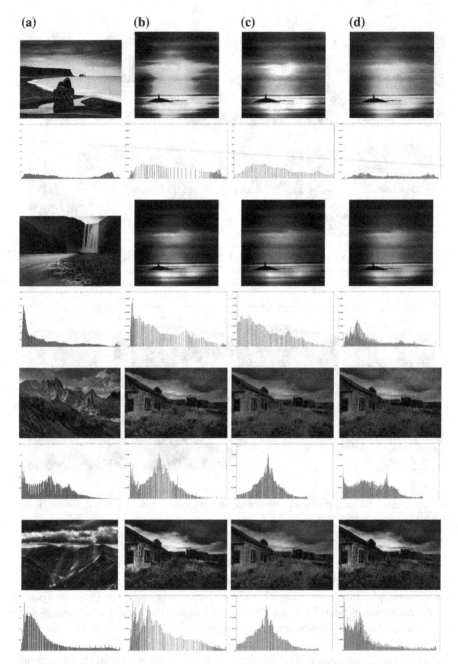

Fig. 5.11 Comparison of algorithms by modified images and their histograms. **a** Exemplar image.
b Modified source image by global histogram matching. **c** Color normalization. **d** Notan-guided
region-wise histogram matching

defined for two Notans. In future work, we can employ a more sophisticated similarity measure between two Notans. For the experimental results in Sect. 5.5, this automatic setting is employed.

5.5 Experimental Results in the Automatic Setting

In Fig. 5.11, we show results by our Notan-guided region-wise histogram matching algorithm and compare with global histogram matching and color normalization. The source Notan is automatically chosen (see description in the previous section). Our new method tends to generate smoother histograms and better controlled dynamic range. The other methods more often yield burned out areas.

Figure 5.12 presents more examples. In the experiments, the number of segments is set to 3 for simple scenes and 6 for complex scenes. Note that more segments require more parameters to be estimated and therefore more computation. We observe that the global histogram matching often yields the artifact of abrupt changes in intensity.

(a)   **(b)**   **(c)**   **(d)**   **(e)**

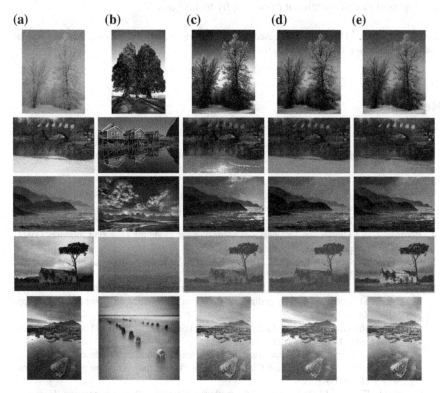

Fig. 5.12 Additional experimental results. **a** The source image. **b** The exemplar. **c** Global histogram matching. **d** Color normalization. **e** Notan-guided region-wise histogram matching

The color normalization method uses a linear mapping function whose growth rate is determined by the variances of the source and the exemplar distributions. A high (or low) growth rate can burn out (or flatten) the final image. Our new method controls better the extreme cases by regulating the transformation parameters.

5.6 Summary

This chapter presented two computerized approaches to provide photographers with on-site composition feedback and enhancement suggestions. The first approach is based on spatial design categorization that places a photo into one or more categories including horizontal, vertical, diagonal, textured, and centered. Such categorization enables retrieval of exemplar photos with similar composition. The second approach utilizes the concept of Notan in visual art for tonal adjustment. A user can improve the aesthetics of a given photo through transforming the dark-light configuration toward that of a target photo. We view this work as just the beginning of a new direction under which principles of composition in visual art are used to guide the development of computational photography techniques.

Acknowledgments This material is based upon work supported by the National Science Foundation under Grant Nos. 0347148 and 0936948.

References

1. Abadpour, A., Kasaei, S.: Color transfer in correlated color space. Proceedings of the 2006 ACM International Conference on Virtual Reality Continuum and Its Applications, pp. 305–309. New York, USA (2006)
2. Adams, A.: The Print. Little Brown, Toronto (1995)
3. Bhattacharya, S., Sukthankar, R., Shah, M.: A coherent framework for photo-quality assessment and enhancement based on visual aesthetics. In: Proceedings of ACM Multimedia Conference, pp. 271–280 (2010)
4. Bouman, C.A.: Cluster: an unsupervised algorithm for modeling Gaussian mixtures (1997) http://www.ece.purdue.edu/~bouman
5. Cohen-Or, D., Sorkine, O., Gal, R., Leyvand, T., Xu, Y.: Color harmonization. ACM Trans. Graph. **25**(3), 624–630 (2006)
6. Datta, R., Joshi, D., Li, J., Wang, J.Z.: Studying aesthetics in photographic images using a computational approach. In: Proceedings of European Conference on Computer Vision, pp. 288–301 (2006)
7. Datta, R., Joshi, D., Li, J., Wang, J.Z.: Image retrieval: Ideas, influences, and trends of the new age. ACM Comput. Surv. **40**(2), 5:1–5:60 (2008)
8. Feininger, A.: Principles of Composition in Photography. Thames and Hudson Ltd (1973)
9. Folts, J.A., Lovell, R.P., Zwahlen, F.C.: Handbook of Photography. Thompson Delmar Learning, New York (2005)
10. Fogarty, J., Forlizzi, J., Hudson, S.E.: Aesthetic information collages: generating decorative displays that contain information. In: Proceedings of ACM Symposium on User Interface Software and Technology, pp. 141–150 (2001)

11. Krages, B.P.: Photography: The Art of Composition. Allworth Press, New York (2005)
12. Lamb, J., Stevens, R.: Eye of the photographer. Soc. Stud. Texan **26**(1), 59–63 (2010)
13. Lawrence, C., Zhou, J.L., Tits, A.L.: User's guide for CFSQP version 2.0: A C code for solving (large scale) constrained nonlinear (minimax) optimization problems, generating iterates satisfying all inequality constraints. Technical Report (1994) http://drum.lib.umd.edu/handle/1903/5496
14. Li, J.: Agglomerative connectivity constrained clustering for image segmentation. Stat. Anal. Data Min. **4**(1), 84–99 (2011)
15. Li, J., Wang, J.Z., Wiederhold, G.: IRM: integrated region matching for image retrieval. In Proceedings of ACM Multimedia Conference, pp. 147–156 (2000)
16. Liu, L., Chen, R., Wolf, L., Cohen-Or, D.: Optimizing photo composition. Comput. Graph. Forum **29**(2), 469–478 (2010)
17. Meer, P., Georgescu, B.: Edge detection with embedded confidence. IEEE Trans. Pattern Anal. Mach. Intell. **23**(12), 1351–1365 (2001)
18. Obrador, P., Anguera, X., Oliveira, R., Oliver, N.: The role of tags and image aesthetics in social image search. In: Proceedings of the ACM SIGMM Workshop on Social Media, pp. 65–72 (2009)
19. Obrador, P., Oliveira, R., Oliver, N.: Supporting personal photo storytelling for social albums. In: Proceedings of ACM Multimedia Conference, pp. 561–570 (2010)
20. Otsu, N.: A threshold selection method from gray-level histograms. IEEE Trans. Syst. Man Cybern. **9**(1), 62–66 (1979)
21. Papadakis, N., Provenzi, E., Caselles, V.: A variational model for histogram transfer of color images. IEEE Trans. Image Process. **20**, 1682–1695 (2011)
22. Paris, S., Durand, F.: A fast approximation of the bilateral filter using a signal processing approach. Int. J. Comput. Vis. **81**(1), 24–52 (2009)
23. Payne, E.: Composition of Outdoor Painting, 7th edn. Deru's Fine Arts, x (2005)
24. Pitie, A.C.K.F., Dahyot, R.: Automated colour grading using colour distribution transfer. Comput. Vis. Image Underst. **107**(1–2), 123–137 (2007)
25. Pitie, F., Kokaram, A.: The linear Monge-Kantorovitch colour mapping for example-based colour transfer. In: Proceedings of the IEEE European Conference on Visual Media Production, pp. 1–9 (2007)
26. Pouli, T., Reinhard, E.: Progressive color transfer for images of arbitrary dynamic range. Comput. Graph. **35**(1), 67–80 (2011)
27. Raybould, B.J.: Notan painting lessons. Virtual Art Academy (2014) http://www.virtualartacademy.com/notan.html
28. Reinhard, E., Ashikhmin, M., Gooch, B., Shirley, P.: Color transfer between images. IEEE Comput. Graph. Appl. **21**(5), 34–41 (2001)
29. Russ, J.C.: The Image Processing Handbook. CRC Press (2006)
30. Sorrel, C.: Nadia camera offers opinion of your terrible photos. WIRED, online, July 26 (2010)
31. Speed, H.: The Practice and Science of Drawing, 3rd edn. Dover Publications, New York (1972)
32. Sternberg, R.J.: Cognitive Psychology. Wadsworth Publishing, Florence (2008)
33. Tai, Y.-W., Jia, J., Tang, C.-K.: Local color transfer via probabilistic segmentation by expectation-maximization. Proc. IEEE Conf. Comput. Vis. Pattern Recognit. **1**, 747–754 (2005)
34. Verhulst, P.F.: A note on population growth. Correspondence Mathematiques et Physiques **10**, 113–121 (1838)
35. Wang, J.Z., Li, J., Wiederhold, G.: SIMPLIcity: semantics-sensitive integrated matching for picture libraries. IEEE Trans. Pattern Anal. Mach. Intell. **23**(9), 947–963 (2001)
36. Warren, B.: Photography: The Concise Guide. Delmar Cengage Learning, New York (2002)
37. Wen, C.-L., Hsieh, C.-H., Chen, B.-Y., Ouhyoung, M.: Example-based multiple local color transfer by strokes. Comput. Graph. Forum **27**, 1765–1772 (2008)
38. Werman, S.P.M., Rosenfeld, A.: A distance metric for multi-dimensional histograms. Comput. Vis. Graph. Image Process. **32**, 328–336 (1985)

39. Xiao, X., Ma, L.: Color transfer in correlated color space. In: Proceedings of the 2006 ACM International Conference on Virtual Reality Continuum and Its Applications, pp. 305–309. New York, NY, USA (2006)
40. Xiao, X., Ma, L.: Gradient-preserving color transfer. Comput. Graph. Forum **28**, 1879–1886 (2009)
41. Yao, L., Suryanarayan, P., Qiao, M., Wang, J.Z., Li, J.: Oscar: on-site composition and aesthetics feedback through exemplars for photographers. Int. J. Comput. Vis. **96**(3), 353–383 (2012)

Part III
Mobile Visual Search and Recognition

Chapter 6
FaceSimile: A Mobile Application for Face Image Search Based on Interactive Shape Manipulation

Li Zhang, Brandon M. Smith and Shengqi Zhu

Abstract Current face image retrieval methods achieve impressive results, but lack efficient ways to refine the search, particularly for geometric face attributes. Users cannot easily find faces with slightly more furrowed brows or specific leftward pose shifts, for example. This creates significant problems, especially for mobile users with small screens, low bandwidth, and awkward keyboard settings. To address this problem, we propose a new face search technique based on shape manipulation that is complementary to current search engines. Users drag one or a small number of contour points, like the bottom of the chin or the corner of an eyebrow, to search for faces similar in shape to the current face, but with updated geometric attributes specific to their edits. For example, the user can drag a mouth corner to find faces with wider smiles, or the tip of the nose to find faces with a specific pose. As part of our system, we propose (1) a novel confidence score for face alignment results that automatically constructs a contour-aligned face database with reasonable alignment accuracy, (2) a simple and straightforward extension of PCA with missing data to tensor analysis, and (3) a new regularized tensor model to compute shape feature vectors for each aligned face, all built upon previous work. Despite the powerful algorithms used in this application, we achieve real-time performance on Apple devices. To the best of our knowledge, our system demonstrates the first face retrieval approach based chiefly on shape manipulation. We show compelling results on a sizeable database of over 10,000 face images captured in uncontrolled environments.

L. Zhang (✉)
Google, 651 North 34th Street, Seattle, WA 98103, USA
e-mail: zhl@google.com

B.M. Smith
Computer Sciences Department, University of Wisconsin,
1210 West Dayton Street, Madison, WI 53706, USA
e-mail: bmsmith@cs.wisc.edu

S. Zhu
Google, 1600 Amphitheatre Parkway, Mountain View, CA 94043, USA
e-mail: sqzhu@google.com

© Springer International Publishing Switzerland 2015
G. Hua and X.-S. Hua (eds.), *Mobile Cloud Visual Media Computing*,
DOI 10.1007/978-3-319-24702-1_6

147

6.1 Introduction

Retrieving one or several desired face images from a large collection has been recently studied in several contexts [1–4]. These works can be roughly grouped into two categories: *example based* (given a query face image, find similar face images) and *attribute based* (given some natural language description, e.g., black hair, find faces with the desired attributes). While these methods achieve impressive results, they lack efficient ways to refine the search, particularly for geometric face attributes. For example, among the search results, there is no efficient way to find a face with a specific type of grin, or a slightly leftward gaze.

In this chapter, we present a new face search technique based on shape manipulation that is complementary to current search engines. For example, by clicking on the tip of the nose and dragging it to the left, our goal is to find faces similar in shape to the current face, but with leftward pose, as shown in Fig. 6.1; by dragging the corner of the mouth, we hope to find smiling faces, etc. Our approach is particularly well suited for geometric face attributes that (1) cannot be easily expressed in natural language or otherwise supported by current face search methods, but (2) can be intuitively specified via a mouse or touchpad interface.

To achieve this goal, we must address the following three challenges:

- *Face alignment.* Although well studied, accurately identifying facial shape contour features (e.g., eyelid contours, mouth contours) in a large database is still a challenging problem, especially for face images captured in uncontrolled environments.
- *User input interpretation.* The user should be able to find his/her desired faces with very few shape edits. However, ambiguities exist. For example, when dragging the corner of the mouth to the right, the user may want to change the pose, but this could also be interpreted as a desire to widen the mouth.
- *Search metric.* Transforming user edits into geometric shape features with which desired faces can be retrieved in the database.

To the best of our knowledge, our system demonstrates the *first* face retrieval approach based chiefly on shape manipulation. As part of our system, we propose three techniques that build upon previous work:

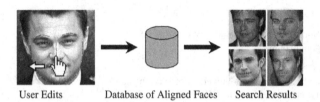

User Edits   Database of Aligned Faces   Search Results

Fig. 6.1 Illustration of our face search technique based on interactive shape manipulation. In this example, the user drags the tip of the nose *leftward* to search for similar faces with *leftward* pose in a sizeable database of aligned faces

- A novel confidence score for face alignment results. This score allows us to automatically reject poor face alignment results in order to construct a sizeable database of reasonably well-aligned faces.
- A simple algorithm of tensor decomposition in the presence of missing data. This algorithm is a straightforward generalization of PCA with missing data.
- A new regularized tensor model of aligned face shape. We use this model to (1) associate a tensor coordinate as shape features to each face, (2) resolve shape manipulation ambiguities so that a user can specify his/her intended face shape with few edits, and (3) find the desired faces in the database.

We have implemented our technique on Apple iPads and iPhones. We next review related work before presenting our system.

6.2 Related Work

Our work is directly inspired by Goldman et al. [5], in which the user can drag points on a face in one frame of a video to retrieve desired faces from other frames. Their system tracks a single person's face in a single video for retrieval purposes, and does not differentiate facial motion induced by pose or expression. Later in [2], Kemelmacher-Shlizerman et al.demonstrate a system which, given a photo of person A, finds a photo of person B with similar expression for a puppetry application. In this system, the query is the appearance descriptor of the user's own face. In our system, a user often only needs to provide a few (1–3) edits to find desired faces. Each database they use is on the order of 1000 faces of a single person. Our test database is 10 times larger, and contains many different people. We have only used shape features for query; including appearance features is complementary and remains part of our future work.

In computer graphics, creating a desired 3D face model is a central challenge. Recent solutions [6–8] generate a face from a small number of user edits. Their goal is different from ours in that they seek to generate a new 3D model from example models, but we hope to find one or several desired existing images. No new images are generated in our system. Technically, they work with 3D models, which eliminates pose as a shape parameter. We work with 2D images, where pose is one parameter used to model the underlying object shape.

Face alignment is one important component of our system; however, face alignment is not our contribution. We implemented Gu and Kanade's face alignment method [9] as part of our system. Rather, we propose a novel method of measuring alignment confidence, which allows us to *automatically* construct a large database of reasonably well-aligned faces. This is important because large databases cannot be easily verified by manual inspection. Human-based computation, e.g., via Amazon Mechanical Turk, may be suitable for such a task, but is beyond the scope of this paper. The recent face alignment paper by Liu et al. [10] also points out the importance of measuring confidence. However, the confidence they use is specific to their objective function. Although their method achieves impressive results, they demonstrate performance on datasets of about 300 examples using congealing. We need to align tens of thousands of images, which would likely be a very slow process if we choose to use a congealing-based approach.

Tensor analysis [11] has been successfully used in vision and graphics to model textures [12, 13], for face image recognition [14], and for 3D face transfer [15]. In this paper, we use tensor analysis to model 2D face contour shapes.

Our tensor analysis builds upon [14], with the addition of a regularization term to deal with situations in which the number of tensor coefficients is greater than the number of user edits. Our regularized tensor analysis differs from the previous probabilistic tensor analysis of [16] in that our method takes a single data tensor as input while theirs assumes multiple data tensors as input.

6.2.1 A Brief Review of Tensor Algebra

We provide a brief summary of tensor algebra to define the notations used in subsequent sections of this paper. Tensor analysis generalizes the widely used Principal component analysis (PCA). Given a data matrix $\mathbf{X}$, PCA decomposes $\mathbf{X}$ as

$$\mathbf{X} = \mathbf{UZV}^{\mathrm{T}} = \sum_{m,n} z_{m,n} u_{:,m} v_{:,n}^{\mathrm{T}}, \tag{6.1}$$

where $z_{m,n}$ is an element in $\mathbf{Z}$; $u_{:,m}$ and $v_{:,n}$ are columns of $\mathbf{U}$ and $\mathbf{V}$, respectively, following MATLAB notation. In the case of PCA, $\mathbf{Z}$ is diagonal, i.e., $z_{m,n} \neq 0$ only if $m = n$. The scalar version of Eq. (6.1) is

$$x_{i,j} = \sum_{m,n} z_{m,n} u_{i,m} v_{j,n}. \tag{6.2}$$

A matrix is a 2D array; tensor analysis more generally operates on a multidimensional array, or a *data tensor*. For example, a 3D data tensor (cube) is $\mathscr{X} = [x_{i,j,k}]$. The right-hand side of the second "=" in Eq. (6.1) can be generalized for tensors as

$$\mathscr{X} = \sum_{l,m,n} z_{l,m,n} u_{:,l} \circ v_{:,m} \circ w_{:,n}, \tag{6.3}$$

where for each (l, m, n)-triple, $u_{:,l} \circ v_{:,m} \circ w_{:,n}$ is the outer product of the three column vectors, the result of which is a data tensor (cube) of the same size as $\mathscr{X}$. A linear combination of such tensors with $z_{l,m,n}$ as combination weights yields $\mathscr{X}$. Similar to Eq. (6.2), the scalar version of Eq. (6.3) is

$$x_{i,j,k} = \sum_{l,m,n} z_{l,m,n} u_{i,l} v_{j,m} w_{k,n}, \tag{6.4}$$

in which, if we fix $z_{:,:,:}$ as well as any two of the three row vectors $u_{i,:}$, $v_{j,:}$, and $w_{k,:}$, $x_{i,j,k}$ is a linear function of the remaining row vector; that is, Eq. (6.4) is a *tri-linear* function.

If the summation in Eq. (6.4) is executed in a particular order, Eq. (6.4) is equivalent to

$$x_{i,j,k} = \sum_n \left(\sum_m \left(\sum_l z_{l,m,n} u_{i,l} \right) v_{j,m} \right) w_{k,n}. \tag{6.5}$$

Each summation in Eq. (6.5) can be viewed as a matrix product, which leads to the matrix form of tensor product as

$$\mathcal{X} = \mathcal{Z} \times \mathbf{U} \times \mathbf{V} \times \mathbf{W}, \tag{6.6}$$

where $\mathcal{Z} = [z_{i,j,k}]$ is the *core tensor*, which usually has a smaller size than $\mathcal{X}$; $\mathbf{U}$, $\mathbf{V}$, and $\mathbf{W}$ are the matrices with u, v, and w in Eq. (6.5) as elements. Since the summation order in Eq. (6.5) can be arbitrarily switched, the tensor product $\times$ in Eq. (6.6) is *commutative*.

Finally, in Eq. (6.4), if we fix j, k and vary the index i, the column vector $x_{:,j,k}$ can be viewed as a degenerate cube, evaluated in the following three equivalent ways:

$$\begin{aligned}
x_{:,j,k} &= \sum_l u_{:,l} \left(\sum_{m,n} z_{l,m,n} v_{j,m} w_{k,n} \right) \\
&= \left(\mathcal{Z} \times v_{j,:} \times w_{k,:} \right) \times \mathbf{U} \\
&= \mathbf{U} \left(\mathcal{Z} \times v_{j,:} \times w_{k,:} \right).
\end{aligned} \tag{6.7}$$

6.3 System Overview

Our face retrieval system consists of the following four components.

- *Face database construction.* We construct a sizable database of aligned faces that exhibit a wide range of pose and facial expression variation. Unfortunately, even state-of-the-art alignment methods [9, 10, 17–19] cannot guarantee perfect results in all cases; we therefore propose a novel confidence score to filter out poor alignment results based on the face alignment method from [9].
- *Tensor model training.* From a set of 2D training face shapes of different poses, expressions, and identities (each shape is represented by a set of points), we form a 4D data tensor $\mathcal{X}$, with each of the four dimensions indexing point vertex, pose, expression, and identity. We decompose the tensor as

$$\mathcal{X} = \mathcal{Z} \times \mathbf{U}_{\text{vert}} \times \mathbf{U}_{\text{pose}} \times \mathbf{U}_{\text{expr}} \times \mathbf{U}_{\text{iden}}. \tag{6.8}$$

We propose a new and simple iterative algorithm to achieve this decomposition in the presence of missing data. Note that the dataset for training the model is much smaller than the database used for searching.

- *Tensor coefficient recovery.* Using the estimated $\mathscr{L}$ and $\mathbf{U}_{\text{vert}}$, we associate each aligned face in the database with three coefficient vectors, $\mathbf{c}_{\text{pose}}$, $\mathbf{c}_{\text{expr}}$, and $\mathbf{c}_{\text{iden}}$ for pose, expression, and identity, respectively. For each search, we also estimate the three coefficient vectors $\mathbf{c}_{\text{pose}}$, $\mathbf{c}_{\text{expr}}$, and $\mathbf{c}_{\text{iden}}$ for the user-specified query shape, which we expect to have few known vertices (corresponding to user edits).
- *Search by tensor coefficient comparison.* The coefficient vectors associated with each face in the database are compared against the coefficient vectors estimated for the query face; the closest face images (according to this tensor coefficient comparison) are retrieved. The user can then edit one of the retrieved faces to refine the search.

More details are presented in the subsequent sections.

6.4 Technical Details

6.4.1 Tensor Decomposition with Missing Data

In order to obtain $\mathscr{L}$, $\mathbf{U}_{\text{vert}}$, $\mathbf{U}_{\text{pose}}$, $\mathbf{U}_{\text{expr}}$, and $\mathbf{U}_{\text{iden}}$, we need a training set in which each subject's face is photographed under a *complete* set of known expressions and poses, along with ground truth shapes. Such a subset of data is difficult to obtain; even highly structured datasets like Multi-PIE [20] have missing faces. Computing tensor decomposition in the presence of missing data is unavoidable in practice. We propose a simple algorithm for this purpose.

We separate a data tensor $\mathscr{X}$ into two parts: $[\mathscr{X}_{\text{known}}, \mathscr{X}_{\text{missing}}]$. For notational convenience, we interchangeably view $\mathscr{X}$ as a multidimensional array or as vector consisting all elements in $\mathscr{X}$ (i.e., $\mathscr{X}(:)$ in MATLAB notation). Without loss of generality, we assume that the vectorized form is arranged such that the missing elements come after the known elements. Under this arrangement, we seek to estimate $\mathscr{X}_{\text{missing}}$, $\mathscr{L}$, $\mathbf{U}_{\text{vert}}$, $\mathbf{U}_{\text{pose}}$, $\mathbf{U}_{\text{expr}}$, and $\mathbf{U}_{\text{iden}}$ by minimizing the following error function:

$$\left\| \mathscr{L} \times \mathbf{U}_{\text{vert}} \times \mathbf{U}_{\text{pose}} \times \mathbf{U}_{\text{expr}} \times \mathbf{U}_{\text{iden}} - \begin{bmatrix} \mathscr{X}_{\text{known}} \\ \mathscr{X}_{\text{missing}} \end{bmatrix} \right\|^2. \tag{6.9}$$

We iterate between the following steps to minimize Eq. (6.9):

1. Fix $\mathscr{X}_{\text{missing}}$ and optimize $\mathscr{L}$, $\mathbf{U}_{\text{vert}}$, $\mathbf{U}_{\text{pose}}$, $\mathbf{U}_{\text{expr}}$, and $\mathbf{U}_{\text{iden}}$. This step is the standard tensor decomposition, as given in [11].
2. Fix all the U's and optimize $\mathscr{X}_{\text{missing}}$ and $\mathscr{L}$. This step is a least squared problem because $\mathscr{L} \times \mathbf{U}_{\text{vert}} \times \mathbf{U}_{\text{pose}} \times \mathbf{U}_{\text{expr}} \times \mathbf{U}_{\text{iden}}$ is linear with respect to $\mathscr{L}$ when all the U's are fixed. More specifically, we use

$$\mathbf{A}\mathscr{X} = \begin{bmatrix} \mathbf{A}_{\text{known}} \\ \mathbf{A}_{\text{missing}} \end{bmatrix} \mathscr{X} \tag{6.10}$$

to represent this linear transformation, and Eq. (6.9) becomes

$$\left\| \begin{bmatrix} \mathbf{A}_{\text{known}} & \mathbf{0} \\ \mathbf{A}_{\text{missing}} & -\mathbf{I} \end{bmatrix} \begin{bmatrix} \mathscr{X} \\ \mathscr{X}_{\text{missing}} \end{bmatrix} - \begin{bmatrix} \mathscr{X}_{\text{known}} \\ \mathbf{0} \end{bmatrix} \right\|^2 . \tag{6.11}$$

This function can be efficiently minimized using the conjugate gradient method, assuming both transformations $\mathbf{A}$ and $\mathbf{A}^{\text{T}}$ can be implemented without explicitly storing the matrix elements. This is indeed the case because $\mathbf{A}\mathscr{X}$ represents $\mathscr{X} \times \mathbf{U}_{\text{vert}} \times \mathbf{U}_{\text{pose}} \times \mathbf{U}_{\text{expr}} \times \mathbf{U}_{\text{iden}}$ and $\mathbf{A}^{\text{T}}\mathscr{X}$ represents $\mathscr{X} \times \mathbf{U}_{\text{vert}}^{\text{T}} \times \mathbf{U}_{\text{pose}}^{\text{T}} \times \mathbf{U}_{\text{expr}}^{\text{T}} \times \mathbf{U}_{\text{iden}}^{\text{T}}$.

In practice, we initialize $\mathscr{X}_{\text{missing}}$ using subsets of face shapes from $\mathscr{X}_{\text{known}}$. That is, for a needed pose i, expression j, and identity k vector $x_{:,i,j,k}$ in $\mathscr{X}_{\text{missing}}$, we gather all vectors in $\mathscr{X}_{\text{known}}$ that share pose i and expression j; the mean average of these vectors is used to initialize $x_{:,i,j,k}$.

6.4.2 Tensor Coefficient as Facial Feature Vector

In this subsection, we present an algorithm that takes a face shape (partial or complete) as input and computes three coefficient vectors describing the pose, expression, and identity of the face. This algorithm is used in two places in our retrieval system. First, it gives each face shape in the database the three vectors as feature vectors. Second, it estimates the three feature vectors from a few user constraints and retrieves faces with similar feature vectors from the database.

Since a user seldom wants to edit every point on the face contour for retrieval, our algorithm needs to be able to handle partial shapes. From Eq. (6.8), we know that a face shape vector $\mathbf{f}$ can be expressed as

$$\mathbf{f} = \mathscr{X} \times \mathbf{U}_{\text{vert}} \times \mathbf{c}_{\text{pose}}^{\text{T}} \times \mathbf{c}_{\text{expr}}^{\text{T}} \times \mathbf{c}_{\text{iden}}^{\text{T}}, \tag{6.12}$$

where the core tensor $\mathscr{X}$ and the vertex basis matrix $\mathbf{U}_{\text{vert}}$ are estimated in Sect. 6.4.1, and $\mathbf{c}_{\text{pose}}$, $\mathbf{c}_{\text{expr}}$, and $\mathbf{c}_{\text{iden}}$ are the coefficient vectors we seek. We break $\mathbf{f}$ into $[\mathbf{f}_{\text{known}}, \mathbf{f}_{\text{unknown}}]$; our goal is to compute all the $\mathbf{c}$ vectors from $\mathbf{f}_{\text{known}}$.

In practice, the dimension of $\mathbf{f}_{\text{known}}$ is often much less than the total number of variables in $\mathbf{c}_{\text{pose}}$, $\mathbf{c}_{\text{expr}}$, and $\mathbf{c}_{\text{iden}}$, which makes the estimation under-constrained. To address this issue, we estimate all of the $\mathbf{c}$'s by minimizing a regularized objective function as follows:

$$\phi(\mathbf{c}_{\text{pose}}, \mathbf{c}_{\text{expr}}, \mathbf{c}_{\text{iden}})$$

$$= \frac{1}{2\sigma^2} \|\mathbf{f}_{\text{known}} - \mathscr{Z} \times \mathbf{U}_{\text{vert}}^{\text{known}} \times \mathbf{c}_{\text{pose}}^{\text{T}} \times \mathbf{c}_{\text{expr}}^{\text{T}} \times \mathbf{c}_{\text{iden}}^{\text{T}}\|^2 \qquad (6.13)$$

$$+ \|\mathbf{c}_{\text{pose}}\|^2 + \|\mathbf{c}_{\text{expr}}\|^2 + \|\mathbf{c}_{\text{iden}}\|^2,$$

where $\mathbf{U}_{\text{vert}}^{\text{known}}$ are the rows in $\mathbf{U}_{\text{vert}}$ that correspond to $\mathbf{f}_{\text{known}}$, and σ^2 is the variance of tensor shape fitting noise, estimated as the average of the squared residual errors after tensor model fitting by minimizing Eq. (6.9).

We minimize Eq. (6.13) using an iterative algorithm. Starting with an initial estimation of $\mathbf{c}_{\text{pose}}$, $\mathbf{c}_{\text{expr}}$, and $\mathbf{c}_{\text{iden}}$, we iteratively hold two of them fixed and update the remaining one until the decrease of Eq. (6.13) is less than 10^{-6} compared to the its value in the last iteration. This algorithm is used both during runtime for retrieval and during the face database construction stage; the initialization of the $\mathbf{c}$'s are described in the following two subsections.

6.4.3 Searching for Faces Using Tensor Coefficients

Using the tensor coefficient vectors $\mathbf{c}_{\text{pose}}$, $\mathbf{c}_{\text{expr}}$, and $\mathbf{c}_{\text{iden}}$ in Sect. 6.4.2, our system enables a user to search images by shape manipulation. For example, starting with one face image, the user can drag the tip of the nose to find images with desired pose; Constraining the locations of multiple points on the face will narrow down the search results.

In general, computing all the $\mathbf{c}$ coefficient vectors from a single user input is underconstrained even with the regularization term in Eq. (6.13). For example, dragging the corner of the mouth may result in a smiling face or a rotated face.

To address this ambiguity, our search interface allows the user to specify whether either pose vector or expression vector or both should be adjusted to satisfy the edit. Given the user specification, only the corresponding coefficient vector is estimated when minimizing Eq. (6.13). Once the coefficient vectors $\mathbf{c}_{\text{pose}}$, $\mathbf{c}_{\text{expr}}$, and $\mathbf{c}_{\text{iden}}$ are known, we use them to construct a face $\mathbf{f}$ using Eq. (6.12) and retrieve its 50 nearest neighbors in the database as results.

6.4.4 Face Alignment Confidence Measure

To support face search by shape manipulation, our system needs automatic face alignment to establish the shape of each face in the database. We implemented the robust face alignment method of Gu and Kanade [9] for this purpose. Being among state-of-the-art methods [9, 10, 17–19], this method indeed produces impressive results on a wide range of real world images, as we demonstrate in Sect. 6.5.1. However, natural face images exhibit a wide range of shape, pose, illumination, and other appearance variation; occlusions, image noise, and motion blur further confound the problem. This method does not guarantee accuracy in all situations.

One approach might be to remain agnostic—to simply allow all aligned faces to exist in the database regardless of their accuracy. However, this reduces the quality of the query results, and it burdens users with the additional task of recognizing and ignoring poorly aligned results. Similarly, manually removing poorly aligned faces from large databases is burdensome if not impractical.

Identifying Poorly Aligned Faces

We instead propose a novel method of measuring alignment confidence, which allows us to *automatically* remove poorly aligned faces from the database. In a nutshell, our method computes a confidence score for each vertex in the aligned shape, filters the scores along the contour, and finally sums up the filtered scores as the overall confidence.

More precisely, the alignment confidence score s_n for the point n is computed as

$$s_n = \exp\left\{-\frac{\rho_n^2}{2d_n}\right\}.$$ (6.14)

d_n is the average distance from point n to its contour neighbors in the shape model (the canonical shape we used is approximately 160 pixels tall, from eyebrows to chin, irrespective of the target face size), ρ_n^2 is found by the alignment algorithm [9] and is the observation variance, or noise level, of landmark n at the end of the matching process. Figure 6.2 shows an illustration of the ρ_n values for an actual alignment result.

In Eq. (6.14), the landmark confidence function maps the raw observation variance to the range [0, 1]. It acts as a robust measure of confidence, with 1 denoting high confidence, and 0 denoting no confidence; landmark locations with very large

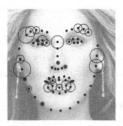

Fig. 6.2 An illustration of Eq. (6.16) for computing the confidence of each alignment. The radius of each *circle* is given by ρ_n as defined in [9]; *large circles* are supposed to indicate low confidence and *small circles* are supposed indicate high confidence. However, in practice they are not perfect due to spurious local image features. Eq. (6.15) aims to eliminate imperfections in these per-landmark confidence measures by taking into account the confidence of nearby points, which will be used in Eq. (6.16)

observation variance are clamped to 0. Empirically, we found that if s_n is large, the alignment for point n is often reliable; however, if s_n is small, the alignment for the point n *may or may not* be reliable, depending on the alignment accuracy of its neighboring points.

To deal with this phenomenon, we filter the point confidence scores using $f(\cdot)$ defined as

$$f(s_n) = \max\{s_n, g(s_n)\}, \tag{6.15}$$

where $g(s_n)$ is a Gaussian filter of the confidence scores along point n's contour, centered on point n, with $\sigma = 1.5$ in units of neighbor rank, i.e., $1 =$ nearest neighbor, $2 =$ second nearest neighbor, etc in one direction.

In Eq. (6.15), the filter aims to eliminate erroneously labeled bad landmark locations. For example, a landmark might have low confidence because of spurious local image features despite its contour neighbors exhibiting high confidence. In such a scenario, the alignment algorithm would significantly reduce the contribution of the low confidence point so that the contour will be driven by the surrounding high confidence neighbors. Assuming the contour is correct, the single low confidence landmark should also be correct, and should have a higher confidence value than it was originally given.

Finally, the overall alignment confidence for a face shape is computed as

$$\bar{s} = \frac{1}{N} \sum_{n=1}^{N} f\{s_n\}, \tag{6.16}$$

where N is the number of landmarks.

We found that the confidence score is strongly correlated with alignment accuracy as shown in Sect. 6.5.2. By comparing the confidence score of each alignment result to a threshold, bad alignment results can be identified and removed from the database.

6.5 Experiments

In this section, we describe in detail the construction of a sizeable and varied database of aligned faces, we demonstrate experimentally that the alignment confidence score described in Sect. 6.4.4 is a good predictor of alignment accuracy, and we show that the tensor model described in Sect. 6.3 allows a user to find his/her desired faces using only one or a few shape edits.

6.5.1 Constructing a Database of Aligned Faces

Our system is designed to search for desired face images in a large database. For experimentation purposes, we constructed a sizeable database of approximately 10,000 aligned faces from the Public Figures (PubFig) dataset [21]. In its entirety, PubFig contains approximately 50,000 images of 200 celebrities from the internet captured in uncontrolled environments.

The faces were aligned using our implementation of [9]. We first trained shape and appearance models using ground truth landmarks provided with the Multi-PIE dataset [20], and 962 additional ground truth landmarks that we supplied (the original set of ground truth landmarks does not include faces with both non-frontal pose and nonneutral facial expression). Approximately, 330 subjects are represented in our training set, with five different poses (±30, ±15, and 0 degrees relative to frontal) and six different expressions (neutral, smile, surprise, squint, disgust, and scream), although approximately half of the possible subject-pose-expression combinations are missing.

For each face, we first use a face detector [22] to estimate of the size of the face in each image. We removed all faces with bounding boxes smaller than 120 pixels in height to ensure the database would contained few low quality images. We ran the face alignment algorithm on the remaining 21,919 images.

Our system relies on face alignment accuracy to return good query results. Therefore, we used a relatively high alignment confidence score threshold to remove all but the most confident 10,000 results from the database. In Fig. 6.3, the results in each column are representative of results with similar alignment confidence score. The score is statistically a good indicator of the alignment accuracy. However, we note that the score is not perfect; outliers do exist. Some good results have uncharacteristically low scores and vice versa, which is quantitatively characterized in Fig. 6.4.

6.5.2 Alignment Confidence Score Performance

The alignment confidence score given in Sect. 4.4.1 should be correlated with the alignment error. A low score should predict large alignment error and vice versa. Here, we give experimental results that confirm this relationship.

We first trained shape and appearance models as in Sect. 5.1, but with subjects 1–20 omitted from the training set. The shape and appearance models were then used to align the 375 images of subjects 1–20. After alignment, we computed (1) the normalized root mean squared error (NRMSE) relative to ground truth, and (2) the alignment confidence score described in Sect. 6.4.4. The NRMSE is given as a percentage, computed by dividing the root mean squared (RMS) error by the height of the smallest bounding box that encompasses the ground truth landmarks in each image. A similar measure is given in [10], but they divide the RMS error by the pupillary distance; this is not invariant under significant pose change and so we do

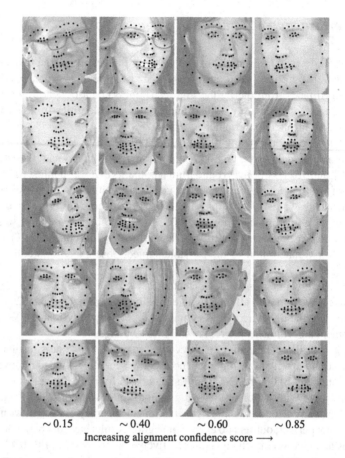

~ 0.15   ~ 0.40   ~ 0.60   ~ 0.85

Increasing alignment confidence score ⟶

Fig. 6.3 Each column shows a selection of alignment results on the PubFig dataset that share approximately the same alignment confidence score. The scores are ordered from *left* to *right*. Each column shows typical results for the associated score. The score is statistically a good indicator of alignment accuracy, as we show in Fig. 6.4 Best viewed electronically

not use it. Figure 6.4a shows that the NRMSE decreases significantly as the alignment confidence score increases.

Although the sets of subjects used for training and testing in the previous experiment were independent, they both came from the same structured database. Similarities exist between these training and testing sets that would not occur naturally. To avoid making erroneous conclusions that might be due to these similarities, we performed the experiment again using the same training set, but a different test set, namely 583 images selected randomly from the PUT face database [23], which exhibits moderate variation in pose and facial expression.

The ground truth landmarks given in the PUT database do not exactly match those given in the Multi-PIE database. However, with few exceptions, corresponding ground truth contours exist. We therefore divide up the PUT contours to obtain a

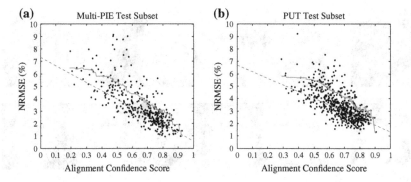

Fig. 6.4 Each data point represents one alignment result. The *y*-axis gives the *normalized root mean squared error* (NRMSE) of each result, and the *x*-axis gives the alignment confidence score, according to Sect. 6.4.4. A good/bad score threshold can be thought of as a boundary that separates "bad" results to the *left* from "good" to the *right*. The *solid red line* gives a 95 % error bound for any given score threshold. That is, for a given score threshold, 95 % of the "good" results have a NRMSE at or below the *red line*. The *dashed blue line* shows the global trend of the best 95 % NRMSE w.r.t. the score, found by dividing the scores into 0.05-width bins, computing the mean average NRMSE among points in each bin under the 95 % error bound, and fitting a line to the averages. We do not show a linear regression fit of all the points in the plot because the tightly clustered points in the lower right corner heavily dominate, and the resulting fit does not reflect the global trend. Best viewed electronically

set of landmark points that very closely match the Multi-PIE ground truth. The six Multi-PIE landmarks not found on any PUT contours (four on the vertical portion of the nose and one near each ear) were omitted in computing the NRMSE. Figure 6.4b similarly shows that the NRMSE decreases significantly as the alignment confidence score increases.

6.5.3 Tensor Model Training

To construct the tensor model, we used 1470 faces (49 identities × 5 poses × 6 expressions) from the Multi-PIE dataset to train the tensor model. Within the tensor model we used 9 bases to represent the point vertices, 14 bases for identity, 3 for pose, and 3 for expression. The number of bases was chosen such that 95 % of the total variance of the original data was retained.

6.5.4 Face Retrieval Performance

In this section, we demonstrate that users only need to edit one or a small number of face points for our system to find desired faces. Figure 6.5 shows the top user-selected

(a)

(b)

(c)

Fig. 6.5 Top user-selected results for three queries. The query images are shown in the *leftmost* column, with user edits illustrated by *yellow arrows*. Five selected results are given to the right of each query image. Each *row* shows one query. **a** One edit. Expression is held constant; the nose tip is dragged left to search for similar faces with slightly leftward pose. **b** Two edits. Pose is held constant; the lips are dragged apart to search for smiling faces. **c** Three edits. Pose is held constant; the lips are pulled together and the cheeck is pulled outward to search for serious expressions

results for three queries. By using a combination of multiple editing and holding expression or pose constant, users can refine their search result in an intuitive way.

We also quantitatively evaluate how many edits on a query image are needed in order to find a target image. To this end, we emulate user edits in our system as follows. We start by picking up query-target image pairs from the database. Each pair of images either share a similar pose but have different expressions, or share a similar expression but have different poses, or are dissimilar in both pose and expression.[1]

Given a pair of query and target images, our testing system randomly orders the landmarks, and edits them one after another according to this order. Each edit moves one landmark from the query to the target image. After each edit, a set of results (top 10) will be retrieved. We calculate the average Euclidean distance between the top 10 results and the desired image. We also calculate the minimum Euclidean distance between the top results and the target image. If the minimum Euclidean distance is zero, it indicates the target is among the top results.

---

[1] When selecting a query-target image pair with a similar expression but different poses, we first randomly pick the target image, then remove all the images whose Euclidean distance is among the nearest one-third. In the remaining images, we select the one whose expression is most similar to the target image by comparing c_{pose} and use it as the query image. We can select a pair with a similar pose but different expressions in a similar way. A pair with both dissimilar pose and dissimilar expressions can be selected randomly.

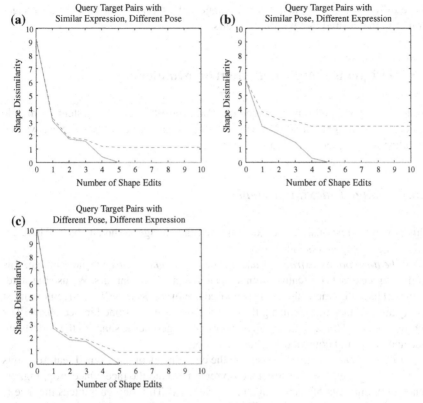

Fig. 6.6 The number of edits needed to find desired faces. The x-axis is the number of edits performed. $x = 0$ corresponds to the original query shape before any edit is applied; the y-axis shows the shape difference between the result shapes and the target shape. The *solid green line* indicates the minimum Euclidean distance between the target and the returned 10 results, so it represents the best among the returned results. The *dashed blue line* indicates the average Euclidean distance. Here in all the tested cases, with fewer than FIVE edits, the target image can be retrieved. Note that the max number of edits in the x-axis is 10, which is only a small portion of the total number (68) of points in the face shape model. In fact, even for 1–2 edits, the decrease in shape difference is significant, which suggests that very often we can roughly get the desired image within 1–2 edits. Each *curve* is computed by averaging over 10 query-target image pairs

Figure 6.6 shows the result, averaged over 10 randomly selected pairs. The x-axis is the number of edits operated. $x = 0$ corresponds to the original query shape before any edit is applied; the y-axis shows the shape difference between the result shapes and the target shape. The solid green line indicates the minimum Euclidean distance between the target and the returned 10 results, so it represents the best shape among the returned results. The dashed blue line indicates the average Euclidean distance. As the number of edits increases, a more accurate shape will be returned. In all tested cases, with fewer than five edits, the target image can be retrieved. Note that, the max number of edits on the x-axis is 10, which is only a small portion of the total number (68) of points in the face shape model. In fact, even for 1–2 edits, the decrease in shape difference is significant, which suggests that very often we can get images similar to the desired one within 1–2 edits.

6.6 Design and Implementation on Mobiles

We have implemented our technique on iPads and iPhones. Our system on mobile devices can be roughly divided into three modules: an offline image indexing system, an online image query server, and a search client.

6.6.1 Image Indexing System

This module is responsible for indexing each face image in the database. There are three major components in this module:

(1) Feature points extraction and shape alignment. For each face image, this module first extracts 68 feature points located along face contours. We use the state-of-the-art face alignment algorithm proposed by Gu and Kanade [9], and remove most poorly aligned face images using the confidence score mentioned in Sect. 6.4.4. The 2D coordinates of these feature points represent the geometric shape of the underlying face and are stored compactly in our database.

(2) Thumbnail generation. Based on the coordinates of the aligned feature points from the above step, we construct a crop region around the face. Once cropping, we generate thumbnails of each image in the database. This step guarantees the face is clearly visible in each thumbnail. The thumbnails provide mobile users with a quick preview and allow them to fine tune their search results using as little bandwidth as possible.

(3) Multilinear model coefficients extraction. We use a multilinear tensor model in Sect. 6.4.2 to represent the transformation of identity, expression, and pose of all face images. This multilinear tensor model is both simple and powerful. Computing the coefficients of each face shape only requires solving a linear system, yet our model is flexible enough to accurately model a wide variety of face shapes and is powerful enough to resolve user edit ambiguities, i.e., whether the expression or the pose should change.

For demonstration purpose, we constructed a sizable database of approximately 10,000 aligned faces from the Public Figures (PubFig) dataset [21]. These images are a subset of about 50,000 images consisting of 200 celebrities captured in uncontrolled environments.

6.6.2 Search Client

The search client is a mobile application that runs on Apple iPad, iPhone, and iPod devices. There are two coexisting user interfaces in this module.

Fig. 6.7 User interface for iPhone (*left*) and iPad (*right*)

(1) Shape representation interface. This is the main area for shape manipulation. Both the image and the recovered face shape contour can be overlaid here. The on-off switches at the bottom of the interface allow users to lock either the pose or expression component, so that shape ambiguity problem mentioned in Sect. 6.4.2 can be resolved.

(2) Thumbnail preview interface. This is the auxiliary area for shape manipulation. Thumbnails that best represent the desired face image are shown here. These thumbnails are fetched from the server by using standard HTTP protocols. They are ranked by both the similarity with the desired shape and the confidence score of the alignment. If any of the thumbnails are chosen here, the original image will be fetched and will be displayed in the shape representation interface with its feature points overlaid.

In order to accommodate different screen sizes, we developed two client applications, one for large-screen devices like the iPad, and another for small-screen devices like the iPhone. A screen capture of each of the user interface is displayed in Fig. 6.7. The iPhone application separates these two interfaces in two tabs to save screen space while the iPad application displays these two interfaces together as two columns.

6.6.3 User-System Interaction

The interaction between user and our system can be summarized in Fig. 6.8. From an initial shape, the user first specifies the type of edits, which can be either a pose change, an expression change, or both. Our system then constructs a search candidate set from the whole image database based on the edit type. This candidate set limits the number of results so that consecutive queries can be as efficient as possible while still maintaining accuracy. Users then drag one or several feature points in the shape representation interface. Our search client application automatically calculates the target coefficients and shape based on the trained tensor model. This calculation can be efficiently implemented by a linear system solver; it can be further sped up by Apple's Accelerator Framework. The target face shape is then used to rank

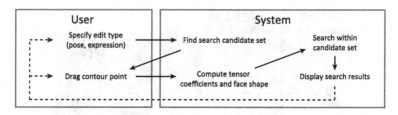

Fig. 6.8 Summary of our system workflow

the candidate set. A set of ranked thumbnail results are displayed to user. These thumbnails serve as a guide for further refinement. If necessary, users can repeat the manipulation process based on any of the candidate result.

6.7 Conclusion and Future Work

In this chapter, we have proposed a new face search technique that aims to address a common problem in face image search. That is, it's difficult to refine face search results based on geometric attributes that are easy to see, but hard to put into words. To the best of our knowledge, our system is the first face retrieval approach based chiefly on shape manipulation. This approach is complementary to current search engines [1–4], and could be used to further refine face search results.

While we have a reasonable confidence measure which helps us to automatically construct a sizeable database, face alignment still needs improvement to further enhance the system performance and utility, both in terms of query accuracy and constructing a database with better face alignments.

Our database is relatively sparse compared to much larger collections [3], which reduces our ability to lock identity in refining search results. In the future, we hope to demonstrate our approach on databases containing millions of face images and videos. To realize this goal, we will need to use a more efficient coefficient search algorithm than our naive linear search.

Although face image retrieval is a key challenge, we note that our approach generalizes well. As part of our future work, we hope to apply our technique to other more general types of image collections. Additionally, we hope to incorporate appearance-based attributes into our system to further improve search results.

References

1. Bitouk, D., Kumar, N., Dhillon, S., Belhumeur, P.N., Nayar, S.K.: Face swapping: Automatically replacing faces in photographs. SIGGRAPH (2008)

2. Kemelmacher-Shlizerman, I., Sankar, A., Shechtman, E., Seitz, S.M.: Being John Malkovich. ECCV (2010)
3. Kumar, N., Belhumeur, P., Nayar, S.: Face tracer: A search engine for large collections of images with faces. ECCV (2008)
4. Wu, Z., Ke, Q., Sun, J., Shum, H.Y.: Scalable face image retrieval with identity-based quantization and multi-reference re-ranking. CVPR (2010)
5. Goldman, D.B., Gonterman, C., Curless, B., Salesin, D., Seitz, S.M.: Video Annotation, Navigation, and Composition. UIST (2008)
6. Lau, M., Chai, J., Xu, Y.Q., Shum, H.: Face poser: Interactive modeling of 3D facial expressions using facial priors. SIGGRAPH (2010)
7. Zhang, L., Snavely, N., Curless, B., Seitz, S.M.: Spacetime faces: high-resolution capture for modeling and animation. SIGGRAPH, pp. 548–558 (2004)
8. Sumner, R.W., Zwicker, M., Gotsman, C., Popović, J.: Mesh-based inverse kinematics. SIGGRAPH (2005)
9. Gu, L., Kanade, T.: A generative shape regularization model for robust face alignment. ECCV (2008)
10. Liu, X., Tong, Y., Weeler, F.W., Tu, P.H.: Facial contour labeling via congealing. ECCV (2010)
11. Lathauwer, L.D., Moor, B.D., Vandewalle, J.: On the best rank-1 and rank-(R1, R2,..., Rn) approximation of higher-order tensors. SIAM J. Matrix Anal. Appl. 21(4), 1324–1342 (2000)
12. Vasilescu, M.A.O., Terzopoulos, D.: TensorTextures: Multilinear image-based rendering. ACM Trans. Gr. 23(3): 336–342. ACM, New York (2004). http://doi.acm.org/10.1145/1015706.1015725
13. Wang, H., Wu, Q., Shi, L., Yu, Y., Ahuja, N.: Out-of-core tensor approximation of multi-dimensional matrices of visual data. ACM Trans. Gr. 24(3): 527–535. ACM, New York (2005). http://doi.acm.org/10.1145/1073204.1073224
14. Vasilescu, M.A.O., Terzopoulos, D.: Multilinear analysis of image ensembles: Tensor faces. ECCV (2002)
15. Vlasic, D., Brand, M., Pfister, H., Popović, J.: Face transfer with multilinear models. SIGGRAPH (2005)
16. Tao, D., Sun, J., Wu, X., Li, X., Shen, J., Maybank, S.J., Faloutsos, C.: Probabilistic tensor analysis with akaike and bayesian information criteria. In: Ishikawa, M., Doya, K. (eds.) Neural Information Processing. Springer, Berlin, Heidelberg (2008) http://dx.doi.org/10.1007/978-3-540-69158-7_82
17. Saragih, J., Lucey, S., Cohn, J.: Face alignment through subspace constrained mean-shifts. CVPR, pp. 1034–1041 (2009). doi:10.1109/ICCV.2009.5459377
18. Tong, Y., Liu, X., Wheeler, F.W., Tu, P.: Automatic facial landmark labeling with minimal supervision. CVPR (2009)
19. Zhu, J., Gool, L.V., Hoi, S.C.H.: Unsupervised face alignment by robust nonrigid mapping. ICCV (2009)
20. Gross, R., Matthews, I., Cohn, J., Kanade, T., Baker, S.: Multi-PIE. In: Proceedings of International Conference on Automation Face Gesture Recognition. 28(5): 807–813 (2010)
21. Kumar, N., Berg, A.C., Belhumeur, P.N., Nayar, S.K.: Attribute and simile classifiers for face verification. ICCV (2009)
22. Rowley, H., Baluja, S., Kanade, T.: Rotation invariant neural network-based face detection. CVPR (1998)
23. Kasiński, A., Florek, A., Schmidt, A.: The PUT face database. Tech. Rep., Poznan University of Technology, Poznan, Poland (2009)

Chapter 7
Exploiting On-Device Image Classification for Energy Efficiency in Ambient-Aware Systems

Mohammed Shoaib, Swagath Venkataramani, Xian-Sheng Hua, Jie Liu and Jin Li

Abstract Ambient-aware applications need to know what objects are in the environment. Although video data contains this information, analyzing it is a challenge *esp.* on portable devices that are constrained in energy and storage. A naïve solution is to sample and stream video to the cloud, where advanced algorithms can be used for analysis. However, this increases communication energy costs, making this approach impractical. In this article, we show how to reduce energy in such systems by employing simple on-device computations. In particular, we use a low-complexity feature-based image classifier to filter out unnecessary frames from video. To lower the processing energy and sustain a high throughput, we propose a hierarchically pipelined hardware architecture for the image classifier. Based on synthesis results from an ASIC in a 45 nm SOI process, we demonstrate that the classifier can achieve minimum-energy operation at a frame rate of 12 fps, while consuming only 3 mJ of energy per frame. Using a prototype system, we estimate about 70 % reduction in communication energy when 5 % of frames are interesting in a video stream.

M. Shoaib (✉) · X.-S. Hua · J. Liu · J. Li
Microsoft Research, Redmond, WA 98052, USA
e-mail: moshoaib@microsoft.com; mohammed.shoaib@microsoft.com

X.-S. Hua
e-mail: xshua@microsoft.com

J. Liu
e-mail: liuj@microsoft.com

J. Li
e-mail: jinl@microsoft.com

S. Venkataramani
School of ECE, Purdue University, West Lafayette, IN 47907, USA
e-mail: venkata0@purdue.edu

© Springer International Publishing Switzerland 2015   167
G. Hua and X.-S. Hua (eds.), *Mobile Cloud Visual Media Computing*,
DOI 10.1007/978-3-319-24702-1_7

7.1 Introduction

Portable devices connect to the physical world through sensors. One rich sensing modality is the visual light field, which is captured by cameras. It provides us information about various things and events around us. Thus, perceiving the environment through a stream of video has the potential to light up a host of new context-aware applications on portable devices. Figure 7.1 illustrates three such examples. First, an on-board camera can help a flying drone detect the presence of obstacles and aid in navigation [1]. Second, a dash-mounted camera can provide real-time driver assistance by identifying traffic signs, pedestrians, lanes, and other automobiles [2, 3]. Third, wearable cameras and smartphones can detect people and objects in front of them, which can help improve service and productivity [4–8] .

Observe that while extracting actionable information from video, a basic requirement is to detect and recognize objects in each frame. Then comes higher level image understanding such as actions, and events. Fortunately, all three of these are rich areas of research and the literature provides many algorithmic options to solve them [9–11]. However, when realizing these techniques in an end-to-end system for portable devices, there are some new trade-offs that we need to make. We discuss some of these next.

7.1.1 System-Level Challenges

Figure 7.2 shows a block diagram of the various steps involved in realizing an ambient-aware system. It comprises computations for object detection, recognition,

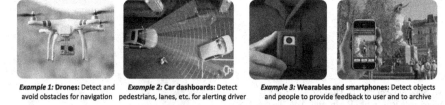

Example 1: Drones: Detect and avoid obstacles for navigation   **Example 2:** Car dashboards: Detect pedestrians, lanes, etc. for alerting driver   **Example 3:** Wearables and smartphones: Detect objects and people to provide feedback to user and to archive

Fig. 7.1 Video processing can enable a range of ambient-aware applications on portable devices

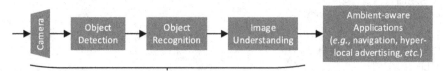

Key Requirements: Real-time performance, high accuracy, and low energy

Fig. 7.2 An end-to-end ambient-aware system involves computations for object detection, recognition, and image understanding. To be useful in a mobile scenario, such systems need to meet strict constraints in performance and energy

and image understanding. Information derived from image understanding is used to drive ambient-aware applications such as the ones described in the previous section. To be realized on portable devices, such systems need to meet three key constraints. First, the most applications require ambient-aware systems to respond in real time. One way to achieve this is to keep some sensor in the system always on. For example, a dash-mounted camera has to detect pedestrians as soon as they appear so that brakes can be applied in time, if necessary. This can be achieved by either keeping the camera always on or using a continually operating motion detector to trigger the camera. Second, these systems must have high algorithmic accuracy. This in turn implies that each step in the sequence to be precise. Third, these systems must be energy efficient when realized on a portable device. This last constraint arises due to the need for mobility in several useful ambient-aware applications.

The three system-level constraints mentioned above lead to interesting design trade-offs. Intuitively, lowering latency hints toward performing all computations locally on the portable device. However, the associated energy costs for this approach can be prohibitive. Recent evaluations with face recognition on Google Glass, an emerging wearable device, validate this behavior. Experiments show that local computations can drain the battery at a speed that is $10\times$ faster than routine use (battery life is lowered from 377 to 38 min) [12, 13]. Similar results have also been observed for other portable devices such as smartphones, drones, and security cameras [14–16]. Another trade-off is between accuracy and energy: accurate algorithms are desirable at each stage but are prohibitive on portable devices due to the high energy costs.

Since it is infeasible to support all computations locally on portable devices, there is an emerging thrust toward realizing hybrid systems. Such systems aim to exploit the growing connectivity of devices together with the computational capabilities of the cloud [17, 18]. Although promising, these hybrid systems face issues along a new dimension—they introduce additional latencies and energy costs due to data communication. Figure 7.3 shows the costs involved in acquiring 3-channel RGB video [at 30 frames-per-second (fps), 2×8b per pixel] and streaming it to the cloud for processing. For the analysis shown, we assume 90 mW power for sensing 1080p/60 fps video and 240 mW for MPEG compression by $10\times$ [19, 20]. We also assume that the power scales with the frame rate and resolution. Further, for communication using the WiFi 802.11 a/g/n protocol, we assume transmission energies of 40 and 10 nJ/b at speeds of 54 and 150 Mbps, respectively [21]. Under these assumptions, for a portable device with a Li-ion battery of capacity 500 mAh (6660 J at 3.7 V), the streaming system model allows operation for only 96 min before requiring a recharge. The recharge time reduces to 78 and 35 min for 720p and 1080p HD image resolutions, respectively. Thus, acquiring raw video on the portable device and streaming it to the cloud for processing is undesirable for continuous operation. Thus, there is a need to dissect the sequence of computations so that some are performed locally on the device and some on the cloud. Our proposed system model is guided by this insight. We present details about it next.

7.1.2 Design Approach

As an alternative to performing all computations in the cloud, we propose to split the sequence so that computations are supported in parts on the device and the cloud. In this section, we present the analysis behind our approach.

Consider the CamVid dataset, which is representative of typical recordings from a portable device [22]. Specifically, the dataset provides multiple recordings from a dash-mounted camera on a car; for illustration purposes, we have randomly chosen one recording, seq05VD, of 3 min. There are many objects of interest in the video recording. Observe from Fig. 7.4 that the frames-of-interest (FoI) (i.e., those that contain relevant objects) comprise only a small percentage of all frames. On average, across all objects, only 10 % of the frames are interesting at 10 fps. At a lower frame rate of 1 fps, this number is reduced to about 1 %. This result shows that just after the object detection step, the amount of useful data (determined by FoI) can be reduced by 90–99 %. Processing through the object-recognition step can further lower the number of informative frames. However, the room for improvement due to this step is low. Thus, in our end-to-end system, we propose to employ computations for object detection (used synonymously with image classification) locally on the portable device, while performing all other computations in the cloud. Through this approach, we will demonstrate that we can substantially reduce the amount of communication energy (and thus the end-to-end system energy). To keep the image classification energy low, we will also show that we need to subtly tweak the algorithmic accuracy as well as develop a dedicated hardware accelerator.

Our system model is shown in Fig. 7.5. Under the same assumptions as those used for Fig. 7.3, we observe that using a local data filter for image classification on the portable device can improve battery lives by up to 5.5× (i.e., battery life improves from 96 min or 1.6 h in Fig. 7.3 to 8.8 h in our case for VGA frames). These energy savings come due to a reduction in the communication energy. Observe that in estimating the gains, we assume that the local filter for image classification reduces useful data frames by 90 % and that it costs an additional 3 mJ/frame. Next, we validate these assumptions and describe the trade-offs that exists between accuracy and energy consumption of the data filter.

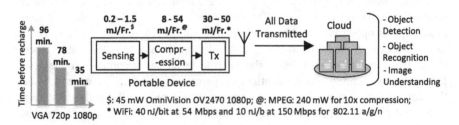

Fig. 7.3 Realizing an end-to-end ambient-aware system through continuous video streaming is infeasible on portable devices

7.2 Algorithm Selection for Data Filtering

Recall from Fig. 7.4 that the FoI reduces with frame rate. Also, note from the figure that once an object is found in a frame, it stays in the camera's field of view for at least 5–10 subsequent frames, when the video is sampled at 30 fps. We call this behavior *persistence*. The value of persistence is shown for the various objects in the CamVid recording on the secondary Y-axis in Fig. 7.4. This high value of persistence hints at the fact that we could lower the frame rate by 5–10× and still detect the presence of interesting objects in the video. Equivalently, we could relax the accuracy of the image classification algorithm so that it detects at least one out of the 5–10 contiguous frames in which the object of interest appears. In our system, we propose to exploit a combination of both of these approaches.

To sustain the battery charge up to a reasonably long duration, we assume a computational energy budget of approx. 3–20 mJ (Fig. 7.5), depending on the image resolution. Assuming a 50 mW budget for VGA (lowest) resolution, this translates to 17 fps, 100 million operations per second (MOPS) [costing 2 mJ/Fr. total, assuming 0.3 μW/OP], and less than 10 MB of memory accesses [costing 1 mJ/Fr. total, assuming 100 pJ/B access energy] per frame. Thus, our energy budget still allows

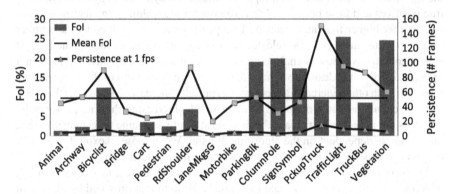

Fig. 7.4 Results from a typical video dataset show that most object persist in the camera's field of view for at least 10 frames. In a recording of approx. 3 min, on average, specific objects appear in ≤10% of the frames at 10 fps and in about 1% of the frames at 1 fps

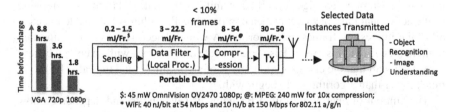

Fig. 7.5 Proposed system model: Perform object detection locally on the device. This approach can increase battery lives by up to 5.5× (i.e., 96 min in Fig. 7.3 to 8.8 h in our case for VGA frames)

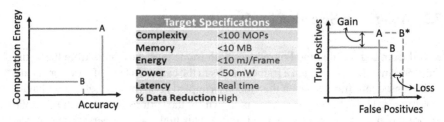

Fig. 7.6 We propose to bias a low-energy algorithm B toward having high true positives at the cost of additional false positives (resulting in an algorithm B*). Gain and loss are annotated for algorithm B* in comparison with algorithm B

room for relaxing the accuracy of the algorithm. We achieve this by employing the technique of biased classifiers. We explain this concept next.

Figure 7.6, in the middle, shows the energy constraints for implementing the detection algorithm locally on the portable device. At the left, the figure also shows two potential algorithm choices that we have for implementing image classification, namely, A and B. Algorithm A has high accuracy but also high computational energy. Algorithm B, on the other hand, has both lower accuracy and energy. On the right, the figure shows two metrics that represent the accuracy of the algorithms, namely, true positives and false positives. Observe how for algorithm B one metric is lower and another higher than algorithm A. True positives are determined by the number of frames transmitted (FT) (or selected) by the algorithm that are among the FoI—it is desirable to have these high. False positives are determined by the FT that are not among the FoI—it is desirable to have these low. Typically, both of these metrics are related to each other, increasing (decreasing) one also increases (decreases) the other. But, the change is not symmetric. In other words, increasing the true positives by x % does not necessarily increase the false positives by the same percentage. In fact, the change is dependent on the algorithm at hand. We propose to exploit this niche property of classification algorithms in tweaking the on-device image classifier.

Our proposal is to bias algorithm B such that it leads us to a new algorithm B*, which has a high true positive rate (potentially close to that provided by algorithm A) at the cost of a higher false positive rate than algorithm B (and algorithm A). For ambient-aware applications, having high true positives is important since the algorithm then does not miss frames that contain objects of interest. The above process thus implies that algorithm B* transmits a few additional frames (comprising of the additional false positives) when compared to algorithm A but is able to detect all of the interesting frames that algorithm A would detect. However, an important point to note is that this higher false positive rate of B* comes with an energy benefit over A—recall that the energy requirements of algorithm B (and thus also B*) were much lower than algorithm A to begin with.

The amount of energy algorithm B* helps us save end-to-end depends on how simple algorithm B* is in comparison to algorithm A. Consider the computational

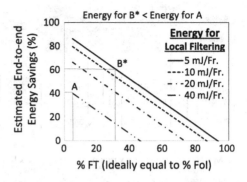

Fig. 7.7 Since algorithm B* has much lower computational energy costs, it provides us higher end-to-end energy savings than algorithm A. Figure adapted from [23]

energy costs for algorithm B* ranging from 5–40 mJ/Fr. Figure 7.7 shows the end-to-end energy savings that are achievable with these potential costs. If algorithm B* costs 40 mJ/Fr. for image classification, end-to-end energy savings are achieved only until the number of frames transmitted (%FT) is ≤40 %. Thus, if %FoI is 10 %, there is an additional room of 30 % for the increasing false positive rate. However, if algorithm B* costs only 5 mJ/Fr. then end-to-end energy savings are achieved until 94 %, resulting in a room of 84 % for the increase in false positive rate. Thus, to maximize the end-to-end energy savings, it makes more sense to choose an algorithm B* that is energy efficient and has a higher false positive rate (like algorithm B*) than one that has higher energy costs and a lower false positive rate (like algorithm A). The image classification algorithm that we select for our system is based on this principle. We present details about it next.

7.3 Low-Energy Algorithm for Image Classification

Recent results have shown that neural network-based algorithms have the potential to provide state-of-art accuracy in image classification as well as in visual recognition [24]. These algorithms employ dynamic decision models that require large memories, high-bandwidth communication links, and compute capacities of up to several GOPS [25–27]. With enormous potential parallelism, such algorithms provide very high accuracies. However, these algorithms are not suited for implementation in our case. This is because, as mentioned earlier, our goal is not to select the algorithm with the highest accuracy but the one with the lowest energy consumption. It is also desirable that the algorithm that we choose be programmable so that it can detect arbitrary objects of interest. We thus choose an algorithm that not only performed reasonably well in the ILSVRC competition, but also that which had a much lower computational complexity [28]. The basic algorithm is illustrated in Fig. 7.8. It comprises four major computational blocks that we describe next.

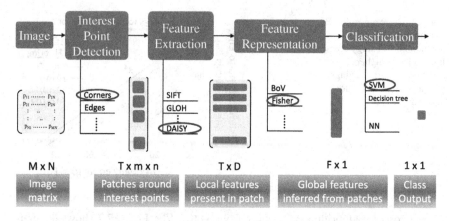

Fig. 7.8 Light-weight algorithm used for image classification on the portable device. At each stage, our selection is shown *circled* and the dimensionality of data is shown at the *bottom*

7.3.1 Interest-Point Detection (IPD)

For each incoming frame, this step helps identify the pixel locations with the most information. Locations typically lie at key-points such as corners, edges, blobs, and ridges. In our case, we utilize the Harris–Stephens algorithm that detects pixel locations on object corners [29]. In this algorithm, a patch of pixels $I(x, y)$ is extracted around each pixel location (x, y) in a grayscale frame I. This patch is subtracted from a shifted patch $I(x + u, y + v)$ centered at location $(x + u, y + v)$, and the result is used to compute the sum-of-squared distances [denoted by $S(x, y)$] using the following formulation:

$$S(x, y) = \Sigma_u \Sigma_v w(u, v)[I(u + x, v + y) - I(u, v)]^2, \tag{7.1}$$

where $w(u, v)$ is a window function (matrix) that contains the set of weights for each pixel in the frame patch. The weight matrix could comprise a circular window of Gaussian (isotropic response) or uniform values. In our case, we pick uniform values since it simplifies implementation. A corner is then characterized by a large variation of $S(x, y)$ in all directions around the pixel at (x, y). In order to aid the computation of $S(x, y)$, the algorithm exploits a Taylor series expansion of $I(u + x, v + y)$ as follows:

$$I(u + x, v + y) \approx I(u, v) + I_x(u, v)x + I_y(u, v)y \tag{7.2}$$

where $I_x(u, v)$ and $I_y(u, v)$ are the partial derivatives of the image patch I at (u, v) along the x and y directions, respectively. Based on this approximation, we can write $S(x, y)$ as follows:

$$S(x, y) \approx \Sigma_u \Sigma_v w(u, v) \cdot [I_x(u, v) \cdot x - I_y(u, v) \cdot y]^2 \approx [x, y] A [x, y]^T \tag{7.3}$$

where A is a structure tensor that is given by the following:

$$\begin{vmatrix} <I_x^2> & <I_xI_y> \\ <I_xI_y> & <I_y^2> \end{vmatrix}. \tag{7.4}$$

In order to conclude that (x, y) is a corner location, we need to compute the eigen-values of A. But, since the exact computation of the eigenvalues is computationally expensive, we can compute the following corner measure $M_{c'}(x, y)$ that approximates the characterization function based on the eigenvalues of A:

$$M_{c'}(x, y) = det(A) - \kappa \cdot trace^2(A). \tag{7.5}$$

To be more efficient, we avoid setting the parameter κ and make use of a modified corner measure $M_c(x, y)$, which amounts to evaluating the harmonic mean of the eigenvalues as follows:

$$M_c(x, y) = 2 \cdot det(A) / [trace(A) + \varepsilon] \tag{7.6}$$

where ε is a small arbitrary positive constant (that is used to avoid division by zero). After computing a corner measure $[M_c(x, y)]$ at each pixel location (x, y) in the frame, we need to assess if is largest among all abutting pixels and if it is above a prespecified threshold; marking it to be a corner if it is. This process is called non-maximum suppression (NMS). The corners thus detected are invariant to lighting, translation, and rotation.

7.3.2 Feature Extraction

The feature-extraction step extracts low-level features from pixels around the inter-est points. Typical classification algorithms use histogram-based feature-extraction methods such as SIFT, HoG, and GLOH. While appearing quite different, many of these can be constructed using a common modular framework consisting of five processing stages, namely G-block, T-Block, S-Block, E-Block, and N-Block [30, 31]. This approach known as the daisy feature-extraction algorithm, thus allows us to adapt one computation engine to represent most other feature-extraction meth-ods depending on tunable algorithmic parameters that can be set at runtime. Figure 7.9 shows a block-level diagram of the daisy feature-extraction module. At each stage, different candidate block algorithms may be swapped in and out to produce new overall descriptors. In addition, parameters that are internal to the candidate features can be tuned in order to maximize the performance of the descriptor as a whole. We next present details about each of the processing stages.

- **Presmoothing (G-block)**: A $P \times P$ patch of pixels around each interest point is smoothed by convolving it with a 2D-Gaussian filter of standard deviation (σ_s).

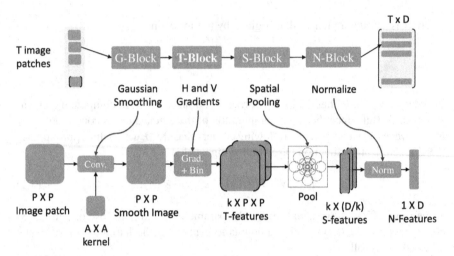

Fig. 7.9 We use the daisy feature-extraction algorithm. It comprises T, S, N, and E processing blocks

- **Transformation (T-block)**: This block maps the smoothed patch onto a length k vector with nonnegative elements. There are four subblocks defined for the transformation, namely, T1, T2, T3, and T4. In our system, we have implemented only the T1 and T2 blocks, with easy extensibility options for T3 and T4.

  - **T1**: At each pixel location (x, y), we compute gradients along both horizontal (Δx) and vertical (Δy) directions. We then apportion the magnitude of the gradient vector into k (equals 4 in T1a and 8 in T1b mode) bins split equally along the radial direction—resulting in an output array of k feature maps, each of size $P \times P$.
  - **T2**: The gradient vector is quantized in a sine-weighted fashion into 4 (T2a) or 8 (T2b) bins. For T2a, the quantization is done as follows: $|\Delta_x| - \Delta_x$; $|\Delta_x| + \Delta_x$; $|\Delta_y| - \Delta_y$; $|\Delta_y| + \Delta_y$. For T2b, the quantization is done by concatenating an additional length 4 vector using Δ_{45}, which is the gradient vector rotated through $45°$.
  - **T3**: At each pixel location (x, y), we apply steerable filters using n orientations and compute the response from quadrature pairs. After this, we quantize the result in a manner similar to T2a to produce a vector of length $k = 4n$ (T3a) and T2b to produce a vector of length $k = 8n$ (T3b). It is also possible that we use filters of second or higher order derivatives and/or broader scales and orientations in combination with the different quantization functions.
  - **T4**: We compute two isotropic difference of Gaussian (DoG) responses with different centers and scales (effectively reusing the G-block). These two responses are used to generate a length $k = 4$ vector by rectifying the positive and negative parts into separate bins as described in T2.

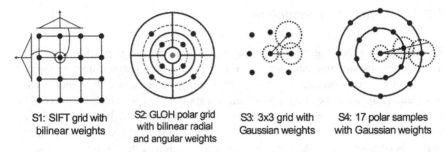

S1: SIFT grid with bilinear weights

S2: GLOH polar grid with bilinear radial and angular weights

S3: 3x3 grid with Gaussian weights

S4: 17 polar samples with Gaussian weights

Fig. 7.10 Examples of the various spatial summation patterns. Figure reproduced from [35]

- *Spatial Pooling (S-block)*: In this stage, we accumulate weighted vectors from the previous stage to give N linearly summed vectors of length k. This process is similar to the histogram approach used other descriptor algorithms in the literature. We concatenate these N vectors to produce a descriptor of length kN. Figure 7.10 shows an overview of the different approaches. We use the following pooling patterns for the vectors:

  - **S1**: Square grid of pooling centers. The overall footprint of this grid is a parameter. The T-block features are spatially pooled by linearly weighting them according to their distances from the pooling centers.
  - **S2**: This is similar to the spatial histogram used in GLOH [32]. We use a polar arrangement of summing regions. The radii of the centers, their locations, the number of rings, and the number of locations per angular segment are all parameters that can be adjusted (zero, 4, or 8) to maximize performance.
  - **S3**: We use normalized Gaussian weighting functions to sum input regions over local pooling centers arranged in a 3×3, 4×4, or 5×5 grid. The sizes and the positions of these grid samples are tunable parameters.
  - **S4**: This is the same approach as S3 but with a polar arrangement of the Gaussian pooling centers instead of being rectangular. We used 17 or 25 centers with the ring sizes and locations being tunable parameters.

- *Embedding (E-block)*: This is an optional stage that is mainly used to reduce the feature vector dimensionality. This comprises multiple substages: principal component analysis (E1), locality preserving projections (E2) [33], locally discriminative embedding (E3) [34], etc. In our design, we have not implemented the E-block but provide an option for extensibility.

- *Post Normalization (N-block)*: This block is used to remove descriptor dependency on image contrast. In the noniterative process, we first normalize the s-block features to a unit vector (dividing by the Euclidean norm) and clip all elements that are above a threshold. In the iterative version of this block, we repeat these steps until a maximum number of iterations have been reached.

7.3.3 Feature Representation

This step allows us to aggregate feature vectors from all image patches to produce a vector of constant dimensionality. Again, there are several algorithmic options for high-level feature representation including the bag-of-visual words, fisher vectors (FV), etc. [36]. We choose the FV, which is a statistical representation obtained by pooling local image features. The FV representation provides high classification performance, thanks to a richer Gaussian mixture model (GMM)-based representation of the visual vocabulary. Next, we provide a description of the FV representation.

Let $I = (x_1, x_2, \ldots, x_T)$ be a set of T feature descriptors (i.e., the daisy features) extracted from an image each of dimensionality D. Let $\Theta = (\mu_k, \Sigma_k, \phi_k, k = 1, 2, \ldots, K)$ be the parameters of a GMM fitting the distribution of the daisy descriptors. The GMM associates each vector x_i to a centroid k in the mixture with a strength given by the following posterior probability:

$$q_{ik} = \frac{exp\left[-\frac{1}{2}(x_i - \mu_k)^T \Sigma_k^{-1}(x_i - \mu_k)\right]}{\Sigma_{t=1}^{K} exp\left[-\frac{1}{2}(x_i - \mu_t)^T \Sigma_k^{-1}(x_i - \mu_t)\right]}. \tag{7.7}$$

For each centroid k, the mean (u_{jk}) and covariance deviation (v_{jk}) vectors are defined as follows:

$$u_{jk} = \frac{1}{T\sqrt{\pi_k}}\Sigma_{i=1}^{T} q_{ik} \frac{xji - \mu jk}{\sigma_{jk}} \tag{7.8}$$

$$v_{jk} = \frac{1}{T\sqrt{2\pi_k}}\Sigma_{i=1}^{T} q_{ik} \left[\left(\frac{xji - \mu_{jk}}{\sigma_{jk}}\right)^2 - 1\right]. \tag{7.9}$$

where $j = 1, 2, \ldots, D$ spans the vector dimensions. The FV of an image I is the stacking of the vectors u_k and then of the vectors v_k for each of the K centroids in the Gaussian mixtures:

$$FV(I) = [\ldots u_k \ldots v_k \ldots]^T. \tag{7.10}$$

To get a good classification performance, the FVs need to be normalized. This is achieved by reassigning each dimension z of an FV to be $|z|^\alpha sign(z)$, where α is a design parameter that is optimized to limit the dynamic range of the normalized FVs. The FVs are normalized a second time by dividing each dimension by the l^2 norm. The normalized FVs thus produced are global feature vectors of size $2KD$.

7.3.4 Feature Classification

To keep the computational costs low, we use a simple margin-based classifier [specifically, a support vector machine (SVM)] to classify the FVs. The classifier thus helps detect relevant frames based on a model that is learned offline using prelabeled data during the training phase. In SVMs, a set of vectors (total N_{SV} vectors), called support vectors, determine the decision boundary. During online classification, the FV is used to compute a distance score (D_S) as follows:

$$D_S = \sum_{i=1}^{N_{SV}} K\left(FV \cdot sv_i\right) \alpha_i y_i - b, \qquad (7.11)$$

where sv_i is the ith support vector; b, α_i, and y_i are training parameters; and the function $K(\cdot)$ is the kernel function, which is a design parameter. In our implementation, we choose polynomial kernels (up to order 3), which are defined as follows:

$$K\left(FV \cdot sv_i\right) = \left(FV \cdot sv_i + \beta\right)^d, \qquad (7.12)$$

where d and β are training parameters. Based on the sign of D_S, an FV is assigned to either the positive (object of interest) or the negative class. To bias the classifier toward having a high true positive rate at the cost of increased false positive rate, we modify the decision boundary using the various training parameters.

7.4 Software Implementation of On-Device Image Classification

We implemented the end-to-end algorithm in C# and parallelized the code using the task parallel library (TPL) provided by the .NET 4.5 framework [37]. To evaluate the algorithm, we used the following four image classification datasets: Caltech256 [38], NORB [39], PASCAL VOC [40], and CamVid [22]. For each of the above datasets, we performed a design-space exploration of the algorithmic parameters to determine the best-performing values. Table 7.1, for instance, summarizes the exploration results for Caltech256. The highlighted row gave the best accuracy and the algorithmic parameters were chosen accordingly. Specifically, the image scale factor was set to 2 along with T14-Rect for the daisy features and third-degree polynomial kernel for the SVM. We also explored other microparameters (not shown in Table 7.1) such as the number of GMM clusters and α scale values for the FVs. After finding the best-performing parameters, we biased the SVM classifier using data resampling so that the end-to-end algorithm has a high true positive rate. In the rest of the article, we use the following two algorithmic performance metrics: (1) *coverage*, which basically represents the true positive rate [but alludes to the FoI that are detected (or covered) by the algorithm], and (2) FT, which represents a combination of the false positives and true positives.

Figure 7.11 shows the FT versus FoI charts for the four datasets. Results are shown at four different coverage levels: 30–50, 50–70, 70–90, and 90–100%. These coverage levels mean that the respective percentage of interesting frames are selected or detected by the algorithm. Like previously mentioned, we bias the classifier to achieve these coverage levels. The error bars shown in the figure represent the vari-

Table 7.1 Design-space exploration of the algorithmic parameters for Caltech256: The highlighted row gave the best performance and the algorithmic parameters were picked accordingly

Img. Scale			Daisy T-Blk				Daisy S-Blk			SVM			Accuracy
1	2	4	T14	T24	T18	T28	Rect	1r8s	2r8s	Lin	Poly3	RBF	
X			X						X		X		0.65
X			X				X			X			0.8
X			X				X				X		0.85
X			X				X					X	0.8
X				X					X		X		0.6
X				X			X				X		0.6
X					X		X				X		0.6
X					X			X			X		0.5
X					X				X		X		0.5
X						X	X				X		0.75
X						X		X			X		0.45
X						X			X		X		0.6
	X		X				X			X			0.8
X	**X**		**X**				**X**				**X**		**0.85**
	X		X				X					X	0.85
	X			X			X				X		0.85
	X					X	X				X		0.8
	X			X					X		X		0.6
	X	X					X				X		0.85
	X			X			X				X		0.8
	X					X	X				X		0.8

ance across different objects of interest. The dotted line along the diagonal indicates the ideal value of FT (=FoI) the different coverage levels. Note that some lines cross over the others in the figure. This is an artifact of our experimental data; we believe that repeating the experiment for more objects (or different combinations of objects) and averaging the results would smooth the trends and remove the cross overs.

From Fig. 7.11, we observe that without any on-device classification, FT is always 100 %; this represents the streaming system model of Fig. 7.3. Further, with local image classification, for a coverage of $\geq 90\%$, we are able to filter out $\sim 70\%$ (FT = 30 %) of the frames (averaged over all datasets) at FoI = 5 %. This number improves dramatically at lower coverage levels (i.e., goes down to 73, 83, and 91 % at coverage levels of 70–90, 50–70, and 30–50 %, respectively). Lower coverage levels are acceptable since typical datasets have substantial persistence (recall that persistence was 10 % at 10 fps in Fig. 7.4). Thanks to high persistence, the probability of detecting at least one frame that contains the object of interest is thus high even at low coverage levels. The large amounts of data filtering that we achieve though local filtering translates directly into big system-level energy savings that we present ahead in Sect. "System-Level Energy Benefits Due to SAPPHIRE".

Although promising from an accuracy perspective, the software implementation of the algorithm fares poorly when it comes to runtime costs. Table 7.2 shows how the algorithmic complexity varies depending on the frame size, number of interest points, classifier model size, (these parameters are dataset dependent). Across all datasets, we find that the mean complexity is quite low: ~ 116 MOPS. However, the

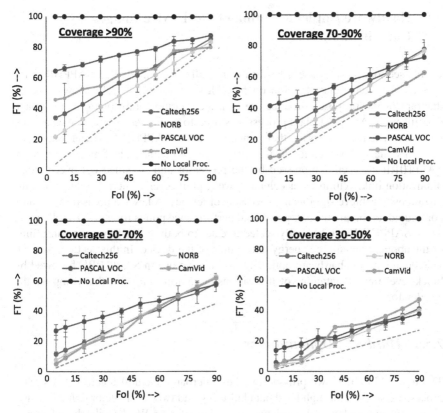

Fig. 7.11 FT, which is $\geq$ FoI at higher coverage values, begins to approach FoI as we relax the coverage levels of the algorithm

Table 7.2 Software implementation of image classification incurs a large processing delay that is unacceptable for real-time context-aware applications

	Caltech256	NORB	PASCAL	CamVid
Frame size	640 × 480	96 × 96	640 × 480	720 × 960
MOPS	161	9	81	211
Time/frame (s)	3.5	0.33	1.6	4.5

Table reproduced from [23]

software runtime on both a desktop (Core i7) and mobile CPU (Snapdragon 800) exceeds 2.5 s/frame on average. This latency comes about because we are unable to fully exploit the inherent parallelism in the algorithm. Since this latency is unacceptable for real-time context-aware applications, we propose to accelerate the image classification algorithm through hardware specialization. We describe this approach next.

7.5 Hardware Implementation of On-Device Image Classification

In this section, we propose a hardware-specialized engine called SAPPHIRE for accelerating image classification on portable devices. Figure 7.12 shows a block diagram of the proposed architecture of a local computation platform for image classification. An ARM-class processor is used to preprocess video frames as they stream in. The raw frames are then handed off to the SAPPHIRE accelerator, which performs image classification in an energy-efficient manner. The frames selected by SAPPHIRE are then compressed by the processor and streamed out over a communication link. Within the accelerator, we exploit several microarchitectural optimizations to achieve significant processing efficiency. A key feature is that it can be configured to obtain different power and performance points for a given application. Thus, SAPPHIRE can be easily scaled to cater to both the performance constraints of the application and the energy constraints of the device. In this section, we provide details on the hardware optimizations that we use in SAPPHIRE followed by block-level implementations of the various computing modules that comprise the accelerator.

7.5.1 Hardware Optimizations

Through SAPPHIRE, we provide two key microarchitectural features: (1) stream processing support through local data buffering and two-level vector reduction, and (2) data-level parallelism through hierarchical pipelining. We describe these features next.

7.5.2 Stream Processing

Our proposed architecture for SAPPHIRE allows for stream processing through two techniques. First, it allows data to be buffered locally, which obviates the need for multiple fetches from external memory. Thus, the required external memory

Fig. 7.12 Proposed use of an accelerator (SAPPHIRE) for image classification on portable devices

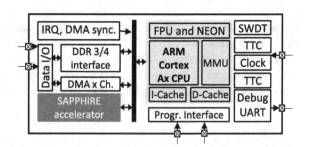

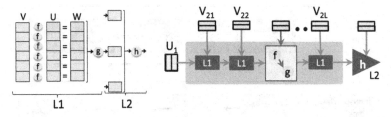

Fig. 7.13 Two-level vector reduction along with local data buffering allows for stream processing on SAPPHIRE

bandwidth requirements of SAPPHIRE are low. Second, we support a feature called two-level vector reduction. This is a commonly occurring computational process in our system wherein vector data is processed in two stages. Figure 7.13 illustrates the concept more generally. In the first level of reduction (i.e., L1), two vectors operands U and V are processed element-wise using a reduction function f. To achieve this, we exploit inter-vector data parallelism (we provide more details about parallelism in Sect. 7.5.3), which enables us to reuse the vector V across all L1 lanes. Thus, the operation can be iteratively completed within a systolic array. In the second level of reduction (i.e., L2), each element of the resulting vector W is processed by another reduction function g. To achieve this, we decompose U and interleave the element-wise operations. A common example of two-level vector reduction is the computation of dot-products between two vectors in the first level followed by multiply-accumulation of the resulting vector in the second level. Thanks to two-level vector reduction, we can avoid refetching data repeatedly from external memory. Thus, both memory bandwidth and local storage are significantly lowered.

7.5.3 Data-Level Parallelism

The image classification algorithm provides abundant opportunity for parallel processing. Since SAPPHIRE operates on a stream of frames, it is throughput limited. Thus, we also exploit data-level parallelism through pipelining. An interesting feature of the algorithm is that the pipelined parallelism is not available at one given level, but rather buried hierarchically across multiple levels of the design. To exploit this parallelism, we develop a novel three-tiered, hierarchically pipelined architecture shown in Fig. 7.14. The timing diagram for hierarchical pipelining is also shown in the figure. Next, we provide details about the functional aspects of the system.

Inter-picture pipeline. This is the topmost tier in the pipeline. Here, we exploit parallelism across successive input video frames. As shown in Fig. 7.14, this stage comprises two parts, namely feature computation and classification. Feature computation includes IPD, daisy feature extraction, and the FV blocks; classification comprises just the SVM. As shown in the timing diagram, while global features of a frame i are being computed, the previous frame i.e., $i - 1$ is concurrently processed by the classifier.

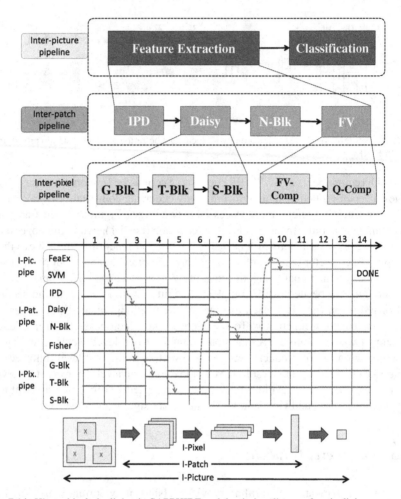

Fig. 7.14 Hierarchical pipelining in SAPPHIRE and the timing diagram for pipelining

Inter-patch pipeline. This is the next tier in the pipeline. Here, we exploit parallelism within each feature-computation stage of the inter-picture pipeline. In this tier, image patches around different interest points are processed concurrently. Thus, this tier comprises the IPD, daisy (G, T, and S blocks only), and the FV modules. Interest points that are found by the IPD are pushed onto a first-in first-out (FIFO) memory, which are then utilized by the daisy subblocks to compute the S-block features. These features are then normalized to produce the full local descriptors at that interest point. The normalized vectors are consumed by the FV block, which iteratively updates the global feature memory. The entire process is repeated until the local memory is empty. It is interesting to note that the stages of computation in this tier cannot be merged with the previous tier since global FV computations require all descriptors (i.e., descriptors at all interest points) to be available before evaluation. Due to this dependency, these tiers must be independently operated.

Inter-pixel pipeline. This is the innermost tier of the hierarchy and is present within the G, T, and S blocks of the inter-patch pipeline. It leverages the parallelism across pixels in a patch by operating them in a pipeline. The three daisy subblocks (i.e., G, T, and S) together compute the S-Block feature output for each image patch in the frame.

To maximize throughput, it is important to balance execution cycles across all tiers of the pipeline. This, however, requires careful analysis since the execution time of each block significantly differs based on the input data and other algorithmic parameters. For instance, the delay of the second tier is proportional to the number of interest points, which varies across different video frames. Thus, in our implementation, we systematically optimize resource allocation for the various blocks based on their criticality to the overall throughput. To better understand the various inter-twined hardware–software trade-offs, we next describe the microarchitectural details of the computational block in SAPPHIRE.

7.5.4 Microarchitecture of Computational Blocks

In addition to pipelining, the algorithm also allows fine-grained parallel implementations within the various processing elements of SAPPHIRE. Many blocks involve a series of two-level vector reduction operations. In our design, we employ arrays of specialized processing elements that are suitably interconnected to exploit this computation pattern. We also employ local buffering at various stages of processing. In this section, we describe the microarchitectural details of the different blocks in SAPPHIRE.

The IPD Block

A block diagram of the hardware architecture for IPD is shown in Fig. 7.15. For every pixel, we retrieve 4 pixels from the neighborhood using the ordering shown in the figure. The pixels are fetched from external memory (8b/pixel) using an address value that is generated by the IPD block. Thus, the external memory bandwidth required for this operation is $4MN \times 8$b/frame, where M and N are the height and width of the grayscale frame. For VGA resolution at 30 fps, this bandwidth would be 281 Mbps and for 720p HD resolution at 60 fps, this would be 1.6 Gbps. Note that this is modest since typical DDR3 DRAMs provide a peak bandwidth of up to several 10 s of Gbps.

The four abutting pixels are then used to compute the gradients along the horizontal and vertical directions, which are buffered into a local FIFO memory of size $W \times 3 \times N \times 18b$ (in a nominal implementation $W = 3$ and the memory is of size 12.7 kB for VGA and 25.3 kB for 720p HD). These gradients are in turn used to evaluate the

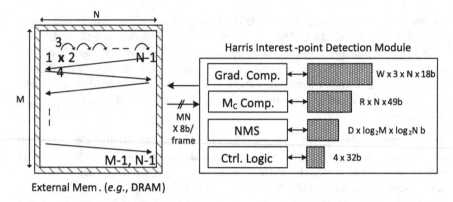

Fig. 7.15 Block diagram of the implemented IPD module: For typical algorithmic parameters, SAPPHIRE requires an external bandwidth of 70.31 Mbps for VGA, 0.46 Gbps for 1080p, and 1.85 Gbps for 4k image resolutions at 30 fps

corner measure (M_c). The data path comprises one CORDIC-based divider besides other simple compute elements. The resulting corner measures are put in a local FIFO of depth R (typically 3). This FIFO is thus of size 9.8 kB for VGA and 19.5 kB for 720p HD. The M_c values are then processed by the NMS block, which pushes the identified interest point locations (both x and y coordinates) onto another local FIFO of depth D (typically 512). Thus, the FIFO capacity is typically equal to 5.2 kB for VGA and 6.1 kB for 720p HD. In conclusion, if all pixels are accessed from external memory, the total bandwidth requirements for the IPD block are: 70.31 Mbps for VGA, 0.46 Gbps for 1080p, and 1.85 Gbps for 4k image resolutions at 30 fps.

The Daisy Feature-Extraction Block

The feature-extraction module is highly pipelined to perform stream processing of pixels. As mentioned above, the entire architecture comprises four processing steps that are heavily interleaved at the pixel, patch, and frame levels. This allows us to exploit the inherent parallelism in the application and perform computations with minimal delay. At a high level, the T-block is a single-processing element that generates the T-block features sequentially. The patterns for spatial pooling in the S-block are stored in an on-chip memory along the borders of the 2D array. The spatially pooled S-Block features are then produced at the output. The number of rows and columns in the G-Block array and the number of lanes in the S-Block array can be adjusted to achieve the desired energy and throughput scalability. Next, we provide more details on each block.

G-Block. Figure 7.16 shows a block diagram of the implemented systolic-array architecture for 2D convolution. Our architecture allows the inputs to be fed only once allowing maximum data reuse, which minimizes the bandwidth requirements

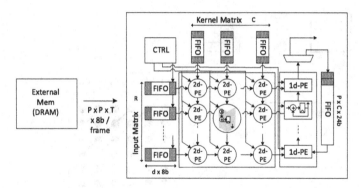

Fig. 7.16 Block diagram of the systolic array architecture used for 2D convolution in the G-block

from external memory. Further, the vector reduction process described above allows us to perform 2D convolution along any direction, with varying stride lengths, and kernel sizes.The systolic array is primarily used in the G-block.

T patches (of size $P \times P$ and centered at locations specified in the IPD output FIFO) are read out from external memory in block sizes of R pixels. In each iterations, these R pixels are processed in $R + 3C$ cycles to produce R processed 2D convolution outputs. The processing core comprises a systolic array of 2D processing elements (PEs), which are basically small multiply-accumulate (MAC) units and internal registers for fast-laning. As shown in Fig. 7.16, R input data vectors and the kernel elements stored in C columns are processed by the 2D PEs sequentially. At any given point in time, the systolic array comprises fully and partially convolved outputs. This aspect is shown in Fig. 7.17. As per the illustration, note in particular that the elements along the diagonal comprise the desired output that will be available after CM cycles. In order to accommodate the partially convolved outputs, we employ a set of 1D PEs (accumulators) along the edge of the 2D array.

The total memory requirements for the block are as follows: $RCd \times$ 8b for the I/O FIFOs of depth d (typically, 16) and $PC \times$ 24b to store the partially convolved outputs. If pixels are refetched after IPD from external memory, then the hardware requires an external memory bandwidth of $TP2 \times$ 8b. However, in our implementation, we avoid going to external memory by adding local buffers between the IPD and feature-extraction blocks.

T, S, and N Blocks. Figure 7.18 shows the block diagram of the T, S, and N blocks. The data path for the T-block comprises gradient-computation and quantization engines for the T1 (a), T1 (b), T2 (a), and T2 (b) modes of operation. In the S-block, we have a configurable number of parallel lanes for the spatial-pooling process. These lanes comprise comparators that read out Np pooling region boundaries from a local memory and compare with the current pixel locations. The output from the S-block is processed by the N-block, which comprises an efficient square-rooting algorithm and division module (based on CORDIC). The T-block outputs are buffered in a local memory of size $6(R + 2) \times$ 24b, and the pooling region bound-

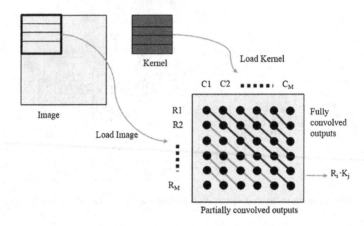

Fig. 7.17 At any given time, the systolic array comprises fully and partially convolved outputs that are reduced by the 1D PEs in the second level of processing

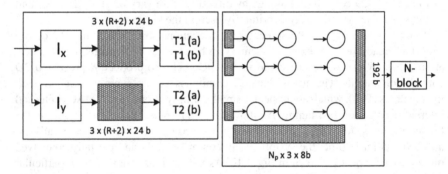

Fig. 7.18 Block diagram of the T, S, and N processing blocks. SAPPHIRE has low internal memory overheads: 207.38 kB for VGA, 257.32 kB for 1080p, and 331.11 kB for 4k image resolutions

aries are stored in a local SRAM memory of size $3Np \times 8b$. The power consumption and performance of the S block can be adjusted by varying the number of lanes in the array. These are called the parallel S-block lanes and we study their impact ahead in the experimental results section (Sect. "Microarchitectural Design-Space Exploration").

All data precisions are tuned to maximize the output signal-to-noise-ratio (SNR) for most images. The levels of parallelism in the system, the output precisions, memory sizes etc., can all be parameterized in the code. In conclusion, assuming no local data buffering between the IPD and daisy feature-extraction modules, the total memory requirements of the feature-extraction block (for nominal ranges) are (assuming 64×64 patch size and 100 interest points): 1.2 kB (4×4 2D array and 25 pooling regions) for a frame resolution of VGA (128×128 patch size and 100 interest points) and 3.5 kB (8×8 2D array and 25 pooling regions) for a frame resolution of 720p HD. Since, in our implementation, we include local buffering between the

IPD and feature-extraction modules, they work in a pipelined manner and thus the external data access bandwidth is completely masked. The total estimated storage capacity for IPD and feature-extraction is 207.38 kB for VGA, 257.32 kB for 1080p, and 331.11 kB for 4k image resolutions

The FV Feature-Representation Block

The microarchitecture of the FV representation block is shown in Fig. 7.19. It comprises three processing elements, namely, Q-compute, FV-compute, and Q-norm compute. We exploit parallelism across GMM clusters by ordering the Q and FV computations in an arrayed fashion. The GMM parameters (i.e., μ, σ, and π) are

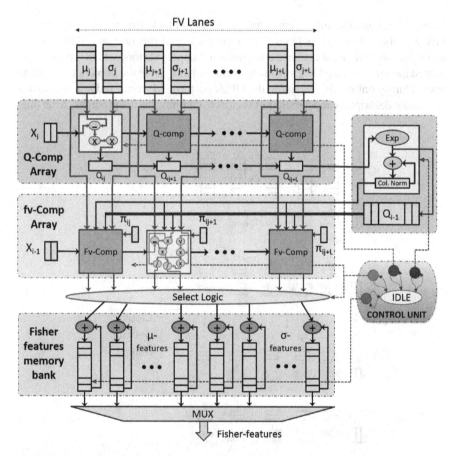

Fig. 7.19 Block diagram of the fisher-vector computation block. It involves three elements: Q computation, Q-norm computation, and FV computation. The GMM parameters are shared across Q and FV computations of successive patches. Figure reproduced from [23]

stored in on-chip streaming memory elements. The daisy feature descriptors come in from the left and are processed by the Q- and FV-compute elements. After one round of processing, the global feature memory is updated. This process is repeated across all GMM clusters—recall that the number of GMM clusters is an algorithmic parameter that is fixed during the initial design-space exploration phase. To maximize throughput, the GMM model parameters are shared across successive feature inputs in the Q- and FV-compute elements. This sharing also saves us memory bandwidth. The power and performance of the FV block can be adjusted by varying the number of lanes in the processing element array. We revisit this aspect in Sect. "Microarchitectural Design-Space Exploration."

The SVM Feature-Classification Block

Figure 7.20 shows the microarchitecture of the SVM block. It comprises two types of PEs, namely, the dot-product unit (DPU) and the kernel-function unit (KFU). These units together realize the distance computation. Support vectors, which represent the trained model, are stored in a streaming memory bank along the borders of the DPU array. During online classification, the DPUs perform L1 vector reduction between the feature descriptors and the support vectors to compute the dot products. After this,

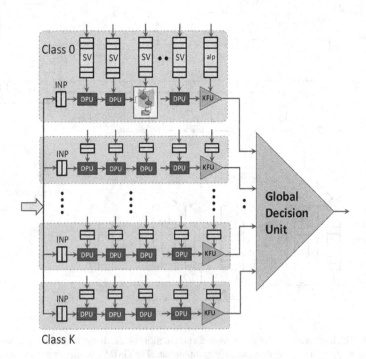

Fig. 7.20 Block diagram of the SVM classification block. Multiple (horizontal) processing lanes allow parallel processing of the FVs

the dot products are streamed out to the KFU, where the kernel function (representing the L2 reduction) and the distance score is computed. In our implementation, we only support linear and polynomial kernels, but provide easy extensibility options for other kernels. Finally, the distance score is used by the global decision unit (GDU) to compute the classifier output. Note that all of the previous operations are independent and can be parallelized. Note also that the execution time of the SVM is proportional to the number of DPU units (SVM lanes).

Through the various microarchitectural and hardware optimizations (e.g., specialized processing elements, parallel stages, and multi-tiered pipelines) mentioned in this section, SAPPHIRE performs efficient image classification. The ability to scale performance and energy by adjusting the various design parameters is also a key attribute of the hardware architecture. We explore this aspect next.

7.6 SAPPHIRE Evaluation

We evaluate the performance and energy consumption of SAPPHIRE in an ASIC implementation. In this section, we describe about our experimental methodology. We then present results at various levels of the design hierarchy.

7.6.1 Experimental Methodology

In this section, we describe our methodology and the benchmarks that we used to evaluate the performance and energy consumption of SAPPHIRE.

Architecture-level evaluation. We implemented SAPPHIRE at the register-transfer logic (RTL) level using Verilog hardware description language (HDL). We synthesized it to an ASIC in a 45 nm SOI process using Synopsys Design Compiler. We used Synopsys Power Compiler and Primetime to estimate the power consumption and delay of SAPPHIRE at the gate level, respectively. The microarchitectural- and circuit-level parameters that we used in our implementation are shown in Table 7.3. Since repeatedly simulating the algorithm at the gate-level was prohibitive in terms of runtime, we developed a cycle-accurate simulation model for the design. This model helped us estimate the hardware performance much more efficiently. For the estimations, we computed the energy consumption of SAPPHIRE as a product of the cycle count, operating frequency, and total power.

System-level energy modeling. We estimated the energy consumption in the end-to-end streaming system model (see Fig. 7.3) as follows:

$$E_{baseline} = E_{sense} + E_{compress} + E_{transmit} \tag{7.13}$$

Table 7.3 Microarchitectural- and circuit-level parameters used in SAPPHIRE

μ Arch. params	Value
G-Blk rows/cols	3/8
S-Blk lanes	1
FV lanes	2
SVM lanes	4
Peak GOPS	29
(Daisy, FV, SVM)	(18.5, 6, 2.5)
Circuit params	Value
Feature size	45 nm SOI
Area	0.5 mm^2
Power (lkg+act)	51.8 mW
Gate count	150k
Frequency	250 MHz

Table reproduced from [23]

where E_{sense}, $E_{compress}$, and $E_{transmit}$ are the energies for sensing, compression, and data transmission, respectively. We estimate the energy of the proposed system model (see Fig. 7.5) as follows:

$$E_{proposed} = E_{sense} + E_{SAPPHIRE} + (1 - \gamma)\left(E_{compress} + E_{transmit}\right) \qquad (7.14)$$

where γ is the defined as the fraction of the filtered frames (i.e., $\gamma = (100 - FT)/100$, where FT is in percentage). To cover a broad spectrum of devices, we estimate each of these energies by assuming a slightly relaxed choice of components (when compared to Figs. 7.3 and 7.5). Specifically, we use the following numbers: a less aggressive low-power OmniVision VGA sensor (100.08 mW) [41], a light-weight MPEG encoder (20 mW and 5× compression) [42], and low-bandwidth 802.11a/g WiFi transmitter (45 nJ/bit at 20 Mbps) [43]. We also assumed a frame rate of 10 fps.

Application benchmarks. We used the four benchmarks mentioned earlier to evaluate the performance of SAPPHIRE. The first three (Caltech256, NORB, and PASCAL VOC) are static image benchmarks, while CamVid is a labeled video dataset. Across these benchmarks, we design SAPPHIRE to detect frames that contain one of 13 objects and filter the rest.

7.6.2 Experimental Results

In this section, we demonstrate the performance and energy savings at the system level due to SAPPHIRE. We also illustrate the impact of parameter tuning on the hardware energy.

System-Level Energy Benefits Due to SAPPHIRE

Like we mentioned before, adding SAPPHIRE saves us communication energy at the cost of some extra computational energy. The energy required by SAPPHIRE is shown in comparison to the other components in Fig. 7.21. Observe that SAPPHIRE achieves a 1.4–3.0× (2.1× on average) improvement in system energy, while capturing over 90 % of interesting frames in the datasets; recall that these numbers are what we used to estimate the battery recharge times in Fig. 7.5. At lower coverage levels, the energy benefits are much higher. For instance, they reach to about 3.6× and 5.1× on an average at 70–90 and 50–70 % coverages, respectively. It is interesting to note that at lower coverage levels, the higher system-level energy savings come about even in the presence of additional communication energy costs. The figure also shows the energy overhead incurred due to SAPPHIRE as a fraction of the total system energy.

Figure 7.22 shows the total energy costs of SAPPHIRE in comparison with the other system components for the different datasets. Compared to the baseline, we see that SAPPHIRE only contributes to about 6 % of the overall system energy. This energy disproportionality between identifying interesting data versus completely transmitting them is key to the applicability of SAPPHIRE. The energy contributions of SAPPHIRE increase to 28 % at lower coverage levels since the overall system energy is also significantly lowered.

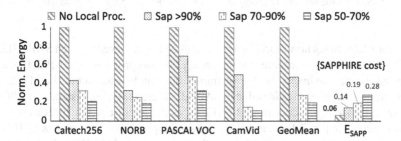

Fig. 7.21 SAPPHIRE costs 6 % overhead but lowers system energy by 2.1×. This overhead increases to 28 % at lower coverage levels, but the overall system energy is also reduced

Fig. 7.22 Comparison between energy costs of SAPPHIRE and other system components

	Caltech256	NORB	Pascal	CamVid
Image Size	640 x 480 24 b/pix	96 x 96 24 b/pix	640 x 480 24 b/pix	960 x 720 24 b/pix
Bits/frame	1.5 Mbits	88 Kbits	1.5 Mbits	3.3 Mbits
E/frame Sense⁺	1.7 mJ	0.06 mJ	1.7 mJ	3.8 mJ
E/frame Compress$	8 mJ	0.27 mJ	8 mJ	8 mJ
E/frame Tx*	66 mJ	2 mJ	66 mJ	149 mJ

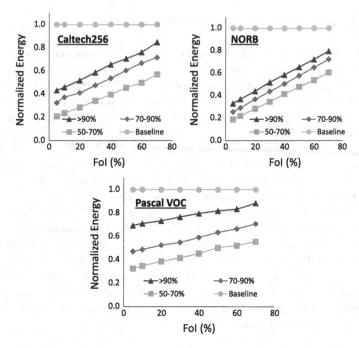

Fig. 7.23 SAPPHIRE saves more energy at lower FoI (typical of appl.). Figure adapted from [23]

Figure 7.23 shows how much energy savings can be achieved through SAPPHIRE at different FoI levels. Observe that the energy benefits provided by SAPPHIRE are bounded by the maximum number of frames that can be filtered out (i.e., FoI). At higher values of FoI, the savings due to SAPPHIRE are lower. For instance, at $\geq 90\%$ coverage, the savings reduce from 2.1 to $1.3\times$ as FoI goes from 5 to 70%. However, as we observed in Fig. 7.4, in most context-aware applications, FoIs are low ($\leq 10\%$). Thus, most systems can benefit substantially by employing SAPPHIRE for local data filtering.

Runtime and Energy Breakdown of SAPPHIRE

Figure 7.24, at the top, shows the percentage contributions to power and runtime, respectively, of the various computational elements in SAPPHIRE. Note that the sum of all runtimes does not equal 100 % since the hardware is pipelined and more than one block may be concurrently active. For these results, we use the microarchitectural configuration of Table 7.3. At the bottom, the figure shows the breakdown in the normalized energy. Observe that the energy proportions for the various computational elements depend on the complexity of the dataset. For instance, number of interest points are high in Caltech256, leading to a higher ($\sim 90\%$) runtime for daisy feature extraction. This is in contrast with NORB, where the SVM classifier is active most

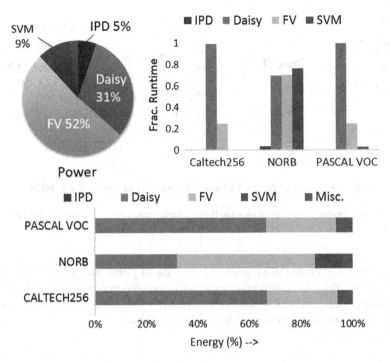

Fig. 7.24 Power, runtime, and energy breakdown of various computational blocks in SAPPHIRE. Figure adapted from [23]

of the time. Thus, we observe that the microarchitectural parameters of SAPPHIRE need to be tuned so that we can optimize the energy consumption for different datasets and applications. We explore this aspect next.

Microarchitectural Design-Space Exploration

We perform an exhaustive search of the design space for the energy-optimal microarchitectural configuration of SAPPHIRE. Figure 7.25a shows a scatter plot of performance [i.e., achievable fps] versus the normalized energy consumption per frame for various architectural configurations. In Fig. 7.25b, the energy per frame is decoupled into two components, namely frame processing time (FPT) and power (the product of these is the energy/frame). The pareto-optimal configurations that minimize the energy consumption are also shown in Fig. 7.25a. The configurations are marked as a tuple comprising the number of parallel lanes in the G-, S-, FV- and SVM-blocks, and the operating frequency of SAPPHIRE. We see from the figure that the pareto-optimal configurations are not obtained by scaling just a single parameter, but a combination. Also, at lower FPS, the increase is FPT outweighs the corresponding decrease in power, thereby resulting in higher energy per frame. At

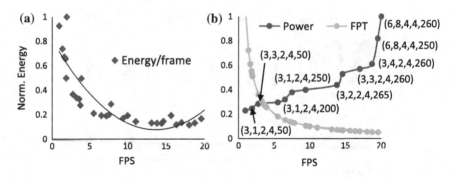

SAPPHIRE config: (*G Rows, S Lanes, FV Lanes, SVM Lanes, Freq. MHz*)

Fig. 7.25 Design space exploration showing the minimum-energy configuration of SAPPHIRE for Caltech256

higher FPS,however, the disproportional increase in power also leads to a higher frame energy. Thus the minimum-energy configuration occurs at an FPS of $\sim$12 for this dataset. Thus, SAPPHIRE allows us to achieve optimal energy configurations depending on the characteristics of the application data.

7.7 Conclusions

A range of emerging applications require portable devices to be continually ambient aware. However, this requires devices to be always on, leading to a large amount of sensed data. Transmitting this data to the cloud for analysis is power inefficient. In this article, we proposed the design of a hybrid system that employs local computations for image classification and the cloud for more complex processing. We chose a light-weight image classification algorithm to keep the energy overheads low. We showed that even with this light-weight algorithm, we can achieve very high true positive rates at the cost of some extra false positives. This approach helped us filter out a substantial number of frames from video data in the device itself. In order to overcome the high processing latency in software, we also proposed a hardware-specialized accelerator called SAPPHIRE. This accelerator allowed us to perform image classification 235$\times$ faster than a CPU with a very low (3 mJ/frame) energy cost. Using multiple levels of pipelining and other architectural innovations, we were able to simultaneously achieve high performance and better energy efficiency in the end-to-end system. Thanks to the resulting communication energy reduction, we showed that our hybrid system using SAPPHIRE can bring down the overall system energy costs by 2.1$\times$. Our system thus has the potential to prolong battery lives of many portable ambient-aware devices.

References

1. D'Andrea, R.: Can drones deliver? IEEE Trans. Autom. Sci. Eng. 138–141 (2014)
2. Randell, C.: Wearable computing: a review. Technical Report Number CSTR-06-004. University of Bristol (2005)
3. Geronimo, D., Lopez, A.M., Sappa, A.D., Graf, T.: Survey of pedestrian detection for advanced driver assistance systems. IEEE Trans. Pattern Anal. Mach. Intell. 32(7), 1239–1258 (2009). doi:10.1109/TPAMI.2009.122
4. Baber, C., Smith, P., Cross, J., Zasikowski, D., Hunter, J.: Wearable technology for crime scene investigation. In: Proceedings of the IEEE International Symposium on Wearable Computers, pp. 138–141 (2005)
5. Mann, S.: WearCam (the wearable camera): personal imaging systems for long-term use in wearable tetherless computer-mediated reality and personal photo/videographic memory prosthesis. In: Proceedings of the IEEE International Symposium on Wearable Computers, pp. 124–131 (1998)
6. Kelly, P., Marshall, S.J., Badland, H., Kerr, J., Oliver, M., Doherty, A.R., Foster, C.: An ethical framework for automated, wearable cameras in health behavior research. Am. J. Prev. Med. 44(3), 314–319 (2013). doi:10.1016/j.amepre.2012.11.006
7. Navab, N.: Developing killer apps for industrial augmented reality. IEEE Comput. Graph. Appl. 24(3), 16–20 (2004)
8. Aleksya, M., Rissanenb, M.J., Maczeya, S., Dixa, M.: Wearable computing in industrial service applications. Int. Conf. Ambient Syst. Netw. Technol. 5, 394–400 (2011). doi:10.1016/j.procs.2011.07.051
9. Weinland, D., Ronfard, R., Boyer, E.: A survey of vision-based methods for action representation, segmentation and recognition. Elsevier Comput. Vis. Image Underst. 115(2), 224–241 (2011). doi:10.1016/j.cviu.2010.10.002
10. Poppe, R.: A survey on vision-based human action recognition. Elsevier Image Vis. Comput. 28(6), 976–990 (2010). doi:10.1016/j.imavis.2009.11.014
11. Crevier, D., Lepage, R.: Knowledge-based image understanding systems: a survey. Elsevier Comput. Vis. Image Underst. 67(2), 161–185 (1997). doi:10.1006/cviu.1996.0520
12. LiKamWa, R., Wang, Z., Carroll, A., Lin, X.F., Zong, L.: Draining our glass: an energy and heat characterization of Google Glass. In: Proceedings of Asia-Pacific Workshop on Systems, Article no. 10, (2014). doi:10.1145/2637166.2637230
13. Ha, K., Chen, Z., Hu, W., Richter, W., Pillai, P., Satyanarayanan, M.: Towards wearable cognitive assistance. In: Proceedings of the International Conference on Mobile Systems, Applications, and Services, pp. 68–81 (2014). doi:10.1145/2594368.2594383
14. Jia, Z., Balasuriya, A., Challa, S.: Vision based target tracking for autonomous land vehicle navigation: a brief survey. Recent Pat. Comput. Sci. 2(1), 32–42 (2009)
15. Soro, S., Heinzelman, W.: A survey of visual sensor networks. Hindawi Advances in Multimedia, Article no. 640386 (2009). doi:10.1155/2009/640386
16. Kyono, Y., Yonezawa, T., Nozaki, H., Keio, M.O., Keio, T.I., Keio, J.N., Takashio, K., Tokuda, H.: EverCopter: continuous and adaptive over-the-air sensing with detachable wired flying objects. In: Proceedings of the ACM Conference on Pervasive and Ubiquitous Computing Adjunct Publication, pp. 299–302 (2013). doi:10.1145/2494091.2494183
17. Kemp, R., Palmer, N., Kielmann, T., Bal, H.: Cuckoo: a computation offloading framework for smartphones. In: Mobile Computing, Applications, and Services. Lecture Notes of the Institute for Computer Sciences, Social Informatics and Telecom. Engineering, vol. 76, pp. 59–79 (2012)
18. Ra, M-R., Sheth, A., Mummert, L., Pillai, P., Wetherall, D., Govindan, R.: Odessa: enabling interactive perception applications on mobile devices. In: Proceedings of the International Conference on Mobile Systems, Applications, and Services, pp. 43–56, (2011). doi:10.1145/1999995.2000000

19. Nishikawa, T., Takahashi, M., Hamada, M., Takayanagi, T., Arakida, H., Machiada, N., Yamamoto, H., Fujiyoshi, T., Matsumoto, Y., Yamagishi, O., Samata, T., Asano, A., Terazawa, T., Ohmori, K., Shirakura, J., Watanabe, Y., Nakamura, H., Minami, S., Kuroda, T., Furuyama, T.: A 60MHz 240mW MPEG-4 video-phone LSI with 16Mb embedded DRAM. IEEE J. Solid-State Circuits **35**, 1713–1721 (2000)
20. Worlds most power-efficient 1080p/60 high definition imag sensor for front-facing camera applications. OV2740 1080p Product Brief. www.ovt.com (2014)
21. Halperin, D., Greenstein, B., Sheth, A., Wetherall, D.: Demystifying 802.11n power consumption. In: Proceedings of the International Conference on Power Aware Computing and Systems, Article no. 1 (2010)
22. Brostow, G., Shotton, J., Fauquer, J., Cipolla, R.: Segmentation and recognition using structure from motion point clouds. In: Proceedings of the European Conference on Computer Vision, pp. 44–57 (2008). doi:10.1007/978-3-540-88682-2_5
23. Venkataramani, S., Bahl, V., Hua, X.-S., Liu, J., Li, J., Phillipose, M., Priyantha, B., Shoaib, M.: SAPPHIRE: an always-on context-aware computer-vision system for portable devices. In: Proceedings of Conference on Design Automation and Test in Europe, to appear (2015)
24. Krizhevsky, A., Sutskever, I., Hinton, G.E.: Imagenet classification with deep convolutional neural networks. In: Proceedings of Neural Information Processing Systems, pp. 1106–1114 (2012)
25. Jin, J., Gokhale, V., Dundar, A., Krishnamurthy, B., Martini, B., Culurciello, E.: An efficient implementation of deep convolutional neural networks on a mobile coprocessor. IEEE Int. Midwest Symp. Circuits Syst. 133–136 (2014). doi:10.1109/MWSCAS.2014.6908370
26. Gokhale, V., Jin, J., Dundar, A., Martini, B., Culurciello, E.: A 240 G-ops/s mobile coprocessor for deep neural networks. IEEE Conf. Comput. Vis. Pattern Recognit. Workshops 696–701 (2014). doi:10.1109/CVPRW.2014.106
27. Chen, T., Du, Z., Sun, N., Wang, J., Wu, C., Chen, Y., Temam, O.: DianNao: a small-footprint high-throughput accelerator for ubiquitous machine-learning. In: Proceedings of the International Conference on Architectural Support for Programming Languages and Operating Systems, pp. 269–284 (2014). doi:10.1145/2541940.2541967
28. Perronnin, F., Sanchez, J., Mensink, T.: Improving the fisher kernel for large-scale image classification. In: Proceedings of the European Conference on Computer Vision, pp. 143–156 (2010)
29. Harris, C., Stephens, M.: A combined corner and edge detector. In: Proceedings of the Fourth Alvey Vision Conference, pp. 147–151 (1988)
30. Winder, S., Hua, G., Brown, M.: Picking the best daisy. In: Proceedings of the International Conference on Computer Vision and Pattern Recognition (2009)
31. Winder, S., Hua, G., Brown, M.: Discriminative learning of local image descriptors. IEEE Trans. Pattern Anal. Mach. Intell. **33**(1), 43–57 (2009). doi:10.1109/TPAMI.2010.54
32. Shotton, J., Johnson, M., Cipolla, R.: Semantic texton forests for image categorization and segmentation. In: Proceedings of the International Conference on Computer Vision and Pattern Recognition, pp. 1–8 (2008). doi:10.1109/CVPR.2008.4587503
33. He, X., Yan, S., Hu, Y., Niyogi, P., Zhang, H.-J.: Face recognition using Laplacian faces. IEEE Trans. Pattern Anal. Mach. Intell. **27**(3), 328–340 (2005)
34. Chen, H.-T., Chang, H.-W., Liu, T.-L.: Local discriminant embedding and its variants. In: Proceedings of the International Conference on Computer Vision and Pattern Recognition, pp. 846–853 (2005). doi:10.1109/CVPR.2005.216
35. Winder, S.A.J., Brown, M.: Learning local image descriptors. In: Proceedings of the International Conference on Computer Vision and Pattern Recognition, pp. 1–8 (2007)
36. Sanchez, J., Perronnin, F., Mensink, T., Jakob, V.: Image classification with the Fisher vector: theory and practice. Int. J. Comput. Vis. **105**(3), 222–245 (2013). doi:10.1007/s11263-013-0636-x
37. Leijen, D., Schulte, W., Burchardt, S.: The design of a task parallel library. In: Proceedings of the Conference on Object Oriented Programming Systems Languages and Applications, pp. 227–242(2009). doi:10.1145/1640089.1640106

38. Griffin, G., Holum, A., Perona, P.: Caltech-256 object category dataset. Caltech Technical Report Number: CNS-TR-2007-001. http://authors.library.caltech.edu/7694 (2011)
39. LeCun, Y., Huang, F.J., Bottou, L.: Learning methods for generic object recognition with invariance to pose and lighting. Proc. Int. Conf. Comput. Vis. Pattern Recognit. (2004). doi:10.1109/CVPR.2004.1315150
40. Everingham, M., Ali, E.S.M., Luc, V.G., Williams, C.K.I., Winn, J., Zisserman, A.: The pascal visual object classes challenge: a retrospective. Int. J. Comput. Vis. 1–39 (2014). doi:10.1007/s11263-014-0733-5
41. OmniVision OV7735 Product Brief. www.ovt.com (2014)
42. Chen, S., Bermak, A., Wang, Y.: A CMOS image sensor with on-chip image compression based on predictive boundary adaptation and memoryless QTD algorithm. IEEE Trans. VLSI Syst. **19**(4), 538–547 (2011)
43. Low Power Advantage of 802.11a/g vs. 802.11b. Whitepaper, Texas Instruments. www.ti.com (2003)

Chapter 8
Compact Deep Neural Networks for Device-Based Image Classification

Zejia Zheng, Zhu Li and Abhishek Nagar

Abstract Convolutional Neural Network (CNN) is efficient in learning hierarchical features from large image datasets, but its model complexity and large memory footprints prevent it from being deployed to devices without a server back-end support. Modern CNNs are always trained on GPUs or even GPU clusters with high-speed computation capability due to the immense size of the network. A device-based deep learning CNN engine for image classification can be very useful for situations where server back end is either not available, or its communication link is weak and unreliable. Methods on regulating the size of the network, on the other hand, are rarely studied. In this chapter we present a novel compact architecture that minimizes the number and complexity of lower level filters in a CNN by separating the color information from the original image. A 9-patch histogram extractor is built to exploit the unused color information. A high-level classifier is then used to learn the features obtained from the compact CNN that was trained only on grayscale image with limited number of filters and the 9-patch histogram extracted from the color information in the image. We apply our compact architecture to Samsung Mobile Image Dataset for image classification. The proposed solution has a recognition accuracy on par with the state-of-the-art CNNs, while achieving significant reduction in model memory footprint. With these advantages, our system is being deployed to the mobile devices.

Z. Zheng (✉)
Michigan State University, 428 South Shaw Lane, Room 3110, East Lansing,
MI 48824, USA
e-mail: zhengzej@msu.edu

Z. Li · A. Nagar
Samsung Research America, 1301 E. Lookout Drive, Richardson, TX 75082, USA
e-mail: zhu1.li@samsung.com

A. Nagar
e-mail: a.nagar@samsung.com

© Springer International Publishing Switzerland 2015
G. Hua and X.-S. Hua (eds.), *Mobile Cloud Visual Media Computing*,
DOI 10.1007/978-3-319-24702-1_8

8.1 Convolutional Neural Network

In recent years commercial and academic datasets for image classification have been growing at an unprecedented pace. The SUN database for scenery classification contains 899 categories and 130,519 images [15]. The ImageNet dataset contains 1000 categories and 1.2 million images [6]. In response to this immensely increased complexity, many researchers have focused on designing even more sophisticated classifiers to effectively capture all the invariant and discriminative features.

Among a great number of available classifiers, Convolutional Neural Network (CNN) is reported to have the leading performance on many image classification tasks. Overfeat, a CNN-based image features extractor and classifier, scored a low 29.8 % error rate in classification and localization task on ImageNet 2013 dataset. Clarifai, a hierarchical architecture of CNN and deconvolutional neural network, achieved an 11.19 % error recognition rate on ImageNet 2013 classification task [16]. CNNs have been reported to have state-of-the-art performance on many other image recognition and classification tasks, including handwritten digit recognition [7], house numbers recognition [11], and traffic signs classification [2].

8.1.1 Network Architecture

Convolutional Neural Network is specifically designed to handle computer vision problems. A typical CNN is presented in Fig. 8.1. It has the following features that differentiate itself from traditional neural networks:

1. Local receptive field. Each neuron in the convolutional layer accepts only a portion of the entire input image. Thus the learned filters only produce the strongest response to a local input pattern, thereby reinforcing the local nature of typical image features.
2. Shared weights. Each neuron in the convolutional layer shares the same set of filters. This architecture ensures that important local features would be detected regardless of their position in the visual field.
3. Subsampling for dimension reduction. Convolutional neural network alternates between the convolutional and pooling layers. Pooling is performed on overlapping or nonoverlapping neighborhoods of the input to reduce the data dimensions and at the same time find the most prominent features.

Combining those three features together, we have the architecture of a typical CNN as is presented in Fig. 8.1.

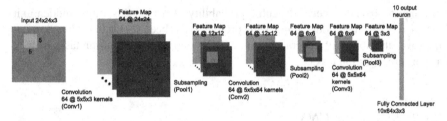

Fig. 8.1   Architecture of a typical CNN. This figure shows the structure of a typical CNN trained on CIFAR-10 dataset

Convolutional Layer

The response map in the convolutional layer is computed using the same set of filters (as is described in the second property of CNN). The convolution operation is expressed as:

$$y^{j(r)} = ReLU(b^{j(r)} + \sum_i k^{ij(r)} * x^{i(r)}) \tag{8.1}$$

where x^i is the ith input map and y^j is the jth output map, k^{ij} is the convolution filter corresponding to the ith input map and the jth output map, and r indicates a local region on the input map where the weights are shared.

Rectifier Linear Unit, also know as ReLU nonlinearity (i.e., $ReLU(x) = max(0, x)$) is used on the obtained feature maps. It is observed that ReLU yields better performance and faster convergence speed when trained by error back propagation [6].

Pooling Layer

As is discussed in the third property of CNN, the pooling layer serves as a mechanism for dimension reduction and feature selection. This layer does not do learning by itself. It takes a small $k \times k$ block from the final feature map of the previous layer and output a single value. The most used pooling methods are max-pooling, where the output is the maximum value of the block, and average pooling, where the output is the average value of the block. There are other pooling methods with good performance on certain tasks [3, 8].

Dropout

Dropout is proposed as an element of the training procedure to reduce overfitting on the training data by preventing coadaptations among neurons [4]. Dropout is performed on each forward passing of a training image, randomly omitting the response of a neuron from the network with a probability of 0.5. In this way a hidden unit cannot rely on other hidden units being present. It has been shown in [4] that dropout improves the ability of generalization in CNNs on image recognition tasks as well as voice recognition tasks.

8.1.2 Size of the CNN

Size of a typical CNN is usually huge. The winning system of ImageNet 2013 classification contest was a deep convolutional neural network million parameters. The ILSVRC 2012 challenge winning CNN system by Krizhevsky has around 60 million parameters [6]. Overfeat, the ILSVRC 2013 challenge winning CNN, has more than 140 million parameters [12]. Owing to their complexity, these networks are always trained on a GPU machine or GPU clusters for better performance. Are all those parameter needed for image classification? Is there a way to train a compact CNN with the same performance as the state-of-the-art architecture?

8.1.3 Filter suppression and selection

In this subsection, we present a novel way to evaluate the contribution of each filter in a high performance compact Convolutional Neural Network. The filters in the first layer of the proposed CNN are selected from a pretrained larger CNN (2 times larger). The selection is based on ranking the contribution of each filter to the final performance of the network.

Filter Suppression

Filter suppression is used to evaluate the importance of each filter. The term *filter suppression* refers to setting the weight of a specific filter to zero. The performance of the *suppressed* network is then evaluated based on the validation dataset. Contribution of this filter is calculated based on the difference between the error recognition rates before and after filter suppression:

$$Contribution = ERR\_suppressed - ERR\_original \qquad (8.2)$$

where ERR stands for error recognition rate, which is the percentage of error recognition in the validation set.

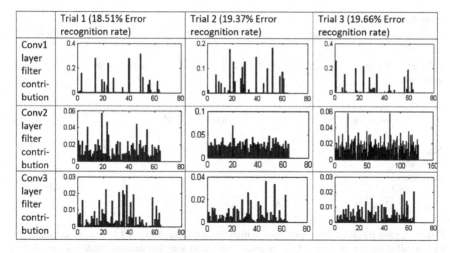

Fig. 8.2 Contribution evaluation for three convolutional neural networks trained on CIFAR-10. For each figure, the x-axis is the index of the filters examined, and the y-axis is the contribution of that filter to the final recognition rate. The contribution of filters in the first convolutional layer varies drastically, indicating that there redundant filters in this layer. Contribution of higher level filters appears to be more uniform compared to the contribution of the filters in the first convolutional layer. The dead filters (more than 50 %) in Conv1 layer can be removed without affecting the final performance

Figure 8.2 shows the contribution evaluation result of three CNNs (with three convolutional layers of the same size) trained on CIFAR-10 dataset. These CNNs are initialized with different parameter (randomly generated) but trained with the same data. The evaluation reveals two important properties of the filters inside a CNN:

1. A large CNN network, though yields good performance during testing, has a considerable amount of *dead* filters in Conv1 layer. By *dead* filters we mean those filters with contribution of 0 % to the recognition rate on the validation dataset. The weight inside those filters can be set to zero without affecting the overall performance of the network.
2. Filters of higher level layers, i.e., Conv2 layer and Conv3 layer, have more averaged contributions to the final performance compared to the filters in the first convolutional layer.

Filter Selection

It is possible that the dead filters in the lower layers, though useless when suppressed individually, are actually important for classification when they are combined together in higher layers. To test that hypothesis, all dead filters are removed in the tested network, including weights that connect the corresponding layer1 feature

Table 8.1 Filter selection result

		Conv1	Conv2	Conv3	Fully Connect	Size	ERR (%)
Original network	Filter size	$5 \times 5 \times 3$	$5 \times 5 \times 64$	$5 \times 5 \times 64$	$7 \times 7 \times 64$	240960	18.51
							19.37
							19.66
	Num. of filter	64	64	64	10		
Network without dead filters	Filter size	$5 \times 5 \times 3$	$5 \times 5 \times 32$	$5 \times 5 \times 64$	$7 \times 7 \times 64$	187360	18.51
							19.37
							19.66
	Num. of filter	32	64	64	10		

Filter selection result on three randomly initialized networks. The dead filters can be removed without affecting performance of the original network, making the network more compact. ERR stands for error recognition rate

map. The recognition rate, as is shown in Table 8.1, remains unchanged compared to the recognition rate of the original network.

8.2 Compact CNN with Color Descriptor

As is discussed in previous section, CNNs give extraordinary performance on image recognition tasks at the cost of extremely large networks powered by GPUs. The large size of CNNs makes it hard to implement such a system onto a mobile device with limited computational resources. Filter suppression and selection reveals that a CNN by itself is not fully exploiting the lower level information from the input images, generating the dead filters as is shown in Table 8.1. Is there a way to maintain the performance while keeping the network small? In this section we present a compact CNN combined with histogram color descriptor. The proposed solution has a recognition accuracy on par with the state-of-the-art CNNs, while achieving significant model memory footprint reduction. Due to these benefits, the proposed solution is being deployed to the mobile devices.

8.2.1 Histogram-based Classification

Color histograms are widely used to compare images despite the simplicity of this method. It has been proven to have good performance on image indexing with relatively small datasets [13]. Color histograms are trivial to compute and tend to be robust against small changes to camera viewpoint, which makes them a good compact image descriptor for device-based image classification task. It was also reported in [1] that the performance of a histogram-based classifier was improved when the higher level classifier was a support vector machine.

However, when applied to large dataset, histogram-based classifiers tend to give poor performance because of high variances within the same category. It is also observed that images with different labels may share similar histograms [10].

In this work, we propose a novel architecture that combines the histogram-based classification method with CNN. The histogram representation of color information helps the CNN to exploit color information in the original image. This means that we can cut down the size of the basic feature detectors (i.e., layer 1 of the CNN). The proposed architecture is introduced in the following section.

8.2.2 Convolutional Neural Networks

We train two CNNs with different number of filters in the first layer: an original version and a compact version. The 'original' network is the exact replicate of the CNN reported in [5], which gives a final error recognition rate of 13 % using multiview testing on CIFAR-10. In this work, however, we only use single view testing when reporting the final result for both the original CNN and compact CNN.

We use the architecture of Krizhevsky et al. [6] to train the *original* CNN in the experiments. We then modified layer 1 by changing the filter size (from $5 \times 5 \times 3$ to $5 \times 5 \times 1$) and the number of filters (from 64 to 32) in later experiments. The details of the experiments are introduced in the next section.

Both the original and the compact CNNs have four convolutional layers. Table 8.2 shows the details of the two networks when trained on cropped images from the Samsung Mobile Image dataset. Our compact CNN is marked in bold font to show the difference. There are only 32 filters in the first layer of the compact CNN while the number is 64 in the original CNN. This cuts down the number of parameters by 50 % in layer 3 (i.e., the second convolutional layer). The final compact CNN has 40 % less parameters to tune compared to the original version.

8.2.3 Color Information

A color is represented by a three-dimensional vector corresponding to a point in the color space. We choose red–green–blue (RGB) as our color space, which is in bijection with the hue–saturation–value (HSV).

HSV may seem attractive in theory for a classifier purely based on histograms. HSV color space separates color component from the luminance component, making the histogram less sensitive to illumination changes. However, this does not seem

Table 8.2 Original and compact CNN architecture

Operation	Layer 1 Conv	Layer 2 Max	Layer 3 Conv	Layer 4 Max	Layer 5 Conv	Layer 6 Conv	Layer 7 Fully connect	Layer 8 Softmax
Original input size	$24 \times 24 \times k$	$24 \times 24 \times 64$	$12 \times 12 \times 64$	$12 \times 12 \times 64$	$6 \times 6 \times 64$	$6 \times 6 \times 32$	$6 \times 6 \times 32$	31×1
Compact input size	$24 \times 24 \times 1$	$24 \times 24 \times 32$	$12 \times 12 \times 32$	$12 \times 12 \times 64$	$6 \times 6 \times 64$	$6 \times 6 \times 32$	$6 \times 6 \times 32$	31×1
Filter size	$5 \times 5 \times k$		$5 \times 5 \times 64$		$3 \times 3 \times 64$	$3 \times 3 \times 32$	$6 \times 6 \times 32$	
Compact filter size	$5 \times 5 \times 1$		$5 \times 5 \times 32$		$3 \times 3 \times 64$	$3 \times 3 \times 32$	$6 \times 6 \times 32$	
Original filter num	64		64		32	32	31	
Compact filter num	32		64		32	32	31	
Pool size		3×3		3×3				
Stride	1×1	2×2	1×1	2×2	1×1	1×1		31×1
Output	$24 \times 24 \times 64$	$12 \times 12 \times 64$	$12 \times 12 \times 64$	$6 \times 6 \times 64$	$6 \times 6 \times 32$	$6 \times 6 \times 32$	31×1	

to be important in practice. Minimal improvement on the performance of a support vector machine was observed when switching from RGB color space to HSV color space [1].

The benefit of using RGB is that the three channels share the same range (i.e., from 0 to 255), making it easier for normalization.

We experiment with three different configurations of the color histogram:

1. Global histogram, 48 bins.
2. 9-patch histogram, 192 bins. The 9 patches are generated as is shown in Fig. 8.3. As CIFAR-10 dataset contains only 32 by 32 images, which makes it harder to extract useful histograms, the number of bins in this setup are 48, 2 × 24, 2 × 24, and 4 × 24.
3. 9-patch histogram, 384 bins. Numbers of bins are doubled compared to the previous setup.

These experiments on histogram configuration are solely carried out on the CIFAR-10 image dataset. This series of experiment serves as a guideline for our experiment on Samsung Mobile Image Dataset.

8.2.4 Combined Architecture

Once the CNN is trained for the classification task with the grayscale version of the training set, we replace the fully connected layer and the softmax layer (i.e., layer 7 and 8 as is shown in Table 8.2) with a new fully connected layer and a new softmax

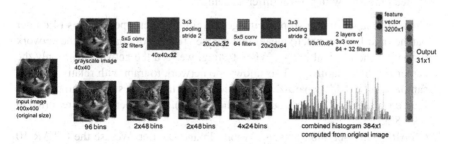

Fig. 8.3 Compact CNN with histogram-based color descriptor. We separate color information from the original image by only feeding the CNN with the grayscale image. Color histogram is combined with the final feature vector. This figure shows how an image from Samsung Mobile Image Dataset is classified as is described in Sect. 8.3.2. Image size and the number of bins in a histogram are reduced accordingly when testing on CIFAR-10. There are only 32 filters in layer 1, selected from the 64 filters in layer 1 of the original network via filter contribution evaluation. The performance of the Compact architecture, therefore, is similar to the original architecture, with the network size 40 % smaller when testing on CIFAR-10, and 20 % smaller when testing on Samsung Mobile Image Database

layer trained on the combined feature vector, using the feature vector from the same training set.

The combined feature vector is generated by Algorithm 1.

Input: image I, total number of patches k
Output: Combined Feature Vector *vec_combined*
segment I into $\{I_i, i = 1, 2, ..., k\}$;
extract histogram vector *hist_vec* from $\{I_i\}$;
resize I to CNN input size, feed I into CNN;
extract layer 6 output *cnn_layer_6_vec* from CNN;
reshape *cnn_layer_6_vec* to a one dimensional vector *cnn_vec*;
vec_combined = concatenate(*cnn_vec*, *hist_vec*);
return *vec_combined*

Algorithm 1: EXTRACT NEW FEATURE VECTOR

With the new feature vector extracted from the training set, we train a new layer 7 (fully connected layer) and layer 8 (softmax layer) based on the combined feature vector extracted from the training set.

8.3 Experiment

The purpose of the work presented is to find a compact architecture by combining handcrafted feature representation with final feature vector from the CNN. To make clear comparison with the existing system, we evaluate the performance of the combined classifier with several different setups:

1. Cropped images and uncropped images. Training on cropped images (4 corner patches and 1 center patch) means that we feed patches of image into the network instead of the original image. When testing, we feed the network with only the center patch of the image. This allows the network to train with relatively more samples, but would jeopardize recognition for certain classes in Samsung Mobile Image Dataset (e.g., upper body and whole body). This experiment is reported in Sect. 8.3.1.
2. CIFAR-10 dataset and Samsung Mobile Image Dataset. We use the CIFAR-10 dataset to test different configurations of histograms and several data augmentation methods in Sect. 8.3.1. The results on CIFAR-10 serves as a guideline for us to construct a compact classifier for the Samsung Mobile Image Dataset, a hierarchical dataset collected at Samsung Research America. The experiment on this new dataset is reported in Sect. 8.3.2.

Details about these experiments are reported in the following section. In short, we found that the proposed compact architecture trained on cropped grayscale image maintains the high accuracy of the original CNN trained on cropped RGB images.

8.3.1 Extracting Histogram-Based Color Feature

CIFAR-10 has been heavily tested with many classification methods. Krivzhevsky et al. [6] achieved a 13 % test error rate when using their ILSVRC 2012 winning CNN architecture (without normalization). By generalizing Hinton's dropout [4] into suppression in weight values instead of activation values, Wan et al. [14] reported an error testing rate of 9.32 %, using their modified Convolutional Neural Network DropConnect. Lin et al. [9] replaced the ReLU convolutional layer in Krizhevsky's architecture [6] with a convolutional multilayer perceptron. They reported a test error rate of 8.8%, currently ranking top on the leader board of classification on CIFAR-10 dataset.

Our experiment in this chapter is still based on Krizhevsky's architecture as is described in [6]. The goal of this paper is to study the contribution of color information to CNN-based image classification, and to seek possible combination between handcrafted feature vector and CNN extracted feature vector to further exploit the low level features with limited number of parameters. For these reasons we apply our modifications to a standard CNN architecture as is provided by Krizhevsky in [6]. We believe that the combined architecture can also be applied to other CNN variants with few modifications.

Getting Histogram

For device-based image classification, a large histogram vector means heavier load for computation. Therefore we only extract a global histogram of a small amount of bins from the original image in our first experiment. The histogram and the final feature vector from the CNN pass are concatenated together as is described in the previous section.

In later trials, we move on to more complicated histograms feature vector extraction configurations instead of just using the global histogram. We extracted histogram feature vectors of different length from 9 patches of the input image. Suppose we are to extract a histogram feature vector of length 384, then the number of bins of each patch would be: 96 bins from the entire image, 48 × 4 bins from the left half, the right half, the top half and the bottom half, 24 × 4 bins from the upper left corner, the upper right corner, the lower left corner and the lower right corner. This procedure is shown in Fig. 8.3. The intention is to precisely reflect the global color information as well as the local color distribution in the extracted features.

Table 8.3 Different histogram configuration result on uncropped images using original CNN (on CIFAR-10)

Input image and hist config.	Top-1 error rate (%)
Grayscale	24.79
Grayscale+global hist (48 bins)	24.95
Grayscale+9 patch hist (192 bins)	24.55
Grayscale+9 patch hist (384 bins)	24.10

Training Methods

Although our CNN architecture is similar to Krivzhevsky's network, we modify some parts of the training procedures in [6] to suit our needs.

As is shown in Table 8.3, we first explore the configuration of histogram vector by adjusting the amount of information the histogram vector contains. In each case, the grayscale CNN, trained on the original architecture remains unchanged. Although global color histogram does not help to improve classification, the 9-patch configuration led to significantly improved performance. One important guideline we observed is that a more detailed histogram (384 bins) gives better classification result compared to rough color information.

When trained on uncropped RGB images using the original architecture, the performance (recognition rate) is 2% worse than the original architecture trained on grayscale images.

When trained with enough images (i.e., after cropping), the CNN trained with RGB images is more accurate, with an error recognition rate of 16.36%. However, the original CNN has 146,368 parameters due to the large number of filters in layer 1 and layer 2. The compact CNN trained on grayscale images has less filters in layer 1 and thus 50% compared to the original CNN, while the error recognition rate rises only by 1%. As a result, the proposed architecture maintains high performance, while the size of the architecture is 40% smaller.

8.3.2 Samsung Mobile Image Dataset

The Samsung Mobile Image Dataset is a large scale collection of mobile phone photographs collected at Samsung Research America. There are 31 classes, with a total 82181 images of different sizes and resolutions.

Class names together with sample images of each class are shown in Fig. 8.4. Instead of just training the network to recognize if a person is in the image, the network is also required to report a general posture (e.g., lying, leaning forward or backward, etc.). The general food category is also divided into three sub categories: the class 'food part 1' contains breads, desserts and bottled/cupped food; the class

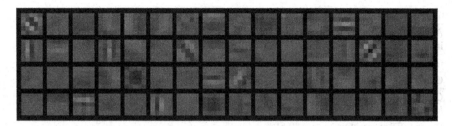

Fig. 8.4 Sample images for Samsung Mobile Image Dataset. This hierarchical image dataset has unclear boundaries among categories. The first level category is presented by colored ovals. Second level categories are presented by the label and a random sample from the training dataset

'food part 2' contains meat and other foods on a plate; the class 'food part 3' consists of pictures about foods on tables. Details of each class can be found in Table 8.6.

We split the dataset by assigning 10 % of the images to the testing set, 10 % to a validation set and 80 % to the training set. After the 384 bins histogram is extracted, each image is then resized into a 48 × 48 grayscale image and then fed to the convolution network. The layer configuration and parameters are the same as is described in Table 8.2. Note that the input image size should be modified accordingly.

Getting Histogram

As the original image contains more detailed information due to the increased image resolution, a global histogram vector is not sufficient to describe the color information with high accuracy.

Guided by the result from our first experiment, we extract a color descriptor of length 384 by concatenating histogram feature vectors from 9 patches of the image as is described in previous experiment (Table 8.4).

Data Augmentation

As is reported in the previous experiment, cropping images leads to more robust features learned by the network. But cropping as is done in [6] may lead to confusion

Table 8.4 Cropped image test result (on CIFAR-10)

Architecture (all on cropped images)	Top-1 error rate (%)	Number of parameters
Grayscale (original)	18.10	143168
Grayscale (compact)	18.95	91168
Grayscale (compact) 9 patch hist (384 bins)	*16.55*	*95008*

Table 8.5 Samsung mobile image test result

Architecture (all on cropped images)	Top-1 error rates (%)	Number of parameters
Grayscale (original)	26.08	230848
Grayscale (compact)	26.06	178848
Grayscale (compact) 9 patch hist (384 bins)	*22.80*	*186528*
Dense SIFT aggregation	30.61	–

Fig. 8.5 Compact CNN layer 1 filter. There are only 32 filters in layer 1 of the proposed architecture. The network learns basic features as edges and corners from the grayscale input. Network trained on grayscale images from Samsung Mobile Image Dataset

when the network needs to distinguish upper body from whole body (class 9 and 10 in Table 8.6). Therefore we flip the images from the uprightwhole class horizontally at a 0.5 probability. The images are then resized and zero-padded to fit the input size of the network (40×40).

Experiment Result

The error recognition rates of different configurations are reported in Table 8.5.

The difference between the error recognition rate of the original architecture (trained on grayscale images) and the compact architecture (trained on grayscale images) is even smaller when using Samsung Mobile Image Dataset (i.e., less than 0.3%). This result indicates that the 64 filters on the first layer learned redundant information. The learned filters are visualized in Figs. 8.5 and 8.6.

It can also be seen from the result that color information boosts the performance of the grayscale CNN (original version and compact version) by as much as 3 % (for compact CNN) and 4 % (for original CNN). Our proposed architecture is neck and neck with the original architecture in recognition, while the proposed architecture is more compact compared to the original version.

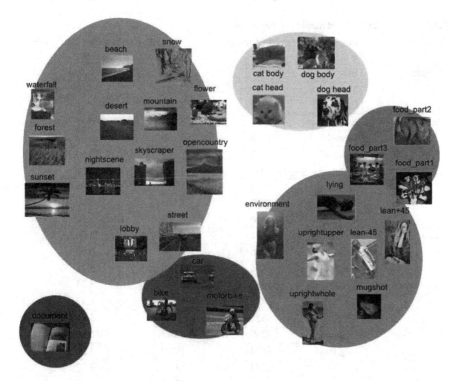

Fig. 8.6 Original CNN trained on RGB images from Samsung Mobile Image Dataset. The network deploys most of its resources in finding color gradient, compared to the filters learned in CNN trained on grayscale images

8.4   Conclusions

In this chapter we introduce the convolutional neural network for image classification. Convolutional neural networks give state-of-the art performance but its application is limited due to its large memory footprint. We present a novel architecture to minimize the size of the network. The proposed architecture combines handcrafted global color information with a convolutional neural network pretrained with thumbnail grayscale images. The proposed architecture has similar recognition capacity compared to state-of-the-art CNNs, quite ahead of the traditional dense SIFT aggregation solution, but with a much smaller network size and complexity that can fit on the mobile devices. We apply our network to Samsung Mobile Image Dataset, a hierarchically organized image dataset. The experiment shows that carefully designed histogram extractor helps to boost the performance of the convolutional neural network. In future work we are investigating a CNN feature map relearning and top-down CNN complexity reduction solution that can further compact the network and improve the accuracy.

Details about the Samsung Mobile Image dataset are included in Table 8.6.

Table 8.6 Class labels and number of images per class

Level 1	Level 2	# of images	Top-1 error rate (%)	Top-2 error rate (%)
Vehicle	Bike	3097	2.64	1.56
	Motorbike	865	6.41	1.79
	Car	2969	21.78	5.37
People	Environment	2713	35.08	6.23
	Lean-45	1271	26.06	10.43
	Lean+45	1277	26.07	10.43
	Lying	1005	23.16	11.58
	Mugshot	3625	16.45	6.45
	Uprightupper	4197	37.01	6.49
	Uprightwhole	3336	37.01	6.49
Food	Food part1	3291	50.00	25.00
	Food part2	2926	20.18	6.02
	Food part3	3168	10.94	3.12
Documents	Document	3080	6.21	3.73
Pets	Cat body	3717	19.13	8.47
	Cat head	3521	5.37	3.95
	Dog body	3769	22.13	10.36
	Dog head	3158	10.39	3.58
Scenery	Flower	3577	4.24	2.12
	Mountain	2838	49.05	13.74
	Skyscraper	2549	49.44	9.20
	Opencountry	1829	31.56	13.78
	Snow	1955	38.34	9.20
	Street	1966	41.82	11.27
	Sunset	2350	60.12	8.90
	Waterfall	1012	4.82	2.19
	Beach	2874	45.26	7.51
	Desert	873	22.22	8.72
	Forest	2667	25.00	5.62
	Lobby	2298	11.48	6.56
	Nightscene	3050	45.51	9.55

References

1. Chapelle, O., Haffner, P., Vapnik, V.N.: Support vector machines for histogram-based image classification. IEEE Trans. Neural Netw. **10**(5), 1055–1064 (1999)
2. Ciresan, D., Meier, U., Schmidhuber, J.: Multi-column deep neural networks for image classification. In: 2012 IEEE Conference on Computer Vision and Pattern Recognition (CVPR). IEEE, pp. 3642–3649 (2012)

3. Deng, L., Abdel-Hamid, O., Yu, D.: A deep convolutional neural network using heterogeneous pooling for trading acoustic invariance with phonetic confusion. In: 2013 IEEE International Conference on Acoustics, Speech and Signal Processing (ICASSP). IEEE, pp. 6669–6673 (2013)
4. Hinton, G.E., Srivastava, N., Krizhevsky, A., Sutskever, I., Salakhutdinov, R.: Improving neural networks by preventing co-adaptation of feature detectors. arXiv preprint arXiv:1207.0580 (2012)
5. Krizhevsky, A.: Learning multiple layers of features from tiny images. Unpublished
6. Krizhevsky, A., Sutskever, I., Hinton, G.E.: Imagenet classification with deep convolutional neural networks. In: Advances in Neural Information Processing Systems, pp. 1097–1105 (2012)
7. LeCun, Y., Denker, J., Henderson, D., Howard, R.E., Hubbard, W., Jackel, L.D.: Handwritten digit recognition with a back-propagation network. In: Advances in Neural Information Processing Systems, Citeseer (1990)
8. Lee, H., Grosse, R., Ranganath, R., Ng, A.Y.: Convolutional deep belief networks for scalable unsupervised learning of hierarchical representations. In: Proceedings of the 26th Annual International Conference on Machine Learning, ACM, pp. 609–616 (2009)
9. Lin, M., Chen, Q., Yan, S.: Network in network. CoRR, abs/1312.4400, 2013
10. Pass, G., Zabih, R.: Histogram refinement for content-based image retrieval. In: Proceedings of the 3rd IEEE Workshop on Applications of Computer Vision, WACV'96. IEEE, pp. 96–102 (1996)
11. Sermanet, P., Chintala, S., LeCun, Y.: Convolutional neural networks applied to house numbers digit classification. In: 21st International Conference on Pattern Recognition (ICPR). IEEE, pp. 3288–3291 (2012)
12. Sermanet, P., Eigen, D., Zhang, X., Mathieu, M., Fergus, R., LeCun, Y.: Overfeat: Integrated recognition, localization and detection using convolutional networks. arXiv preprint arXiv:1312.6229 (2013)
13. Swain, M.J., Ballard, D.H.: Indexing via color histograms. In: Active Perception and Robot Vision. Springer, pp. 261–273. (1992)
14. Wan, L., Zeiler, M., Zhang, S., LeCun, Y., Fergus, R.: Regularization of neural networks using dropconnect. In: Proceedings of the 30th International Conference on Machine Learning (ICML-13), pp. 1058–1066 (2013)
15. Xiao, J., Hays, J., Ehinger, K.A.: Aude Oliva, and Antonio Torralba. Sun database: Large-scale scene recognition from abbey to zoo. In: 2010 IEEE conference on Computer vision and pattern recognition (CVPR). IEEE, pp. 3485–3492. (2010)
16. Zeiler, M.D., Fergus, R.: Visualizing and understanding convolutional neural networks. arXiv preprint arXiv:1311.2901 (2013)

Chapter 9
Assistive Text Reading from Natural Scene for Blind Persons

Chucai Yi and Yingli Tian

Abstract Text information serves as an understandable and comprehensive indicator, which plays a significant role in navigation and recognition in our daily lives. It is very difficult to access this valuable information for blind or visually impaired persons, in particular, in unfamiliar environments. With the development of computer vision technology and smart mobile applications, many assistive systems are developed to help blind or visually impaired persons in their daily lives. This chapter focuses on the methods of text reading from natural scene as well as their applications to assist people who are visually impaired. With the research work on accessibility for the disabled, the assistive text reading technique for the blind is implemented in mobile platform, such as smart phone, tablet, and other wearable device. The popularity and interconnection of mobile devices would provide more low-cost and convenient assistance for blind or visually impaired persons.

9.1 Introduction

With the development of computer vision technology and smart mobile applications, many assistive systems are developed to help blind or visually impaired persons in their daily lives. This chapter focuses on the methods of text reading from natural scene as well as their applications to assist people who are visually impaired. With the research work on accessibility for the disabled, the assistive text reading technique for the blind is implemented in mobile platform, such as smart phone, tablet, and other wearable device. The popularity and interconnection of mobile devices would provide more low-cost and convenient assistance for blind or visually impaired persons.

C. Yi
HERE North America, 425 W Randolph St, Chicago, IL 60606, USA
e-mail: gschucai@gmail.com

Y. Tian (✉)
The City College of New York, Convent Avenue at 138th Street,
New York, NY 10031, USA
e-mail: ytian@ccny.cuny.edu

© Springer International Publishing Switzerland 2015
G. Hua and X.-S. Hua (eds.), *Mobile Cloud Visual Media Computing*,
DOI 10.1007/978-3-319-24702-1_9

Of the 314 million visually impaired persons worldwide, 45 million are blind [1]. In the United States, the 2008 National Health Interview Survey (NHIS) reported that an estimated 25.2 million adult Americans (over 8 %) are blind or visually impaired [2]. This number is increasing rapidly as the baby boomer generation ages. With the help of guide cane and guide dog, visually impaired persons perceive surrounding environments by hearing, smell, or touch, so that they are able to discern objects by shape and material, and avoid obstacles in the way-finding process.

However, it is beyond their capabilities to acquire text information from natural scene. Some office buildings and public facilities do provide blind-assistant signage in Braille. However, in most cases, text information in natural scene is prepared for people with normal vision, in the form of printed fonts at a signage board.

Text information serves as an understandable and comprehensive indicator, which plays a significant role in navigation and recognition in our daily lives. It is very difficult to access this valuable information for blind or visually impaired persons, in particular, in unfamiliar environments. However, recent developments in computer vision, digital cameras, and portable computers make it feasible to develop camera-based assistive products to help them. These blind-assistant systems usually combine computer vision technology with other existing commercial products such OCR, GPS systems.

This chapter is organized as follows. Section 9.2 introduces the related work on the requirements of blind users and the available effective methods of scene text extraction. Section 9.3 presents a technical framework of scene text extraction. Section 9.4 describes two blind-assistant prototype systems of text recognition respectively for handheld object recognition and indoor navigation. Section 9.5 introduces blind-assistant system design for accessibility on mobile platform.

9.2 Related Work

A blind-assistant system should be comfortable to wear, portable, efficient, low-cost, and user-friendly. These basic requirements are closely associated with the system design and implementation. Many blind-assistant systems have been developed [3–8]. In general, a blind-assistant system contains three main components: capture, process, and feedback. More descriptions of the blind-assistant system interface design will be presented later in this chapter.

The *capture* component of a blind-assistant system is to help blind user perceive surrounding objects. For example, white cane can be considered as a simple *capture* component. It perceives surrounding objects by touch, and it is portable and easy to hold. In computer vision-based blind-assistant systems, the *capture* component is usually a camera, which can be attached to a wearable device, so that the blind or visually impaired persons can conveniently take it everywhere. To clearly capture surrounding objects in different distances, some systems [9] took multiple cameras with different viewpoints and focuses. In most cases, the cameras are attached to a sunglass [10] or a helmet [6, 11]. Many wearable cameras, such as Autographer [12],

MeCam [13], Looxcie [14], and GoPro [15] have developed for portable photography or entertainment, but they can also be used in blind assistance. The Google-glass [16] may also be used as a basic device to capture data in blind assistance. Recently, RGBD cameras that are able to capture depth information were often used in blind-assistant navigation [17] or indoor scene indexing [18].

The *process* component of a blind-assistance system is to extract valuable information, which can be provided to blind persons to recognize surrounding objects or find their ways to destination. The image/video data captured by cameras provides large amount of information about the surrounding objects in natural scenes, in which text serves as the most straightforward and informative indicators. Thus in this chapter, as one of the main tasks of the *process* component, we will focus on extracting surrounding text information for blind or visually impaired users. Our research group has developed a series of computer vision-based methods for blind people to recognize signage [19] and object labels [20], recognize objects, and clothes patterns [21–23], independently access and navigate unfamiliar environments [9, 24–26]. Tian et al. developed a proof-of-concept computer vision-based way-finding aid for blind people to independently access unfamiliar indoor environments [27]. We also developed several methods and prototype systems [10, 28] to extract text information from natural scenes. Scene text extraction is usually divided into two steps: detection and recognition. Text detection is to find out image regions containing text characters and strings. Text detection algorithms [29–32] were mostly involved in color uniformity, gradient distribution, and edge density of text regions. Text recognition is to transform the image-based text information into readable text codes [33–35]. Text recognition algorithms were mostly based on the design of feature representation for text character recognition, and the combination of vision-based recognition and lexicon-based model for word recognition.

The *feedback* component of a blind-assistant system is to provide the extracted information in an acceptable way to the blind users. The feedback should satisfy several requirements of blind or visually impaired persons who are located in an unfamiliar environment or hold an unfamiliar object. It must be simple, in time, and understandable. A straightforward way of information feedback is indicative speech, which transforms the vision-based information into audio-based information so that the blind or visually impaired persons can hear it. Many systems adopted this scheme [8, 10, 36]. In addition, many sonar-based systems were designed to help blind person avoid obstacles [37–41]. The ultrasound is transmitted and received to measure the distances and directions of possible obstacles that reflect it, and the blind or visually impaired persons can obtain real-time notifications. However, these systems cannot provide vision-based information like text signage. In addition to acoustical feedback, such as audio and speech, some systems designed haptic feedback based on regular vibration of a wearable device. The device used for haptic feedback can be a helmet [11], finger [42], or tongue display unit in the mouth [42–45].

9.3 Scene Text Extraction

In this section, we describe the technical framework of scene text extraction that contains two main steps: text detection and text recognition.

9.3.1 Scene Text Detection

To extract text information from camera-based natural scene images, first, we need to separate the contours or blobs that possibly contain text characters from background outliers. These possible text characters are defined as candidate characters. In our framework, two algorithms are developed to detect candidate characters, which are respectively associated with contours and blobs of text characters.

Candidate Character Detection

A. Contours in Edge Map

Candidate characters normally generate regular and closed contours in the edge map of scene image. Thus a straightforward method of detecting candidate characters is to first generate all object contours in a scene image, and then find out the contours probably generated by scene text characters.

We apply Canny edge detector [46] to acquire the edge map of a natural scene image. In low-level image processing, a contour is defined as a set of connected edge pixels. Figure 9.1 illustrates the detected contours in a natural scene image. Among these contours, some geometrical constraints are defined to detect the contours of candidate characters.

Both Canny edge detection and object contour generation are computationally efficient. However, without predefined constraints like color uniformity to analyze the blobs, the contours of candidate characters would be mixed with the contours of background objects, and it is difficult to distinguish them. A more effective operator is presented in next section to extract candidate characters.

B. Maximum Stable Extremal Region

In addition to contours in specific geometrical constraints, candidate characters and their attachment surfaces are usually painted with uniform color. Thus, we can extract these candidate characters in the form of blobs, which include not only the contour but also torso information.

Maximum stable extremal region (MSER) operator was proposed in [47], which has been used as a blob detection technique for a long time in computer vision field. MSER is defined based on an extension of the definitions of image and set. Let image I be a mapping such that $I : D \subseteq \mathbb{Z}^2 \to S$, where D denotes the set of all pixels in the image, and S is a totally ordered set with reflexive, antisymmetric and transitive

(a)   **(b)**

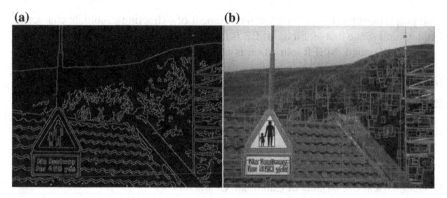

Fig. 9.1 **a** Canny edge map of a scene images. **b** Bounding boxes of object contours in the form of connected edge pixels, obtained from edge map

Fig. 9.2 **a** Canny edge map of a scene images. **b** Bounding boxes of object contours in the form of connected edge pixels, obtained from edge map

properties. It means each pixel in an image is mapped into a value, and each pair of pixels can be in comparison with each other through their respective values. In real applications, this value is defined as pixel gray intensity.

An adjacent relation is defined as A. For two neighboring pixels a_i and a_{i+1}, we have $a_i A a_{i+1}$ if and only if $|I(a_{i+1}) - I(a_i)| \leq Threshold$, where $I(a_i)$ denotes the mapped gray intensity at pixel a_i. Then, an MSER region Q is defined as a contiguous subset of D, such that for each $p, q \in Q$, there is a sequences $p, a_1, a_2, a_3, \ldots, a_n, q$, where $p A a_1, a_1 A a_2, \ldots, a_i A a_{i+1}, \ldots, a_n A q$. Here, A represents the intensity difference and p, q or a_i is in the form of 2-dimensional vector, representing the x-coordinate and y-coordinate of an image pixel. As shown in Fig. 9.2, MSER generates connected components of text characters in a scene image, while edge map only gives the contours of text characters. Further, MSER map filters out the foliage thoroughly.

Since MSER cannot confirm the intensity polarity of text and attachment surface, that is, not able to distinguish white-text-in-black-background from black-text-in-white-background, both text and attachment surface will be extracted as candidate characters in MSER map. However, attachment surface components can be easily removed by defining some geometrical properties. Moreover, MSER has several specific properties compatible with the requirement of extracting candidate characters from natural scene image. First, MSER is invariant to affine transformation of image intensities. Second, MSER extraction is very stable since a region is selected only if its support is nearly the same over a range of thresholds. Third, MSER is scale-invariant and is able to extract candidate characters in multiple scales without any preprocesses of original natural scene image.

MSER extraction is efficient enough to satisfy mobile applications, because its time complexity in the worst case is $O(n)$ where n represents the number of pixels in the image. However, in our experiments, MSER blob detection usually takes about 2–3 times the computational time as contour search in edge map.

C. Geometrical Constraints of Candidate Characters

Not all contours in an edge map and not all blobs generated by MSER operator come from text characters, which also compose that from non-text background outliers.

To remove the non-text background outliers from the set of candidate characters, we define a group of geometrical constraints. In these constraints, a candidate characters C, in the form of either contour or blob, is described by several geometrical properties: $height(.)$, $width(.)$, $coorX(.)$, $coorY(.)$, $area(.)$, and $numInner(.)$, which represent height, width, centroid x-coordinates, centroid y-coordinates, area, and the number of inner candidate characters respectively.

We define a group of geometrical constraints based on above measurements to ensure that the preserved candidate characters are real text characters as possible. Since we will further perform text string layout analysis and text structure modeling to remove false positive candidate characters, the constraints defined in this step are not very strict.

$$height(C) > 15 pixels$$
$$0.3 \leq \frac{width(C)}{height(C)} \leq 1.5$$
$$numInner(C) \leq 4 \tag{9.1}$$
$$\frac{1}{10} \cdot ImageWidth \leq coorX(C) \leq \frac{9}{10} \cdot ImageWidth$$
$$\frac{1}{10} \cdot ImageHeight \leq coorY(C) \leq \frac{9}{10} \cdot ImageHeight$$

The involved geometrical constraints are presented in Eq. (9.1). First of all, the candidate character component cannot be too small, and otherwise we will treat it as background noise. It also means that our whole framework of scene text extraction requires enough resolution of camera-captured scene text image. Second, the aspect ratio of a character should be located in a reasonable range. Under a threshold of aspect ratio, we might also remove some special text characters like 1, but it is very possible to restore this false removal by generating text strings. Third, we define some constraints related to the number of nested candidate character components as presented in [48]. Fourth, we observe that many background outliers obtained from the above partition methods are located at the boundaries of scene images. Thus, the candidate character components whose centroids are located at the $1/10$ boundary of the images are not taken in account in further processes.

The constraints in Eq. (9.1) do not depend on any learning models to decide the parameters as in [29, 49]. Instead, all the involved geometrical constraints are weak conditions, with the preservation of true text characters in higher priority than the removal of false positive background outliers. Therefore, only the obvious background outliers are filtered by the geometrical constraints. The remaining false positive candidate characters will be handled in the extraction of text string.

Text String Detection

A set of candidate character components is created in the form of contours or blobs from an input image. Most candidate characters are not true scene text characters but non-text background objects in uniform color or some portions of an object under uneven illumination. Geometrical constraints as described in last section cannot remove them, so we design more discriminative layout characteristics of scene text from high-level perspective. Text in natural scene mostly appears in the form of words and phrases instead of single characters. It is because words and phrases are more informative text information, while single character usually serves as a sign or symbol. Words and phrases are defined as text strings, and we attempt to find out possible text strings by combining neighboring candidate characters. Therefore, in this chapter, we define a text string as a combination of neighboring candidate characters.

In this section, a method named as adjacent character grouping is presented in [50] to detect text strings among the extracted candidate characters. Text strings in natural scene images usually appear in horizontal alignment and each character in a text string has at least one sibling at adjacent positions. Furthermore, a text character and its siblings in a text string have similar sizes and proper distances. Therefore, the idea of adjacent character grouping is removing the candidate characters that do not have any siblings.

In adjacent character grouping method, the main problem is how to decide whether two candidate characters C_1 and C_2 are sibling characters. According to our observations and statistical analysis of text strings, we define three geometrical constraints as follows:

(1) Considering the approximate horizontal alignment of text strings in most cases, the centroid of candidate character C_1 should be located between the upper-bound and lower-bound of the other candidate character C_2.

(2) Two adjacent characters should not be too far from each other despite the variations of width, so the distance between two connected components should not be greater than T_2 times the width of the wider one.

(3) For text strings aligned approximately horizontally, the difference between y-coordinates of the connected component centroids should not be greater than T_3 times the height of the higher one.

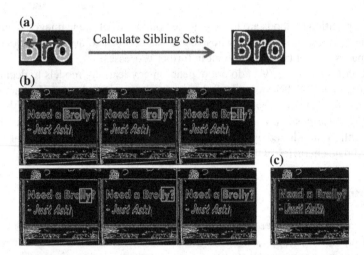

Fig. 9.3 **a** Sibling group of the connected component r where B comes from the *left sibling set* and o comes from the *right sibling set*; **b** Merge the sibling groups into an adjacent character group corresponding to the text string Brolly?; **c** Two detected adjacent character groups marked in *red* and *green* respectively [50]

In our applications, we set the thresholds $T_1 = 0.5$, $T_2 = 3$, $T_3 = 0.5$. For each candidate character C_i, a sibling set $S(C_i)$ is generated, where $1 \leq i \leq |\mathbb{C}|$ and $|\mathbb{C}|$ represents the number of candidate characters obtained from image partition.

First, an empty sibling set is initialized as $S(C_i) := \phi$. We transverse all candidate characters except C_i itself. If a candidate character C_i' satisfies all above constraints with C_i, we add it into the sibling set as $S(C_i) := S(C_i) \cup \{C_i'\}$. Second, all the sibling sets compose a set of adjacent groups $\Lambda = \{A_i | A_i := S(C_i)\}$, where a sibling set is initialized to be adjacent group A. Third, the set of adjacent groups is iteratively updated by merging the overlapping adjacent groups. An adjacent group is a group of candidate character components that are probably character members of a text string. As Eq. (9.2), if two adjacent groups A_i and A_j in Λ have intersection, they will be merged into one adjacent group. This merging operation is iteratively repeated until no overlapping adjacent groups exist.

In the resulting set of adjacent groups, each adjacent group A_i is a set of candidate characters in approximate horizontal alignment, which will be regarded as a text string, as shown in Fig. 9.3. Then, a bounding box is generated for each adjacent group to represent the region of a localized text string in natural scene image.

$$\forall A_i, A_j \in \Lambda, \quad \text{if} \quad A_i \cap A_j \neq \phi,$$
$$\text{then} \quad A_i := A_i \cup A_j \quad \text{and} \quad A_j := \phi \tag{9.2}$$

9.3.2 Scene Text Recognition

The extraction of candidate character and text string is able to efficiently localize most text strings from natural scene image. However, to acquire valuable text information for blind or visually impaired persons, there are still two problems to be solved. First, above steps of text character and string extraction are pixel-based processing and statistic-based parameter setting, and they will bring in many false text strings from the natural scene image with complex background. Second, for true text strings, a method or off-the-shelf system is required to recognize the text information in it, which transforms the image-based text information into readable text codes. To solve these two problems, feature representations related to inner text structure are designed in two different ways.

Text String Classification

In the first problem of scene text recognition, feature representation is proposed to model structural insights of text characters and strings. At first, each text string, localized by above steps in last section, is defined as a sample. It may be a positive sample, which means this region truly contains text information. It may also be a negative sample, which means that this region is generated by background outliers, e.g., some texture similar to text character, such as bricks, window grids and foliage, and some objects rendered by specific illumination change, as shown in Fig. 9.4. To distinguish text from non-text outlier, we design text structure-related feature representations by using Haar-like block patterns and feature maps. Figure 9.5 illustrates the flowchart of the text string classification process.

To extract structural information from these samples, Haar-like filters are designed in the form of block patterns, as shown in Fig. 9.6. Each block pattern consists of white regions and gray regions in specific ratio. It will be resized into the same size as a sample, and used as a mask. Then specific calculation metrics are defined based on these block patterns for extracting structural features.

A simple idea of feature extraction is to apply these block patterns directly to the text string samples, and calculate Haar-like features from intensity values of the

Fig. 9.4 Some examples of text string samples in the form of image patches

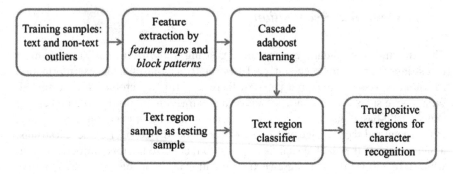

Fig. 9.5 Diagram of the proposed Adaboost learning-based text string classification algorithm

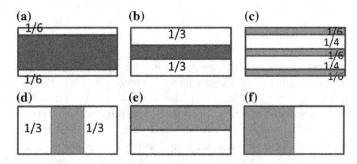

Fig. 9.6 Some examples of Haar-like block patterns to extract text structural features. Features are obtained by the absolute value of mean pixel values in *white regions* minus those in *black regions*

image patches. However, unlike face detection [51], the sole intensity values cannot completely represent structure of text strings.

To model text structure, we design a set of feature maps for the samples, in which the physical meaning of each pixel is transformed from intensity value to some measurements related to text structure. The structure-related measurements are mostly based on gradient, edge density, and stroke. The involved feature maps include gradient, stroke width, stroke orientation, and edge density [10].

In feature map of a text string sample, each pixel is transformed from intensity to some measurements related to text structure. Each pixel reflects text structural configuration from a local perspective. By tuning the parameters of generating feature maps under a design scheme, we can obtain multiple feature maps. In our framework, we design 3 gradient maps, 2 stroke width maps, 14 stroke orientation maps, and 1 edge distribution map, to which 6 Haar-like block patterns are applied for calculating feature values. Each combination of a feature map, a block pattern and a calculation scheme [28] is developed into a weak classifier in Adaboost learning model. By using the localized regions in above text detection steps as training samples, Adaboost learning model selects an optimized subset of weak classifiers and weighted combine them to effectively classify text from non-text outlier. This classifier is actually an optimized combination of a subset of weak classifiers.

Scene Text Character Recognition

In the second problem of scene text recognition is to transform image-based text information into readable text codes. A straightforward way is to apply off-the-shelf optical character recognition (OCR) software [52–54] to the text strings. However, most OCR systems are designed for scan documents or hand-written recognition, and they are not robust to background interference and various text patterns. Thus, we also propose a feature representation for recognizing total of 62 categories of scene text characters (STCs), which include 10 digits (0–9) and 26 English letters in both upper (A–Z) and lower cases (a–z).

The most significant role in STC recognition is to work out a multi-class classifier to predict the category of a given STC. In our system, Chars74K [55] dataset is adopted to train this multi-class classifier. Figure 9.7 illustrates some examples of STCs cropped from text strings. We observe that the STCs have irregular patterns and similar structure to each other.

A feature representation is designed to model the representative structure of each of the 62 STC categories and the discriminative structure between STC categories. Each STC sample is mapped into its feature representation in the form of a vector. Then, it is input into SVM learning model to obtain the multi-class classifier. Figure 9.8 demonstrates the whole process of STC recognition.

First, low-level features are extracted from STC image patches to describe appearance and structure of STCs from all 62 STC categories. Through performance evaluations of 6 state-of-the-art low-level feature descriptors [56], our framework selects

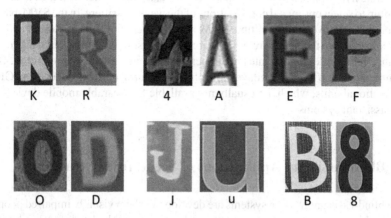

Fig. 9.7 Some examples of STCs cropped from text strings. Most STCs have similar structure to another counterpart

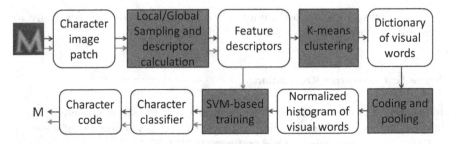

Fig. 9.8 Some examples of STCs cropped from text strings. Most STCs have similar structure to another counterpart

Histogram of oriented gradient [57] descriptor applied to the key points sampled from STC image patches.

Second, key-point sampling and feature coding/pooling play a significant role. We made a comparative study of several methods of key-point sampling and schemes of feature coding/pooling [56]. In dense sampling, soft-assignment coding and max pooling scheme obtain the best performance. However, the global sampling obtains even better performance, which uses the whole character patch as a key-point neighborhood window to extract features. In global sampling, key-point detection, coding, and pooling process are all skipped to largely reduce information loss.

Third, STC recognition depends on SVM-based training and testing over the STC samples. While the learning process in text string classification is to select the representative combinations of feature maps, Haar-like block patterns and calculation schemes to distinguish text from non-text, the learning process in STC prediction treats the feature representation vector of an STC sample as a point in feature space, which describes the STC structure. Thus, we would adopt SVM learning model [58] to generate hyper-planes in feature space as STC classifier, rather than the Adaboost algorithm to select optimized combinations of the weak classifiers. In the SVM-based learning process, we adopt multiple SVM kernels, including Linear Kernel and χ^2 Kernel, to evaluate the feature representations of STC structure. In recent work, deep learning framework demonstrates better performance in scene text recognition. But the implementation of the multilayer convolutional neutral network depends on GPU computational units, which are usually not available for wearable mobile devices in blind-assistant systems.

9.4 Blind-Assistant Applications of Scene Text Extraction

Many blind-assistant reading systems are developed to help visually impaired people reading object bar code or documents through some wearable devices. A big limitation is that it is very hard for blind users to find the position of the bar code and to correctly point the bar code reader at the bar code.

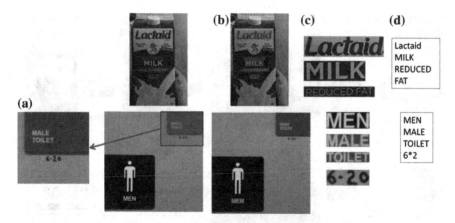

Fig. 9.9 Two examples of text extraction by the prototype system from camera-captured images. *Top* a milk box; *Bottom* a men bathroom signage. **a** Camera-captured images; **b** localized text strings (marked in *blue*); **c** text strings cropped from image; **d** text codes recognized by OCR [10]

To assist blind or visually impaired people to read text from handheld objects, a camera-based text reading prototype is developed to track the object of interest within the camera view and extract print text information from the object label. Our framework of scene text extraction can effectively handle complex background and multiple text patterns, and obtain text information from both hand-held objects and nearby signage, as shown in Fig. 9.9. Two corresponding blind-assistant applications are developed on the basis of scene text extraction.

9.4.1 Reading Text Labels for Hand-Held Object Recognition

In most assistive reading systems, users have to position the object of interest within the center of the cameras view. To ensure the handheld object be captured within the camera view, we use a wide-angle camera to accommodate users with only approximate aim. However, this wide-angle camera will also capture many other text objects (for example, while shopping at a supermarket). To extract the handheld object from the camera image, we develop a motion-based scheme to acquire a region of interest (ROI) of the object by asking the blind user shakes the object for a couple of seconds. This scheme is based on background subtraction-based motion detection [27]. Then we perform scene text extraction from only this ROI, including detecting text strings and recognizing text codes. In the end, the recognized text codes are output to blind users in audio or speech. To present how our prototype system works, a flowchart is presented in Fig. 9.10.

A prototype system of scene text extraction is designed and implemented in PC platform and Mobile platform [27, 59]. This system consists of three main components: scene capture, data processing, and audio output. The scene capture component

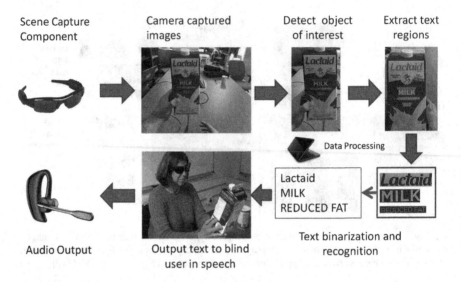

Fig. 9.10 Flowchart of prototype system to read text from handheld objects for blind users [10]

collects surrounding scenes or objects and generates high-quality image frames. The data processing component is used for deploying our proposed framework of scene text extraction. The audio output component is to inform the blind user of recognized text codes. This simple hardware configuration proves the portability of the assistive text reading system. The prototype system has been used to assist blind or visually impaired people to recognize handheld object as described, as shown in Fig. 9.11.

To evaluate the performance of hand-held object recognition system, following the Human Subjects Institutional Review Board approval, we recruited 10 blind persons to collect a dataset of reading text on handheld objects. The blind user wore a camera attached on sunglasses to capture images of the objects in his/her hand, as illustrated in Fig. 9.11. The resolution of the captured image is 960×720. There were 14 testing objects for each person, including grocery boxes, medicine bottles, books, etc. They

Fig. 9.11 Prototype system assists blind user read text information from handheld objects, including the detected text strings in cyan and the recognized text codes

were required to keep head (where the camera is fixed) stationary for a few seconds and subsequently shake the object for an additional couple of seconds to allow our system detect the object of interest based on the motion. Then, the user rotated each object several times to ensure the main text on the object are exposed and captured. We manually extracted 116 captured images and labeled 312 text regions of object labels.

In our evaluations, a region is correctly detected if the ratio of the overlapping area of a detected text region and its ground truth region is no less than 3/4. Experiments demonstrate that 225 of the 312 ground truth text regions are correctly detected by our localization algorithm. Some examples of extracted scene text from handheld objects are illustrated in Fig. 9.12, proving that our proposed framework is suitable for real applications. To further improve the accuracy of text detection and recognition, the practical system would restrict the range of possible recognized words by a prior dictionary of common words that are frequently printed in handheld objects. The extracted text results are output by audio only if it has close edit distance to some word in the dictionary.

Currently, the system efficiency mainly depends on the efficiency of scene text extraction in each image or video frame. However, through the design of parallel processing for text extraction and device input/output, the efficiency of this assistant reading system can be further improved. That is, speech output of recognized text in the current frame and localization of text strings in the next image are performed simultaneously.

9.4.2 Reading Text Signage for Indoor Navigation

A blind-assistant prototype system is designed for hand-held object recognition in last section. It can be further extended to indoor navigation, by extracting indicative information from surrounding text signage in indoor environment. In most cases, indoor navigation is to guide blind users to a targeted destination such as an office, a restroom, or an elevator entrance. All of them have doors by a signage with a room name or a room number. The people with normal vision can refer a floor plan map to find their ways, but blind or visually impaired people cannot acquire this information. Thus our proposed prototype system can perceive their current location and generate a proper path from current location to their destination. The hardware of this prototype system is similar to the system of handheld object recognition in last section, including a wearable camera, a process unit, and audio output device. However, the system implements indoor navigation by adding the door detection.

In indoor environments, doors, and elevators serve as important landmarks and transition points for way finding. They also provide entrance and exit information. Thus, an effective door detection method plays an important role in indoor navigation. We develop the vision-based door detection method [60] to localize doors for blind users. This method depends on a very general geometric door model, describing the general and stable features of a door frame edges and corners, as shown in Fig. 9.13.

(a)

(b)

Fig. 9.12 **a** Some results of text detection on the blind user-captured dataset, where localized text regions are marked in *blue*. **b** Two groups of enlarged text regions, binarized text regions, and word recognition results from *top* to *bottom* [10]

Our method can handle complex background objects and distinguish doors from other door-like shapes such as bookshelves. After detecting doors, scene text extraction is performed within the door region or its immediately neighboring region to obtain text information related to room names and room numbers, as shown in Fig. 9.14. Both the localization and navigation processes are based on accurate scene text extraction. Fortunately, the indoor environment mostly does not contain too much background interferences, and the text signage has relatively fixed pattern, e.g., room number contains only digits in print format, and restroom is usually marked by MEN, WOMEN, or RESTROOM. Thus, the proposed scene text extraction will adapt its parameters to this indoor navigation application.

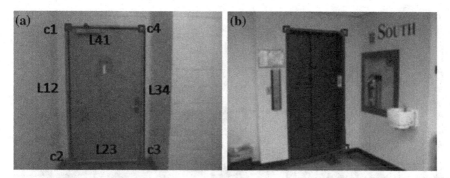

Fig. 9.13 a Edges and corners are used for door detection. **b** Door detection under cluttered background

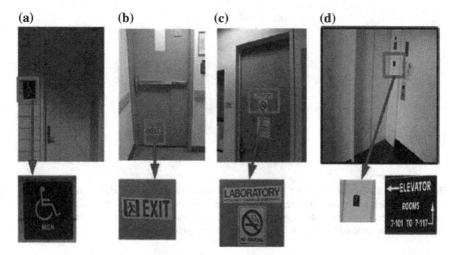

Fig. 9.14 Indoor objects (*top row*) and their associated text information (*bottom row*): **a** a bathroom, **b** an exit, **c** a lab room, **d** an elevator. Text information (*bottom row*) can be extracted to help blind or visually impaired persons find their ways [24]

By using the extracted information from text signage, blind or visually impaired person can better perceive his/her current location and surrounding environment. Furthermore, most buildings have floor plan maps as tourist guide. A floor plan map contains room numbers and relative locations of the offices, restrooms, and elevator entrances. The data of floor plan map can be combined with the extracted text information to figure out blind-assistant navigation prototype in unfamiliar buildings.

A prototype design of floor plan-based way-finding system can be found in [9]. A floor plan map is first parsed into a graph, in which a room is defined as a node (see Fig. 9.15). Each pair of nodes is connected, and an available path of way finding is defined for each connection. For example, in Fig. 9.15c, the yellow line corresponds to a proper path marked in yellow in Fig. 9.15b from room 632 to room 623. According

(a)   (b)

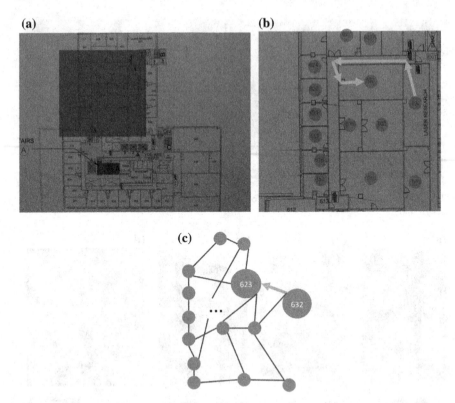

(c)

Fig. 9.15 a An example of a floor plan of our building, where the *blue shaded region* will be analyzed. **b** Each room number is regarded as a node, and the path from room 632 to room 623 is marked in *yellow*. **c** The abstract graph of the floor plan map, where the *yellow line* indicates a connection from node 632 to node 623, corresponding the *yellow path* in (**b**)

to the length and the number of turning corners of the path, a cost value is assigned to its corresponding connection in the graph. In this weighted graph, the current location of a blind user is regarded as a starting point while his/her destination is regarded as an ending point. In the navigation process, our system finds out a path with minimum cost value and then generates the corresponding path to destination based on the floor plan map.

9.5 Blind-Assistant System Interface Design

The interface design always plays a significant role in the development a blind-assistant system. A well-developed system should provide safe, comfortable, and efficient services that are compatible with the daily life of blind or visually impaired persons. Our research group invited 10 visually impaired persons to survey user interface preference [61]. These 10 persons are all well educated, employed (or retired after employment), and familiar with blind-assistant technology. Through a questionnaire, we collect their advices and requirements of blind-assistant systems. The associated problems and solutions of interface design will be presented in this section according to the three main components of blind-assistant system as described in Sect. 9.2, which are *capture*, *process* and *feedback*.

The *capture* component of a compute vision-based blind-assistant system is normally a wearable camera, which is attached to a sunglass, helmet, kneepad, or wrist. These wearable cameras should satisfy specific requirements of blind or visually impaired persons. First, they should be easy and comfortable to put on and take off. Although the wearable devices are light and compatible with human face or body, almost all the users will choose to take them off if not necessary. Second, they should be easy to control. Based on our survey about this issue, most blind or visually impaired persons prefer button control rather than voice recognition, because the latter one is not reliable in noisy situations. Third, they should be able to capture relatively high-quality images or videos for information retrieval. Thus the camera focus should be adaptive to most indoor environments. It is difficult for blind or visually impaired persons to stand still for waiting for the calibration process because they cannot know the quality of the image. In addition, our group designed a method of selecting high-quality frames from blind captured videos [62].

The *process* component of a blind-assistant system is the process unit of the technical framework and algorithm implementation. Although it is not directly related to the user interface design, it is very important to reduce the computational complexity of the technical algorithms and optimize the codes to ensure the efficiency of the whole system for real-time processing as well as to reduce the power consumption of the processing unit. For example, the framework should be able to save and search the historical data of blind-assistant recognition or navigation in specific buildings or scenes. Since a system belongs to one specific blind user, he/she would be able to directly obtain previous results when entering the same building or a scene again. Also the framework should be developed into a query-based system, rather than a notification-based system. It means that the system will not generate continuous notifications but keep sleep until the user wakes it. When the blind or visually impaired persons did not need the help of the system, the notifications would become useless noise.

About the *feedback* component of a blind-assistant system, first, the feedback should be simple, so that the users are able to obtain the most informative feedback within the shortest time. For example, in object recognition, it should adopt only two or three common-use words to describe an object or its main characteristic. Second, the feedback should be in time, that is, neither too early nor too late, so that the users are able to make decisions at the reasonable time window. Third, the feedback should be understandable. For example, it is improper to say a door is located 3 m in front with 10-degree deviation to the right, because the blind or visually impaired persons cannot measure the distance and orientations in an unfamiliar environment. It would be much better to navigation them to be close enough to the object and then tell them use their hands or white canes to touch it. The blind or visually impaired persons prefer speech communication with the system rather than the haptic feedback such as vibration. In addition, the feedback from users should be included in the *process* component.

9.6 Conclusions and Discussions

In this chapter, we focus on assistive text reading from natural scenes since text signage plays an important role in blind-assistant recognition and navigation applications. However, scene text extraction is still an open research topic to be addressed. It is a challenging task to extract text information from natural scene images for several reasons. First, the frequency of occurrence of text information in natural scene image is usually very low, and text information is always buried under all kinds of non-text outliers in cluttered background of natural scenes. Thus background removal plays a significant role in text detection. Second, even though image regions containing text characters are detected from complex background, current optical character recognition (OCR) systems do not work well on the recognition of scene text, because they are mostly designed for scan documents. More effective feature representations and more robust models are required to improve the performance of scene text recognition. Unlike the text in scan documents, scene text usually appears in multiple colors, fonts, sizes and orientations.

In Sect. 9.2, we have reviewed several computer vision-based blind-assistant applications, including the technical framework, user interface design, and prototype systems. We described a framework of scene text extraction in Sect. 9.3. First edge-based contour and MSER-based connected components are extracted as candidate characters while removing large amount of non-text background outliers, and then text string alignment is applied to filter out the false positive candidate characters. Next, feature representations are designed to describe text structure, on the basis of gradient distribution, stroke width and orientation, edge density, and color uniformity, to remove false text strings. At last, feature representations are designed to recognize each text character of the text strings, on the basis of HOG descriptor.

The proposed framework of scene text extraction is involved in two blind-assistant applications in Sect. 9.4, handheld object recognition and indoor navigation. In these applications, scene text extraction is transplanted into mobile platforms, and combined with other techniques. In a practical blind-assistant system, the user interface design is very important as well as the algorithm framework. In our design, a blind-assistant system consists of three components, which are capture, process, and feedback. According to the survey of blind or visually impaired persons who are familiar with blind-assistant technology, we summarize the requirements of the three components respectively in Sect. 9.5.

In future, we will further improve the accuracy of scene text extraction algorithm, making it adaptive to more complex environments for more reliable practical application. Also we will make the algorithms more compatible with mobile applications. Furthermore, more interactions with blind or visually impaired people will be performed to better understand their requirements and design more robust and user friendly blind-assistant interface.

Acknowledgments This work was supported in part by NSF grants EFRI-1137172, IIP-1343402, and FHWA grant DTFH61-12-H-00002.

References

1. 10 facts about blindness and visual impairment, World Health Organization: Blindness and Visual Impairment (2009)
2. Advance Data Reports from the National Health Interview Survey. http://www.cdc.gov/nchs/nhis/nhis_ad.htm (2008)
3. Dakopoulos, D., Bourbakis, N.G.: Wearable obstacle avoidance electronic travel aids for blind: a survey. IEEE Trans. Syst. Man Cybern. Part C-Appl. Rev. **40**, 2535 (2010)
4. Yi, C., Flores, R., Chincha, R., Tian, Y.: Finding objects for assisting blind people. Netw. Model. Anal. Health Inf. Bioinform. **2**(2), 71–79 (2013)
5. Schauerte, B., Martinez, M., Constantinescu, A., Stiefelhagen, R.: An assistive vision system for the blind that helps find lost things. In: ICCHP (2012)
6. Caperna, S., Cheng, C., et al.: A navigation and object location device for the blind. Techical report, University of Maryland (2009)
7. Hub, A., Diepstraten, J., Ertl, T.: Design and development of an indoor navigation and object identification system for the blind. In: Proceedings of the ACM SIGACCESS Conference on Computer and Accessibility (2004)
8. Bigham, J., Jayant, C., Miller, A., White, B., Yeh, T.: VizWiz: LocateIt enabling blind people to locate objects in their environments. In: Proceedings of the CVPR Workshop Computer Vision Applications for the Visually Impaired (2010)
9. Joseph, S., Zhang, X., Dryanovski, I., Xiao, J., Yi, C., Tian, Y.: Semantic indoor navigation with a blind-user oriented augmented reality. In: IEEE International Conference on Systems, Man, and Cybernetics (2013)
10. Yi, C., Tian, Y., Arditi, A.: Portable camera-based assistive text and product label reading from hand-held objects for blind persons. IEEE/ASME Trans. Mechatron. **19**(3), 808–817. http://dx.doi.org/10.1109/TMECH.2013.2261083 (2014)
11. Mann, S., Huang, J., Janzen, R., Lo, R., Rampersad, V., Chen, A., Doha, T.: Blind naviation with a wearable range camera and vibrotactile helmet. In: ACM-MM (2011)
12. Autographer. http://www.autographer.com/home
13. MeCam. http://www.mecam.me/
14. Looxcie. http://www.looxcie.com/
15. GoPro. http://www.gopro.com
16. Google glass. https://www.google.com/glass/start (2014)
17. Lee, Y.H., Medioni, G.: A RGB-D camera based navigation for the visually impaired. In: RGB-D: Advanced Reasoning with Depth Camera Workshop (2011)
18. Wang, Z., Liu, H., Wang, X., Qian, Y.: Segment and Label Indoor Scene Based on RGB-D for the Visually Impaired, Multimedia Modeling. Lecture Notes in Computer Science, vol. 8325, pp. 449–460. Springer, New York (2014)
19. Wang, S., Yi, C., Tian, Y.: Signage detection and recognition for blind persons to access unfamiliar environments. J. Comput. Vis. Image Process. **2**(2) (2012)
20. Ye, Z., Yi, C., Tian, Y.: Reading labels of cylinder objects for blind persons. In: IEEE International Conference on Multimedia and Expo (ICME) (2013)
21. Yuan, S., Tian, Y., Arditi, A.: Clothing matching for visually impaired persons. Technol. Disabil. **23**, 75–85 (2011)

22. Hasanuzzaman, F., Yang, X., Tian, Y.: Robust and effective component-based banknote recognition for the blind. IEEE Trans. Syst. Man Cybern.-Part C: Appl. Rev. **42**, 1021–1030 (2012)
23. Yang, X., Yuan, S., Tian, Y.: Assistive clothing pattern recognition for visually impaired people. IEEE Trans. Hum.-Mach. Syst. **44**(2), 234–243 (2014)
24. Tian, Y., Yang, X., Yi, C., Arditi, A.: Toward a computer vision-based wayfinding aid for blind persons to access unfamiliar indoor environments. Mach. Vis. Appl. **24**, 521–535 (2012)
25. Pan, H., Yi, C., Tian, Y.: A primary travelling assistant system of bus detection and recognition for visually impaired people. In: IEEE Workshop on Multimodal and Alternative Perception for Visually Impaired People (MAP4VIP), in conjunction with ICME (2013)
26. Wang, S., Pan, H., Zhang, C., Tian, Y.: RGB-D image-based detection of stairs, pedestrian crosswalks and traffic signs. J. Vis. Commun. Image Represent. (JVCIR) **25**, 263–272 (2014). http://dx.doi.org/10.1016/j.jvcir.2013.11.005
27. Tian, Y., Senior, A., Lu, M.: Robust and efficient foreground analysis in complex surveillance videos. Mach. Vis. Appl. **23**(5), 967–983 (2012)
28. Yi, C., Tian, Y.: Assistive text reading from complex background for blind persons. In: The 4th International Workshop on Camera-Based Document Analysis and Recognition (CBDAR) (2011)
29. Yao, C., Bai, X., Liu, W., Ma, Y., Tu, Z.: Detecting text of arbitrary orientations in natural images. In: IEEE Conference on Computer Vision and Pattern Recognition (2012)
30. Epshtein, B., Ofek, E., Wexler, Y.: Detecting text in natural scene with stroke width transform. In: IEEE Conference on Computer Vision and Pattern Recognition (2010)
31. Nikolaou, N., Papamarkos, N.: Color reduction for complex document images. Int. J. Imaging Syst. Technol. **19**, 14–26 (2009)
32. Phan, T., Shivakumara, P., Tan, C.: A Laplacian method for video text detection. In: International Conference on Document Analysis and Recognition, pp. 66–70 (2009)
33. Shi, C., Wang, C., Xiao, B., Zhang, Y., Gao, S., Zhang, Z.: Scene text recognition using part-based tree-structured character detection. In: IEEE Conference on Computer Vision and Pattern Recognition, pp. 2961–2968 (2013)
34. Weinman, J., Learned-Miller, E., Hanson, A.: Scene text recognition using similarity and a lexicon with sparse belief propagation. IEEE Trans. Pattern Anal. Mach. Intell. **31**(10), 1733–1746 (2009)
35. Mishra, A., Alahari, K., Jawahar, C.: Top-down and bottom-up cues for scene text recognition. In: IEEE Conference on Computer Vision and Pattern Recognition (2011)
36. Seeing with Sound The vOICe. http://www.seeingwithdound.com/
37. Bousbia-Salah, M., Redjati, A., Fezari, M., Bettayeb, M.: An ultrasonic navigation system for blind people. In: IEEE International Conference on Signal Processing and Communications (ICSPC), pp. 1003–1006 (2007)
38. Kao, G.: FM sonar modeling for navigation. Technical report, Department of Engineering Science, University of Oxford (1996)
39. Kuc, R.: A sonar aid to enhance spatial perception of the blind: engineering design and evaluation. IEEE Trans. Biomed. Eng. **49**(10), 1173–1180 (2002)
40. Laurent, B., Christian, T.: A sonar system modeled after spatial hearing and echo locating bats for blind mobility aid. Int. J. Phys. Sci. **2**(4), 104–111 (2007)
41. Morland, C., Mountain, D.: Design of a sonar system for visually impaired humans. In: The 14th International Conference on Auditory Display, June 2008
42. Velazquez, R.: Wearble assistive devices for the blind, Chapter 17. In: Lay-Ekuakille, A., Mukhopadhyay, S.C. (eds.) Wearable and Autonomous Biomedical Devices and Systems for Smart Environment: Issues and Characterization. LNEE, vol. 75, pp. 331–349. Springer, New York (2010)
43. BrainPort lets you see with your tongue, might actually make it to market. http://www.engadget.com/2009/08/14/brainport-lets-you-see-with-your-tongue-might-actually-make-it/
44. Chebat, D.R., Rainville, C., Kupers, R., Ptito, M.: Tactile visual acuity of the tongue in early blind individuals. NeuroReport **18**(18), 1901–1904 (2007)

45. Khoo, W., Knapp, J., Palmer, F., Ro, T., Zhu, Z.: Designing and testing wearable range-vibrotactile devices. J. Assist. Technol. **7**, 102–117 (2013)
46. Canny, J.: A computational approach to edge detection. IEEE Trans. Pattern Anal. Mach. Intell. **PAMI-8**, 679–698 (1986)
47. Matas, J., Chum, O., Urban, M., Pajdla, T.: Robust wide baseline stereo from maximally stable extremal regions. In: British Machine Vision Conference, pp. 384–396 (2002)
48. Kasar, T., Kumar, J., Ramakrishnan, A.: Font and background color independent text binarization. In: Camera-Based Documentation Analysis and Recognition, pp. 3–9 (2007)
49. Neumann, L., Matas, J.: A method for text localization and detection. In: Asian Conference on Computer Vision (2010)
50. Yi, C., Tian, Y.: Text string detection from natural scenes by structure-based partition and grouping. IEEE Trans. Image Process. **20**(9), 2594–2605 (2011)
51. Viola, P., Jones, M.: Robust real-time face detection. Int. J. Comput. Vis. **57**, 137–154 (2004)
52. Nuance. Nuance Omnipage. http://www.nuance.com/for-business/by-product/omnipage/index.htm
53. Abbyy. http://finereader.abbyy.com/
54. Smith, R.: An overview of the Tesseract OCR engine. In: International Conference on Document Analysis and Recognition (2007)
55. de-Campos, T., Babu, B., Varma, M.: Character recognition in natural images. In: International Conference on Computer Vision Theory and Applications (2009)
56. Yi, C., Yang, X., Tian, Y.: Feature representations for scene text character recognition: a comparative study. In: International Conference on Document Analysis and Recognition (2013)
57. Dalal, N., Triggs, B.: Histogram of oriented gradients for human detection. In: Proceedings of IEEE Conference on Computer Vision and Pattern Recognition (2005)
58. Burges, C.J.C.: A tutorial on support vector machine for pattern recognition. Data Min. Knowl. Discov. **2**, 121–167 (1998)
59. Yi, C., Tian, Y.: Scene text recognition in mobile applications by character descriptor and structure configuration. IEEE Trans. Image Process. **23**(7), 2972–2982 (2014)
60. Yang, X., Tian, Y.: Robust door detection in unfamiliar environments by combining edge and corner features. In: IEEE Conference on Computer Vision and Pattern Recognition Workshop on Computer Vision Applications for Visual Impaired (2010)
61. Arditi, A., Tian, Y.: User interface preferences in the design of a camera-based navigation and wayfinding aid. J. Vis. Impair. Blind. **107**(2), 118–129 (2013)
62. Tian, L., Yi, C., Tian, Y.: Detecting good quality frames in videos captured by a wearable camera for blind navigation. In: IEEE Conference on Bioinformatics and Biomedicine, pp. 334–337 (2013)

Chapter 10
Mobile Image Search: Challenges and Methods

Xin Yang and K.T. Tim Cheng

Abstract The proliferation of camera-equipped mobile devices with enhanced mobile computing power and network connectivity results in a rising demand for mobile image search. Although image search has been studied extensively over the last few decades, most existing solutions, developed for desktops and server platforms, are not suitable for mobile devices. In this chapter, we provide an overview of challenging issues unique in mobile search scenarios and present several techniques addressing these challenges. Specifically, we focus the discussion on: (1) robust, distinctive, and fast feature extraction on mobile devices, (2) compact indexing structure for efficient feature matching, and (3) multimodel context-aware data fusion for improving performance of mobile image search.

10.1 Introduction

Mobile devices such as smartphones and tablets have experienced phenomenal growth. Their computing power has grown enormously and the connectivity of smartphones has also gone through rapid evolution. A wide range of radios including cellular broadband, Wi-Fi, Bluetooth, and NFC available in today's smartphones enable users to communicate with other devices, interact with the Internet, and exchange their data with and running their computing tasks in the clouds. The abundance of camera-equipped mobile devices and low-latency data networks has led to an increasing demand for mobile image search. A mobile image search system, which has the ability to identify objects in a picture and use the recognized object as a starting point for search (often referred to as 'query-by-image'), can support a wide range

X. Yang (✉)
Department of Electronics and Information Engineering, Huazhong University
of Science and Technology, Wuhan 430074, Hubei, China
e-mail: xinyang@umail.ucsb.edu

K.T.T. Cheng
Department of Electrical and Computer Engineering, University of California,
Santa Barbara, CA 93106, USA
e-mail: timcheng@ece.ucsb.edu

© Springer International Publishing Switzerland 2015
G. Hua and X.-S. Hua (eds.), *Mobile Cloud Visual Media Computing*,
DOI 10.1007/978-3-319-24702-1_10

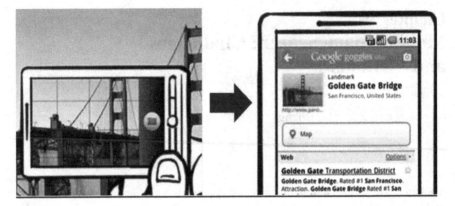

Fig. 10.1 An example of a search of a famous landmark on mobile devices (*Source* Google Goggles.)

of mobile applications. For instance, a user can take a picture of a famous landmark to search for information about it (as shown in Fig. 10.1), a picture of a product's barcode or a book cover to search for online stores selling the product/book, a picture of a movie poster to view reviews or to find tickets at nearby theatres, or a picture of a restaurant menu in French for translation to English. Such a query-by-image capability allows users to search for items without typing any text. For its image-based translation capability, the app recognizes printed text and uses optical character recognition (OCR) to produce a snippet and then translate it into another language.

Image search has been studied extensively for several decades. To improve scalability, efficiency, and accuracy, the three key performance metrics of image search, a number of algorithms for image representation and indexing have been developed [1–3]. Most of the existing solutions are based on and optimized for the laptop, desktop, and server platforms and the unique challenges and opportunities presented by a mobile scenario have not been thoroughly analyzed. In the following, we first present a general pipeline for image search, and then we discuss the main challenges for image search on mobile devices. Then, we present some existing solutions and finally conclude the chapter by pointing out some promising directions for mobile image search.

10.2 Pipeline

A conventional image search pipeline (Fig. 10.2) consists of two phases: (1) offline database construction and (2) online image search. In the offline phase, feature extraction is performed for every database image. An indexing structure which encodes feature descriptors of all database images is constructed. Popular indexing methods for efficient and scalable image search include locality sensitive hashing (LSH) and

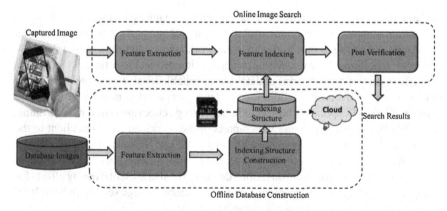

Fig. 10.2 A general pipeline for image search on mobile devices

bag-of-words (BOW) model. More details about these two methods will be provided in Sect. 10.4. In the online search phase, features of a captured image are first extracted, each of which is then used to query the database using an indexing structure for finding a matching feature in the database. The database image which has the most matching features with the capture image is considered as candidate targets. Postverification (using methods such as RANdom SAmple Consensus, RANSAC, [4]) and PROgressive Sample Consensus (PROSAC) [5] is then conducted among candidate images to find the most relevant images to the query image.

The performance of feature extraction and indexing algorithms greatly affect the user experience of mobile image search apps. Ideally, we demand (1) highly robust and distinctive image features which can provide good search accuracy even for large databases and meanwhile can be extracted efficiently on mobile devices, and (2) a compact indexing structure which can be stored on mobile devices in order to avoid network latency for accessing data on a server. However, each of these goals remains challenging in mobile scenarios despite advances in image search algorithms as well as mobile hardware. For example, mobile CPUs are still not fast enough to achieve real-time performance for compute-intensive image processing operations, such as feature extraction. Popular feature extraction algorithms (e.g., SIFT [6], which is widely used for image search) require a large amount of floating point operations, which is slow to compute on mobile CPUs. In addition, limited memory space of mobile embedded system (i.e., 1–2 GB, shared by all apps and the OS, for today's smartphones and tablets) could be a limiting factor when extracting features for an image search. This is because feature extraction such as SIFT often requires large sets of intermediate data to be stored in memory as analysis is performed sequentially. The total amount of memory usage of each stage grows linearly with the size of the original image. For moderate- to high-resolution images, this process could easily exhaust memory resources. Limited storage space of mobile devices also prohibits indexing structure of a large database from being stored locally on a mobile device. As a result, most existing systems employ a client–server architecture. That is, sending the captured image or processed image data (e.g., image features) to a server (or a cloud) via Internet and performing feature indexing and post verification on the server side. The client–server mode may suffer from network latency and thus cannot meet the efficiency requirement for image search apps which demand real-time performance. In practice, according to the size of databases, available local storage and computing resources, and performance requirements, developers need to make decisions for a number of issues to optimize the user experience (e.g., choosing different algorithms, offloading different amount and which parts of the workload from the client to the server side, etc.). In the following, we first elaborate key challenges in mobile image search. In Sect. 10.4, we present some potential solutions addressing the challenges in feature extraction and indexing on mobile devices. We also present existing efforts for fusing multimodel context-aware information for mobile image search. In Sect. 10.5, we conclude the paper and discuss some future work.

10.3 Challenges

Mobile devices differ from general computing environments in several aspects. The design of a mobile image search system must take into account the following inherent limitations of mobile devices:

(a) **Lower Processing Power of CPU**. The design objectives of modern mobile application processors are more than just performance. Priority is often given to other factors such as low power consumption and a small form factor. Although the performance of mobile CPUs has achieved greater than 30X improvement within a short period of recent 5 years (e.g., ARM quad-core Cortex A-15 in 2014 vs. ARM 11 single-core in 2009), today's mobile CPU cores are still not powerful enough to achieve real-time performance for compute-intensive vision tasks such as sophisticated feature extraction and indexing algorithms. Graphics processing units (GPUs), which have been built into most application processors, can help speed up processing via parallel computing [7, 8], but most feature extraction and indexing algorithms are designed to be executed sequentially and cannot fully utilize the capability of GPU cores in a mobile application processor.

(b) **Less Memory Capacity**. Mobile devices have less memory and lower memory bandwidth than desktop systems. The memory of today's high-end smartphones, such as Samsung Galaxy S5, is limited to 2GB of SDRAM and the memory size of mid- and entry-level phones is even smaller. This level of memory sizes is not sufficient for performing local image search using a large database. In order to realize efficient image search, the entire indexing structure of a database needs to be loaded and reside in main memory. The total amount of memory usage for an indexing structure usually grows linearly with the number of database images. For a database of a moderate size (e.g., tens of thousands of images), or a large size (e.g., millions of images), the indexing structure itself could easily exhaust memory resources. Several scalable mobile image search systems [9, 10] employ the client–server model to handle large databases. That is, sending the captured image or processed image data (e.g., image features) to a server (or a cloud) via Internet, performing feature indexing and post verification on the server side, and then sending the search results and associated information back to the mobile device. While Wi-Fi is a built-in feature for almost all mobile devices, connection to high-bandwidth access points is still not available anyplace, neither anytime. For connection to data networks, today's mobile devices rely on a combination of mobile broadband networks including 3G, 3.5G, and 4G. These networks, while providing acceptable network access speed for most apps, cannot support real-time responses for apps demanding a large amount of data transfer. Moreover, advanced mobile broadband networks still have limited availability in areas not having dense populations.

(c) **Small Screen Size**. Modern high-end smartphones boast displays which measure slightly less than seven inches diagonally. However, this size is still much smaller than that of a common desktop or laptop. Smaller screens greatly limit the amount of information that can be presented to a user. As a result, it requires a more effective display of search results and higher search accuracy in order to achieve satisfactory user experience.

(d) **Noisy Query**. The search precision for content-based image search still has significant room for improvement. Particularly in the mobile scenario, a user's query photo can be noisy due to clutter, occlusions, and large viewpoint changes. Therefore, a visual search on a large-scale database with noisy images based on a noisy query cannot achieve high accuracy. Modern smartphones, equipped with various sensors (e.g., GPS, accelerometer gyroscope, magnetometer, etc.), can provide various forms of context information. Mobile search systems can incorporate such context information to improve image search's accuracy, efficiency, and scalability. However, context information captured by a mobile device's sensors is noisy as well. Integrating such noisy context information into vision-based image search methods that can robustly improve accuracy and efficiency is not a trivial task at all.

10.4 Methods

In this section, we introduce recent work addressing some of the challenges that face mobile image search. Specifically, we describe existing solutions for (1) extracting robust and distinctive features efficiently on mobile devices (Sect. 10.4.1); (2) constructing compact indexing structure which can be stored locally on mobile devices or can facilitate precise and fast matching feature retrieval from a large database in the cloud (Sect. 10.4.2); and (3) fusing multimodel context information to improve search accuracy and reduce computational complexity (Sect. 10.4.3).

10.4.1 Robust, Distinctive, and Fast Feature Extraction on Mobile Devices

Local features (an example shown in Fig. 10.3a) have been widely used in many computer vision and pattern recognition apps. In contrast to global feature extraction which generates a single feature vector for an entire image, local feature extraction generates a set of high-dimensional feature vectors for an image. Local feature extraction typically consists of two steps: (1) interest point detection, also referred to as local feature detection, which selects a set of salient points in an image, and (2) interest point description, also referred to as local feature description, which transforms a small image patch around a feature point into a vector representation suitable for further processing. In comparison with a global feature representation, local features are more robust to various geometric and photometric transformations, occlusion, and background clutters and thus more suitable for mobile image search.

Local features' efficiency, robustness, and distinctiveness significantly affect the user experience and performance of a mobile image search system. In this section, we give an overview of mobile interest point detection and description. Due to space limitation, we only review some most representative methods, which do not represent a comprehensive survey.

Interest Point Detection

An interest point detector is an operator which attributes a saliency score to each pixel of an image and then chooses a subset of pixels with local maximum scores. A good detector should provide points that have the following properties: (1) *repeatability (or robustness)*, i.e., given two images of the same object under different image conditions, a high percentage of points on the object in both images can be chosen, (2) *distinctiveness*, i.e., the neighborhood of a detected point should be sufficiently informative so that the point can be easily distinguished from other detected points, (3) *efficiency*, i.e., the detection in a new image should be sufficiently fast to support real-time applications, and (4) *quantity*, i.e., a typical image should contain a

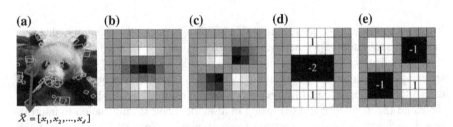

(a)   **(b)**   **(c)**   **(d)**   **(e)**

$\bar{X} = [x_1, x_2, ..., x_J]$

Fig. 10.3 **a** An exemplar image overlaid with detected local features. **b** and **c** are the discretized and cropped Gaussian second-order partial derivative in the y-direction and the xy-direction, respectively; **d** and **e** are SURF box filter approximation for L_{yy} and L_{xy}, respectively

sufficient number of detected points to cover a target object, so that it can be recognized using these detected points even under partial occlusion.

There exist a wide variety of interest point detectors. Some lightweight detectors [11] aim at high efficiency to target applications which demand real-time performance and/or mobile hardware platforms with limited computing resources. However, the performance of these detectors is relatively poor. As a result, it requires postverification to exclude false matches in the subsequent matching phase which often incurs a nontrivial runtime. Therefore, their overall runtime efficiency is not necessary high. On the other hand, several high-quality feature detectors [6, 12, 13] have been developed with a primary focus on robustness and distinctiveness. These detectors' ability to accurately localize correct targets from a large database makes them suitable for large-scale image search. However, the computational complexity of these detectors is usually very high, making them inefficient on a mobile device. Some recent efforts, e.g., [14], adapt these feature detection algorithms with respect to mobile platforms and optimize their performance and efficiency for mobile image search. In the following, we review the most representative methods for the lightweight detector, the high-quality detector, and algorithm adaptation. A thorough survey on local feature-based detectors can be found in [15].

a. Lightweight Detector: FAST

The FAST (Features from Accelerated Segmented Test) detector, proposed by Rosten and Drummond [11], is popular due to its highly efficient processing pipeline. The basic idea of FAST is to compare 16 pixels located on the boundary of a circle (radius is 3) around a central point, each of which is numbered from 1 to 16 clockwise. If the intensities of n consecutive pixels are all higher or all lower than that of the central pixel and n is greater than a predefined minimum threshold, then the central pixel is labeled as a potential feature point and n is defined as the response value for the central pixel. The final set of feature points is determined after applying a *nonmaximum suppression* step, which selects a potential point as a feature point if its response value is the local maximum within a small region. Because the FAST detector only involves a set of intensity comparisons with few arithmetic operations, it is highly efficient.

The FAST detector is not invariant to scale changes. To achieve scale invariance, Rublee et al. [16] employed a scale pyramid to an image and detected FAST feature points at each level in the pyramid. FAST could produce large responses along edges, leading to lower repeatability and distinctiveness compared to high-quality detectors such as SIFT [6] and SURF [12, 13]. To address this limitation, Rublee et al. further employed a Harris corner measure to order the FAST feature points and discard those with small responses to the Harris measure.

b. High-Quality Detector: SURF

The SURF (Speeded Up Robust Feature) detector, proposed by Bay et al. [12, 13], is one of the most popular high-quality point detectors in the literature. It is scale-invariant and based on the determinant of the *Hessian* matrix $H(X, \sigma)$:

$$H(X, \sigma) = \begin{bmatrix} L_{xx}(X, \sigma) & L_{xy}(X, \sigma) \\ L_{xy}(X, \sigma) & L_{yy}(X, \sigma) \end{bmatrix} \tag{10.1}$$

where $X = (x, y)$ is a pixel location in an Image I, σ is a scale factor, $L_{xx}(X, \sigma)$ is the convolution of the Gaussian second-order derivative in the x direction, similarly for L_{yy} and L_{xy} (see Fig. 10.3b, c).

To speed up the computation, a SURF detector approximates the Gaussian second-order partial derivatives with a combination of box filter responses (see Fig. 10.3d, e), computed using the integral image technique [17]. Denoting the approximated derivatives as D_{xx}, D_{xy} and D_{yy}, the approximate Hessian determinant can be expressed as:

$$\det \left(H_{approx} \right) = D_{xx} D_{yy} - (0.9 D_{xy})^2 \tag{10.2}$$

A SURF detector computes Hessian determinant values for every image pixel i over scales using box filters of a successively larger size, yielding a determinant pyramid for the entire image. Then it applies a $3 \times 3 \times 3$ local maximum extraction over the determinant pyramid to select interest points' locations and corresponding salient scales.

To achieve rotation invariance, SURF relies on gradient histograms to identify a dominant orientation for each detected point. An image patch around each point is rotated to its dominant orientation before computing a feature descriptor. Specially, the dominant orientation of a SURF detector is computed as follows. First, the entire orientation space is quantized into N histogram bins, each of which represents a sliding orientation window covering an angle of $\pi / 3$. Then SURF computes gradient responses of every pixel in a circular neighborhood of an interest point. Based on the gradient orientation of a pixel, SURF maps it to the corresponding histogram bins and adds its gradient response to these bins. Finally, the bin with the largest responses is utilized to calculate the dominant orientations of interest points.

Comparing to FAST, SURF point detection involves much more complex computations and, thus, is much slower than FAST. The runtime limitation of SURF is further exacerbated when running a SURF detector on a mobile platform. Table 10.1 compares the runtime performance of a FAST detector and a SURF detector running on a single CPU core in a mobile device (Motorola Xoom1) and a laptop (Thinkpad T420) respectively. Running a FAST detector takes 170 ms on a Motorola Xoom1 (whose application processor consists of dual-core ARM Cortex-A9) and 40 ms on

Table 10.1 Comparison of FAST and SURF detectors on mobile device and PC

Time detector	Mobile device (ms)	PC (ms)	Speedup
FAST detector	170	40	4x
SURF detector	2156	143	15x

an i5-based Thinkpad, yielding a 4x speed gap. However, running a SURF detector on them takes 2156 and 143 ms respectively, indicating a 15x speed gap.

FAST is more efficient, but less robust and distinctive than SURF. As a result, FAST usually fails to achieve satisfactory performance for mobile image search apps which still demand sufficiently high search accuracy from a large database and the ability of handling content with large photometric/geometric changes.

c. Algorithm Adaptation: Accelerating SURF on Mobile Devices

There are several techniques aiming at improving SURF's efficiency. They include exploiting coherency between consecutive frames [18], employing graphics processing units (GPUs) for parallel computing, and optimizing various aspects of the implementation [8]. A solution proposed in [14] analyzes the causes for a SURF detector's poor efficiency and large overhead on a mobile platform, and propose a set of techniques to adapt the SURF algorithm to a mobile platform. Specially, two mismatches between the computations used in the SURF algorithm and common mobile hardware platforms are identified as the sources for its significant performance degradation:

- *Mismatch between SURF's data access pattern and a mobile platform's small cache size.* A SURF detector relies on an integral image and accesses it using a sliding window of successively larger size for different scales. But a 2D array is stored in a row-based fashion in memory (cache and DRAM), not in a window-based fashion; pixels in a single sliding window reside in multiple memory rows (illustrated in Fig. 10.4a). The data cache size of a mobile application processor (AP), typically 32KB for today's devices, is too small to cache all memory rows

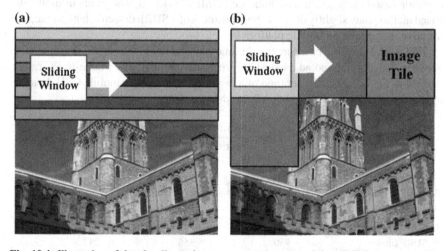

Fig. 10.4 Illustration of data locality and access pattern in **a** the original SURF detector, and **b** the tiled SURF. Each color represents data stored in a unique DRAM row. In the original SURF, a sliding window needs to access multiple DRAM rows, leading to frequent cache misses, while in tiled SURF, all required data within a sliding window can be cached

for pixels involved in one sliding window, leading to cache misses and cache line replacements and, in turn, incurring expensive memory access.

- *Mismatch between a huge amount of data-dependent branches in the SURF algorithm and high pipeline hazard penalty of the mobile platform.* To identify a dominant orientation, a SURF detector analyzes a gradient histogram. During this analysis, every pixel around an interesting point is mapped to corresponding histogram bins via a set of branch operations, i.e., "If-then-Else" expressions. The total number of pixels involved in this analysis is huge and thus the entire process involves an enormous amount of data-dependent branch operations. However, the branch predictor and the speculation of out-of-order execution of an ARM-based mobile CPU core are less sophisticated that of a laptop, desktop, or server processor. Consequently, it incurs higher pipeline hazard penalties, yielding significant performance degradation.

To address the problem caused by the mismatch between the data access pattern of SURF and the small cache size of a mobile CPU, a tiled SURF was proposed in [14] which divides an image into tiles (illustrated in Fig. 10.4b) and performs point detection for each tile individually to exploit local spatial coherences and reduce external memory traffic. To avoid pipeline hazards penalties, two solutions were proposed in [14] to remove data-dependent branch operations. The first solution is to use an alternative implementation: instead of using "If-then-Else" expressions, a lookup table is used to store the correlations between each orientation and the corresponding histogram bins. This alternative does not change the functionality and other computations, but trades memory for speed. The second solution is to replace the original gradient histogram method with a branching-free orientation operator based on gradient moments (i.e., GMoment) [19]. The gradient-moment-based method may slightly degrade the robustness of a SURF detector, but can greatly improve its runtime on mobile platforms.

Tables 10.2 and 10.3 compare the runtime cost and the Phone-to-PC runtime ratio between the original and adapted SURF, respectively [14]. The Phone-to-PC ratio, defined in Eq. (10.3), is the runtime of a program running on a mobile CPU divided by that on a desktop CPU, which reflects the speed gap between them.

$$Phone\text{-}to\text{-}PC \ ratio = \frac{\text{runtime on a mobile platform}}{\text{runtime on an x86-based PC}} \qquad (10.3)$$

Table 10.2 Runtime cost comparison on three mobile platforms

Time (ms)	Droid	Thunderbolt	Xoom1
U-SURF	1310	525	461
U-SURF tiling	930	356	243
O-SURF	7700	2495	2156
O-SURF lookup table	4264	1820	1178
O-SURF GMoment	1516	613	519
O-SURF tiling + GMoment	1053	404	269

Table 10.3 Speed ratio comparison on three mobile platforms

Phone-to-PC ratio (x)	Droid	Thunderbolt	Xoom1
U-SURF	20	8	7
U-SURF tiling	14	7	4
O-SURF	54	17	15
O-SURF lookup table	18	7	6
O-SURF GMoment	19	8	7
O-SURF tiling + GMoment	13	7	3

The evaluation experiments were performed on three mobile devices: a Motorola Droid which features an ARM Cortex-A8 processor, an HTC Thunderbolt which uses a Scorpion processor, and a Motorola Xoom1 which uses a dual-core ARM Cortex-A9 processor. The first two rows of Tables 10.2 and 10.3 compare the runtime cost and the Phone-to-PC ratio of upright SURF (U-SURF) without and with tiling. As expected, tiling can greatly reduce runtime cost by 29–47 %. It reduces the Phone-to-PC ratio by 12.5–42.9 % on these three devices. The reduction in Phone-to-PC ratio indicates that the mismatch between the data access pattern and a small cache size of a mobile CPU causes more severe runtime degradation on mobile CPUs than desktop CPUs. So alleviating this problem is critical for performance optimization when porting algorithms to a mobile CPU. The 3rd–5th rows of Tables 10.2 and 10.3 compare the results of oriented SURF (O-SURF) with branch operations, O-SURF using a lookup table and using *GMoment* [19], respectively, which show that using a lookup table or using the *GMoment* method can greatly reduce the overall runtime and the Phone-to-PC ratio on three platforms. The reduction in the Phone-to-PC ratio further confirms that branch hazard penalty has a much greater runtime impact on a mobile CPU than on a desktop CPU. Choosing proper implementations or algorithms to avoid such penalties is critical for a mobile task. The last rows of Tables 10.2 and 10.3 show the results of applying both adaptation ideas to O-SURF: the runtime of SURF on mobile platforms can be reduced by 6X–8X.

Local Feature Description

Once a set of interest points has been extracted from an image, their content needs to be encoded in descriptors that are suitable for matching. In the past decade, the most popular choices for this step are the SIFT and the SURF descriptors. SIFT and SURF have successfully demonstrated their high robustness and distinctiveness in a variety of computer vision applications. However, the computational complexity of the SIFT descriptor is too high for real-time applications with tight runtime constraints. While SURF accelerates SIFT by 2X–3X, it is still not sufficiently fast for real-time applications running on a mobile device. In addition, SIFT and SURF are high-dimensional real-value vectors which demand large storage space and high computing power for matching. The booming development of real-time mobile apps has stimulated significant advances in binary descriptors that are more compact, and faster to compute than SURF-like features while maintaining a satisfactory feature quality. Notable work includes BRIEF [8] and its variants rBRIEF [16], BRISK [20], FREAK [21], and LDB [22–24]. In the following, we review three representative descriptors: SURF, BIREF, and LDB.

a. SURF: Speed Up Robust Features

The SURF descriptor aims to achieve robustness to lighting variations and small positional shifts by encoding the image information in a localized set of gradient statistics. Specifically, each image patch is divided into 4×4 grid cells. In each cell, SURF computes a set of summary statistics $\sum d_x$, $\sum |d_x|$, $\sum d_y$, and $\sum |d_y|$, resulting in a 64-dimensional descriptor. The first-order derivatives d_x and d_y can be calculated very efficiently using box filters and integral images.

Motivated by the success of SURF, a further optimized version proposed in [8] takes advantage of the computational power available in CUDA [25]-enabled graphics cards. This GPUSURF implementation has been reported to perform feature extraction for a 600×480 image at a frame rate up to $20\,Hz$, thus making feature extraction an affordable processing step. However, to date, most mobile GPU cores do not support CUDA. Furthermore, mobile GPU cores, in addition to being much less powerful than desktop GPU chips, share the same external memory and memory buses with CPU cores and other heterogeneous cores in the application processor. Thus porting an implementation from desktop-based GPUs to mobile GPUs remains a tedious task with unpredictable performance gain [26, 27].

b. BRIEF: Binary Robust Independent Elementary Features

The BRIEF descriptor, proposed in [28], primarily aims at high-computational efficiency for construction and matching, and a small footprint for storage. The basic idea of BRIEF is to directly generate bit strings by simple binary tests comparing pixel intensities in an image patch. More specifically, a binary test τ is defined and performed on a patch p of size $S \times S$ as

$$\tau(p; x, y) = \begin{cases} 1 & \text{if } I(p, x) < I(p, y) \\ 0 & \text{otherwise} \end{cases} \tag{10.4}$$

where $I(p, x)$ is the pixel intensity at location $x = (u, v)^T$. Choosing a set of $n_d(x, y)$-location pairs uniquely defines the binary test set and consequently leads to an n_d-dimensional bit string that corresponds to the decimal counterpart of

$$\sum_{1 \leq i \leq n_d} 2^{i-1} \tau(p; x_i, y_i) \tag{10.5}$$

By construction, the tests of Eq. (10.5) consider only the information at single pixels; therefore, the resulting BRIEF descriptors are very sensitive to noises. To increase

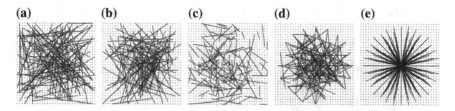

Fig. 10.5 Different approaches to choose the test locations. Sampling (X, Y) locations from a patch of size $S \times S$ according to **a** a uniform distribution $(-\frac{s}{2}, \frac{s}{2})$, **b** an isotropic Gaussian distribution $(0, \frac{1}{25}S^2)$, **c** a nonisotropic Gaussian distribution $X \sim (0, \frac{1}{25}S^2)$, $Y \sim (x_i, \frac{1}{25}S^2)$, **d** random distribution, **e** from a coarse polar grids. Courtesy of [28]

the stability and repeatability, the authors proposed to smooth pixels of every pixel pairs using Gaussian or box filters before performing the binary tests.

The spatial arrangement of binary tests greatly affects the performance of the BRIEF descriptor. In [28], the authors experimented with five sampling geometries for determining the spatial arrangement, as shown in Fig. 10.5a–e. Experimental results demonstrate that the tests which are randomly sampled from an isotropic Gaussian distribution—Gaussian $(0, \frac{1}{25}S^2)$ where the origin of the coordinate system is the center of a patch and S is the patch size—give the highest recognition rate.

BRIEF and its enhanced versions of BRIEF [16, 20, 21] are very efficient to compute, store, and to match (simply computing the Hamming distance between descriptors via XOR and bit count operations). These runtime advantages make these binary descriptors attractive for real-time applications and handheld devices. However, they often utilize overly simplified information, i.e., only intensities of a subset of pixels within an image patch, and thus have low discriminative ability. Lack of distinctiveness results in a huge number of false matches when matching against a large database. Expensive postverification methods (e.g., RANdom SAmple Consensus (RANSAC) [4]) are usually required to discover and validate matching consensus, increasing the runtime of the entire process.

c. LDB: Local Difference Binary

LDB (Local Difference Binary), a binary descriptor, achieves similar computational speed and robustness as BRIEF and other state-of-the-art binary descriptors, yet offering greater distinctiveness. The better quality of LDB is achieved through three schemes. First, LDB utilizes average intensity I_{avg} and first-order gradients, d_x and d_y, of grid cells within an image patch. Specifically, the internal patterns of the image patch is captured through a set of binary tests, each of which compares the I_{avg}, d_x and d_y of a pair of grid cells (illustrated in Fig. 10.6a, b). The average intensity and gradients capture both the DC and AC components of a patch, thus they provide a more complete description than other binary descriptors. Second, LDB employs a multiple gridding strategy to encode the structure at different spatial granularities (Fig. 10.6c). Coarse-level grids can cancel out high-frequency noise while fine-level grids can capture detailed local patterns, thus enhancing distinctiveness. Third, LDB

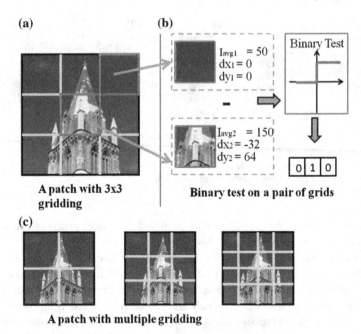

Fig. 10.6 Illustration of LDB extraction. **a** An image patch is divided into 3×3 equal-sized grids. **b** Compute the intensity summation (I), gradient in x and y directions (d_x and d_y) of each patch, and compare I, d_x and d_y between every unique pair of grids. **c** 3-level gridding (with 2×2, 3×3, and 4×4 grids) is applied to capture information at different granularities

leverages a modified AdaBoost method [23] to select a set of salient bits. The modified AdaBoost targets the fundamental goal of idea binary descriptors: minimizing distance between matches while maximizing them between mismatches, optimizing the performance of LDB for a given descriptor length. Computing LDB is highly efficient: relying on integral images, the average intensity, and first-order gradients of each grid cell can be obtained by only 4–8 add/subtract operations.

Accelerating Feature Extraction via Mobile GPU Cores

Mobile application processor includes embedded graphics processing unit (GPU) cores and other hardware accelerators in addition to the CPU cores. GPUs allow for large quantities of instructions to be executed in parallel and efficient for floating point operations. While originally intended for rendering 2D and 3D graphics, GPUs have been at the core of a branch of study known as general-purpose computation on graphics processing units (GPGPU) [29]. GPGPU technology extends the programmability of GPUs to enable nongraphics applications with high parallelizability to run more efficiently than on a CPU. In the context of mobile image search, where sequential feature extraction algorithms are often used, In order to employ GPGPU, feature extraction algorithms need to be broken up into smaller subtasks which can be executed in parallel. Several efforts have been made to improve the parallelization of feature extraction. For example, in [30], a number of stages in the SIFT algorithm are parallelized to run on consumer desktop GPUs, decreasing runtime by a factor of 10. However, it should be pointed out that mobile GPUs have very different characteristics compared to desktop GPUs: a mobile GPU has fewer cores, smaller graphics memory, lower GPU bus bandwidth, sharing the same memory bus with mobile CPUs, and variant architecture when compared to a desktop GPU. To fully utilize the mobile GPUs, new feature extraction algorithms must be devised with the aim to be executed concurrently. It is also necessary to characterize the computing capability of the target mobile CPU-GPU platform in order to identify the condition that offloading tasks to GPU cores leads to an optimized performance [7].

10.4.2   Compact Indexing Structure for Fast Matching on Mobile Devices

To search relevant database images for a captured image, an image search system matches each feature descriptor in the captured image to database features to find the query feature's nearest neighbor (NN). If the similarity between a feature and its NN being above a predetermined threshold and they comply with a geometric model, this feature pair is considered a matched pair. The database object which has most matched features to the captured image is considered as the recognized object.

Fast and accurately retrieving the NN of a local feature from a large database is the key to efficient and accurate image search, ensuring a satisfactory user experience and scalability for mobile image search apps. Two popular techniques commonly used for large-scale NN matching are Locality Sensitive Hashing (LSH) and bag-of-words (BOW) matching.

LSH: Locality Sensitive Hashing

LSH [31] is widely used for approximate NN search. The key of LSH is a hash function, which maps similar descriptors into the same bucket of a hash table and distinct descriptors into different buckets. To find the NN of a query descriptor, we first retrieve its matching bucket and then check all the descriptors within the matched bucket using a brute-force search.

For binary features, the hash function can simply be a subset of bits from the original bit string; descriptors with a common sub-bit-string are casted to the same table bucket. The size of the subset, i.e., the hash key size, determines the upper bound of the Hamming distance among descriptors within the same buckets. To improve the detection rate of NN search based on LSH, two techniques, namely *multitable* and *multiprobe*, are usually used. The multitable technique stores the database descriptors in several hash tables, each of which leverages a different hash function. In the query phase, the query descriptor is hashed into a bucket of every hash table and all descriptors in each of these buckets are then further checked for matching. Multitable improves the detection rate of NN search at the cost of higher memory usage and longer matching time, which is linearly proportional to the number of hash tables used. Multiprobe examines both the bucket in which the query descriptor falls and its neighboring buckets. While multiprobe would result in more matching checks of database descriptors, it actually requires fewer hash tables than multitable and thus incurs lower memory usage. In addition, it allows a larger key size and in turn smaller buckets and fewer matches to check per bucket.

Bag-of-Words Matching

Bag-of-Words (BoW) matching [3] is an effective strategy to reduce memory usage and support fast matching via a scalable indexing scheme such as an inverted file. Typically, BoW matching quantizes local image descriptors into visual words and then computes the image similarity by counting the frequency of words co-occurrences. However, it completely ignores the spatial information which may degrade the accuracy. To address this limitation of BoW matching, several approaches have been proposed to compensate the loss of spatial information. For example, geometric verification [32], designed for general image-matching applications, verifies local correspondences by checking their homography consistency. Wu et al. presented a bundling feature matching scheme [33] for partial-duplicate image detection. In their approach, sets of local features are bundled into groups by maximally stable extremal regions (MSER) [34] detected regions, and robust geometric constraints are then enforced within each group. Spatial pyramid matching [35], which considers approximate global geometric correspondences, is another scheme to enforce geometric constraints for more accurate BoW matching. This scheme partitions the image into increasingly finer sub-regions and computes histograms of local features detected within each sub-region. To compute the similarity between two images, the distance between histograms at each spatial level is weighted and summed together. These above-mentioned schemes yield more reliable local-region matches by enforcing various geometric constraints. However, these schemes are very compute-expensive. Thus, for real-time mobile image search, the indexing procedure based on these methods must be conducted on the server side or in the cloud.

10.4.3 Fusing Multimodel Context-Aware Information for Mobile Image Search

At present, the processing power and memory capacity of mobile devices are still too limited for image search apps solely relying on sophisticated visual feature extraction and matching methods. Modern smartphones have equipped a wide range of sensors, e.g., compass, accelerometer, gyroscope, GPS, etc. greatly enrich the devices' functionalities and provide various forms of context information to facilitate image search. For instance, Global Position System (GPS) location is important information for landmark images. In the meanwhile, a growing fraction of images in image databases are tagged with geographical information. As of February 2009, there are more than 100 million geotagged images on Flickr [36]. By leveraging GPS to identify the location of a mobile devices and utilizing a compass (or in combination with other sensors) to determine the direction that the device is heading to, an image search system could retrieve related images which have similar geotagged and direction information as the query image.

The problem, however, is that built-in sensors usually lack sufficient accuracy, thus cannot provide satisfactory performance for search tasks. For instance, since GPS drift can be as much as 100 meters, in densely built areas or using a noisy and large-scale database, more false positive images from surrounding locations will be included. Several studies proposed to combine these vision-based and sensor-based methods. For example, in [10], authors proposed two modes, parallel and serial, to integrate location information in a mobile landmark image search system. In parallel mode, query data from content and location is processed independently, and then the results are combined together through a linear combination approach. In serial mode, location information is first applied to narrow down the search space, and then results will be refined and re-ranked based on visual information. Serial integration can significantly reduce the search scope for the captured landmark, which in turn will greatly improve search precision and speed. However, it may also incur the risk of losing some true positives, i.e., a worse recall, due to the absence of location tags. Another work fuse visual and GPS information is presented in [37]. In this work, the authors proposed to combine visual tracking and GPS for outdoor building visualization. The user can place virtual models on Google Earth and the app can retrieve and visualize them based on the user's GPS location.

The trend of integrating more sensors into mobile devices has not stopped yet. For example, Google has just released a new mobile platform, Tango, which integrates six Degree-of-Freedom motion sensors, depth sensors, and high-quality cameras. Amazon has announced their new Fire phone which includes four cameras tucked into the front corners of the phone, in additional to other motion sensors. Advances in mobile hardware offer the opportunities to gain richer contextual information surrounding a mobile device and in turn open a door for new approaches to best utilizing all available multimodel information.

10.5 Conclusions

The advancement of mobile technology, in terms of hardware computing power, seamless connectivity to the cloud and fast computer vision algorithms, have raised image search into the mainstream of mobile apps. Following the widespread popularity of a handful of killer image search applications already commercially available, it is believed that mobile image search will expand exponentially in the next few years. The advent of mobile image search will have a profound and lasting impact on the way people use their smartphones and tablets. These emerging mobile image search apps will turn our everyday world into a fully interactive digital experience, from which we can see, hear, feel and even smell the information in a different way. This emerging direction will push the industry toward truly ubiquitous computing and a technologically converged paradigm.

The scalability, accuracy, and efficiency of the underlying techniques (i.e., feature extraction and indexing) are key factors influencing user experience of mobile image search apps. New algorithms in computer vision and pattern recognition, such as lightweight feature extraction, have been developed to provide efficiency, compactness on low-power mobile devices, and meanwhile maintain sufficiently good accuracy. Several efforts are also made to analyze particular hardware limitations for executing existing feature extraction and indexing algorithms on mobile devices and explore adaption techniques to address these limitations. In addition to advances in the development of lightweight computer vision algorithm, a variety of sensors have been integrated into modern smartphones, enabling location recognition (e.g., via GPS) and device tracking (e.g., via gyroscope, accelerometer, and magnetometer) at little computational cost. However, due to large noise of low-cost sensors equipped in today's smartphones, the accuracy of location recognition is usually low and cannot meet the requirement for apps which demand high accuracy. Fusing visual information with sensor data is a promising direction to achieve both high accuracy and efficiency, and we shall see an increasing amount of research work along this direction in the near future.

References

1. Yang, X., Zhu, Q., Cheng, K.-T.: Near-duplicate detection for images and videos. In: ACM Workshop on Large Scale Multimedia Retrieval and Mining, Beijing, October 2009
2. Jegou, H., Douze, M., Schmid, C.: Packing bag-of-features. In: International Conference on Computer Vision, September 2009
3. Sivic, J., Zisserman, A.: Video Google: a text retrieval approach to object matching in videos. In: Proceedings of International Conference on Computer Vision, vol. 2, pp. 1470–1477 (2003)
4. Fischler, M.A., Bolles, R.C.: Random sample consensus: a paradigm for model fitting with applications to image analysis and automated cartography. Commun. ACM **24**, 381–395 (1981)
5. Chum, O., Matas, J.: Matching with PROSAC—progressive sample consensus. Proc. Comput. Vis. Pattern Recognit. **1**, 220–226 (2005)
6. Lowe, D.G.: Distinctive image features from scale-invariant keypoints. Int. J. Comput. Vis. **60**(2), 91–110 (2004)
7. Cheng, K.T., Yang, X., Wang, Y.-C.: Performance optimization of vision apps on mobile application processor. In: International Conference on Systems, Signals and Image Processing (IWSSIP), Bucharest, Romania, 7–9 July 2013
8. Terriberry, T.B., French, L.M., Helmsen, J.: GPU accelerating speeded-up robust features. In: Proceedings of the 3D Data Processing, Visualization and Transmission (2008)

9. Xie, X., Lu, L., Jia, M.L., Li, H., Seide, F., Ma, W.Y.: Mobile search with multimodel queries. Proc. IEEE **96**(4), 589–601 (2008)
10. Yang, X., Pang, S., Cheng, K.-T.: Mobile image search with multimodel context-aware queries. In: ACM International Workshop on Mobile Vision, June 2010
11. Rosten, E., Drummond, T.: Machine learning for high speed corner detection. In: Proceedings of the European Conference on Computer Vision (2006)
12. Bay, H., Ess, A., Tuytelaars, T., Gool, L.V.: SURF: speeded-up robust features. In: Proceedings of the European Conference on Computer Vision (2006)
13. Bay, H., Ess, A., Tuytelaars, T., Gool, L.V.: Speeded-up robust features. In: Proceedings of the Conference on Vision and Image Understanding, vol. 110(3), June 2008
14. Yang, X., Cheng, K.T.: Accelerating SURF detector on mobile devices. In: ACM International Conference on Multimedia, Nara, Japan, October 2012
15. Tuytelaars, T., Mikolajczyk, K.: Local invariant feature detectors: a survey. J. Found. Trends Comput. Graph. Vis. **3**, 177–280 (2008)
16. Rublee, E., Rabaud, V., Konolige, K., Bradski, G.: ORB: an efficient alternative to SIFT or SURF. In: Proceedings of the International Conference on Computer Vision (2011)
17. Simard, P., Bottou, L., Haffner, P., LeCun, Y.: Boxlets: a fast convolution algorithm for signal processing and neural networks. In: Proceedings of the Neural Information Processing Systems (NIPS) (1998)
18. Ta, D.N., Chen, W.C., Gelfand, N., Pulli, K.: SURFTrac: efficient tracking and continuous object recognition using local feature descriptors. In: Proceedings of the Conference on Vision and Pattern Recognition (2009)
19. Rosin, P.L.: Measuring corner properties. J. Comput. Vis. Image Underst. **73**(2), 291–307 (1999)
20. Leutenegger, S., Chli, M., Siegwart, R.: BRISK: binary robust invariant scalable keypoints. In: Proceedins of the Computer Vision on Pattern Recognition (2011)
21. Alahi, A., Ortiz, R., Vandergheynst, P.: FREAK: fast retinal keypoint. In: Proceedings of the Computer Vision on Pattern Recognition (2012)
22. Yang, X., Cheng, K.T.: Local difference binary for ultrafast distinctive feature description. IEEE Trans. Pattern Anal. Mach. Intell. **36**(1), 188–194 (2014)
23. Yang, X., Cheng, K.T.: Learning optimized local difference binaries for scalable augmented reality on mobile devices. IEEE Trans. Vis. Comput. Graph. **20**(6), 852–865 (2014)
24. Yang, X., Cheng, K.T.: LDB: an ultrafast feature for scalable augmented reality on mobile device. In: Proceedings of International Symposium on Mixed and Augmented Reality, pp. 49–57 (2012)
25. CUDA: http://www.nvidia.com/object/cuda_home_new.html
26. Wang, Y.-C., Cheng, K.-T.: Energy and performance characterization of mobile heterogeneous computing. In: IEEE Workshop on Signal Processing System, Canada, October 2012
27. Wang, Y.-C., Cheng, K.-T.: Energy-optimized mapping of application to smartphone platform—a case study of mobile face recognition. In: IEEE Workshop of Embedded Computer Vision, USA (2011)
28. Calonder, M., Lepetit, V., Strecha, C., Fua, P.: BRIEF: binary robust independent elementary features. In: Proceedings of the European Conference on Computer Vision (2010)
29. GPGPU: http://gpgpu.org/developer
30. Sinha, S., Frahm, J., Pollefeys, M., Genc, Y.: GPU-based video feature tracking and matching. In: Workshop on Edge Computing Using New Commodity Architectures (2006)
31. Gionis, A., Indyk, P., Motwani, R.: Similarity search in high dimensions via hashing. In: Proceedings of International Conference on Very Large Databases, pp. 518–529 (1999)
32. Philbin, J., Chum, O., Isard, M., Sivic, J., Zisserman, A.: Object retrieval with large vocabularies and fast spatial matching. In: Proceedings of Computer Vision and Pattern Recognition, pp. 1–8 (2007)
33. Wu, Z., Ke, Q.F., Isard, M., Sun, J.: Bundling features for large scale partial-duplicate web image search. In: Proceedings of Computer Vision and Pattern Recognition, pp. 25–32 (2009)

34. Matas, J., Chum, O., Urban, M., Pajdla, T.: Robust wide baseline stereo from maximally stable extremal regions. In: Proceedings of British Machine Vision Conference, pp. 384–396 (2002)
35. Lazebnik, S., Schmid, C., Ponce, J.: Beyond bags of features: spatial pyramid matching for recognizing natural scene categories. In: Proceedings of IEEE Conference on Computer Vision and Pattern Recognition, pp. 2169–2178 (2006)
36. Kleban, J., Moxley, E., Xu, J.J., Manjunath, B.S.: Global annotation on georeference photographs. In: ACM International Conference on Image and Video Retrieval, Greece, July 2009
37. Naimark, L., Foxlin, E.: Circular data matrix fiducial system and robust image processing for a wearable vision-inertial self-tracker. In: Proceedings of the International Symposium on Mixed and Augmented Reality, pp. 27–36 (2002)

Part IV
Cloud Visual Computing and Mobile Applications

Chapter 11
CloudCV: Large-Scale Distributed Computer Vision as a Cloud Service

**Harsh Agrawal, Clint Solomon Mathialagan, Yash Goyal,
Neelima Chavali, Prakriti Banik, Akrit Mohapatra,
Ahmed Osman and Dhruv Batra**

Abstract We are witnessing a proliferation of massive visual data. Unfortunately, scaling existing computer vision algorithms to large datasets leaves researchers repeatedly solving the same algorithmic, logistical, and infrastructural problems. Our goal is to democratize computer vision; one should not have to be a computer vision, big data, and distributed computing expert to have access to state-of-the-art distributed computer vision algorithms. We present CloudCV, a comprehensive system to provide access to state-of-the-art distributed computer vision algorithms as a cloud service through a web interface and APIs.

H. Agrawal (✉) · C.S. Mathialagan · Y. Goyal · N. Chavali · P. Banik ·
A. Mohapatra · D. Batra
Virginia Tech, Blacksburg, VA, USA
e-mail: harsh92@vt.edu

C.S. Mathialagan
e-mail: mclint@vt.edu

Y. Goyal
e-mail: ygoyal@vt.edu

N. Chavali
e-mail: gneelima@vt.edu

P. Banik
e-mail: prakriti@vt.edu

A. Mohapatra
e-mail: akrit@vt.edu

D. Batra
e-mail: dbatra@vt.edu

A. Osman
Imperial College London, London, UK
e-mail: ahmed.osman99@gmail.com

© Springer International Publishing Switzerland 2015
G. Hua and X.-S. Hua (eds.), *Mobile Cloud Visual Media Computing*,
DOI 10.1007/978-3-319-24702-1_11

11.1 Introduction

A recent World Economic Form report [1] and a New York Times article [2] declared data to be a new class of economic asset, like currency or gold. Visual content is arguably the fastest growing data on the web. Photo-sharing web sites like Flickr and Facebook now host more than 6 and 90 billion photos (respectively). Every day, users share 200 million more images on Facebook. Every minute, users upload 72 hours or 3 days worth of video to Youtube. Besides consumer data, diverse scientific communities (Civil and Aerospace Engineering, Computational Biology, Bioinformatics, Astrophysics, etc.) are also beginning to generate massive archives of visual content [3–5], without necessarily having access to the expertise, infrastructure, and tools to analyze them.

This data revolution presents both an opportunity and a challenge. Extracting value from this asset will require converting meaningless data into perceptual understanding and knowledge. This is challenging but has the potential to *fundamentally change the way we live*—from self-driving cars bringing mobility to the visually impaired, to in-home robots caring for the elderly and physically impaired, to augmented reality with Google-Glass-like wearable computing units.

11.1.1 Challenges

In order to convert this raw visual data into knowledge and intelligence, we need to address a number of key challenges:

- **Scalability**. The key challenge for image analysis algorithms in the world of big data is scalability. In order to fully exploit the latest hardware trends, we must address the challenge of developing fully distributed computer vision algorithms. Unfortunately, scaling existing computer vision algorithms to large datasets leaves researchers repeatedly solving the same infrastructural problems: building and maintaining a cluster of machines, designing multithreaded primitives for each algorithm and distributing jobs, precomputing and caching features, etc.

  Consider, for instance the recent state-of-the-art image categorization system by the Google/Stanford team [6]. The system achieved an impressive 70 % relative improvement over the previous best known algorithm for the task of recognizing 20,000 object categories in the Imagenet dataset [7]. To achieve this feat, the system required a sophisticated engineering effort in exploiting model parallelism and had to be trained on a cluster with 2,000 machines (32,000 cores) for one week. While this is a commendable effort, lack of such an infrastructural support and intimate familiarity with parallelism in computer vision algorithms leaves most research groups marginalized, computer vision experts and nonexperts alike.

- **Provably Correct Parallel/Distributed Implementations**. Designing and implementing efficient and provably correct parallel computer vision algorithms is extremely challenging. Some tasks like extracting statistics from image collections are *embarrassingly parallel*, i.e., can be parallelized simply by distributing the images to different machines. This is where framework such as MapReduce have demonstrated success. Unfortunately, most tasks in computer vision and machine learning such as training a face detector are not embarrassingly parallel—there are data and computational dependencies between images and various steps in the algorithm. Moreover, for each such parallel algorithm, researchers must repeatedly solve the same low-level problems: formulating parallelizable components in computer vision algorithms, designing multithreaded primitives, writing custom hardware wrappers, implementing mechanisms to avoid race conditions, deadlocks, etc.

- **Reusability**. Computer vision researchers have developed vision algorithms that solve specific tasks but software developers building end-to-end system find it extremely difficult to integrate these algorithms into the system due to different software stacks, dependencies, and different data format. Additionally, hardware designers have developed various dedicated computer vision processing platforms to overcome the problem of intensive computation. However, these solutions have created another problem: heterogeneous hardware platforms have made it time-consuming and difficult to port computer vision systems from one hardware platform to another.

11.1.2 CloudCV: Overview

In order to overcome these challenges, we are building **CloudCV**, a comprehensive system that will provide access to state-of-the-art distributed computer vision algorithms on the cloud (Fig. 11.1).

CloudCV today consists of a group of virtual machines running on Amazon Web Services capable of running large number of tasks in a distributed and parallel setting. Popular datasets used are already cached on these servers to facilitate researchers trying to run popular computer vision algorithms on these datasets. Users can access these services through a web interface which allows user to upload a few images from either Dropbox or local system and obtain results real time. For larger datasets, the system enables to embed CloudCV services into a bigger end-to-end system by utilizing Python and MATLAB APIs. Since the APIs are fairly easy to install through standard package managers, the researchers can now quickly run image analysis algorithms on huge datasets in a distributed fashion without worrying about infrastructure, efficiency, algorithms, and technical know-how. At the back end, on recieving the list of images and the algorithm that needs to be executed, the server distributes these jobs to worker nodes that process the data in parallel and communicate the results to the user in real time. Therefore, the user does not need to wait

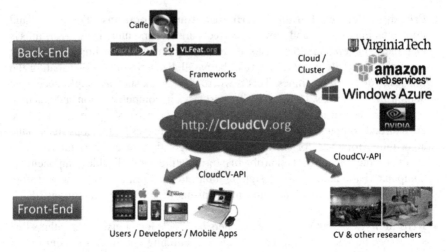

Fig. 11.1 Overview of CloudCV

for the processing to finish on the entire dataset and can monitor the progress of the job due to real-time updates.

11.1.3 Application

CloudCV will benefit three different audiences in different ways:

- **Computer vision researchers**: who do not have resources to or do not want to reinvent a large-scale distributed computer vision system. For such users, CloudCV can serve as a unified data and code repository, providing cached version of all relevant data representations and features. We envision a system where a program running on CloudCV simply "calls" for a feature; if it is cached, the features are immediately loaded from distributed storage (HDFS [8]); if it is not cached, then the feature extraction code is run seamlessly in the background and the results are cached for future use. Eventually, CloudCV becomes the ultimate repository for "standing on the shoulders of giants".
- **Scientists who are not computer vision experts**: but have large image collections that need to be analyzed. Consider a biologist who needs to automate the process of cell counting in microscopy images. Today such researchers must find computer vision collaborators and then invest in the logistical infrastructure required to run large-scale experiments. CloudCV can eliminate both these constraints, by providing access to state-of-the-art computer vision algorithms *and* compute time on the cloud.
- **Nonscientists**: who simply want to learn about computer vision by demonstration. There is a tremendous demand from industry professionals and developers for learning about computer vision. Massive Open Online Classes (MOOCs) like

Udacity and Coursera have demonstrated success. CloudCV can build on this success by being an important teaching tool for learning computer vision by building simple apps on the cloud. Imagine a student writing four lines of code in CloudCV development environment to run a face detector on a stream of images captured from his laptop webcam.

11.2   Related Efforts

Before describing the architecture and capabilities of CloudCV, let us first put it in context of related efforts in this direction. Open-source computer vision software can be broadly categorized into three types:

- General-Purpose Libraries: There are a number of general-purpose computer vision libraries available in different programming languages:

  - C/C++: OpenCV [9], IVT [10], VXL [11]
  - Python: OpenCV (via wrappers), PyVision [12]
  - .NET: AForge.NET [13].

  The most comprehensive effort among these is OpenCV, which is a library aimed at real-time computer vision. It contains more than 2500 algorithms and has been downloaded 5 million times by 47 K people [9]. The library has C, C++, Java, and Python interfaces and runs on Windows, GNU/Linux, Mac, iOS, and Android operating systems.
- Narrow-Focus Libraries: A number of toolboxes provide specialized implementations for specific tasks, e.g., Camera Calibration Toolbox [14], Structure from Motion toolboxes [15–17], Visual Features Library [18], and deep learning frameworks such as Caffe [19], Theano [20, 21], Torch [22], etc.
- Specific Algorithm Implementations: released by authors on their respective web sites. Popular examples include object detection [23], articulated body pose estimation [24], graph cuts for image segmentation [25], etc.

Unfortunately, all three source code distribution mechanisms suffer from at least one of these limitations:

1. **Lack of Parallelism**: Most of the existing libraries have a fairly limited or no support for parallelism. OpenCV and VLFeat, for instance have multithreading support, allowing programs to utilize multiple cores on a single machine. Unfortunately, modern datasets are so large that no single machine may be able to hold all the data. This makes it necessary to distribute jobs (with computational and data dependencies) on a cluster of machines. CloudCV will have full support for three levels of parallelism: (i) single machine with multiple cores; (ii) multiple machines in a cluster with distributed storage; and (iii) "cloudbursting" or dynamic allocation of computing resources via a professional elastic cloud computing service (Amazon EC2 [26]).

2. **Burden on the *User* not the Provider**: Today, computer vision libraries place infrastructural responsiblities squarely on the user of these systems, not the provider. The user must download the said library, resolve dependencies, compile code, arrange for computing resources, parse bugs, and faulty outputs. CloudCV will release the user of such burdens—the user uploads the data (or points to a cached database in the repository) and simply specifies what computation needs to be performed.

Finally, we stress that CloudCV is not another computer vision toolbox. Our focus is not on reimplementing algorithms, rather we build on the success of comprehensive efforts of OpenCV, Caffe, and others. Our core contribution will be to provide fully distributed implementations on the cloud and make them available as a service.

Efforts Closest to the Goal of CloudCV: There are multiple online services which provide specific algorithms such as face, concept, celebrity [27] or provide audio and video understanding [28], personalized object detectors [29]. Unlike these services, CloudCV is an open-source architecture that aims to provide the capability to run a user's own version of CloudCV on cloud services such as Amazon Web Services, Microsoft Azure, etc.

11.3 CloudCV Back-End Infrasructure

In this section, we describe in detail all the components that form the back-end architecture of CloudCV.

The back-end system shown in Fig. 11.2 mainly consists of a web server that is responsible for listening to incoming job requests and sending real-time updates to the user. A job scheduler takes these incoming jobs and distributes them across number of worker nodes. The system uses a number of open-source frameworks to ensure an efficient design that can scale to a production system.

11.3.1 Web Servers

The back end consists of two servers that are constantly listening for incoming requests. We use a Python-based web framework which handles Hypertext Transfer Protocol (HTTP) requests made by the web interface or the APIs. These requests contain details about the job such as list of images, which executable to run, executable parameters, user information, etc. One drawback to HTTP requests is that it allows only a single request–response pair, i.e., for a given request the server can only return one response after which the connection breaks and the server cannot communicate with the client unless client sends a request. This leads to serious limitations because a persistent real-time connection cannot be established for the server to send updates

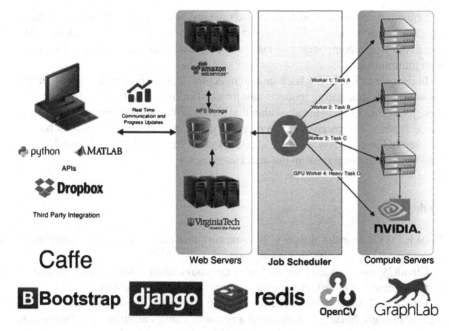

Fig. 11.2 Users can access CloudCV using a web interface, Python, or MATLAB API. The back end consists of web servers which communicates with the client in real time through HTTP and WebSockets. The job schedule at the master node distributes incoming jobs across multiple computer servers (worker nodes)

to the user. To solve this problem, we use the WebSocket protocol (Socket.IO) on top of another server (Node.js).

Django

CloudCV uses Django [30] which is a high-level Python HTTP web framework that is based on the Model View Controller (MVC) pattern. MVC defines a way of developing software so that the code for defining and accessing data (the model) is separate from request routing logic (the controller), which in turn is separate from the user interface (the view).

A key advantage of such an approach is that components are loosely coupled and serve single key purpose. The components can be changed independently without affecting the other pieces. For example, a developer can change the URL for a given part of the application without affecting the underlying implementation. A designer can change a page's HTML code without having to touch the Python code that renders it. A database administrator can rename a database table and specify the change in a single place, rather than having to search and replace through a dozen files.

Scaling up to serve thousands of web request is a crucial requirement. Django adopts a "share nothing" philosophy in which each part of the web stack is broken down into single components so that inexpensive servers can be added or removed with minimum fuss.

In the overall CloudCV back-end architecture, Django is responsible for serving the web pages, translating requests into jobs and calling the job scheduler to process these jobs. The output of the algorithm that the job is running is pipelined to a message queue system. The receiver of the message queue system sends the output back to the user. In CloudCV, the message queue system is Redis and the receiver is Node.js; both of these are explained in the next two sections.

Node.js

Node.js [31] is an event-driven web framework that excels in real-time applications such as push updates and chat applications.

CloudCV uses Node.js for real-time communication with the user so that all updates related to a particular job can be communicated to the user.

Unlike traditional frameworks that use the stateless request–response paradigm such as Django, Node.js can establish a two-way communication with the client so that server can send updates to the client without the need for the client to query the server to check for updates. This is in contrast to the typical web response paradigm, where the client always initiates communication. Real-time communication with the client is important because completing a job that contains large amounts of data will take some time and delaying communication with the client until the end of job makes for a poor user experience and having the client query the server periodically is wasteful.

The de facto standard for building real-time applications, Node.js applications is via Socket.IO [32]. It is an event-based bidirectional communication layer which abstracts many low-level details and transports, including AJAX long polling and WebSockets, into a single cross-browser compatible API. Whenever an event is triggered inside Node.js server, an event callback mechanism can send a response to the client.

Redis

One of the use cases of real-time communication with the user is the ability to send algorithm output to the user during execution. To make this possible, there needs to be a system in place that can pipeline the algorithm output to the Node.js server, which is responsible for communicating the output back to client.

In case of CloudCV, this system is Redis [33], a high-performance in-memory key-value data store. Since the data is stored in RAM (in-memory), looking up keys and returning a value are very fast.

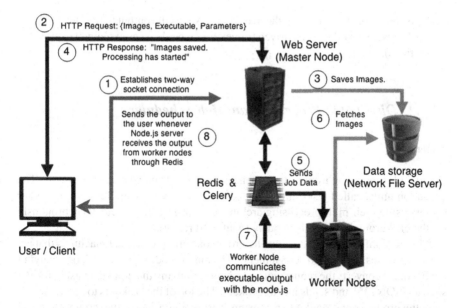

Fig. 11.3 Flow describing the execution of a job starting from the user connecting to the CloudCV system to the back end sending results to the user during execution of the job in real time

Redis can also act as a message queue between two processes—worker process executing a particular algorithm and the Node.js server. Whenever a text output is generated by the executable, the worker process sends the output string through Redis. Node.js triggers an event whenever it receives the message from the message queue. The message consists of the output string, and the socket id of the client to which this output needs to be sent. Consequently, the event handler sends the output string to the user associated with that particular socket id.

Figure 11.3 describes the process of executing a job in detail. The flow is as follows:

1. At the start of a job, the user establishes a two-way socket connection with the server. Each user is recognized by the unique socket id associated with this connection.
2. The details about the job such as list of images to process, name of the functionality that needs to be executed and its associated parameters are sent to the server using HTTP request.
3. The server saves the image in the database and sends a response back to the user.
4. The server then distributes the job to worker nodes by serializing all the data. An idle worker node pops the job from the queue, fetches the image from the network file server, and starts executing the functionality associated with the job.
5. Whenever the executable generates an output, the worker node informs the master node by sending the generated output through a message queue.

6. Upon receiving the message, the master node sends the output to the client. This is made possible by the event-driven framework of Node.js (as explained in previous sections).

11.3.2 Distributed Processing and Job Scheduler

Celery

Celery [34] is an asynchronous task queue based on distributed message passing. The execution units, called tasks, are executed concurrently on a single or more worker servers using their multiprocessing architecture. Tasks can execute asynchronously (in the background) or synchronously (wait until ready).

CloudCV infrastructure contains heterogenous group of virtual machines that act as worker nodes, also called "consumers". The master node ("producer") on receiving a job request converts the request into a task by serializing the input data using format such as JSON [35] and sends it to a "broker". The job of the broker is to receive a task from the producer and send it to a consumer. Broker consists of two components: an exchange and queues. Based on certain bindings or rules, exchange sends each task to a particular queue. For instance, GPU-optimized tasks (such as image classification Sect. 11.4.1 are sent to "Classification Queue" which are then processed by worker nodes that have GPUs. On the other hand, image stitching tasks that utilize multiple CPUs are sent to CPU-only machines via "Image Stitching Queue". A queue is simply a buffer that stores the messages (Fig. 11.4).

This protocol is known as AMQP Protocol [36] and Celery abstracts away details of the protocol efficiently, allowing the system to scale.

GraphLab

GraphLab [37] is a high-level abstraction for distributed computing that efficiently and intuitively expresses data and computational dependencies with a sparse data graph. Unlike other abstractions such as MapReduce, computation in GraphLab is expressed as a vertex program, which is executed in parallel on each vertex (potentially on different machines), while maintaining data consistency between machines and appropriate locking.

We implemented a parallel image stitching algorithm by creating GraphLab wrappers for the image stitching pipeline in OpenCV [9], a widely used open-source computer vision library. The implementation is open source and is available in the GraphLab's computer vision toolkit [38].

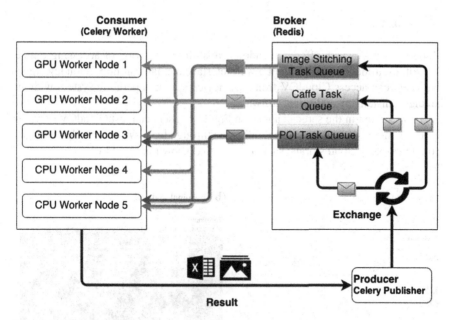

Fig. 11.4 Celery flow chart

11.3.3   Caffe—Deep Learning Framework

Caffe [19] is a deep learning framework initially developed by the Berkeley Vision group and now an open-source project with multiple contributors. In performance tests, it consistently ranks as of the fastest Convolution Neural Network (CNN) implementations available online. Caffe is widely used in academic research projects, industrial applications pertaining to vision, speech, etc. A number of state-of-the-art models implemented in Caffe are publicly available for download.

CloudCV uses Caffe at the back end to provide services such as classification, feature extraction, and object detection. CloudCV also allows adding a new category to a pretrained CNN model without retraining the entire model and is described in detail in Sect. 11.4.3.

11.3.4   Front-End Platforms

CloudCV computer vision algorithms are accessible via three front-end platforms: (1) Web interface, (2) Python APIs, and (3) MATLAB APIs.

Web Interface

Modern web browsers offer tremendous capabilities in terms of accessing online content, multimedia, etc. We built a web interface available at http://cloudcv.org so that users can access CloudCV from any device via any operating system without having to install any additional software.

As illustrated in the screen capture in Fig. 11.5, users can test CloudCV services by trying them out on a few images uploaded through local system or upload images from third-party cloud storage such as Dropbox (shown in Fig. 11.6).

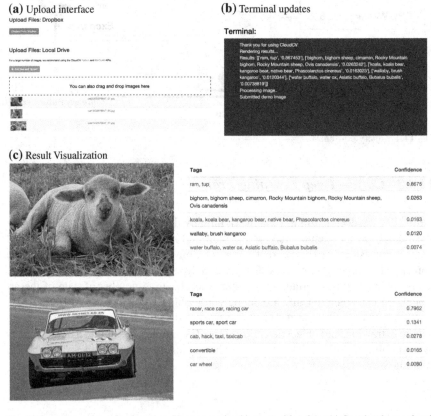

Fig. 11.5 **a** shows the upload section. User can upload images either from his/her dropbox or local disk, **b** shows the terminal which receives real-time progress updates from the server, and **c** shows the visualization interface for a given job. Note in this case the task was classification and the result displays category and corresponding confidence for a given image

Fig. 11.6 The web interface allows user to upload images and save features or models files inside his/her Dropbox account. **a** Shows the upload interface where a user can select one or multiple images and **b** shows the save interface where the user can save all the data generated for the given job inside Dropbox. In this example, the user was trying to save features extracted in the form of Mat files inside Dropbox account

We are also working on providing user authentication such that users can have access to all the trained models, training images, and job history. This will enable the user to seamlessly transfer data across multiple data sources.

Python API

To enable building end-to-end applications on top of CloudCV, we make our services accessible via a Python API.

Python has seen significant growth in terms of libraries developed for scientific computation because of its holistic language design. It also offers interactive terminal and user interface which makes data analysis, visualization, and debugging easier.

Loading necessary packages: To use the CloudCV Python API, a user only needs to import the PCloudCV class.

```
from pcloudcv import PCloudCV
import utility.job as uj
import json
import os
```

At this point, the pcloudcv object may be used to access the various functionalities provided in CloudCV. These functionalities are detailed in Sect. 11.4.

Setting the configuration path: When used in the above manner, the user needs to provide details about the job (executable name, parameter settings, etc.) for each such API call. In order to reduce this burden, our API includes a *configuration file* that stores all such necessary job information. The contents of this configuration file are shown below.

```
1   {
2       "exec": "classify",
3       "maxim": 500,
4       "config": [
5           {
6               "name": "ImageStitch",
7               "path": "dropbox:/1/",
8               "output": "/home/dexter/Pictures/
                    test_download",
9               "params": {
10                  "warp": "plane"
11              }
12          },
13          {
14              "name": "classify",
15              "path": "local: /home/dexter/
                    Pictures/test_download/3",
16              "output": "/home/dexter/Pictures/
                    test_download",
17              "params": {
18              }
19          },
20          {
21              "name": "features",
22              "path": "local: /home/dexter/
                    Pictures/test_download/3",
23              "output": "/home/dexter/Pictures/
                    test_download",
24              "params": {
25                  "name": "decaf",
26                  "verbose": "2",
27              }
28          }
29      ]
30  }
```

The user may simply provide the full path to the configuration file.

```
#full path of the config.json file
config_path = os.path.join(os.getcwd(),                    )
dict = {        :            }
```

Creating PCloudCV object: To run a job, the user simply needs to create a PCloudCV object. The constructor takes the path to the configuration file, a dictionary that contains optional settings for input directory, output directory, and executable, and a boolean parameter that tells the API whether the user wishes to login to his/her account using third-party authorization—Google accounts or Dropbox. If the boolean parameter is false, then the job request is treated as anonymous.

```
p = PCloudCV(config_path, dict, True)
p.start()
```

MATLAB API

MATLAB is a popular high-level language and interactive environment that offers high-performance numerical computation, data analysis, visualization capabilities, and application development tools. MATLAB has become a popular language in academia, especially for computer vision researchers, because it provides easy access to thousands of low-level building block functions and algorithms written by experts in addition to those specifically written by computer vision researchers. Therefore, CloudCV includes a MATLAB API, as shown in the screenshot Fig. 11.7.

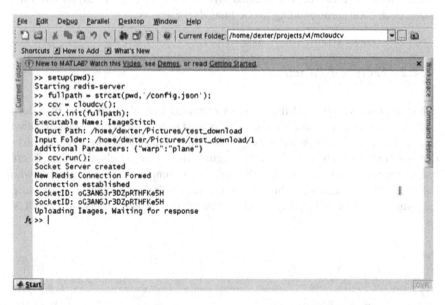

Fig. 11.7 MATLAB API Screenshot: Users can access CloudCV services within MATLAB. These APIs run in background such that while the user is waiting for a response, the user can run other tasks and the API call is non-blocking. The figure shows the screenshort of the MATLAB API

11.4   CloudCV Functionalities

We now describe the functionalities and algorithms currently implemented in CloudCV.

11.4.1   Classification

"Image Classification" refers to predicting the class labels of objects present in an image. This finds myriad applications in visual computing. Knowing what object is visible to the camera is an immense capability in mobile applications. CloudCV image classification tackles this problem in the cloud. The classification API can be invoked to get a list of top five objects present in the image with the corresponding confidence scores.

CloudCV classification implementation uses the "caffenet" model (bvlc_reference_caffenet in Caffe) shown in Fig. 11.8 which is based on AlexNet [39] architecture. The AlexNet architecture consists of five convolutional layers and three fully connected layers. The last fully connected layer (also known as fc8 layer) has 1000 nodes, each node corresponding to one ImageNet category.

11.4.2   Feature Extraction

It has been shown [40, 41] that features extracted from the activation of a deep convolutional network trained in a fully supervised fashion on an image classification task (with a fixed but large set of categories) can be utilized for novel generic tasks that may differ significantly from the original task of image classification. These features are popularly called DeCAF features. A computer vision researcher who just needs DeCAF features on his dataset, is currently forced to set up the entire deep learning framework, which may or may not be relevant to them otherwise. CloudCV

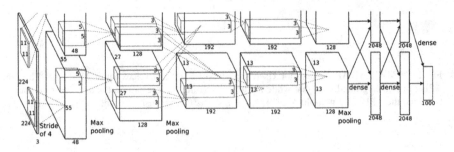

Fig. 11.8 Caffenet model architecture

alleviates this overhead by providing APIs that can be used to extract DeCAF features on the cloud and then download them as a "mat" file for further use.

CloudCV feature extraction implementation uses the same architecture as Fig. 11.8. The DeCAF features are the activations in the second-last fully connected layer (also known as fc7 layer), which consists of 4096 nodes. The caffenet model uses the fc7 activations computed from 10 sub-images—4 corner regions, the center region, and their horizontal reflections. Therefore, the output is a matrix of size 10,4096.

11.4.3 Train a New Category

The classification task described above is limited to a predefined set of 1000 ImageNet categories. In a number of situations, a user may need a classification model with categories other than ImageNet but may not have sufficient data or resources to train a new model from scratch. CloudCV contains a "Train a New Category" capability that can be used to efficiently add new categories to the existing caffenet model with 1000 ImageNet categories (Figs. 11.9, 11.10, and 11.11).

The new model is generated by appending additional nodes in the last fully connected layer (fc8 layer) of the existing caffenet model. Each new node added corresponds to a new category. The weights and biases for these additional nodes are computed using Linear Discriminant Analysis (LDA), which is equivalent to learning a Gaussian Naive Bayes classifier with equal covariance matrices for all categories. All other weights and biases are kept same as the existing caffenet model.

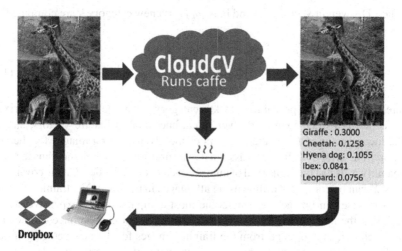

Fig. 11.9 Classification pipeline

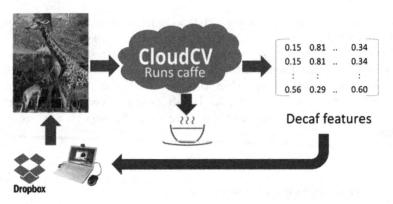

Fig. 11.10 Feature extraction pipeline

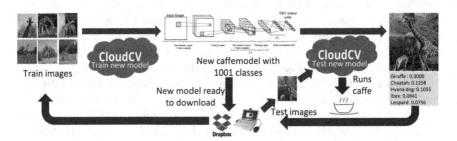

Fig. 11.11 Train a new category pipeline

The LDA weight vector (w_k) and bias (b_k) for a new category k are computed as:

$$w_k = \Sigma^{-1}\mu_k$$
$$b_k = \log \pi_k - \frac{1}{2}\mu_k^T \Sigma^{-1}\mu_k \tag{11.1}$$

where, π_k is the prior probability of kth category, Σ is the covariance matrix of fc7 (second-last fully connected layer in caffenet model) feature vectors, and μ_k is the mean vector of fc7 feature vectors of the given training images for the new category. The prior distribution is assumed to be uniform for this demo, thus the prior probability π_k is just the reciprocal of number of categories. Notice that the covariance matrix Σ can be computed offline using all images in the ImageNet training dataset, and its inverse can be cached. This is the most computationally expensive step in calculating the new parameters (weights and biases), but is done once offline. The mean vector μ_k is computed from the training images for the new category in real time. Thus, a new category can be added to the network instantaneously!

We have also experimented with fine-tuning the softmax layer, and the entire network from this LDA initialization, however, that is useful only when significant training data is available for the new category.

11.4.4 VIP: Finding Important People in Group Images

When multiple people are present in a photograph, there is usually a story behind the situation that brought them together: a concert, a wedding, a presidential swearing-in ceremony (Fig. 11.12), or just a gathering of a group of friends. In this story, not everyone plays an equal part. Some person(s) are the main character(s) and play a more central role.

Consider the picture in Fig. 11.13a. Here, the important characters are the couple who appear to be the British Queen and the Lord Mayor. Notice that their identities and social status play a role in establishing their positions as the key characters in that image. However, it is clear that even someone unfamiliar with the oddities and eccentricities of the British Monarchy, who simply views this as a picture of an elderly woman and a gentleman in costume receiving attention from a crowd, would consider those two to be central characters in that scene.

Figure 11.13b shows an example with people who do not appear to be celebrities. We can see that two people in foreground are clearly the focus of attention, and two others in the background are not. Figure 11.13c shows a common group photograph, where everyone is nearly equally important. It is clear that even without recognizing the identities of people, we as humans have a remarkable ability to understand social roles and identify important players.

Goal. The goal of CloudCV VIP is to *automatically predict the importance of individuals in group photographs*. In order to keep our approach general and applicable to any input image, we focus purely on visual cues available in the image, and do not

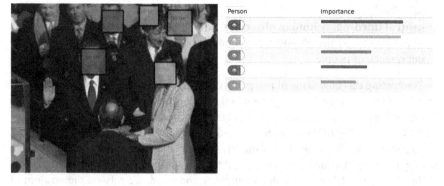

Fig. 11.12 VIP: Predict the importance of individuals in group photographs (without assuming knowledge about their identities)

(a) **(b)** **(c)**

Fig. 11.13 Who are the most important individuals in these pictures? **a** the couple (the British Queen and the Lord Mayor); **b** the person giving the award and the person receiving it play the main role; **c** everyone seems to be nearly equally important. Humans have a remarkable ability to understand social roles and identify important players, even without knowing identities of the people in the images

assume identification of the individuals. Thus, we do not use social prominence cues. For example, in Fig. 11.13a, we want an algorithm that identifies the elderly woman and the gentleman as the two most important people that image without utilizing the knowledge that the elderly woman is the British Queen.

A number of applications can benefit from knowing the importance of people. Algorithms for im2text (generating sentences that describe an image) can be made more humanlike if they describe only the important people in the image and ignore unimportant ones. Photo cropping algorithms can do "smart-cropping" of images of people by keeping only the important people. Social networking sites and image search applications can benefit from improving the ranking of photos where the queried person is important. Intelligent social robots can benefit from identifying important people in any scenario.

Who is Important? In defining importance, we can consider the perspective of three parties (which may disagree):

- **the photographer**, who presumably intended to capture some subset of people, and perhaps had no choice but to capture others;
- **the subjects**, who presumably arranged themselves following social interpersonal rules; and
- **neutral third-party human observers**, who may be unfamiliar with the subjects of the photo and the photographer's intent, but may still agree on the (relative) importance of people.

Navigating this landscape of perspectives involves many complex social relationships: the social status of each person in the image (an award winner, a speaker, the President), and the social biases of the photographer and the viewer (e.g., gender or racial biases); many of these cannot be easily mined from the photo itself. At its core, the question itself is subjective: if the British Queen "photo-bombs" while you are taking a picture of your friend, is she still the most important person in that photo?

In CloudCV VIP, to establish a quantitative protocol, we rely on the wisdom of the crowd to estimate the "ground-truth" importance of a person in an image. Our

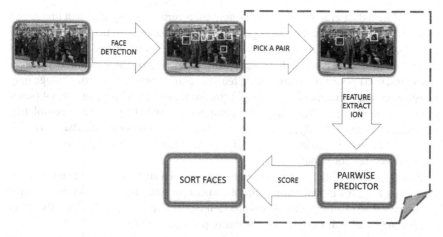

Fig. 11.14 VIP pipeline

relative importance models are trained using real-valued importance scores obtained using Amazon Mechanical Turk.

Pipeline. The basic flow of CloudCV VIP is shown in Fig. 11.14. First, face detection is performed using third-party face detectors. In our published work [42], we used Sky Biometry's API [43] for face detection. CloudCV VIP uses OpenCV [44] to avoid network latency. For every pair of detected faces, features are extracted that describe the relative configuration of these faces. These features are fed to our pretrained regressors to derive a relative importance score for this pair. Finally, the faces are sorted in descending order of importance. The models and features are described in detail in Mathialagan et al. [42]. In order to be fast during test time, CloudCV VIP does not use DPM-based pose features.

11.4.5 Gigapixel Image Stitching

The goal of *Image Stitching* is to create a composite panorama from a collection of images. The standard pipeline [45] for Image Stitching, consists of four main steps:

1. Feature Extraction: distinctive points (or keypoints) are identified in each image and a feature descriptor [46, 47] is computed for each keypoint.
2. Image/Feature Matching: features are matched between pairs of images to estimate relative camera transformations.
3. Global Refinement: of camera transformation parameters across all images.
4. Seam Blending: seams are estimated between pairs of images and blending is performed.

Consider a data graph $G = (V, E)$ where each vertex corresponds to a image and two vertices are connected by an edge if the two images overlap in content, i.e., capture a part of the scene from two viewpoints. In the context of this graph, different steps of the stitching pipeline have vastly different levels of parallelism. Step 1 (feature extraction) is *vertex parallel* since features extraction at each vertex/image may be run completely independently. Step 2 (image/feature matching) and step 4 (seam blending) are *edge parallel* since these computations may be performed completely independently at each edge in this graph. Together these steps are *data parallel*, where parallelism is achieved simply by splitting the data onto different machines with no need for coordination.

Step 3 (global refinement) is the most sophisticated step since it is not embarrassingly parallel. This global refinement of camera parameters, involves minimizing a nonlinear error function (called reprojection error) that necessarily depends on all images [48], and ultimately slows the entire pipeline down.

We formulate this optimization as a "message-passing" operation on the data graph—each vertex simply gathers some quantities from its neighbors and makes local updates to its camera parameters. Thus, different image can be processed on different machines as long as they communicate their camera parameters to their neighbors.

Thus, while this pipeline may not be data parallel, it is *graph parallel* show in Fig. 11.15b, meaning that data and computational dependencies are captured by a sparse undirected graph and all computation can be written as *vertex programs*. It is clear that thinking about visual sensing algorithms as vertex programs is a powerful abstraction.

The CloudCV image stitching functionality can be accessed through the web interface, a screenshot of which is shown in Fig. 11.16.

(a)

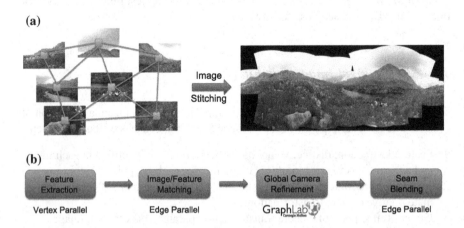

(b)

Fig. 11.15 Gigapixel image stitching. **a** Data graph and panorama. **b** Stitching pipeline

(a)   (b)

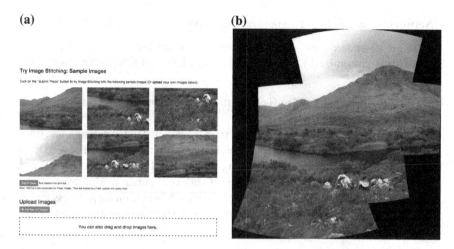

Fig. 11.16 Image stitching web interface. **a** Sample images and upload interface. **b** Result for the sample images

11.5 Future Work

11.5.1 Deep Learning GPU Training System—DIGITS

Convolutional Neural Networks (CNNs) have attracted significant interest from researchers in industry and academia, which has resulted in multiple software platforms for configuring and training CNNs. Most notable software platforms are Caffe, Theano, Torch7, and CUDA-Convnet2.

Recently, NVIDIA^TM released DIGITS [49], an interactive Deep Learning GPU Training System, which provides access to the rich set of functionalities provided by Caffe [19] through an intuitive browser-based graphical user interface. DIGITS complements Caffe functionality by introducing an extensive set of visualizations commonly used by data scientists and researchers. Moreover since DIGITS runs as a web service, this facilitates seamless collaboration between large teams enabling data, trained CNNs model and results in sharing.

DIGITS Overview

A typical workflow of DIGITS can be summarized as follows:

- **Data Source**: First the user has to upload the database to be used for training and validation to DIGITS. Currently, the database of image have to be stored on the same local machine hosting DIGITS.

- **Network Architecture**: Two options are supported for network architecture:
  - to use a standard network architecture such as AlexNet [50],
  - create a customized CNN where user can define each layer and associated parameters.

  DIGITS also provides a tool to visualize the CNN architecture for visual inspection of the network topology.
- **Training and Visualization**: Users can train the newly defined network and track its progress real time. The learning rate and accuracy of the model can be seen from real-time graph visualizations as training progresses. The user can abort training anytime if he suspects there is bug in the network configuration. Moreover similar to Caffe, DIGITS save multiple snapshots of the CNN as training progress giving the user the option to use specific snapshots to generate feature extraction.

Integrating DIGITS with CloudCV

CloudCV classification functionality uses Caffe as the software platform to train and configure CNN. One of the main objectives of CloudCV is to enable nonexperts the ability to use computer vision algorithms as a service through a rich set of API. In future work we will integrate CloudCV functionalities with DIGITS intuitive graphical user interface to provide an end-to-end system that can train a model, classify, or extract features from these trained model, visualize results, etc. Future work includes:

- Integrating the DIGITS codebase with CloudCV.
- Currently, DIGITS only support creating training data on the host machine. We plan to further extend data sources to include cloud storage such as Dropbox and Amazon S3.
- Integerating DIGITS with Scikit-learn [51]—a rich machine-learning Python library—to train different classifiers (Support Vector Machine, etc.) on features extracted from intermediate layers of a CNN. Users will be able to tune the parameters of the classifier and see improvement in real time.
- Extending Visualizations provided by DIGITS to include side-by-side plots to visualize performance of different classifiers on a specific dataset.
- Supporting for a user workspace, where each registered user can have a private workspace. User data like job history, previous datasets, pretrained models, previous outputs will be saved.

Acknowledgments This work was partially supported by the Virginia Tech ICTAS JFC Award, and the National Science Foundation CAREER award IIS-1350553. The views and conclusions contained herein are those of the authors and should not be interpreted as necessarily representing the official policies or endorsements, either expressed or implied, of the U.S. Government or any sponsor.

References

1. Big data, big impact: New possibilities for international development. World Economic Forum Report (2012) http://www.weforum.org/reports/big-data-big-impact-new-possibilities-international-development
2. Lohr, S.: The age of big data. New York Times (20102) http://www.nytimes.com/2012/02/12/sunday-review/big-datas-impact-in-the-world.html?pagewanted=all
3. Berriman, G.B., Groom, S.L.: How will astronomy archives survive the data tsunami? Queue 9(10), 21:20–21:27 (2011)
4. Kvilekval, K., Fedorov, D., Obara, B., Singh, A., Manjunath, B.: Bisque: a platform for bioimage analysis and management. Bioinformatics 26(4), 544–552 (2010)
5. Strickland, N.H.: Pacs (picture archiving and communication systems): filmless radiology. Arch. Dis. Child. 83(1), 82–86 (2000)
6. Le, Q., Ranzato, M., Monga, R., Devin, M., Chen, K., Corrado, G., Dean, J., Ng, A.: Building high-level features using large scale unsupervised learning. In: International Conference in Machine Learning (2012)
7. Deng, J., Dong, W., Socher, R., Li, L.-J., Li, K., Fei-Fei, L.: ImageNet: a large-scale hierarchical image database. CVPR (2009)
8. Shvachko, K., Kuang, H., Radia, S., Chansler, R.: The hadoop distributed file system. In: Proceedings of the 2010 IEEE 26th Symposium on Mass Storage Systems and Technologies, pp. 1–10 (2010)
9. Bradski, G., Kaehler, A.: Learning OpenCV: Computer Vision with the OpenCV Library. O'Reilly (2008). http://opencv.org
10. Integrating Vision Toolkit. http://ivt.sourceforge.net/
11. The Vision-*something*-Libraries. http://vxl.sourceforge.net/
12. Bolme, D.S., O'Hara, S.: Pyvision—computer vision toolkit (2008) http://pyvision.sourceforge.net
13. AForge.NET Image Processing Lab. http://www.aforgenet.com/
14. Bouguet J.Y.: Camera calibration toolbox for Matlab (2008) http://www.vision.caltech.edu/bouguetj/calib_doc/
15. Furukawa, Y.: Clustering Views for Multi-view Stereo (CMVS). http://grail.cs.washington.edu/software/cmvs/
16. Snavely, N.: Bundler: Structure from Motion (SfM) for Unordered Image Collections. http://phototour.cs.washington.edu/bundler/
17. Wu, C.: VisualSFM : a visual structure from motion system. http://www.cs.washington.edu/homes/ccwu/vsfm/
18. Vedaldi, A., Fulkerson, B.: VLFeat: an open and portable library of computer vision algorithms (2008) http://www.vlfeat.org/
19. Jia, Y., Shelhamer, E., Donahue, J., Karayev, S., Long, J., Girshick, R., Guadarrama, S., Darrell, T.: Caffe: convolutional architecture for fast feature embedding (2014) arXiv preprint arXiv:1408.5093
20. Bastien, F., Lamblin, P., Pascanu, R., Bergstra, J., Goodfellow, I.J., Bergeron, A., Bouchard, N., Bengio, Y.: Theano: new features and speed improvements. In: Deep Learning and Unsupervised Feature Learning NIPS 2012 Workshop (2012)
21. Bergstra, J., Breuleux, O., Bastien, F., Lamblin, P., Pascanu, R., Desjardins, G., Turian, J., Warde-Farley, D., Bengio, Y.: Theano: a CPU and GPU math expression compiler. In: Proceedings of the Python for Scientific Computing Conference (SciPy) (2010)
22. Torch:A scientific computing framework for LUAJIT. http://torch.ch/
23. Felzenszwalb, P.F., Girshick, R.B., McAllester, D.: Discriminatively trained deformable part models, release 4. http://www.cs.brown.edu/~pff/latent-release4/
24. Yang, Y., Ramanan, D.: Articulated pose estimation with flexible mixtures-of-parts. CVPR, pp. 1385–1392 (2011)
25. Kolmogorov, V., Zabih, R.: What energy functions can be minimized via graph cuts? PAMI 26(2), 147–159 (2004)

26. Amazon elastic compute cloud (amazon ec2). http://aws.amazon.com/ec2/
27. Orbeus rekognition. https://rekognition.com/
28. Clarifai. http://www.clarifai.com/
29. vision.ai. http://vision.ai/
30. Django: the web framework for perfectionists with deadlines. https://www.djangoproject.com/
31. Node.js. https://nodejs.org/
32. Socket.IO. http://socket.io/
33. Redis. http://redis.io/
34. Celery: distributed task queue. http://www.celeryproject.org/
35. javaScript Object Notation. http://torch.ch/
36. Advanced Message Queueing Protocol. https://www.amqp.org
37. Low, Y., Gonzalez, J., Kyrola, A., Bickson, D., Guestrin, C., Hellerstein, J.M.: Graphlab: a new parallel framework for machine learning. In: UAI (2010)
38. The Graphlab Computer Vision Toolkit. http://graphlab.org/toolkits/computer-vision/
39. Krizhevsky, A., Sutskever, I., Hinton, G.: Imagenet classification with deep convolutional neural networks. NIPS (2012)
40. Donahue, J., Jia, Y., Vinyals, O., Hoffman, J., Zhang, N., Tzeng, E., Darrell, T.: Decaf: a deep convolutional activation feature for generic visual recognition. ICML (2014)
41. Razavian, A.S., Azizpour, H., Sullivan, J., Carlsson, S.: CNN features off-the-shelf: an astounding baseline for recognition (2014) arXiv preprint arXiv:1403.6382
42. Mathialagan, C.S., Batra, D., Gallagher, A.C.: Vip: finding important people in group images. In: Computer Vision and Pattern Recognition (2015)
43. SkyBiometry. https://www.skybiometry.com/
44. Bradski, G.: The OpenCV library (2000)
45. Brown, M., Lowe, D.: Automatic panoramic image stitching using invariant features. IJCV **74**(1), 59–73 (2007)
46. Bay, H., Ess, A., Tuytelaars, T., Van Gool, L.: Speeded-up robust features (surf). Comput. Vis. Image Underst. **110**(3), 346–359 (2008)
47. Lowe, D.G.: Distinctive image features from scale-invariant keypoints. Int. J. Comput. Vision **60**(2), 91–110 (2004)
48. Triggs, B., Mclauchlan, P., Hartley, R., Fitzgibbon, A.: Bundle adjustment—a modern synthesis. Vision Algorithms: Theory and Practice. Lecture Notes in Computer Science, vol. 1883, pp. 298–372. Springer, Berlin (1999)
49. NVIDIA DIGITS interactive deep learning gpu training system. https://developer.nvidia.com/digits. Accessed 1 June 2015
50. Krizhevsky, A., Sutskever, I., Hinton, G.E.: Imagenet classification with deep convolutional neural networks. In: Advances in Neural Information Processing Systems, pp. 1097–1105 (2012)
51. Pedregosa, F., Varoquaux, G., Gramfort, A., Michel, V., Thirion, B., Grisel, O., Blondel, M., Prettenhofer, P., Weiss, R., Dubourg, V., Vanderplas, J., Passos, A., Cournapeau, D., Brucher, M., Perrot, M., Duchesnay, E.: Scikit-learn: machine learning in python. J. Mach. Learn. Res. **12**, 2825–2830 (2011)

Chapter 12
Cloud-Based Mobile Experience Sharing Through Automatic Multimedia Blogging

Hongzhi Li and Xian-Sheng Hua

Abstract The rapid developments of smart mobile devices, wireless networks, and cloud computing have extended mobile phones with much more functionalities rather than only being used as voice communication tools. With an increasing trend, more and more people are using camera phones to record and share their daily experiences due to its mobility and realtiming. Camera phones are true multimedia devices capable of managing acquisition, processing, transmission, and presentation of multiple modal data, such as image, video, audio, and text information, as well as rich contextual information like location, direction, and velocity from the equipped sensors. All these provide sufficient information and channel to effectively share peoples experiences. However, due to the complexity and structureless of the raw multimedia and contextual data, experience sharing is still a nontrivial task. There is still lack of efficient tools that supports mobile, rapid, and realtime experience sharing. In this paper, we will propose a mobile + cloud system enabling rapid and near-realtime experience sharing through automatic blogging and microblogging, which are based on multimodal media content analyses and syntheses. An experimental system shows the effectiveness and efficiency of the proposed scheme.

12.1 Introduction

Smart mobile devices such as camera phones typically will be carried by people most of the time. These devices are true multimedia devices that acquire, process, transmit and present text, image, video, and audio data using both media input (camera and other sensors) and output (screen and speaker) channels. However, due to the limitations in computation, storage, display, and camera, multimedia applications and systems have not been adequately supported on mobile devices. Recently, the

H. Li (✉)
Deptartment of Computer Science, Columbia University, New York, NY, USA
e-mail: hongzhili@cs.columbia.edu

X.-S. Hua
Microsoft Research, New York, NY, USA
e-mail: xshua@microsoft.com

© Springer International Publishing Switzerland 2015
G. Hua and X.-S. Hua (eds.), *Mobile Cloud Visual Media Computing*,
DOI 10.1007/978-3-319-24702-1_12

291

rapid development on cloud computing, high-resolution camera/display, 3G/Wi-Fi net networks, informative sensors, (such as GPS, gravity sensor, and compass), and more powerful CPU, largely mitigated these limitations. In particular, the support of cloud computing platform has become an essential factor especially for scalable and connected mobile multimedia technologies, applications and systems, due to its powerful support on computation, storage and networking.

With all these developments, more and more people are using camera phones to record and share personal experiences with friends and relatives. However, archiving and sharing multimedia experience data is a nontrivial task, and there is still no such a tool that can support these functionalities, especially in an efficient, mobile, and realtime manner. In this paper, we will propose such a system, Melog, standing for mobile/multimedia experience blogging, which leverages both the advantages of mobile devices and cloud computing platforms. We use near-realtime blogging and microblogging as the exemplary forms for experience archiving and sharing, which can be automatically generated based on analyzing the multimedia and contextual data captured from the mobile devices and mined from the Internet.

Travel blog is one of the most popular and convenient ways to share travel experiences with others. In general, people have to take advantage of PC to share records captured by mobile phones, cameras, and camcorders. It generally takes a long time to organize those records and difficult to be accomplished in realtime, therefore, we are unlikely able to share travel experiences with others during the trip. Though microblog, such as Twitter, is more flexible and has better mobility and realtiming in experience sharing, it is still difficult to compose multimedia microblog content effectively on mobile devices. Fortunately, more and more mobile devices have been equipped with sensors like GPS and compass, and with the help of 3G and Wi-Fi network accessing and mobile-cloud computing, it is possible to share travel experience automatically during the trip, even in realtime or near-realtime.

12.1.1 Related Work

We next review existing efforts on mobile multimedia blogging, which can be categorized into three paradigms: manual photo blogging, text-free automatic photo blogging, and text-rich automatic photo blogging.

Manual mobile blogging approaches commonly provide an interface on the mobile devices for inputting and/or selecting the content for the travel blog, then the manually created blog can be pushed into the blog web site. An example of the first paradigm is Nokia Life Blog [7], which allows users to select photos taken by camera phones and input text to create a travel blog, and then can be published on the Web via SMS, MMS, or email.

Although this kind of approaches make it possible to share travel experiences near-realtime through mobile devices directly, they are difficult to be used in practice due to inputting text on mobile devices is tedious, especially when people want to publish a group of photos.

Alternatively, the second paradigm, text-free automatic blogging, releases users from text inputting, instead, it organizes photos by space-time order and displays photos on a map without using additional text. For example, space-time travel blogging [1] displays photos on the map and shows their taken location, which are obtained from a GPS sensor. GeoLife [11] analyzes GPS data and shows photos taken during a trip on a map by time order. It provides a social networking service based on location as well.

Space-time travel blogging and GeoLife focus on how to use photos sequences with time and location information to share experience with others on a map. They failed to provide more information about the trip, especially lacking of text description when manual text inputs are not available. Besides, it cannot reflect users affections to photos, spots or the entire trip, and the blog style is monotonous.

The most closely related work to Melog is Travelog [5], which falls into the third paradigm, text-rich automatic blogging. It provides a relatively friendly interface to help users create a travel blog in an automatic (or semi-automatic) manner. Users are able to publish a travel blog by choosing a photo from the camera phone while related text information, such as, annotation, weather, and related links, can be automatically mined from the Internet, users profile and SnapToTell service [6]. However, the quality of the text information highly depends on the performance of the automatic annotation algorithm and the SnapToTell services, which are actually still challenging problems. Moreover, users still needs to manually select photos to he share, and the style and content of the travel blogs are fixed and in lack of flexibility.

To summarize, the first paradigm needs too much manual effort, and the blog presentation and content in the second paradigm are not rich and flexible enough. The quality of the blog content by the third paradigm highly depends on some challenging technologies thus not stable as well as photo selection still needs much human effort in this paradigm.

12.1.2 Our Approach

The work presented in this paper provides an automatic and intelligent application to generate and publish travel blog and microblog almost in realtime. The main idea of our approach is to summarize the trip intelligently without disturbing users other operations and share the experience in almost realtime during the trip. What the user needs to do is just using camera phones to capture photos, videos, and audios, while the Melog system will take care almost all the things (though interactions are also allowed). The main advantages of Melog system are:

- Easy to use: Almost fully automatic and very few manual input is required.
- Fast to share: Sharing travel experience with friends almost in realtime.
- Convenient to recall: Travel experiences are well organized and easy to recall.
- Less interruptive to travel: Almost no need to take consideration how to share the experience.

The rest of this paper is organized as follows. Section 12.2 provides an overview of system architecture. The method of automatic travel blog generation and presentation will be introduced in Sect. 12.3. The microblog generation scheme is presented in Sect. 12.4. Section 12.5 introduces the database organization. Section 12.6 gives experiment details and evaluation results, followed by concluding remarks in Sect. 12.7.

12.2 Melog System Architecture

First, we define a place as a *spot of interest* (SOI) where people tend to take photos. It may be a sightseeing spot, a building, or any objects or scenes that people are interested in taking photos for. We build in one or more sample photos for each SOI in the system, which are some representative photos taken in the SOI. Then, we define knowledge as a property set of a subject, where a subject could be a SOI or a sample photo associated with the SOI. Knowledge describes the key features of a subject. SOIs and sample photos contain some knowledge to descript their property and content, which will be used in the process of blog generation.

Figure 12.1 illustrates the system architecture of our system which contains two components: the client application on mobile devices and the service in the cloud. Photos, videos, and audios are captured on the mobile client, and then those multimedia travel records will be uploaded to a platform in the cloud with sensor data captured by the devices (say, GPS data).

During a trip, microblog generation and publishing can be either triggered in three modes: fully automatically (FA), semi-automatically (SA), or manually (M). Users location information will be recorded automatically and sent to the location analysis platform in the cloud to analyze the users moving status. When location analysis platform finds that the user is leaving a SOI spot and has taken some photos there, a microblog about this spot will be generated and published into users microblog or blog website automatically in the FA model. While in SA model, the user will be asked to review the content, edit the content if necessary, and decide whether to

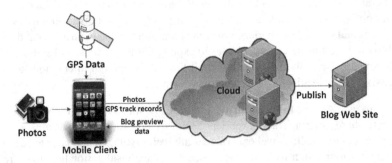

Fig. 12.1 Melog system architecture

publish. In M mode, the user can manually trigger a blog or microblog generation and publishing process.

When finished the trip, the user can choose to generate a complete travel blog about this trip using our system. After the travel blog is generated, a blog preview and modification tool can be executed in the mobile client to allow people edit the travel blog when necessary. Moreover, there is an affection evaluation system in our application. Users can set up some affection variables and style predilections to generate travel blogs that can reflect the users affection about the trip and are with preferred presentation styles.

12.2.1 Services in the Cloud

Several services are deployed in the cloud to support data transmission, storage, analysis, processing, and presentation. The complex computing will be executed in the cloud and the result will be sent to the mobile client.

There are three services running on the cloud side. First, there is a file service to support the file uploading and storage. Second, a users location capturing and analyzing service is built to record and analyze users location and moving status. At third, a blog generation service is running to create and publish travel blogs and microblogs.

12.2.2 Application on Mobile Client

The application in mobile client supports collecting travel records, preview, and edit the travel blogs. Users can also configure the system parameters in mobile client to decide, such as, whether to generate and publish the microblog during the trip, style of the blog, and affection of the travel blog, etc. The user interface of Melog is shown in Fig. 12.2.

The mobile application will monitor users photo folder on the client. When a new photo is taken, the mobile application will obtain the location information from GPS sensor and then upload it with its supported information (such as location information, taken time, owner id, session id) to the file service on the cloud server. There is a separate thread recording the users location at short intervals in mobile client. Those records will be uploaded to the cloud at the same intervals. When user finishes his trip, he can use the application in mobile client to preview and modify the complete travel blog generated by the cloud service.

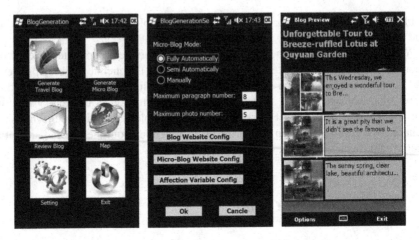

Fig. 12.2 User interface of melog

12.3 Travel Blog Generation

In this section, we will introduce the method of generating the travel blog after a trip, while microblog generation, which involves users moving status analysis, will be detailed in Sect. 12.4. Travel blog generation service is running on the cloud, which can be divided into four steps. First, we will select representative photos from all of photos taken in the trip. Using location information and the content of photos, we can retrieve knowledge from our knowledge database. With the knowledge and photos location information, we get a rough organization of the travel blog data or called paragraph metadata set. Then according to the content of article structure template, we organize related information into blog metadata. After we get the blog metadata, blogging text will be generated based on the natural language generation module. Finally, we will use the presentation template, blog metadata and text to create a complete travel blog.

12.3.1 Photo Selection and Knowledge Retrieval

In this section, we introduce how to select the representative photos and determine the spots of interests which are visited by users during the trip, and how to retrieve knowledge from the knowledge database.

Photo Clustering with Location Information

It is reasonable to assume that a user will take more photos in a spot the user is interested in. We can get a rough structure about the users trip through clustering photos with its location information. In general, a photo cluster center should be near a SOI and in the ideal case, one cluster center corresponds to one SOI. But in practice, user may photograph a spot near another spot or take photos between two spots. Therefore, we choose fuzzy c-means clustering algorithm [2] to cluster photos. Using this algorithm, we can get a group of coefficients which represent the possibility of the photo belongs to each cluster.

Mapping Spots of Interest to Clusters

Detecting visited SOIs from the photo clusters is the key process of travel blog generation. This step finds candidate visited SOIs by computing the physical distance between a SOI and a photo cluster, which is obtained from the associated GPS data. The main idea is to choose the nearest SOI for each the photo cluster based on GPS distance. First, set an interval $[\alpha, \beta]$ and an ideal number of chosen SOI γ for each cluster. The SOIs which the distance from the cluster center is less than a will be chosen immediately. If the number of selected SOIs n is less than γ, we will choose at most $(\gamma - n)$ the nearest SOIs from those whose distance from the cluster center is less than β. After assigning SOIs to each cluster, we get all of selected SOIs as candidate SOIs. We can expect that those candidate SOIs have a great possibility that the user has visited them during the trip, but it cannot be absolutely determined now. We will double check them using the method introduced in the next.

Photo Selection Using Sample Photos

This step refines the visited SOI list obtained from last step through comparing photos in the matched cluster with the sample photos of the SOI. If at least one pair of photos (one from the cluster and one from sample photo set of the SOI) matches well, we can determine the SOI is visited by the user. Otherwise, it can be inferred that the user did not visit this SOI or just walked through it but without taking any photos. In current implementation, this type of SOIs will be ignored in blog generation.[1]

12.3.2 Paragraph Metadata and Blog Metadata

Paragraph Metadata (PM) contains the necessary data (such as photos, knowledge, and some other properties) to create a single paragraph of the travel blog. After photos are selected for each candidate SOI, paragraph metadata can be created based on the information of those SOIs. It consists of selected photos and knowledge from

---

[1] Alternatively we may also detect the fact of visited without taking photos through GPS traces, and may also be reflected in the text part of the blog.

a single SOI. We also compute several properties for each PM, such as average time of the selected photos and the weight of paragraph.

Blog Metadata (BM) consists of the properties of the travel blog and a list of PM. An article structure template is defined to control the structure of the travel blog, such as the maximal number of photos in each paragraph, the maximal number of paragraph and the order of paragraphs, etc. BM can be created by the paragraph metadata set with an article structure template.

12.3.3 Blogging Text Generation

The text in travel blog is used to introduce the visited spot, the content of photos and the users experience. We developed a knowledge-and affection-based nature language generation system to generate text for each blog paragraph. In general, as mentioned in [9], natural language generation (NLG) system has three stages including six tasks. Based on this stages division, we come up with a method to realize the affective NLG system.

12.3.4 Blog Presentation

When the blog content is ready, a presentation template is used to represent the travel blog. Presentation template is a standard html file with some custom tags which defines the style of a travel blog. The presentation template can be chosen from database according to the type of travel blogs and users affection variable, and then the custom tags will be replaced with the real data to generate the travel blog.

Photo Collage

Photo collage is used to show a group of photos in order to make the blog more interesting and lively. Several photo collage methods can be adopted in our Melog system.

Simple photo collage rules are applied when the number of photos is small (say, less than four). We can also use existing approaches like Picture Collage [10] and Auto Collage [4] to show multiple photos in one synthesized picture.

Link to Photosynth

In some case, user may like to capture a large number of photos around the same place. A 3D scene can be reconstructed by a group of photos using Photosynth [8] [12].

We can detect the number and content of photos taken in the same place. If the number and quality of photos are satisfied to create a new Photosynth, we will create one in Bing Map [3] and add a link Browse more in Photosynth in travel blog.

12.4 Micro-Blog Generation

In this section, we will introduce another method to share travel experience in realtime by creating and publishing the microblog.

Comparing with the method of travel blog generation, microblog generation process is more like to create a one paragraph travel blog with a single photo. The key point of microblog generation is to understand the users moving state and detect when the user have visited a spot that is, the user is leaving for a new spot and thus a microblog for the just-visited spot will be published automatically (FA mode) or semi-automatically (SA model).

12.4.1 Understand the Users Moving State

Figure 12.3 shows an example of a users travel route during he arrived at and left a spot. Every red point in the figure stands for the location information obtained from the GPS sensor by a certain time interval. A location sequence L is defined to denote the location points in the trip. The first location point is L(0) and the current location point is denoted by L(i). The location points will be added into L with the users moving. We compute a weight for each new location point by

$$W(i) = \sum_{j=0}^{i-1} \frac{1}{\sigma\sqrt{2\pi}} e^{\frac{-dis(i,j)}{2\sigma^2}} * time(i,j) \tag{12.1}$$

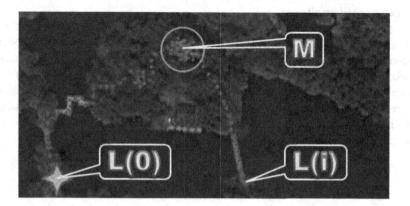

Fig. 12.3 A Sample travel route

where dis(i,j) is the distance between location point i and j; σ is the coefficient; time(i,j) = 1 if the time interval between i and j is less than 5 min, otherwise, time(i,j) = 0.

The change of W can reflect users moving state. If W begin to increase a relative great value, it means the user is stopped or walks slowly. Then, if W holds a relative great value for some time, it means the user stays at a place. When W begins to decrease, it means the user left the place or changed the moving state from slowly moving or stop to walking as usual. When it is detected that W begins to increase, and then hold on a relative great value, finally decreases to the average value, we mark this process as M, which means the user visited a spot during the time of M. If some photos are captured during M, we also find the SOI near the center of the location points recorded at M and Melog system is configured in the FA or SA model, the microblog will be created using the microblog generation service.

12.4.2 Create and Publish the Micro-Blog

Microblog generation is similar with the travel blog generation. We can regard microblog as a one paragraph and one photo travel blog. The same method is used to create paragraph metadata and blog metadata. The number of words in microblog will be limited by NLG system. After the microblog was generated, it will be published into the users microblog website through the APIs provided by the microblog website.

12.5 Database Organization

We organize SOI information, knowledge, and sample photos, etc. into a database. Since most of operation of Melog is based on the database, the performance, and quality of travel blog generation highly depends on the database. The database can be constructed manually but only one time (though could be updated when necessary), and can be used by all users.

Alternatively, we can also use automatic or semi-automatic method to build the database by mining the data from Flickr, search engine and other webpages. SOIs and sample photos can be built by clustering images with location information from Flickr, and then, some general introduction about those SOIs and sample photos will be generated through webpage analyzing technology. Finally, the special information about each SOI can be added manually. On the other hand, the database can also be built manually by leveraging grassroots users on the Internet given an appropriate manual or semi-automatic tool.

12.6   Experiment and Evaluations

In this section, we conducted extensive experiments to evaluate the proposed scheme, including both subjective and objective evaluations. We first evaluate the performance of the SOI selection and the photo selection, and then investigated the performance of Melog system. At last, we have a comparison between Melog system and Travelog system [5]. We invited eight users to evaluate our Melog system. They were asked to use our Melog application and service to record and share the travel experiences of their real trips. In the experiment, each user takes about 70 photos on the average and 10 places (each contains multiple SOIs) are visited. We build the ground truth of candidate SOI selection and candidate photo selection for each scenic spot by hand to evaluate the performance of SOI and photo selection.

12.6.1   Evaluate the Spot of Interest Selection

According to the travel records of participants, the Ground truth is built for each group of data. We mark up the spot as correct if the user visited it, and others are wrong. The average precision and average recall are computed. The result of average precision is 1^2 and the result of average recall is 0.858. The miss selected SOI is caused by the strict strategy we used in photo retrieval process, since we have to guarantee the accuracy of photo selection first. Therefore, some SOIs did not get any photos in photo retrieval process and they were ignored.

12.6.2   Evaluation of Photo Selection and Text Generation

Photo selection is very important to the travel experience sharing. We evaluate the performance of image selection by checking whether the selected photos match with the text, since the text is generated based on the knowledge from the SOI and sample photos. If the text and photo are well matched, it means the photo is currently selected. A web application is built to collect the evaluations from participants. The web application will choose one photo with its text from the generated travel blog and ask the participants if the text is well described the photo. The answers from participants will be stored in our database. We got the average accuracy of photo-text matching is 0.927. It means the most of photos are correctly selected and the text is also well generated. An example of part of the travel blog is shown in Fig. 12.4.

---

[2] As both location information and photo content are used to select SOIs in our system, the selected SOIs are accurate and could hardly be imprecise, though it is possible that there will be slight inaccuracies in practical application because of the proximity of two spots.

Fig. 12.4 An example of part of the travel blog

12.6.3 Evaluation of the Entire Melog System

We invited the eight participants (as the users of the Melog system) to evaluate the Melog system during their trip. They were asked following questions to evaluate the performance of Melog system and the quality of generated blog.

Q1: Is it convenient to generate a travel blog using this application?

Q2: Are photos in travel blog selected reasonable?

Q3: Is the text in travel blog natural?

Q4: Does the blog well summarize your trip?

And then, we invited the other 30 participants (as the readers of the travel blogs) to evaluate the travel blogs generated in our experiment as blog visitors, where the following questions were asked.

Q5: Is the travel blog interesting and good looking?

Q6: Is the text in travel blog natural?

Q7: Does the micro-blog help you understand more about your friends trip?

Users were asked to give a score ranging from 1 (the worst) to 5 (the best) to each of these questions. Figure 12.5 shows the average scores of this evaluation, which shows quite encouraging results. We also found the satisfaction degree of the text in travel blog (corresponds to question Q3 and Q6) is relatively lower than the

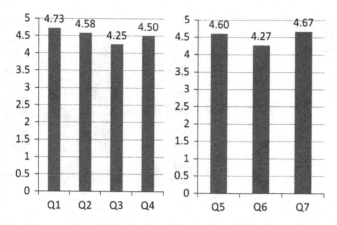

Fig. 12.5 Evaluation result of melog system

evaluation of other aspects. In fact, affective natural language generation is still a changing problem. We will find a better way to generate the affective text in our future work. In general, users are actually very satisfied with our application according to the evaluation.

12.6.4 Comparison

As afore mentioned, Travelog [5] is the most relevant effort to Melog. Therefore, some users are invited to evaluate the operation and the generated travel blog of these two systems. Participants were asked to score the following questions about the two applications:

Q8: The content of blog is rich and well organized.
Q9: The travel blog is pleasant to the read in terms of the presentation style.
Q10: The process of travel blog generation is fast and convenient.

As the result shown in Fig. 12.6, it can be seen that the performance of Melog is obviously better than those of the Travelog system.

In addition, the estimated time of creating and publishing a travel blog by Melog system is about 15 s (begin at the user wants to generate a travel blog and end with the travel blog is published, including the time of downloading the preview data and confirming), while the time of Travelog is 66.5 s (mentioned in [5]) without considering the time of selecting photos and typing the title of travel blog. Moreover, the time for microblog creating and publishing in Melog can be ignored as it is running at the background as an automatic service.

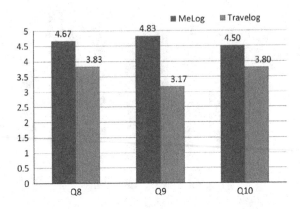

Fig. 12.6 Evaluation result of the comparison between MeLog and travelog.

12.7 Conclusions

In this paper, we have proposed a new mobile multimedia application to help users record and share travel experiences by analyzing the GPS data and photos captured in the trip. We provided an easy and widely accepted method, automatic blogging, to share travel experience with others. We focus on how to reduce users input, create the travel blog intelligently and share the travel experience in realtime. With this application, user can focus on enjoying the happiness of travel itself without many interruptions. Recording, sharing, and recalling travel experiences become more natural and easier. In the future work, we will use more methods to share the travel experience such as organize the travel photos into a video with some presentation methods. New types of travel blog organization approaches, such as image classification based ones, will also be used in the future system.

References

1. Bamford, W., Coulton, P., Edwards, R.: Space-time travel blogging using a mobile phone. In: Proceedings of the International Conference on Advances in Computer Entertainment Technology. ACM, p 8. (2007)
2. Bezdek, J., Ehrlich, R., et al.: FCM: the fuzzy c-means clustering algorithm. Comput. Geosci. **10**(2–3), 191–203 (1984)
3. BingMap. http://www.bing.com
4. Bordeaux, L., Hamadi, Y., Blake, A., Rother, C.: AutoCollage. ACM trans. graph. **25**(3), 847 (2006)
5. Cemerlang, P., Lim, J., You, Y., Zhang, J., Chevallet, J.: Towards automatic mobile blogging. In: IEEE International Conference on Multimedia and Expo, pp. 2033–2036 (2006)
6. Lim, J., Chevallet, J., Merah, S.: Snaptotell: Ubiquitous information access from camera. In: Workshop on Mobile and Ubiquitous Information Access (2004)
7. NokiaLifeBlog. http://press.nokia.com/pr/200603/10381815.html
8. Photosynth. http://photosynth.net
9. Reiter, E., Dale, R.: Building applied natural language generation systems. Nat. Lang. Eng. **3**(01), 5787 (1997)

10. Wang, J., Quan, L., Sun, J., Tang, X., Shum, H.: Picture collage. In: IEEE Computer Society Conference on Computer Vision and Pattern Recognition, vol. 1 (2006)
11. Zheng, Y., Chen, Y., Xie, X., Ma, W.: GeoLife2. 0: a location-based social networking service. In: proceedings of International Conference on Mobile Data Management (2009)
12. Li, H., Zhu, W.: mPano: cloud-based mobile panorama view from single picture. Proc. SPIE 8856, Applications of Digital Image Processing XXXVI, 88560D, September 26 (2013)

Chapter 13
Automatic Visual Pattern Discovery via Cohesive Subgraph Mining

Gangqiang Zhao and Junsong Yuan

Abstract One category of videos usually contains the same thematic pattern, e.g., the spin action in skating videos. The discovery of the thematic pattern is essential to understand and summarize the video contents. This article addresses two critical issues in mining thematic video patterns: (1) automatic discovery of thematic patterns without any training or supervision information, and (2) accurate localization of the occurrences of all thematic patterns in videos. The major contributions are twofold. First, we formulate the thematic video pattern discovery as a cohesive subgraph selection problem by finding a subset of visual words that are spatio-temporally collocated. Then spatio-temporal branch-and-bound search can locate all instances accurately. Second, a novel method is proposed to efficiently find the cohesive subgraph of maximum overall mutual information scores. Our experimental results on challenging commercial and action videos show that our approach can discover different types of thematic patterns despite variations in scale, view-point, color, and lighting conditions, or partial occlusions. Our approach is also robust to the videos with cluttered and dynamic backgrounds.

13.1 Introduction

One category of videos usually shares the same thematic pattern. Such a thematic pattern can be the visual object that is frequently highlighted in the video, e.g., the product logo in a commercial video, or a specific event that appears commonly, e.g., spin action in skating videos. It is of great interests to discover thematic patterns in videos as they are essential to the understanding and summarization of the video contents.

G. Zhao (✉) · J. Yuan
School of Electrical and Electronic Engineering, Nanyang Technological University,
Singapore, Singapore
e-mail: gqzhao@ntu.edu.sg

J. Yuan
e-mail: jsyuan@ntu.edu.sg

© Springer International Publishing Switzerland 2015   307
G. Hua and X.-S. Hua (eds.), *Mobile Cloud Visual Media Computing*,
DOI 10.1007/978-3-319-24702-1_13

Even though tremendous progress has been made for the frequent pattern mining over a decade [6], there are three major challenges for mining thematic visual pattern in videos. First, visual patterns generally exhibit large variabilities in their visual appearances. Different instances of the same thematic pattern may vary significantly due to viewpoint and illumination changes, scale changes, partial occlusion, not to mention the large variations of videos events. Second, visual patterns have complex structures. Different visual items (image patches) can be correlated due to temporal and spatial dependency and co-occurrences. Finally, it is challenging to locate the thematic pattern accurately in the cluttered and dynamic video scenes. Therefore, it is difficult and time consuming, even for human beings, to find the thematic patterns in videos accurately.

To deal with the above challenges, some recent approaches have been proposed to discover common objects in images [3, 14, 21, 27, 30]. Despite a moderate success, these image-based methods cannot be extended to video data directly. For example, to represent the images using the transaction data, Russell et al. have proposed to segment the image multiple times [21]. However, it is very difficult, if not impossible, to segment the video sequences multiple times due to the high computational cost. Besides, the thematic video object may be small and hidden in the cluttered background, while existing object discovery approaches usually assume the object dominates the whole image [27]. Furthermore, for thematic event, it is important to take its spatiotemporal characteristics into consideration, while previous image-based methods only deal with spatial patterns [34].

We propose a novel thematic video pattern discovery method that addresses the challenges mentioned above. A video sequence is characterized by a number of key frames and each frame is composed of a collection of local visual features. After clustering the features into visual words, we measure the pairwise relationship between two words using the mutual information criterion and represent the relationship of all words as an affinity graph. The thematic pattern becomes a cohesive subgraph which has the maximum overall mutual information score and this subgraph can be obtained efficiently by the proposed mining approach. In addition, to identify the thematic pattern, we perform an efficient bounding box search to locate all of the instances of the thematic pattern.

The benefits of our method are threefold. First, our method is a pure data-driven approach and can discover the thematic video patterns automatically by mining the cohesive subgraph. Second, by applying the branch-and-bound search, our method can accurately locate all instances of the thematic patterns in cluttered and dynamic video scenes. Last but not least, by incorporating an affinity graph to describe the spatial or spatiotemporal contextual relationships of visual features, the proposed cohesive subgraph mining is robust to local feature errors, e.g., quantization errors of visual words or the miss detection of local feature. The experimental results on challenging commercial videos and action datasets show that our approach can discover the thematic pattern despite its variations due to scale, view-point, color, and lighting condition changes. It can also accurately locate the thematic patterns in the cluttered and dynamic video scenes.

A preliminary version of this article was published in [33]. The current version described here differs from the former in several ways, including: the detailed description of the cohesive subgraph mining algorithm; further analysis and discussion of the whole approach; as well as the introduction of more related works about visual pattern discovery.

13.2   Related Work

Most existing common pattern discovery methods fall into one of the three categories: frequent pattern mining-based methods, topic model-based methods, and subgraph matching-based methods. Frequent pattern mining-based methods first translate each image into a collection of "visual words" and then discover the common pattern through frequently co-occurring words mining [22, 28, 30]. To represent each image using the transaction data, [30] considers the spatial K-nearest neighbors (K-NN) of each local features as a transaction record. However, it is difficult to select the size K of the nearest neighborhood as there is no a priori knowledge about the thematic pattern scale. Reference [22] proposes both a priori-based and pattern-growth approaches for mining spatial co-orientation image patterns, which refer to the spatial objects that occur frequently and collocate with the same orientation among each other. However, this method only deals with the spatial relations of image patterns. The frequent pattern mining algorithms are summarized in [6].

Topic model-based methods discover the common pattern through topic discovery [4, 21, 24]. To represent the images using the transaction data, [21] segments the image multiple times. However, even though each image is segmented multiple times, the common object is often not well segmented due to multiple objects or the cluttered background. After obtaining a pool of segments from all images, object topics are discovered using Latent Dirichlet Allocation model (LDA) [1] and the most supportive topic is selected as the common topic. The segments corresponding to the common topic are selected as the common objects.

Traditional subgraph matching methods characterize an image as a graph or a tree composed of visual features. Then, the common pattern is discovered by graph or tree matching [7, 27]. However, the existing approaches require the training step and have high computational cost. Different with subgraph matching methods, we characterize all key frames using an affinity graph of all visual features and find the thematic pattern by cohesive subgraph mining. Our method is a pure data-driven approach and can discover the thematic video patterns without any training step. Recently, [28] employs the subgraph (max clique) mining technology as the top-down graph-based approach for frequent pattern mining. However, this subgraph mining algorithm is designed specifically for the proposed *pattern graph*.

Besides discovering common patterns from images, there is also recent work in discovering common patterns from video sequences [13]. This method needs supervision information about the common patterns and user labeling to initialize the search, thus it is not fully unsupervised. In addition, the visual pattern discovery can be combined with co-segmentation algorithms [8, 20, 26, 32]. Other related works can also be found in a recent survey of visual pattern discovery [25].

13.3 Thematic Pattern Discovery

To discover the thematic patterns from videos, visual features are extracted from key frames and clustered into visual words first. Then, we build an affinity graph to capture the pairwise relationships of the visual words in all key frames. Next, the cohesive subgraph corresponding to the thematic pattern is discovered by the proposed mining method. Finally, instances of the thematic pattern are located using the branch-and-bound method. Figure 13.1 illustrates the main steps of our method. The following subsections describe details about these steps.

13.3.1 Preliminaries

Our method first extracts a set of local visual features from the key frames, e.g., the SIFT features [15] or spatial-temporal interest point (STIP) features [10]. Each visual

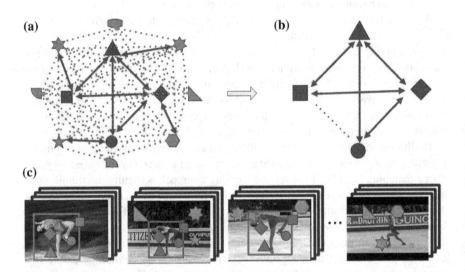

Fig. 13.1 Illustration of the main steps in our method. First, the pairwise relation between the visual words in all key frames is characterized by an affinity graph (**a**), where the *red arrows* indicate the positive affinity value between two words, while the *green-dashed lines* indicate the negative affinity value. The thematic pattern corresponds to the cohesive subgraph which has the maximum overall affinity score. **b** Represents the discovered cohesive subgraph. Using the branch-and-bound search, the thematic pattern is located and highlighted by the *red bounding box* in (**c**)

feature in key frame I_m is described as a feature vector $\phi_m(\mathbf{u}) = [\mathbf{u}, \mathbf{d}]$, where the 3D vector $\mathbf{u}$ is its spatial location and temporal order, and the high-dimensional vector $\mathbf{d}$ encodes the visual appearance of this feature. Then, a key frame I_m is represented by a set of visual features $I_m = \{\phi_m(\mathbf{u}_1), \ldots, \phi_m(\mathbf{u}_p)\}$. Clustering algorithms, such as k-means, group the features in $\{I_m\}_{m=1}^{M}$ according to the similarity between their appearance vectors, yielding N visual words $\Pi = \{W_1, W_2, \ldots, W_N\}$. The features clustered to word W_i are named as instances of word W_i. We denote this representation as the following induced feature-word set:

Definition 1 (*Induced Feature-word Set*)
The induced feature-word set is defined as $\{\boldsymbol{\Phi}_{mi}\}_{m=1}^{M}{}_{i=1}^{N}$, where $\boldsymbol{\Phi}_{mi} = \{\phi_{mi}\}$ represents all instances of word W_i in key frame I_m, *and* ϕ_{mi} is one of these features.

The relation of all visual words can be represented by an affinity graph, where each edge represents the relation between two words, as shown in Fig. 13.1a. As is customary, we represent the affinity graph with the corresponding affinity matrix A. Given two words W_i and W_j, the affinity relationship between them is intuitively defined as following.

Definition 2 (*Pairwise Affinity*)
The affinity value $A_{i,j}$ describes the chance of two words W_i and W_j belonging to the same thematic pattern. While $A_{i,j} \geq 0$ implies that the two words have a high probability of being in the same thematic pattern, and $A_{i,j} \leq 0$ otherwise.

The estimation of the pairwise affinity will be discussed in Sect. 13.3.2. The affinity of all wordpairs are concatenated as a $N \times N$ symmetric matrix A.

13.3.2 Pairwise Affinity Measurement

Given the visual words representation, we can estimate the affinity $A_{i,j}$ between each wordpair $\mathscr{P} = \{W_i, W_j\}$. Existing works demonstrate that word co-occurrence is an important criterion for common pattern discovery [5, 21]. However, due to the inherent complexity of a visual pattern, visual words that co-occur frequently do not always suggest an accurate and meaningful affinity relationship. Even if a word-pair appears frequently, it is not clear whether such co-occurrences are statistically significant or just by chance. Therefore, inspired by the work [30], we employ the point-wise mutual information criterion to estimate the affinity relationship of two words:

$$S(\mathscr{P}) = \log\left(\frac{Pr(\mathscr{P})}{Pr(W_i) \times Pr(W_j)}\right), \tag{13.1}$$

where $Pr(\mathscr{P})$ is the joint probability of wordpair $\mathscr{P}$ and $Pr(W_i)$ is the individual probability of word W_i. This quantity can take on both negative and positive values and is zero if W_i and W_j are independent. Its value is positive if W_i and W_j are positively correlated, while it is negative if they are negatively correlated.

To estimate the probability $Pr(\mathscr{P})$ and $Pr(W_i)$, simply checking their occurrence frequency is far from sufficient. Even in the same key frame, one instance of a visual word may belong to the thematic pattern while the other instance of the same visual word may belong to the background. This situation is very common especially for some frequent visual words. Therefore, we first employ the stop list method to discard the most frequent visual words that occur in almost all key frames, as these visual words often have limited discriminative power [21].

Ideally, two words corresponding to the same pattern need to not only co-occur in different key frames, but also maintain a consistent spatial relationship. But in practice, it is difficult to catch this kind of consistency because (1) the appearance variations and (2) the enormous computational cost involved in exploring the huge solution space, given the variations in location, scale, and the number of thematic patterns. So we assume the features belong to the same thematic pattern should be close in the same key frame. We count the number of effective occurrence of $\mathscr{P}$ as:

$$\mathscr{N}(\mathscr{P}) = |\{m : D_{min}(\phi_{mi}, \phi_{mj}) < \Lambda_D\}|, \tag{13.2}$$

where $D_{min}(\phi_{mi}, \phi_{mj})$ represents the minimal distance between instances of W_i and W_j in key frame I_m, and Λ_D is a threshold. For spatiotemporal features, $D_{min}(\phi_{mi}, \phi_{mj})$ should also consider the temporal information. The number of effective occurrence of each word $\mathscr{N}(W_i)$ is also obtained as:

$$\mathscr{N}(W_i) = |\{m : \exists j, D_{min}(\phi_{mi}, \phi_{mj}) < \Lambda_D\}|. \tag{13.3}$$

Instances of W_i and W_j that satisfy $D_{min}(\phi_{mi}, \phi_{mj}) < \Lambda_D$, will be added to $\hat{\boldsymbol{\Phi}}_{mi}$ and $\hat{\boldsymbol{\Phi}}_{mj}$, respectively. The set $\hat{\boldsymbol{\Phi}}_{mi} \subseteq \boldsymbol{\Phi}_{mi}$ represents the visual features of key frame I_m which contribute to the estimation of $\mathscr{N}(W_i)$.

Based on the point-wise mutual information criterion, the wordpair affinity value is:

$$A_{i,j} = \log \left(\frac{\mathscr{N}(\mathscr{P})/M}{\mathscr{N}(W_i)/M \times \mathscr{N}(W_j)/M} \right). \tag{13.4}$$

If W_i and W_j do not have any effective co-occurrence, $A_{i,j}$ is set a negative value τ.

13.3.3 Thematic Pattern Discovery by Cohesive Subgraph Mining

In order to discover thematic patterns from videos, we consider the integrity and uniqueness of the visual pattern's representation. In other words, the thematic pattern is composed of a specific group of words. Therefore, following this intuition, we represent the thematic pattern as the cohesive subgraph and denote this subgraph using its vertices set Ω, where elements of Ω are the words belong to the same thematic pattern. We define the affinity potential function of the subgraph Ω as $f(\Omega) = \sum_{W_i, W_j \in \Omega} A_{i,j}$ and the solution to the following optimization problem gives the maximum cohesive subgraph:

$$\Omega^* = arg \max_{\Omega \subseteq \Pi} f(\Omega), \tag{13.5}$$

i.e., the subgraph that has the largest affinity potential is the maximum cohesive subgraph. As each thematic pattern is presented by a subgraph, we can discover them one by one. After one pattern is discovered, the features belong to this pattern will be removed and another pattern can be found.

When obtaining the affinity matrix A for all wordpairs, the subset optimization problem in Eq. 13.5 is converted to a binary optimization problem. Given, a subgraph Ω, let $\mathbf{x} = \{x_i\}_{i=1}^N$ with $x_i \in \{-1, 1\}$ represents its indicator vector. When $x_i = 1$, word W_i belongs to subgraph Ω, and vice versa. As the indicator vector $\mathbf{x}$ and the subgraph Ω correspond to each other, Eq. 13.5 can be rewritten as:

$$\mathbf{x}^* = arg \max_{\mathbf{x}} \ f(\mathbf{x}) = \frac{1}{4}(1 + \mathbf{x})^T A(1 + \mathbf{x}),$$
$$s.t. \ x_i \in \{1, 1\}, i = 1, \ldots, N, \tag{13.6}$$

where $f(\mathbf{x}) = \frac{1}{4}(1 + \mathbf{x})^T A(1 + \mathbf{x})$ is the objective function. Equation 13.6 is a binary quadratic programming (BQP) problem. Since A may not be the positive definite matrix, the objective function $f(\mathbf{x})$ can be nonconvex, thus it is a NP problem. Section 13.4 describes the proposed solution of this problem.

13.3.4 Thematic Pattern Localization

After obtaining the cohesive subgraph Ω^*, we can locate the thematic patterns in videos via the occurrences of their corresponding visual features. The instance of thematic pattern is located by assigning each pixel a corresponding confidence score. For a pixel $\mathbf{u}$, if its corresponding feature is assigned to one word in the cohesive subgraph Ω^*, we set its confidence score a positive value. Otherwise, we set it a negative value. This is reasonable as these pixels have low chances to be part of a thematic pattern. In other words, we assign the confidence score to each pixel $\mathbf{u}$ in key frame I_m as:

$$C(m, \mathbf{u}) = \begin{cases} 1 & if \ \phi_m(\mathbf{u}) \in \hat{\boldsymbol{\Phi}}_{mi} \wedge W_i \in \Omega^* \\ v & else \end{cases}, \tag{13.7}$$

where v is a predefined small negative value. After obtaining the confidence score $C(m, \mathbf{u})$, we locate the instances of thematic pattern using a bounding box. To speed up the localization process for 2D thematic patterns, we apply the branch-and-bound search proposed in [9]. To locate the 3D thematic patterns (e.g., actions), the 3D branch-and-bound search solution is employed [31].

13.4 Cohesive Subgraph Mining Algorithm

To solve the proposed BQP problem in Eq. 13.6, we first reformulate it as the continuous optimization problem and then obtain the solution based on the fixed point iteration procedure and the perturbation technique.

To solve Eq. 13.6, we observe that a binary constraint $x_i \in \{-1, 1\}$ is always equivalent to an equilibrium constraint, i.e., $-1 \leq x_i \leq 1$, $(1 + x_i)(1 - x_i) = 0$. Furthermore, this equilibrium constraint is implied by the nonlinear complementarity problem (NCP) function $\psi(1 + x_i, 1 - x_i) = 0$ [2]. In the implementation, we select the popular Fischer–Burmeister function $\psi(a, b) = \sqrt{a^2 + b^2} - (a + b)$ and obtain the differentiable constraint functions:

$$\psi(1 + x_i, 1 - x_i) = \sqrt{2 + 2x_i^2} - 2 = 0. \tag{13.8}$$

To simplify the representation, we denote the Fischer–Burmeister function of Eq. 13.8 as $\psi(x_i)$. By combining Eqs. 13.6 and 13.8, we reformulate the original BQP problem as the following continuous optimization problem:

$$\mathbf{x}^* = arg \max_{\mathbf{x}} f(\mathbf{x}),$$
$$s.t. \quad \psi(x_i) = 0, i = 1, \dots, N, \tag{13.9}$$
$$\mathbf{x}^T \mathbf{x} = N,$$

whose global maximizer offers an exact solution of Eq. 13.6. We see that $\psi(x_i)$ has incorporated the constraint $\mathbf{x}^T \mathbf{x} = N$ and it is kept here on purpose. Figure 13.2 shows the feasible regions of two constraints.

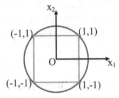

Fig. 13.2 Illustration of the feasible regions of Eq. 13.9 in two dimension space. The first constrain compels the solution lies in the four corners of the *square* while the second constrain relaxes the feasible region to a *circle* of radius one

To deal with the $\psi(x_i)$ constraint, we introduce the quadratic penalty $\sum_{i=1}^{N} \psi^2(x_i)$ into the objective function:

$$\mathbf{x}^* = arg \max_{\mathbf{x}} \; F(\mathbf{x}, \beta) = f(\mathbf{x}) - \frac{\beta}{2} \sum_{i=1}^{N} \psi^2(x_i),$$

$$s.t. \quad \mathbf{x}^T \mathbf{x} = N, \tag{13.10}$$

where $\beta > 0$ is a penalty parameter. To solve the optimization problem of Eq. 13.10 with a specific penalty parameter β, we look at its Lagrangian: $\mathcal{L}(\mathbf{x}, \beta, \lambda) = f(\mathbf{x}) - \frac{\beta}{2} \sum_{i=1}^{N} \psi^2(x_i) - \lambda(\mathbf{x}^T \mathbf{x} - N)$. By taking the derivative and setting $\frac{\partial \mathcal{L}(\mathbf{x}, \beta, \lambda)}{\partial \mathbf{x}} = 0$, we obtain:

$$\frac{1}{2} A(1 + \mathbf{x}) - \beta \sum_{i=1}^{N} \psi(x_i) \psi'(x_i) = 2\lambda \mathbf{x}, \tag{13.11}$$

$$\mathbf{x}^T \mathbf{x} = N.$$

Solving Eq. 13.11 explicitly is difficult. Therefore, as suggested by [29], we employ a fixed point iteration procedure to obtain the solution $\mathbf{x}$. By adding the $-\frac{\beta}{2} \sum_{i=1}^{N} \psi^2(x_i)$ into objective function, it can not only incorporate the constraint but also obtain a concave objective function when the penalty parameter β is large enough, as presented in the following lemma.

Lemma 1 *By adding the $-\frac{\beta}{2} \sum_{i=1}^{N} \psi^2(x_i)$ into objective function, we can obtain a concave objective function $F(\mathbf{x}, \beta)$ when the penalty parameter β is large enough:*

$$F(\mathbf{x}, \beta) = f(\mathbf{x}) - \frac{\beta}{2} \sum_{i=1}^{N} \psi^2(x_i), \tag{13.12}$$

where $f(\mathbf{x}) = \frac{1}{4}(1 + \mathbf{x})^T A(1 + \mathbf{x})$ and $\psi(x_i) = \sqrt{2 + 2x_i^2} - 2$.

The appendix section shows the proof of Lemma 1. This advantage greatly contributes to the searching for an optimal solution or a favorable suboptimal solution of Eq. 13.6 via a sequence of maximization with an increasing penalty parameter.

To explore the neighborhood of the solution for different β, we also perturb the matrix A by a small quantity and hope that this change could lead to a better solution. The perturbation of matrix A is obtained by adding an $N \times N$ perturbation matrix P, where entries of the matrix P ($0 \leq P_{ij} \leq 1$) are randomly generated based on the values of the $\mathbf{x}$ vector. The proposed subgraph mining algorithm is summarized in Alg 1. The maximum cohesive subgraph is obtained according to the best solution found after all iterations.

Algorithm 1 Cohesive sub-graph mining
---
input : Matrix A, number of iterations K, penalty parameter β_0, perturbation threshold δ.
output: the maximum cohesive sub-graph Ω^*

1 construct random solution x
   $\mathbf{x}_{best} = \mathbf{x}$, $A_t = A$
   for $k = 1$ *to* K **do**
2       $A = A_t$, $\beta = \beta_0{}^k$, $\mathbf{x} = \mathbf{x}_{best}$
     /*find the solution $\mathbf{x}^a$ with original matrix A */
     $\mathbf{x}^a = arg \max_{\mathbf{x}} \ f(\mathbf{x}) - \frac{\beta}{2}\sum_{i=1}^{N} \psi^2(x_i)$
     if $f(\mathbf{x}^a) > f(\mathbf{x}_{best})$ **then**
3          $\mathbf{x}_{best} = \mathbf{x}^a$
4   **end**
5   /* obtain the perturbation matrix P */
     for $i = 1$ *to* N **do**
6   produce a small random value δ' while $|\delta'| \leq \delta$
        set i^{th} row and i^{th} column of P as $(x^a{}_i)^2 \delta'$
7   **end**
8       $A = A + P$
     /*find the solution $\mathbf{x}^b$ with perturbed matrix A */
     $\mathbf{x}^b = arg \max_{\mathbf{x}} \ f(\mathbf{x}^a) - \frac{\beta}{2}\sum_{i=1}^{N} \psi^2(x^a{}_i)$
     if $f(\mathbf{x}^b) > f(\mathbf{x}_{best})$ **then**
9          $\mathbf{x}_{best} = \mathbf{x}^b$
10   **end**
11 **end**
12 obtain sub-graph Ω^* based on $\mathbf{x}_{best}$

13.5 Evaluation

To evaluate our approach, we test it on challenging commercial videos and action video collections for thematic pattern discovery. In addition, we compare the proposed approach with the state-of-the-art methods [18, 21].

13.5.1 Video Dataset

In the first experiment, we discover thematic objects from twenty video sequences downloaded from YouTube.com. We test our method on the video sequences one by one. Each video sequence is one advertisement, where the length of videos range from 7 to 41 s. In the second experiment, we apply our method to five action video collections to discover the thematic actions. Two of them (i.e., Hand Clap and Hand Wave) come from MSR action dataset [31] and the other two (i.e., Jumping Jack and Golf Swing) come from UCF action dataset [19]. The last one (Figure Skating Spin) is downloaded directly from YouTube.com. We test our method on the video collections one by one. In each video collection, around half of the videos contain the thematic actions. It is possible that one video sequence contains multiple types of actions and some video sequences do not contain any actions.

13.5.2 Experimental Setting

Several parameters should be set first. The distance threshold Λ_D is set according to the size of each key frame, i.e., we set $\Lambda_D = 0.33W$, where W denotes the width of the video frame. If two visual words do not have any co-occurrence in the datasets, their affinity value is set to be -3, i.e., $\tau = -3$. For the cohesive subgraph mining algorithm, the number of iterations is set to be 20, i.e., $K = 20$, the penalty parameter is set to be 1.1, i.e., $\beta_0 = 1.1$, and the perturbation threshold is set to be a very small number, i.e., $\delta = 0.01$. All these parameters are fixed in our experiments. All the experiments are performed on a Xeon 2.67 GHz PC and our approach is implemented in Matlab.

To quantify the performance of the proposed approach, we manually labeled the ground truth bounding boxes of the instances of thematic patterns in each dataset. For commercial videos, the bounding boxes locate the $2D$ subimages in each key frame. For action video collections, the bounding boxes are $3D$ subvolumes which define the spatial and temporal range of actions. The discovered bounding boxes are decided by the the branch-and-bound search method [9, 31]. Let DR and GT be the discovered bounding boxes and the bounding boxes of ground truth, respectively. The performance is measured by two criteria: $precision = \frac{|GT \cap DR|}{|DR|}$ and $recall = \frac{|GT \cap DR|}{|GT|}$. By combining $precision$ and $recall$, we use a single $F\text{-}measure$ as the metric for performance evaluation [27]. $F\text{-}measure = \frac{2 \times recall \times precision}{recall + precision}$ is the weighted harmonic mean of $precision$ and $recall$. To calculate the $F\text{-}measure$ value for one video, the $F\text{-}measure$ value is first calculated for each key frame and then the average value of all key frames is used to evaluate the whole video. The $F\text{-}measure$ value for action video collections is also obtained similarly.

13.5.3 Thematic Object Discovery from Videos

Many commercial videos contain the thematic objects, e.g., the Starbucks logo in a commercial video of Starbucks coffee. Such a thematic object usually appears frequently, and the discovery of it is essential for understanding and summarizing the video contents. The employed videos are 24 frames per second and we sample key frames from each video at two frames per second, and discover the instances of thematic objects from these extracted key frames. For each video sequence, we only discover the first thematic object, i.e., the thematic object corresponding to the maximum cohesive subgraph. To locate instances of thematic object in each key frame, the confidence score of nonthematic pixels is set to -0.0001, i.e., $v = -0.0001$.

Table 13.1 Numbers of key frames and thematic object instances in each video sequence

Seq.	1	2	3	4	5	6	7	8	9	10	11	12	13	14	15	16	17	18	19	20
FNo.	40	46	14	59	24	60	27	28	19	59	82	31	59	59	40	33	32	49	57	59
INo.	18	22	13	16	21	13	15	19	18	21	33	22	30	9	35	15	17	21	15	17

Fig. 13.3 Sample results of thematic object discovery. For each dataset, we only discover the first thematic object, i.e., the thematic object corresponding to the maximum cohesive subgraph. The first column of each row shows the thematic pattern. Each of the top four rows shows the result of thematic object discovery from a single commercial video. The last row shows the result of thematic object discovery from collections of commercial videos. The discovered thematic objects are located by the *red bounding boxes*, and the frames without bounding boxes contain non thematic objects

In our visual words representation, SIFT local features are extracted from each key frame. For each sequence, the local features are quantized into 1000 visual words by the k-means clustering. The number of visual words is selected experimentally. The top 10 % frequent visual words that occur in almost all key frames are discarded in the experiments. Table 13.1 summarizes the information of twenty video sequences. For each sequence, the number of key frames (*FNo.*) and the ground truth number of thematic object instances (*INo.*) are shown in the first and second rows, respectively.

Figure 13.3 show some sample results of thematic object discovery. In the video sequences, the thematic objects are subject to variations introduced by partial occlusions, scale, viewpoint, and lighting condition changes. It is possible that one video sequence contains multiple thematic objects and some frames do not contain any thematic objects. We also count the number of correctly detected instances of thematic object *CNo.* and the number of falsely detected instances of thematic object *WNo.* for each sequence. Their ratios to the ground truth number of thematic object

Table 13.2 The performance comparison when using different numbers of visual words

Number of Words	400	800	**1000**	1200	1600
F-measure	0.36	0.60	**0.63**	0.59	0.53

instances are calculated as $CorrectRatio = \frac{CNo.}{INo.}$ and $FalseRatio = \frac{WNo.}{INo.}$. Figure 13.5a illustrates the *Correct Ratio* and *False Ratio* of all 20 videos and the average *Correct Ratio* of twenty videos is about 94 % while the average *False Ratio* is about 3 %.

Table 13.2 illustrates the performance comparison when the number of visual words varies. The average *F-measure* value of all twenty sequences is shown. It can be found that the best performance is obtained when the features are clustered into 1000 visual words Moreover, our method is also able to find thematic objects from video collections, as shown in the last row of Fig. 13.3. These results show that the proposed approach performs well for discovering identical thematic objects from video sequences.

13.5.4 Thematic Action Discovery from Video Collections

Discovering actions in the video space is much more complicated than discovering objects in the image space. In this experiment, we discover the thematic action from five different action video collections. For each video collection, we only discover the first thematic action, i.e., the thematic action corresponding to the maximum cohesive subgraph. In our visual words representation, spatial-temporal interest points (STIPs) are extracted from each video sequences [10]. For each video collections, the local features are quantized into 300 visual words by the k-means clustering. The top 10 % frequent visual words that occur in almost all videos are discarded in the experiments.

The numbers of video sequences in five collections are 29, 32, 18, 23, and 20, respectively. The numbers of video sequences which contain the thematic actions are 19, 18, 10, 14, and 12, respectively. Figure 13.4 shows some sample results of thematic action discovery. In the video sequences, the actions are subject to the intra-pattern variations of actions, such as scale and speed variations, and dynamic and cluttered backgrounds and even partial occlusions. Figure 13.5c illustrates the *Correct Ratio* and *False Ratio* of all five video collections and the average *Correct Ratio* of five video collections is about 90 % while the average *False Ratio* is about 9 %. Figure 13.5d illustrates the *F-measure* of all 5 video collections. These mining results show that the proposed approach performs well for mining thematic actions from video collections.

Fig. 13.4 Sample results of thematic action discovery. From *top to bottom*, the actions are Hand Clap, Hand Wave, Jumping Jack, Golf Swing, and Figure Skating Spin, respectively. The discovered thematic actions are located by the *red bounding boxes*, and the videos without bounding boxes contain non thematic actions. The cohesive STIP features are also shown, and most of them are inside the bounding box

13.5.5 Comparison with Other Approaches

We compare our thematic pattern discovery method with two other methods: (1) topic discovery approach and (2) dominant set mining approach. The topic discovery approach [21] is the state-of-the-art approach for object categorization and object discovery. To discover thematic actions from action video collections, we employ the LDA model [21] directly and select the most supportive topic as the thematic action topic. In the second method, we use the dominant set mining approach as described in [18]. As this method only provides the probability of each word that belongs to the dominant set, we have to set a probability threshold to decide whether one word is selected or not. Therefore, we select the same number of words as the proposed method,

As shown in Fig. 13.5b, our proposed approach outperforms both topic discovery approach and dominant set mining approach in terms of the *F-measure* for thematic object discovery, with an average score of 0.63 (Proposed) compared to 0.47 (Dominant set mining) and 0.32 (Topic discovery), respectively. The topic discovery approach does not consider the spatial relationship of the visual features and its results highly depend on the performance of the key frame segmentation. Due to multiple objects and the cluttered background per key frame, performing a reliable segmentation is not a trivial task. In this case, topic discovery approach only obtains a very coarse discovery of the thematic object, which is far from being satisfactory. The dominant set mining can obtain good results in several video datasets. However,

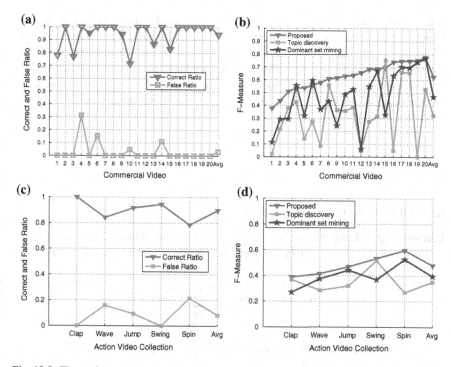

Fig. 13.5 The performance evaluation of the proposed approach: **a** shows the *Correct Ratio* and *False Ratio* for each video; **b** shows the performance comparison of our approach (Proposed), topic discovery approach (Topic discovery) [21] and dominant set mining approach (Dominant set mining); **c** shows the *Correct Ratio* and *False Ratio* for each action video collection; **d** shows the performance comparison of three approaches for action video collections

in the thematic pattern mining applications, there is no a priori knowledge about the size of dominant set. On the contrary, the proposed method can achieve a much better result. The same conclusion can be drawn for thematic action discovery, as shown in Fig. 13.5d. These comparisons clearly demonstrate the advantages of the proposed thematic pattern mining technique.

13.6 Conclusion

Thematic pattern discovery in videos is a challenging problem due to the possibly large visual pattern variations and the prohibitive computational cost to explore the candidate set without a priori *knowledge*. By representing the affinity relations of all words as a graph, we formulate the thematic pattern discovery problem as a novel cohesive subgraph mining problem and obtain its solution by solving the binary quadratic programming problem. Our approach has the ability to identify the thematic pattern and accurately locate its instances in the cluttered and dynamic video scenes. Experiments on challenge commercial videos and action video collections show that our method is efficient, robust, and accurate. Future work can be carried out to test the cohesive subgraph mining algorithm on other applications, such as video clustering and categorization. In addition, our method can be extended to consider more cues like the video saliency [16], object shape [11] and the weakly supervised information about the visual patterns [12, 13, 23].

13.7 Appendix

In Sect. 13.4 of the paper, we give the Lemma 1.

Lemma 1 *By adding the* $-\frac{\beta}{2} \sum_{i=1}^{N} \psi^2(x_i)$ *into objective function, we can obtain a concave objective function* $F(\mathbf{x}, \beta)$ *when the penalty parameter* β *is large enough:*

$$F(\mathbf{x}, \beta) = f(\mathbf{x}) - \frac{\beta}{2} \sum_{i=1}^{N} \psi^2(x_i), \qquad (13.13)$$

where $f(\mathbf{x}) = \frac{1}{4}(1 + \mathbf{x})^T A (1 + \mathbf{x})$ *and* $\psi(x_i) = \sqrt{2 + 2x_i^2} - 2$.

Proof To prove $F(\mathbf{x}, \beta)$ is a concave function, we transform it as:

$$-F(\mathbf{x}, \beta) = -f(\mathbf{x}) + \frac{\beta}{2} \sum_{i=1}^{N} \psi^2(x_i). \qquad (13.14)$$

Now, we prove $-F(\mathbf{x}, \beta)$ is a convex function when the parameter β is large enough.

First, we observe that $-f(\mathbf{x})$ is a twice continuously differentiable function, and its definition domain $[-1, 1]^N$ is a compact set. Second, consider the first and second order differential of penalty term $\psi^2(x_i)$:

$$(\psi^2(x_i))' = 4x_i \left(1 - \frac{2}{\sqrt{(2 + 2x_i^2)}}\right), \qquad (13.15)$$

and

$$(\psi^2(x_i))'' = 4 \left(1 - \frac{4}{\sqrt{(2 + 2x_i^2)^3}}\right). \qquad (13.16)$$

We can conclude that for all $x_i \notin [-\sqrt{2^{\frac{1}{3}} - 1}, \sqrt{2^{\frac{1}{3}} - 1}]$, $(\psi^2(x_i))'' > 0$ and this implies $\psi^2(x_i)$ is strictly convex for all $x_i \notin [-\sqrt{2^{\frac{1}{3}} - 1}, \sqrt{2^{\frac{1}{3}} - 1}]$.

Denote $\sum_{i=1}^{N} \psi^2(x_i)$ as $\Psi(x)$, then its Hessian matrix $\nabla_{xx}^2 \Psi(x)$ is:

$$\begin{bmatrix} (\psi^2(x_1))'' & \cdots & 0 \\ \vdots & \ddots & \vdots \\ 0 & \cdots & (\psi^2(x_N))'' \end{bmatrix}. \tag{13.17}$$

Now, it is easy to see that the minimum eigenvalue λ_{min} of $\nabla_{xx}^2 \Psi(x)$ is greater than ε for all $x_i \notin [-\sqrt{2^{\frac{1}{3}} - 1}, \sqrt{2^{\frac{1}{3}} - 1}], i = 1, \ldots, N$, where $\varepsilon = \lambda_{min} - \delta$ and $\delta > 0$ is an arbitrary small value.

Based on these two observations and the following lemma, $-F(\mathbf{x}, \beta)$ is a convex function when the parameter β is large enough. Consequently, $F(\mathbf{x}, \beta)$ is a concave function when the parameter β is large enough.

Lemma 2 *Suppose that $f : V \to \mathbb{R}$ is a twice continuously differentiable function with $V \subseteq \mathbb{R}^n$ being a compact set and $\Psi : X \to \mathbb{R}$ is a twice continuously differentiable function such that the minimum eigenvalue of its Hessian matrix $\nabla_{xx}^2 \Psi(x)$ is greater than ε for all $x \in X$, where $X \subset V$. Then, there exists a constant $\hat{\beta}$ such that, when $\beta > \hat{\beta}$, $f(\mathbf{x}) + \beta \Psi$ is a strictly convex function on X.*

Proof Its proof can be found in Theorem 2.5 of [17].

Acknowledgments This project is supported in part by MoE Tier-1 grant "Exploring Visual Relevance to Construct a Holistic Picture of Online News".

References

1. Blei, D.M., Ng, A.Y., Jordan, M.I.: Latent dirichlet allocation. J. Mach. Learn. Res. **3**, 993–1022 (2003). doi:10.1162/jmlr.2003.3.4-5.993
2. Chen, C., Mangasarian, O.L.: A class of smoothing functions for nonlinear and mixed complementarity problems. Comput. Optim. Appl. **5**, 97–138 (1996). doi:10.1007/BF00249052
3. Chum, O., Matas, J.: Large-scale discovery of spatially related images. IEEE Trans. Pattern Anal. Mach. Intell. **32**(2), 371–377 (2010). doi:10.1109/TPAMI.2009.166
4. Du, L., Buntine, W.L., Jin, H.: Sequential latent dirichlet allocation: Discover underlying topic structures within a document. In: Proceedings of the 2010 IEEE International Conference on Data Mining, ICDM '10, pp. 148–157. IEEE Computer Society (2010). doi:10.1109/ICDM. 2010.51
5. Gao, J., Hu, Y., Liu, J., Yang, R.: Unsupervised learning of high-order structural semantics from images. In: IEEE 12th International Conference on Computer Vision, ICCV 2009, Kyoto, Japan, September 27–October 4, 2009, pp. 2122–2129 (2009). doi:10.1109/ICCV.2009.5459465
6. Han, J., Cheng, H., Xin, D., Yan, X.: Frequent pattern mining: current status and future directions. Data Min. Knowl. Discov. **15**, 55–86 (2007). doi:10.1007/s10618-006-0059-1. http://portal.acm.org/citation.cfm?id=1275092.1275097
7. Hong, P., Huang, T.S.: Spatial pattern discovery by learning a probabilistic parametric model from multiple attributed relational graphs. Discrete Appl. Math. **139**(1–3), 113–135 (2004). doi:10.1016/j.dam.2002.11.007

8. Kim, G., Xing, E.P.: Jointly aligning and segmenting multiple web photo streams for the inference of collective photo storylines. In: Proceedings of the 2013 IEEE Conference on Computer Vision and Pattern Recognition, CVPR '13, pp. 620–627. IEEE Computer Society, Washington, DC (2013). doi:10.1109/CVPR.2013.86

9. Lampert, C.H., Blaschko, M.B., Hofmann, T.: Efficient subwindow search: a branch and bound framework for object localization. TPAMI **31**(12), 2129–2142 (2009). doi:10.1109/TPAMI. 2009.144

10. Laptev, I.: On space-time interest points. Int. J. Comput. Vision **64**(2–3), 107–123 (2005). doi:10.1007/s11263-005-1838-7

11. Lee, Y.J., Grauman, K.: Shape discovery from unlabeled image collections. In: 2009 IEEE Computer Society Conference on Computer Vision and Pattern Recognition (CVPR 2009), 20–25 June 2009, Miami, Florida, USA, pp. 2254–2261 (2009). doi:10.1109/CVPRW.2009. 5206698

12. Li, Q., Wu, J., Tu, Z.: Harvesting mid-level visual concepts from large-scale internet images. In: Proceedings of the 2013 IEEE Conference on Computer Vision and Pattern Recognition, CVPR '13, pp. 851–858. IEEE Computer Society, Washington, DC (2013). doi:10.1109/CVPR.2013. 115

13. Liu, D., Hua, G., Chen, T.: A hierarchical visual model for video object summarization. TPAMI (2010). http://doi.ieeecomputersociety.org/10.1109/TPAMI.2010.31

14. Liu, J., Liu, Y.: Grasp recurring patterns from a single view. In: Proceedings of the 2013 IEEE Conference on Computer Vision and Pattern Recognition, CVPR '13, pp. 2003–2010. IEEE Computer Society, Washington, DC (2013). doi:10.1109/CVPR.2013.261

15. Lowe, D.G.: Distinctive image features from scale-invariant keypoints. Int. J. Comput. Vision **60**(2), 91–110 (2004). doi:10.1023/B:VISI.0000029664.99615.94

16. Luo, Y., Zhao, G., Yuan, J.: Thematic saliency detection using spatial-temporal context. In: Proceedings of the 2013 IEEE International Conference on Computer Vision Workshops, ICCVW '13, pp. 347–353. IEEE Computer Society, Washington, DC (2013). doi:10.1109/ ICCVW.2013.53

17. Ng, K.M.: A continuation approach for solving nonlinear optimization problems with discrete variables. Ph.d. Dissertation, Stanford University (2002)

18. Pavan, M., Pelillo, M.: Dominant sets and pairwise clustering. TPAMI **29**, 167–172 (2007). doi:10.1109/TPAMI.2007.10

19. Rodriguez, M.D., Ahmed, J., Shah, M.: Action MACH a spatio-temporal maximum average correlation height filter for action recognition. In: 2008 IEEE Computer Society Conference on Computer Vision and Pattern Recognition (CVPR 2008), 24–26 June 2008, Anchorage, Alaska (2008). doi:10.1109/CVPR.2008.4587727

20. Rubinstein, M., Joulin, A., Kopf, J., Liu, C.: Unsupervised joint object discovery and segmentation in internet images. In: Proceedings of the 2013 IEEE Conference on Computer Vision and Pattern Recognition, CVPR '13, pp. 1939–1946. IEEE Computer Society, Washington, DC (2013). doi:10.1109/CVPR.2013.253

21. Russell, B.C., Freeman, W.T., Efros, A.A., Sivic, J., Zisserman, A.: Using multiple segmentations to discover objects and their extent in image collections. In: Proceedings of the 2006 IEEE Computer Society Conference on Computer Vision and Pattern Recognition, CVPR '06, vol. 2, pp. 1605–1614. IEEE Computer Society (2006). doi:lDOIurl10.1109/CVPR.2006.326

22. Shan, M.K., Wei, L.Y.: Algorithms for discovery of spatial co-orientation patterns from images. Expert Syst. Appl. **37**, 5795–5802 (2010). doi:10.1016/j.eswa.2010.02.028

23. Tang, K., Sukthankar, R., Yagnik, J., Fei-Fei, L.: Discriminative segment annotation in weakly labeled video. In: Proceedings of the 2013 IEEE Conference on Computer Vision and Pattern Recognition, CVPR '13, pp. 2483–2490. IEEE Computer Society, Washington, DC (2013). doi:10.1109/CVPR.2013.321

24. Wang, D., Li, T., Ding, C.: Weighted feature subset non-negative matrix factorization and its applications to document understanding. In: ICDM10, pp. 541–550. IEEE Computer Society (2010). http://dx.doi.org/10.1109/ICDM.2010.47

25. Wang, H., Zhao, G., Yuan, J.: Visual pattern discovery in image and video data: a brief survey. Wiley Interdiscip. Rev.: Data Min. Knowl. Discov. **4**(1), 24–37 (2014). doi:10.1002/widm. 1110

26. Wang, L., Hua, G., Sukthankar, R., Xue, J., Zheng, N.: Video object discovery and co-segmentation with extremely weak supervision. In: Proceeding of the European Conference on Computer Vision (2014)

27. Todorovic, S., Ahuja, N.: Unsupervised category modeling, recognition, and segmentation in images. IEEE Trans. Pattern Anal. Mach. Intell. **30**(12), 2158–2174 (2008). doi:10.1109/ TPAMI.2008.24

28. Xie, Y., Yu, P.S.: Max-clique: A top-down graph-based approach to frequent pattern mining. In: ICDM10, pp. 1139–1144. IEEE Computer Society (2010). http://dx.doi.org/10.1109/ICDM. 2010.73

29. Xu, J., Yuan, J., Wu, Y.: Learning spatio-temporal dependency of local patches for complex motion segmentation. Comput. Vis. Image Underst. **115**, 334–351 (2011). doi:10.1016/j.cviu. 2010.11.010

30. Yuan, J., Wu, Y., Yang, M.: From frequent itemsets to semantically meaningful visual patterns. ACM SIGKDD (2007). http://doi.acm.org/10.1145/1281192.1281284

31. Yuan, J., Liu, Z., Wu, Y.: Discriminative video pattern search for efficient action detection. IEEE Trans. Pattern Anal. Mach. Intell. **33**(9), 1728–1743 (2011). doi:10.1109/TPAMI.2011. 38

32. Zhang, D., Javed, O., Shah, M.: Video object co-segmentation by regulated maximum weight cliques. In: Proceeding of the European Conference on Computer Vision (2014)

33. Zhao, G., Yuan, J.: Discovering thematic patterns in videos via cohesive sub-graph mining. In: Proceedings of the 2011 IEEE 11th International Conference on Data Mining, ICDM '11, pp. 1260–1265. IEEE Computer Society, Washington, DC (2011). doi:10.1109/ICDM.2011.55

34. Zhao, G., Yuan, J.: Mining and cropping common objects from images. In: Proceedings of the International Conference on Multimedia, MM '10, pp. 975–978. ACM, New York (2010). doi:10.1145/1873951.1874127

Part V
Mobile Multiple Sensor Fusion

Chapter 14
Absolute Scale Estimation of 3D Monocular Vision on Smart Devices

Christopher Ham, Simon Lucey and Surya Singh

Abstract This paper presents a novel solution to the metric, scaled reconstruction of objects using any smart device equipped with a camera and an inertial measurement unit (IMU). We propose a batch, vision centric approach which only uses the IMU to estimate the metric scale of a scene reconstructed by any algorithm with Structure from Motion like (SfM) output. IMUs have a rich history of being combined with monocular vision for robotic navigation and odometry applications. These IMUs require sophisticated and quite expensive hardware rigs to perform well. IMUs in smart devices, however, are chosen for enhancing interactivity—a task which is more forgiving to noise in the measurements. We anticipate, however, that the ubiquity of these "noisy" IMUs makes them increasingly useful in modern computer vision algorithms. Indeed, we show in this work how an IMU from a smart device can help a face tracker to measure pupil distance, and an SfM algorithm to measure the metric size of objects. We also identify motions that produce better results and, using a high frame rate camera, gain insight to how the performance of our method is affected by the quality of the tracking output.

14.1 Introduction

Obtaining a metric, scaled reconstruction of the 3D world is a problem that has largely been ignored by the computer vision community when using monocular or multiple uncalibrated cameras. This ignorance is well founded, Structure from

---

Source available at http://github.com/kitizz/monocular_scale.

C. Ham (✉) · S. Lucey
Robotics Institute, Carnegie Mellon University, Pittsburgh, PA, USA
e-mail: cwham@andrew.cmu.edu

S. Lucey
e-mail: slucey@cs.cmu.edu

S. Singh
Robotics Design Lab, University of Queensland, Brisbane, QLD, Australia
e-mail: spns@uq.edu.au

© Springer International Publishing Switzerland 2015
G. Hua and X.-S. Hua (eds.), *Mobile Cloud Visual Media Computing*,
DOI 10.1007/978-3-319-24702-1_14

329

Motion (SfM) [5] dictates that a 3D object/scene can be reconstructed up to an ambiguity in scale. The vision world, however, is changing. Smart devices (phones, tablets, etc.) are low cost, ubiquitous and packaged with more than just a monocular camera for sensing the world. Even digital cameras are being bundled with a plethora of sensors such as GPS (global positioning system), light intensity and IMUs (intertial measurement units).

The idea of combining measurements of an IMU and a monocular camera to make metric sense of the world has been well explored by the robotics community [7, 8, 11, 14, 15, 21]. Traditionally, however, the community has focused on odometry and navigation which requires accurate and as a consequence expensive IMUs while using vision largely in a periphery manner. IMUs on modern smart devices, in contrast, are used primarily to obtain coarse measurement of the forces being applied to the device for the purposes of enhancing user interaction. As a consequence costs can be reduced by selecting noisy, less accurate sensors. In isolation they are largely unsuitable for making metric sense of the world.

In this paper we explore an offline vision centric strategy for obtaining metric reconstructions of the outside world using noisy IMUs commonly found in smart devices. Specifically, we put forward a strategy for estimating everything about the world using vision except scale. We rely only on the IMU for the scale estimate. The strength of our strategy lies in the realisation that when the entire subject remains in the frame, scale does not change over time. Assuming that IMU noise is largely uncorrelated and there is sufficient motion during the collection of the video, we hypothesise that such an approach should converge eventually towards an accurate scale estimate even in the presence of significant amounts of IMU noise.

Applications in Vision: By enabling existing vision algorithms (operating on IMU-enabled digital cameras such as smart devices) to make metric measurements of the world, they can be improved and new applications are discovered. Figure 14.1 demonstrates how the lack of metric scale not only introduces ambiguities in SfM style applications, but in other common tasks in vision such as object detection. For example, a standard object detection algorithm could be employed to detect a toy dinosaur in a visual scene. However, what if the task is not only to detect the type of toy, but to disambiguate between two similar toys that differ only in scale? Unless the shot contains both toys (see right-most image in Fig. 14.1) or some other reference object, there would be no simple way visually to separate them. Similarly, a pedestrian detection algorithm could know that a doll is not a person. In biometric applications, an extremely useful biometric trait for separating people is the scale of the head (e.g. pupil distance), which goes largely unused by current facial recognition algorithms. Alternatively, a 3D scan of an object using a smart device could be 3D printed to precise dimensions using our approach combined with SfM algorithms.

Contributions: In this paper, we make the following contributions.

- We propose an elegant batch-style objective for recovering scale with a noisy IMU and monocular vision. A strength of our approach is that it can be seamlessly integrated with any existing vision algorithm that is able to obtain accurate SfM

Toy 1: *"Toy Story Roarin' Rex"*, height = 27cm

Toy 2: *"Toy Story Rex Figure"*, height = 12cm

Fig. 14.1 Scale ambiguities can introduce detection ambiguities. These two toys are similar in shape but vary greatly in size. How could a toy detector know the difference if they are not in the same shot or share a common reference?

style camera motion matrices, and the 3D structure of the object of interest up to an ambiguity in scale and reference frame (Sect. 14.3.2).

- A strategy for automatically aligning video and IMU input on a smart device. Most[1] smart devices do not synchronise the IMU and video. A strength of our alignment strategy, which takes advantage of gravity rather than removing it, is that it is independent of device and operating system (Sect. 14.3.3).
- We provide insight to exactly how high frame rate devices are able to help our algorithm. The performance of our algorithm is highly dependent on the quality of the tracking algorithm estimating the camera poses. A more highly densely sampled vision signal appears to have negligible direct effect on our algorithm. We show that the performance boost our method enjoys from high frame rate devices is purely a result of better tracking.

We demonstrate the utility of our approach for obtaining metric scale across a number of visual tasks such as obtaining a metric reconstruction of a checkerboard, estimating pupil distance, and obtaining a metric 3D reconstruction of an object. This is the first work of its kind, to our knowledge, to get such accurate (in all our experiments, we achieved scale estimates within 1–2 % of ground truth) scaled metric reconstructions using a canonical smart device's monocular camera and IMU.

---

[1] We tested our proposed approach on both iOS and Android smart devices, neither of which provided global timestamps for the video input.

14.2 Related Work

Non-IMU Methods: There are ways to obtain a metric understanding of the world using monocular vision on a smart device that do not require an IMU. They all pivot on the idea of obtaining a metric measurement of something already observed by the vision algorithm and propagating the corresponding scale. There are a number of apps [9, 16] which achieve this using vision. However, they all require some kind of external reference in order to estimate the metric scale factor of the vision, such as credit cards or knowing the height of the camera from the ground (assuming the ground is flat).

Online IMU Methods: Our paper in many ways overlaps with existing robotics literature for combining monocular camera and IMU inputs. It differs in that many of these algorithms are focussed on navigation and odometry, and so the algorithms must execute in real time.

Works by Jones et al. [7], Nützi et al. [14], Weiss et al. [21] and Li et al. [11] all show how the camera motion of any visual SLAM (simultaneous localisation and mapping) algorithm can be fused with accelerometer and gyroscope measurements using a Kalman Filter. The IMU measurements (at 100 Hz or more) are integrated to estimate motion and errors are corrected each time the SLAM is updated (20 Hz).

Weiss et al. [21] take the idea a step further by automatically detecting failures in the SLAM output and use only the IMU until the SLAM algorithm recovers. The objectives of Weiss' work are similar to ours in that their implementation is modular to any SLAM algorithm that provides position and orientation, and they assess the quality of the scale estimate in their results.

Li et al. [11] account for rolling shutter distortion that occurs in low-quality cameras. Unlike the above-mentioned methods they do apply their approach to a smart device. However, they still focus mainly on navigation and the odometry. SLAM feature tracking, and sensor fusion are all tightly integrated and non-modular.

Martenelli [12] presents a rigorous observability analysis of the fundamentals of the fusion of vision and IMU data. He explores many different cases and determines what is observable in each case. Of particular interest to this paper, he presents a solution for finding tracked feature point locations, the starting velocity, the gravity vector and the accelerometer bias if the number of tracks features is at least 2 and the number of camera frames is at least 5. The locations of the feature points should be at the correct absolute scale.

For visual–inertial odometry, the robotics community approaches the use of vision with trepidation [3, 14, 21]. Indeed, even the state-of-the-art large-scale SLAM algorithms [13, 21] still suffer from sudden failures, whereas IMUs will continue to function under almost any circumstance. Vision and IMUs both suffer from a different kind of drift, IMUs drift due to biases in the measurements, and vision drifts due to the piecewise reconstruction of the scene (hallways, rooms and streets, for example). With emphasis on being real time a common paradigm is to rely primarily on the IMU, and attempt to correct for its drift when vision is available.

In contrast, our work relies purely on vision to reconstruct the camera motions and scene up to scale while the IMU is used only to recover scale. This is possible because we focus on applications where neither odometry nor being real time is necessary. We are more interested in being able to reconstruct objects that can fit in the camera's field of view and need not be reconstructed in a piecewise fashion. Consequently the vision suffers from negligible, if any, drift in scale (an important assumption that our method requires for good performance). Also, by processing sequences in batch we can discard frames in which the vision tracking has failed.

Batch IMU Methods: Batch methods are advantageous, as they do not require close integration with the vision algorithm when computing scale. They can oftentimes give more accurate estimates of scale, as they attempt to solve the problem using all the data at the same time (i.e. in batch) unlike online methods. Offline methods have a further advantage in that they allow a "plug and play" strategy for incorporating various object-centric vision algorithms (e.g. face trackers, checkerboard trackers, etc.) with little to no modification.

Jung and Taylor [8] present an offline method to fuse IMU and camera data in batch using spline approximations, with only a handful of camera frames being used to estimate the camera trajectory. Like previous online works, the focus of this work was on recovering odometry. We believe that one of the core motivations for the use of splines was to reduce computational requirements. Splines allow the data to be broken up into "epochs", reducing the dimensionality of the final problem, however this also reduces the resolution. This causes problems if the camera is moving too quickly.

Skoglund et al. [15] propose another offline method that enhances an SfM problem by including IMU data in the objective. The camera and IMU are high quality and secured to a custom rig. The IMU motion is first integrated so that its trajectory can be compared with that of the camera's. Unlike with smart devices, the high sampling rate and quality of sensors allows this to be done without introducing too many compounding errors. An estimation of scale is obtained but is not the central focus of the work.

Tanskanen et al. [19] demonstrate a pipeline for real-time metric 3D reconstruction where the scale estimation is broken into multiple batch problems. However, they never discuss the accuracy of the metric scale estimation. Finite segments of large motions are detected heuristically and estimates for the displacement measured by the IMU and by the camera are compared. An estimation of the scene scale is obtained by executing a batch least squares which minimises the difference between these two displacement estimates. This is accurate enough to help increase the robustness of the 3D reconstruction but the accuracy of the dimensions of the final model is unclear.

14.3 Recovery of Scale

Using SfM (Structure from Motion) algorithms, or algorithms tailored for specific objects (such as checkerboards, faces, cars) we can determine the relative 3D camera pose and scene accurately up to scale. This section describes a batch, vision centric approach which, other than the camera, only uses a smart device's IMU to estimate the metric scale. All that is required from the vision algorithm is the position of the centre of the camera, and its orientation in the scene.

14.3.1 In One Dimension

The scale factor from vision units to real units is time invariant and so with the correct assumptions about noise, an estimation of its value should converge to the correct answer with more and more data. Let us consider the trivial one-dimensional case

$$\arg\min_{s} \; \eta\{s\mathbf{H}_V\nabla^2\mathbf{p}_V - \mathbf{D}\mathbf{H}_I\mathbf{a}_I\} \tag{14.1}$$

$$\text{s.t.} \quad s > 0,$$

where $\mathbf{p}_V$ is the position vector containing samples across time of the camera in vision units. $\mathbf{a}_I$ is the metric acceleration measured by the IMU. ∇^2 is the discrete temporal double derivative operator. $\mathbf{H}_V$ and $\mathbf{H}_I$ are low-pass convolutional matrices for the visual and inertial accelerations, respectively. They have the same cut-off frequency and are each designed for their respective sampling rates. They are applied before $\mathbf{D}$ downsamples the IMU signal to the same sampling rate as the vision. Scale by definition must be greater than zero, we include this here to remain general to the method used to solve the problem. $\eta\{\}$ is some penalty function; the choice of $\eta\{\}$ depends on the noise of the sensor data. This could commonly be the $\ell2$-norm^2, however we remain agnostic to entertain other noise assumptions. Downsampling is necessary since IMUs and cameras on smart devices typically record data at 100 and 30 Hz, respectively. Applying a low pass before downsampling reduces the effects of aliasing.

The approach here allows us to be modular with the way camera motion is obtained and allows us to compare accelerations rather than positions. This idea differs from work such as [10, 19] which incorporates the scale estimation into an SfM algorithm by comparing the position of the camera with the position integrated from IMU data (prone to drift and compounding errors).

Equation 14.1 makes the following assumptions: (i) measurement noise is unbiased and Gaussian (in the case that $\eta\{\}$ is $\ell2$-norm^2), (ii) the IMU only measures acceleration from motion, not gravity, (iii) the IMU and camera samples are temporally aligned and have equal spacing. In reality, this is not the case. First, IMUs (typically found in smart devices) have a measurement bias that is variant to temperature [1]. Second, acceleration due to gravity is omnipresent. However, most smart device APIs provide a "linear acceleration" which has gravity removed. Third, smart device APIs provide a global timestamp for IMU data but timestamps on video frames are relative to the beginning of the video, and so we cannot trivially obtain their alignment. These timestamps do reveal, however, that the spacing between samples in all cases is uniform with little variance. Section 14.3.4 describes the method used to temporally align the data (Figs. 14.2, 14.3, 14.4 and 14.5).

These facts allow us to modify our assumptions: (i) when used over a period of 1–2 min IMU noise is Gaussian and has a constant bias, (ii) the "linear acceleration" provided by device APIs is sufficiently accurate, (iii) the IMU and camera measurements have been temporally aligned and have equal spacing.

For simplicity, we let the acceleration of the vision algorithm, $\mathbf{a}_V = \nabla^2 \mathbf{p}_V$. Given the modified assumptions, we introduce a bias factor into the objective

$$\arg\min_{s,b} \eta \{s\mathbf{H}_V\mathbf{a}_V - \mathbf{D}\mathbf{H}_I(\mathbf{a}_I - \mathbf{1}b)\}. \qquad (14.2)$$

Note that we also omit the $s > 0$ constraint from Eq. 14.1 as it unnecessarily complicates the objective. If a solution to s is found that violates this constraint the solution can be immediately discounted.

Fig. 14.2 The smart device is oscillating in one axis. *Orange solid line* scaled vision acceleration. *Grey dashed line* IMU acceleration

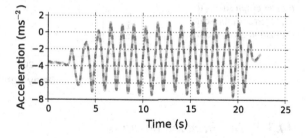

Fig. 14.3 The smart device is oscillating primarily along the Z-axis of the device in a 3D world. *Orange solid line* scaled vision acceleration. *Grey dashed line* IMU acceleration

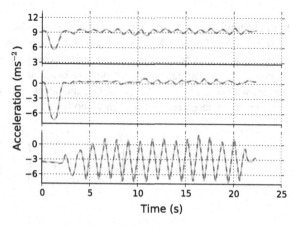

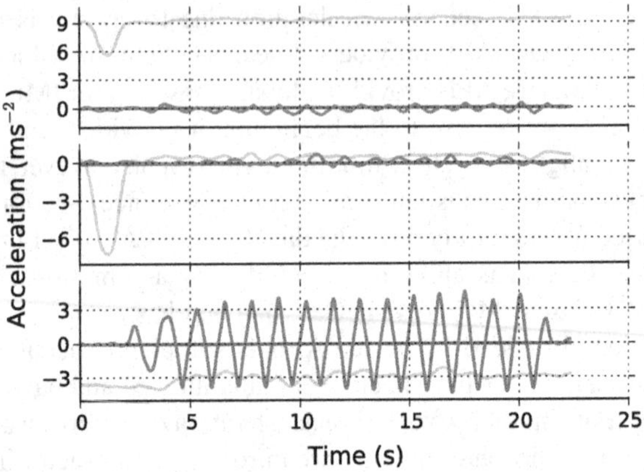

Fig. 14.4 The objective in 3D space can be thought of as separating the three components of acceleration observed by the accelerometer. Visualised here in the local reference frame. Scale: motion observed by vision (*grey*). Bias: locally almost-constant offset in IMU internals (*green*). Gravity: globally constant offset (*orange*)

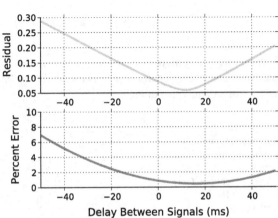

Fig. 14.5 The *top graph* shows the residual of the least-squares optimisation problem as a function of the delay of the camera signal from the IMU signal. The golden section search finds that a delay of 12 ms minimises the residual. The *bottom graph* shows the actual error of the scale estimation given the same delays

14.3.2 In Three Dimensions

In the following subsection, we consider the case where the smart device is moving and rotating in 3D space. Most SfM algorithms will return the position and orientation of the camera in scene coordinates, and IMU measurements are in local, body-centric coordinates. To compare them we need to orient the acceleration measured by the camera with that of the IMU. We define the acceleration matrix such that each row is the (x, y, z) acceleration for each video frame

$$\mathbf{A}_V = \begin{pmatrix} a_x^1 & a_y^1 & a_z^1 \\ \vdots & \vdots & \vdots \\ a_x^F & a_y^F & a_z^F \end{pmatrix} = \begin{pmatrix} \mathbf{a}_1^\mathsf{T} \\ \vdots \\ \mathbf{a}_F^\mathsf{T} \end{pmatrix}. \tag{14.3}$$

Then we rotate the vectors in each row to obtain the body-centric acceleration measured by the vision algorithm and apply the low-pass filter

$$\hat{\mathbf{A}}_V = \mathbf{H}_V \begin{pmatrix} \mathbf{a}_1^\mathsf{T} \mathbf{R}_V^1 \\ \vdots \\ \mathbf{a}_F^\mathsf{T} \mathbf{R}_V^F \end{pmatrix} \tag{14.4}$$

where F is the number of video frames, $\mathbf{R}_V^f$ is the orientation of the camera in scene coordinates at the fth video frame.

Similarly to $\mathbf{A}_V$, we form an $N \times 3$ matrix of IMU accelerations, $\hat{\mathbf{A}}_I$, where N is the number of IMU measurements. We apply the low-pass filter and downsample to match the vision signal

$$\hat{\mathbf{A}}_I = \mathbf{H}_I \mathbf{A}_I \tag{14.5}$$

We also need to ensure that IMU measurements are spatially aligned with the camera coordinate frame. Since the camera and IMU are on the same circuit board, this is an orthogonal transformation, $\mathbf{R}_I$, that is determined by the API used by the smart device [2, 6]. We use the rotation to find the IMU acceleration in local camera coordinates.

This leads to the following objective, noting that antialiasing and downsampling have no effect on constant bias

$$\arg\min_{s, \mathbf{b}} \eta \{ s \cdot \hat{\mathbf{A}}_V + \mathbf{1} \otimes \mathbf{b}^\mathsf{T} - \mathbf{D} \hat{\mathbf{A}}_I \mathbf{R}_I \}. \tag{14.6}$$

14.3.3   The Omnipotency of Gravity

The final component of acceleration measured by the accelerometer is gravity. In previous sections, it has been assumed that this component can be ignored using the "linear acceleration" IMU measurement available on most smart device platforms. Often, this measurement comes from a real-time Kalman filter that depends on gyroscopic and magnetometer sensors.

In this section we show how the objective can be modified to solve for acceleration due to gravity. By removing the black box that is the smart device's filtering algorithm, the performance of our algorithm no longer depends on the filter's quality. The new objective can be thought of as separating the three components measureable by the accelerometer: actual motion, internal bias and gravity.

We assume the magnitude of gravity to be constant and $9.81\,\mathrm{ms}^{-2}$, and we wish to solve for its direction in visual scene coordinates. We introduce a 3D vector, $\mathbf{g}$, and constrain its magnitude, leaving it two degrees of freedom. In order to include it in the objective it must by oriented to the smart device's local reference frame.

$$\hat{\mathbf{G}} = \begin{pmatrix} \mathbf{g}^{\mathsf{T}}\mathbf{R}_V^1 \\ \vdots \\ \mathbf{g}^{\mathsf{T}}\mathbf{R}_V^F \end{pmatrix} \tag{14.7}$$

$$\underset{s,\mathbf{b},\mathbf{g}}{\arg\min} \quad \eta\{s\hat{\mathbf{A}}_V + \mathbf{1} \otimes \mathbf{b}^{\mathsf{T}} + \hat{\mathbf{G}} - \mathbf{D}\hat{\mathbf{A}}_I\mathbf{R}_I\}$$

$$\text{subject to } \|\mathbf{g}\| = 9.81\,\text{ms}^{-2} \tag{14.8}$$

where $\mathbf{g}$ is linear in $\hat{\mathbf{G}}$.

14.3.4 Temporal Alignment

Temporal alignment is important for accurate results. Equations 14.2 and 14.6 assume that the camera and IMU measurements are temporally aligned. This subsection describes a method, that is greatly assisted by gravity, to determine the delay between the signals and thus align them for processing.

When collecting data on the smart device, video recording is started before IMU measurements. The time from when the camera is requested to the time that recording starts can vary significantly and can take up to three seconds on some devices. IMU measurements start much more quickly; in practice the delay between the first video frame and the first IMU measurement keeps below 100 ms.

In order to evaluate the residual for a given delay, we allow the downsampling matrix, $\mathbf{D}$, to be formed so that it linearly interpolates the input vectors, shifted smoothly by delay, d.

$$r(d) = \underset{s,\mathbf{b},\mathbf{g}}{\inf} \quad \eta\{s \cdot \hat{\mathbf{A}}_V + \mathbf{1} \otimes \mathbf{b}^{\mathsf{T}} + \hat{\mathbf{G}} - \mathbf{D}(d)\hat{\mathbf{A}}_I\mathbf{R}_I\}$$

$$\text{subject to } \|\mathbf{g}\| = 9.81\,\text{ms}^{-2} \tag{14.9}$$

We bind the possible delay to between 0 and 100 ms and make the assumption that the residual of the objective is strictly unimodal in this range. The optimum delay is found by minimising $r(d)$ using the golden section search. The solution to the problem returns the optimum values for scale, bias and gravity at this delay. In practice, we found that including gravity in the solution is very helpful in conditioning the problem due to the magnitude and slow speed of its signal (see Sect. 14.3.3).

14.3.5 High Frame Rate Cameras

At the time of writing, devices are emerging that are capable of high frame rates at relatively high resolutions. The iPhone 6 can capture video at 240 fps at a resolution of 1280×720 pixels, for example.

In the latest version of the iOS API the highest sampling rate available for the IMU is 100 Hz. This leads to an unusual situation where the *vision* must be temporally downsampled in order to match the rate of the IMU. The delay must be negative since the delay of the IMU is the lead of the vision.

$$\underset{s,b,g}{\arg\min} \quad \eta\{s\mathbf{D}(-d)\hat{\mathbf{A}}_V + \mathbf{1} \otimes \mathbf{b}^\mathsf{T} + \mathbf{D}(-d)\hat{\mathbf{G}} - \hat{\mathbf{A}}_I\mathbf{R}_I\}$$

$$\text{subject to } \|\mathbf{g}\| = 9.81\,\text{ms}^{-2} \tag{14.10}$$

14.3.6 Solving the Objective

The optimisation problem described in Eq. 14.8 remains general to the choice of objective function and constrains the gravity vector. This section describes how an alternating direction method of multipliers (ADMM) [4] can be used to solve the problem for different objective functions.

Frobenius and Least Squares Norm

If the objective function is the Frobenius norm, $\eta\{X\} = \|X\|_F^2$, we can simplify the problem by vectorising the input and turning it into a constrained least-squares problem. We vectorise the axes such that the first third of the vector is x, the second third is y and the final third is z.

The scale and bias components are straight forward linear extractions from Eq. 14.8. The gravity component is less trivial and requires some rearranging. Equation 14.11 shows how the x, y and z components of the visual rotations are stacked into one $(3F \times 3)$ matrix, $\mathbf{R}_g$, such that $\mathbf{R}_g\mathbf{g} = \text{vec}(\hat{\mathbf{G}})$.

$$\mathbf{R}_V^f = \begin{bmatrix} \mathbf{r}_x^f, & \mathbf{r}_y^f, & \mathbf{r}_z^f \end{bmatrix}$$

$$\mathbf{R}_g = \begin{bmatrix} \mathbf{r}_x^1, \ldots, \mathbf{r}_x^F, & \mathbf{r}_y^1, \ldots, \mathbf{r}_y^F, & \mathbf{r}_z^1, \ldots, \mathbf{r}_z^F \end{bmatrix}^\mathsf{T} \tag{14.11}$$

We define the vectorised problem as

$$\mathbf{M} = \left[\text{vec}(\hat{\mathbf{A}}_V),\ \mathbf{1} \otimes \mathbf{I},\ \mathbf{R}_g \right] \tag{14.12}$$

$$\mathbf{x} = [s;\ \mathbf{b};\ \mathbf{g}] \tag{14.13}$$

$$\mathbf{v} = \text{vec}(\mathbf{D}\hat{\mathbf{A}}_I \mathbf{R}_I) \tag{14.14}$$

$$\underset{\mathbf{x}}{\arg\min}\ \|\mathbf{M}\mathbf{x} - \mathbf{v}\|_2^2$$

$$\text{subject to } \|\mathbf{x}\| \in \mathcal{C} \tag{14.15}$$

where the set $\mathcal{C}$ is the set where the magnitude of the gravity component of $\mathbf{x}$ is $9.81\,\text{ms}^{-2}$.

This can be formed as a constrained ADMM

$$\underset{\mathbf{x}}{\arg\min}\ \|\mathbf{M}\mathbf{x} - \mathbf{v}\|_2^2 + f(\mathbf{z})$$

$$\text{subject to } \mathbf{x} - \mathbf{z} = 0 \tag{14.16}$$

where f is the indicator function for $\mathcal{C}$.

We form the scaled augmented Lagrangian

$$L_\rho(\mathbf{x}, \mathbf{z}, \mathbf{y}) = \|\mathbf{M}\mathbf{x} - \mathbf{v}\|_2^2 + f(\mathbf{z}) + \frac{\rho}{2}\|\mathbf{x} - \mathbf{z} + \mathbf{y}\|_2^2. \tag{14.17}$$

The updates for the scaled ADMM problem are

$$\mathbf{x}_{k+1} := \underset{\mathbf{x}}{\arg\min}\ \|\mathbf{M}\mathbf{x} - \mathbf{v}_k\|_2^2 + \frac{\rho}{2}\|\mathbf{x} - \mathbf{z}_k + \mathbf{y}_k\|_2^2$$

$$\mathbf{z}_{k+1} := \Pi_{\mathcal{C}}(\mathbf{x}_{k+1} + \mathbf{y}_k)$$

$$\mathbf{y}_{k+1} := \mathbf{y}_k + \mathbf{x}_{k+1} + \mathbf{z}_{k+1}$$

where $\Pi_{\mathcal{C}}$ is a Euclidean projection of the input onto the set, $\mathcal{C}$. Here, the gravity component is scaled so that its magnitude is $9.81\,\text{ms}^{-2}$.

The solution converges once the update delta of the scale component of $\mathbf{x}$ is below a desired percentage (often $0.01\,\%$).

$L_{2,1}$ Norm

In the context of this paper, the $L_{2,1}$ norm $(\eta\{\mathbf{X}\} = \|\mathbf{X}\|_{2,1} = \sum_{f=1}^{n} \|\mathbf{X}_f\|_2)$ is used to penalise the unsquared magnitude of the 3D error between the measured IMU acceleration and the acceleration estimated from vision at each frame. This makes it less prone to outliers than the Frobenius norm which penalises the square of the magnitude.

We break up the vision and IMU acceleration matrices into their vectors per frame

$$\hat{\mathbf{A}}_V = \left[\hat{\mathbf{a}}_V^1, \ldots, \hat{\mathbf{a}}_V^F \right]^\mathsf{T} \tag{14.18}$$

$$\mathbf{D}\hat{\mathbf{A}}_I \mathbf{R}_I = \left[\hat{\mathbf{a}}_I^1, \ldots, \hat{\mathbf{a}}_I^F \right]^\mathsf{T}. \tag{14.19}$$

This allows us to the pose the optimisation problem in the following way:

$$\underset{s,\mathbf{b},\mathbf{g}}{\arg\min} \sum_{f=1}^F \| s\hat{\mathbf{a}}_V^f + \mathbf{b} + (\mathbf{R}_V^F)^\mathsf{T}\mathbf{g} - \hat{\mathbf{a}}_I^f \|_{2,1}$$

subject to $\|\mathbf{g}\| = 9.81 \, \text{ms}^{-2}$ \hspace{2cm} (14.20)

We condense the above problem so that we are solving for $\mathbf{x}$ as defined by Eq. 14.13

$$\mathbf{M}^f = \left[\hat{\mathbf{a}}_V^f, \; \mathbf{I}_3, \; (\mathbf{R}_V^F)^\mathsf{T} \right] \tag{14.21}$$

s.t. $\mathbf{M}^f \mathbf{x} = s\hat{\mathbf{a}}_V^f + \mathbf{b} + (\mathbf{R}_V^F)^\mathsf{T}\mathbf{g}.$

From this we express the problem in a way that is ready to be solved as an ADMM

$$\underset{\mathbf{x}}{\arg\min} \sum_{f=1}^F \| \mathbf{v}^f \|_{2,1} + f(\mathbf{z})$$

subject to $\mathbf{x} - \mathbf{z} = 0$ \hspace{2cm} (14.22)

$$\mathbf{v}^f - \mathbf{M}^f \mathbf{x} + \hat{\mathbf{a}}_I^f = 0.$$

We form the scaled augmented Lagrangian

$$L_\rho(\mathbf{x}, \mathbf{z}, \mathbf{V}, \mathbf{y}, \mathbf{U}) = f(\mathbf{z}) + \frac{\rho}{2} \| \mathbf{x} - \mathbf{z} + \mathbf{y} \|_2^2$$

$$+ \sum_{f=1}^F \| \mathbf{v}^f \|_{2,1} + \frac{\rho}{2} \| \mathbf{v}^f - \mathbf{M}^f \mathbf{x} + \hat{\mathbf{a}}_I^f + \mathbf{u}^f \|_2^2 \tag{14.23}$$

where $\mathbf{V} = \left[\mathbf{v}^1, \ldots, \mathbf{v}^F \right]^\mathsf{T}$ and $\mathbf{U} = \left[\mathbf{u}^1, \ldots, \mathbf{u}^F \right]^\mathsf{T}.$

The updates for the ADMM problem are

$$\mathbf{x}_{k+1} := \arg\min_{\mathbf{x}} \frac{\rho}{2}\|\mathbf{x} - \mathbf{z}_k + \mathbf{y}_k\|_2^2 + \sum_{f=1}^{F} \frac{\rho}{2}\|\mathbf{v}_k^f - \mathbf{M}^f\mathbf{x} + \hat{\mathbf{a}}_I^f + \mathbf{u}_k^f\|_2^2$$

$$\mathbf{z}_{k+1} := \Pi_{\mathcal{C}}(\mathbf{x}_{k+1} + \mathbf{y}_k)$$

$$\mathbf{V}_{k+1} := \arg\min_{\mathbf{V}} \sum_{f=1}^{F} \|\mathbf{v}^f\|_{2,1} + \frac{\rho}{2}\|\mathbf{v}^f - \mathbf{M}^f\mathbf{x}_{k+1} + \hat{\mathbf{a}}_I^f + \mathbf{u}_k^f\|_2^2$$

$$\mathbf{y}_{k+1} := \mathbf{y}_k + \mathbf{x}_{k+1} + \mathbf{z}_{k+1}$$

$$\mathbf{u}_{k+1}^f := \mathbf{u}_k^f + \mathbf{v}_{k+1}^f - \mathbf{M}^f\mathbf{x}_{k+1} + \hat{\mathbf{a}}_I^f$$

The $\mathbf{V}$-update can be solved using the $L_{2,1}$ proximal operator [18]

$$\text{Let } \mathbf{q}_k^f = \mathbf{M}^f\mathbf{x}_{k+1} - \hat{\mathbf{a}}_I^f - \mathbf{u}_k^f \tag{14.24}$$

$$\mathbf{v}_{k+1}^f := \max\left(1 - (\rho\|\mathbf{q}_k^f\|_2)^{-1}, 0\right)\mathbf{q}_k^f \tag{14.25}$$

14.3.7 Using Echolocation

For certain applications, it may be known that there is a large planar surface in the scene. For example, the table that a scanned object is sitting on, or a person scanning their face with the front camera could be facing a wall. With some prior on the orientation of the plane and an assumption of the speed of sound, echolocation can be used to collect an additional source of measurements for estimating the scale of the vision.

To obtain data required for echolocation, the phone's speaker emits chirps while recording the sequence. By default on iOS, the audio is recorded at the same time as the video and is properly synchronised.

Timing

In order to estimate the echolocation distance, we need to be able to accurately measure the time taken for the chirp to reach the microphone after being emitted. First, we need to be able to detect and timestamp chirp events in the audio signal. This is done using a correlation filter and noting the time at which peaks occur in the signal (see Fig. 14.8). Chirps are a popular choice in echolocation applications because they provide a temporal accuracy similar to impulses, but require less instantaneous power [17]—volume in this context—in order to cover the same distance (see Fig. 14.6).

Fig. 14.6 A chirp is similar to an impulse, in that it contains all frequencies of equal magnitude; except that the phase changes linearly with respect to the frequencies

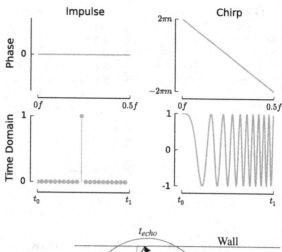

Fig. 14.7 The speaker and microphone are typically at different ends of the phone, with the microphone next to the camera. The *red arrows* show the different paths a chirp takes from the speaker to the microphone

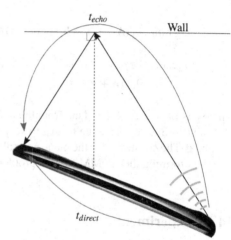

Additionally, we are able to take advantage of the arrangement of hardware on an iPhone, which is also typical of many other smart devices. The speaker is at the bottom end of the phone and there is a microphone positioned very closely to the rear camera sensor (see Fig. 14.7). When a chirp is emitted near enough to a surface, Fig. 14.8 shows how the microphone will detect two instances of the chirp. The first as it comes directly from the speaker to the microphone, and the second as it echos from the nearby surface. If we know distance between the speaker and microphone we can find the exact emission time. The timestamp of the second chirp provides the exact detection time.

We can include the echolocation distance estimates, d_{mic}, in the optimisation problem to help improve the accuracy of the scale estimation. In this case we assume that the normal of the table's surface, $\hat{n}$, is aligned with gravity and facing up

Fig. 14.8 The raw audio data is correlated with the expected chirp signal. This filtered response is processed to find times of the direct and echo events, t_{direct} and t_{echo}

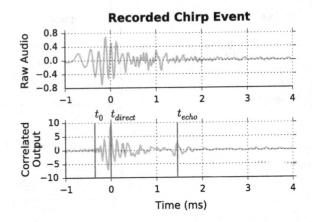

$$\underset{s,b,g,e}{\arg\min}\ \eta\{s\hat{\mathbf{A}}_V + \mathbf{1} \otimes \mathbf{b}^\mathsf{T} + \hat{\mathbf{G}} - \mathbf{D}\hat{\mathbf{A}}_I\mathbf{R}_I\} + \tfrac{\lambda}{2}\|s\mathbf{P}\cdot\hat{\mathbf{n}} + e - d_{mic}\|_2^2$$

$$\text{subject to} \quad \|\mathbf{g}\| = 9.81\,\text{ms}^{-2} \tag{14.26}$$

$$9.81\hat{\mathbf{n}} + \mathbf{g} = \mathbf{0} \tag{14.27}$$

where e is the offset of the plane from the vision's origin.

Note that $\hat{\mathbf{n}}$ is kept separate from $\mathbf{g}$ to keep the problem from becoming nonlinear in s and $\mathbf{g}$. The constraint for the plane normal and gravity is naturally accommodated for when forming the ADMM for this problem.

14.4 Experiments

In the following experiments, sensor data is collected from an iPhone 6 using a custom built application. Unless otherwise specified, the application records video at 240 frames per second while logging IMU data at 100 Hz to a file and the device is twisted along its Z-axis at the beginning to help properly estimate gravity. These files are then processed in batch as described in the experiments. For all the experiments the camera's intrinsic calibration matrix has been determined beforehand.

The choice of $\eta\{\}$ depends on the assumptions of the noise in the data. In many cases we obtained good empirical performance with least squares (Sect. "Frobenius and Least Squares Norm"). However, we also entertained the use of the $L_{2,1}$ norm, being less sensitive to outliers, to investigate the validity of the Gaussian noise assumption.

We obtain camera motion in three different ways: (i) track a checkerboard of unknown size, (ii) use pose estimation of a face-tracking algorithm, (iii) use the output of an SfM algorithm.

14.4.1   Checkerboard Experiments

On an iPad, we assess the accuracy of the scale estimation described in Sect. 14.3.2 and the types of trajectories that produce the best results. Using a chessboard allows us to be agnostic from objects and obtaining the pose estimation from chessboard corners is well researched. We used OpenCV's *findChessboardCorners* function, solve for an initial camera pose with *solvePnP* function, and refine the pose estimation using a batch optimisation which also applies a smoothness reward to the translation of the camera in world coordinates. The refinement helps reduces noise that is amplified when applying a second-order differential to obtain the camera acceleration.

Motions

The trajectories in these experiments were chosen in order to test the trajectories that work best, the frequencies that help the most, and the required amplitude of the motions. They can be placed into the three following categories (shown in Fig. 14.9):

(a) Orbit Around: The camera remains the same distance to the centroid of the object while orbiting around,
(b) In and Out: The camera moves linearly towards and away from the object,
(c) Side Ways: The camera moves linearly and parallel to the object's plane,

We recorded multiple sequences with different oscillatory motions to find which ones perform best. We identify three main components that define a motion.
Trajectory: The shape of the trajectory that the camera follows (see above).

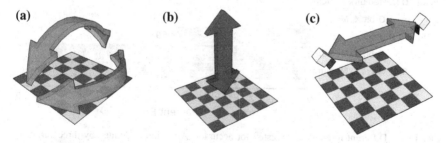

Fig. 14.9 The above diagrams show the different categories of trajectories. The accuracies of different combinations of these trajectories are assessed. In each case, the camera is always looking at the subject. **a** Orbit Around. **b** In and Out. **c** Side Ways

Displacement: The end-to-end distance the camera moves along the trajectory.
Speed: The effective frequency of the actual motion. In some sequences the camera is held still at each end of the trajectory. This is necessary for the fastest motions, without it the low-pass filter will remove a lot of the motion data.

In testing, we observed that In and Out trajectories were consistently accurate for a large range of displacements and speeds. For fast and accurate scale estimation the object should be kept in view at all times for good tracking and the phone should undergo high accelerations in order to keep the signal-to-noise ratio of the IMU measurements high. This is the easiest to acheive with In and Out motions since the device always remains in between the user and the object. For Side Ways and Orbit trajectories the device needs to be rotated to keep the object in its view. This is a challenging task without a lot of practice.

Since In and Out trajectories produce more consistent results, we focus on variations of displacement and speed with this trajectory in the experiments in this paper. In order to gain a good insight about the quality of different motions we look at the final error of sequences after 15 s of motion (Fig. 14.10), and at how quickly the errors converge to less than 2 and 1 % with respect to the number of seconds of data used (Fig. 14.11).

In and Out trajectories with at least 40 cm of displacement result in the most accurate scale estimations and converge within 2 % with less than 6 s of data. When the displacement is too small, slower speeds do not induce enough acceleration and higher speeds that do are filtered out by the low-pass filter (see Sect. "Low Pass" for more details). The Orbit Y and Side Ways Y motions provide no useful scale estimations. In these trajectories, it is much easier to induce motion blur caused by rotational shaking of the device, reducing the tracking accuracy. While the Orbit X

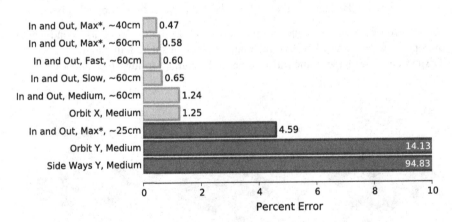

Fig. 14.10 Different motions were tested for accuracy. A motion is defined by three variables: trajectory (see Fig. 14.9), displacement of the camera during the trajectory, and speed (low ≈ 0.3 Hz, medium ≈ 0.5 Hz, fast ≈ 0.7 Hz, max is as fast as the person is able to cover the displacement). A *star* indicates that the camera was held still for a short time at the extreme of each oscillation

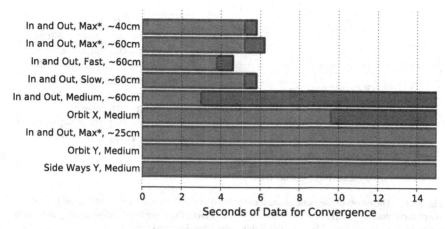

Fig. 14.11 The speed of convergence of motions is also an important factor. The time taken for each sequence to converge within 2 and 1 % is shown in *grey* and *orange*, respectively. The accuracy converges most quickly when the phone is moved as quickly as possible. In and Out motions with at least 40 cm of displacement converge to within 2 % with just 6 s of data

Fig. 14.12 The error of best sequence from Fig. 14.10 is plotted as function of the number of seconds of data used from the recording. We note that more data helps improve the accuracy. We avoid compounding errors by not integrating the IMU signal

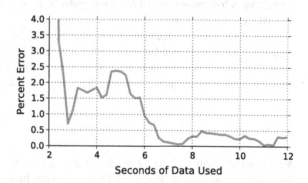

motion shows low error after 15 s, it converges within 2 % much more slowly than the other In and Out motions.

Figure 14.12 shows the error of the best sequence from the motions experiments as a function of the number of seconds of data used. We show that, overall, the accuracy only continues to increase with more data. By comparing *accelerations* instead of displacement, our method remains insensitive to bias in the accelerometer measurements which would otherwise lead to unstable compounding errors.

Low Pass

When downsampling either the IMU or the vision acceleration to match the lowest sampling rate, we first apply a low-pass filter that is much lower than the Nyquist of the new sampling rate. We do this because the double differentiation operator is a

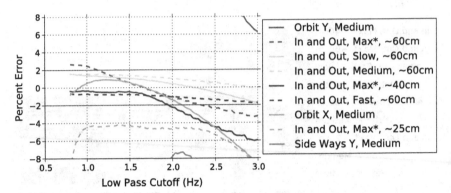

Fig. 14.13 The errors of the same sequences from Fig. 14.10 versus the low-pass cut-off frequency. We observe that 1.2–1.7 Hz returns consistent results before the noise from differentiating the vision signal begins to dominate. The *horizontal thin solid blue line* marks ±2 %

type of high-pass filter and greatly amplifies noise in the original vision signal. This means that a low-pass filter of the same cut-off frequency must be applied to both the IMU acceleration and vision acceleration signals.

Figure 14.13 demonstrates this in practice. The signed errors of the motion sequences are plotted as a function of the low-pass frequency chosen. We find that 1.2–1.7 Hz provides consistent results. With the cut-off frequency too high, noise from the double differentiation causes the scale to be underestimated.

$L_{2,1}$ Norm

We investigate how the use of the $L_{2,1}$ norm affects the performance of the same checkerboard sequences. Figure 14.14 reveals very little change from Fig. 14.10. If the Gaussian noise assumption on the residuals (IMU vs. vision acceleration) is incorrect we would expect to see a notable difference.

14.4.2 Face Experiments

A fast, in-house face tracker was used to track 49 facial keypoints and outputs an estimation of the face's 3D structure. The initial camera poses are generated using OpenCV's *solvePnP()*. The camera poses are refined using a batch optimisation which rewards smoothness of the camera trajectory. The 3D face structure is also refined by making use of the same face model used in the tracker.

Figure 14.15 visualises the accuracy of the interpupillary distance (IPD) at snapshots through the sequence. In this sequence, the device is twisted through 90° to help with gravity estimation and then moved In and Out at max speed while pausing

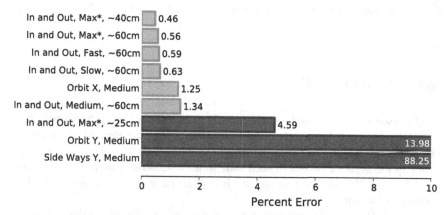

Fig. 14.14 The same sequences from Fig. 14.10 are processed using the $L_{2,1}$ norm objective. Very little difference suggests that the Gaussian noise assumption of the signals is sufficient

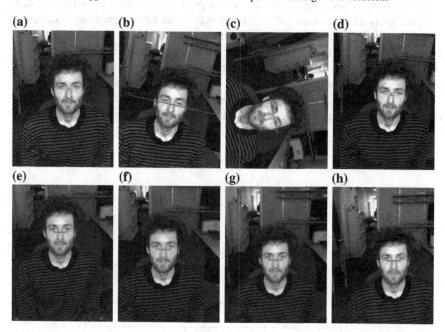

Fig. 14.15 The white ruler in each frame shows our algorithm's estimation of interpupillary distance given the data up to that point in time. The estimation converges once the phone undergoes translation after 3 s. True pupil distance is 64.0 mm; final estimated pupil distance is 64.1 mm (0.16 % error). **a** 0.0 s, 0.0 mm. **b** 1.0 s, 421.9 mm. **c** 2.0 s, 154.3 mm. **d** 3.0 s, −0.0 mm. **e** 4.0 s, 66.0 mm. **f** 5.0 s, 63.1 mm. **g** 6.0 s, 62.8 mm. **h** 7.0 s, 64.1 mm

at each extreme of the oscillation. We see that at 7 s the error of the IPD is only 0.1 mm.

14.4.3 High Frame Rate

All of the sequences recorded for this paper have been recorded at a high frame rate of 240 Hz. The high frame rate allows the camera to be accelerated much faster, which provides a higher signal-to-noise ratio from the IMU data. This is critical for obtaining the accurate results in such little time demonstrated in this work—most smart device IMUs are low cost and much less precise than those typically used in robotics applications.

Figure 14.16 shows the error of two sequences as function of the downsampled frame rate. The new framerates come from either sampling every nth frame of video before tracking or sampling every nth camera pose estimate after tracking. The new effective frame rate becomes $240/n$. The most important and interesting observation is that the accuracy of the scale estimate changes very little if the tracker does not track frame to frame, or if the camera poses are downsampled after tracking. Intuitively, one would expect that highly sampled camera poses are helpful when calculating the camera acceleration with finite differences. Instead, this shows that the performance of our algorithm is dependent simply on the quality of the tracking. The high frame rate leads to higher quality tracking in two ways. First, the frame exposure time is

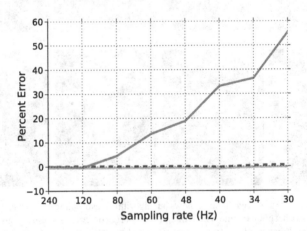

Fig. 14.16 We observe that the performance of our algorithm is far more dependent on the pose estimation of the tracker than the sampling rate itself. The best checkerboard sequence from Sect. "Motions" (*orange*) is tracked at different rates. The face sequence from Sect. 14.4.2 is either tracked at a different rate (*grey solid*) or the final camera poses are sampled at a different rate (*grey dashed*). Since the face-tracking algorithm relies on frame-to-frame tracking, it begins to perform poorly below 120 Hz when the tracking frame rate is lowered

much shorter, reducing motion blur. Second, the frame-to-frame deltas are much smaller and easier to track.

14.4.4   Structure from Motion

For this experiment the camera poses were obtained using VideoTrace [20], an interactive structure from motion and modelling package. The cube is modelled in Video-Trace so that its dimensions are in vision coordinates. Our algorithm estimates the absolute scale of the sequence and we compare the dimensions of the scaled cube with its real dimensions.

Figure 14.17 shows the labelled dimensions of the cube in vision units and scaled metric units. The estimated size of the cube is 56.5 mm; its true size is 57.5 mm. The error in the final estimate is 1 mm or 1.74 %.

14.4.5   Echolocation

Most devices do not yet have a high-speed camera on board, and so time spent recording a sequence cannot be reduced simply by moving the device more quickly. This section investigates how echolocation using the onboard speaker and microphone can be used to greatly help the scale estimation.

The sequences in this experiment were recorded using an Android device at a resolution of 1280 × 720 and frame rate of 30 frames per second. This camera is more prone to motion blur and so the device needs to be moved more slowly to keep the tracking performance high. Figure 14.18 shows how the inclusion of echolocation

Fig. 14.17 The VideoTrace package is used to create a 3D model of a 57.5 mm cube. After resizing the model the estimated dimensions are 56.5 mm (1 mm error)

0.269 vision units, 56.5mm

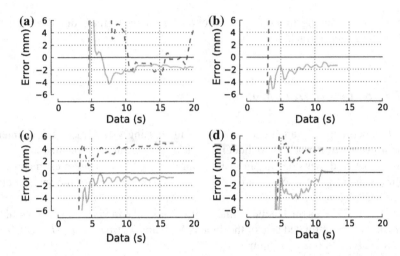

Fig. 14.18 At 30 frames per second, it is not possible to shorten the convergence time by moving the camera faster. These plots show how echolocation can be used to greatly reduce the amount of data required for good performance. **a** Person 1—In and Out. **b** Person 2—In and Out. **c** Person 3—In and Out. **d** Person 4—In and Out

data can significantly improve the accuracy of the scale estimation. At this frame rate, it would ordinarily require one minute of data for acceptable results. Here, each sequence converges to less than 2 mm error within 15 s.

14.5 Conclusion

This paper has presented a batch technique for obtaining the metric scale of the SfM-like output from a vision algorithm using only the IMU on a smart device with less than 2 % error. We have made three main contributions that make this possible. First, we realised that by comparing the acceleration of the camera in vision units with the acceleration of the IMU (which we know to be metric), we can find the optimum scale factor to minimise their difference. Second, we have described a method to align sensor measurements which do not have a common timestamp origin (typical on smart device platforms) that uses acceleration from gravity to help condition the alignment. Finally, we showed how high frame rate devices can significantly improve the scale estimation and used this to demonstrate the importance of good tracking for our algorithm.

References

1. Aggarwal, P., Syed, Z., Niu, X., El-Sheimy, N.: A standard testing and calibration procedure for low cost MEMS inertial sensors and units. J. Navig. **61**(02), 323–336 (2008)
2. Android Documentation: SensorEvent—Android Developers. http://goo.gl/fBFBU (2013)
3. Armesto, L., Tornero, J., Vincze, M.: Fast ego-motion estimation with multi-rate fusion of inertial and vision. Int. J. Robot. Res. **26**(6), 577–589 (2007)
4. Boyd, S., Parikh, N., Chu, E., Peleato, B., Eckstein, J.: Distributed optimization and statistical learning via the alternating direction method of multipliers. Found. Trends® Mach. Learn. **3**(1), 1–122 (2011)
5. Hartley, R.I., Zisserman, A.: Multiple View Geometry in Computer Vision, 2nd edn. Cambridge University Press, Cambridge. ISBN: 0521540518 (2004)
6. iOS Documentation: UIAcceleration Class Reference. http://goo.gl/iwJjKN (2010)
7. Jones, E., Vedaldi, A., Soatto, S.: Inertial structure from motion with autocalibration. In: Workshop on Dynamical Vision (2007)
8. Jung, S.H., Taylor, C.J.: Camera trajectory estimation using inertial sensor measurements and structure from motion results. In: IEEE International Conference on Computer Vision and Pattern Recognition (CVPR), vol. 2, pp. II–732. IEEE (2001)
9. Kamens, B.: RulerPhone—Photo Measuring. AppleAppStore, http://goo.gl/CRaIOk (2010–2013)
10. Konolige, K., Agrawal, M., Sola, J.: Large-scale visual odometry for rough terrain. In: Robotics Research, pp. 201–212. Springer, Berlin (2011)
11. Li, M., Kim, B.H., Mourikis, A.I.: Real-time motion tracking on a cellphone using inertial sensing and a rolling-shutter camera. In: IEEE International Conference on Robotics and Automation (ICRA), pp. 4712–4719 (2013)
12. Martinelli, A.: Vision and IMU data fusion: closed-form solutions for attitude, speed, absolute scale, and bias determination. IEEE Trans. Robot. **28**(1), 44–60 (2012)
13. McDonald, J., Kaess, M., Cadena, C., Neira, J., Leonard, J.J.: Real-time 6-DOF multi-session visual SLAM over large-scale environments. Robot. Auton. Syst. **61**(10), 1144–1158 (2013)
14. Nützi, G., Weiss, S., Scaramuzza, D., Siegwart, R.: Fusion of IMU and vision for absolute scale estimation in monocular SLAM. J. Intell. Robot. Syst. **61**(1–4), 287–299 (2011)
15. Skoglund, M., Sjanic, Z., Gustafsson, F.: Initialisation and estimation methods for batch optimisation of inertial/visual SLAM. Technical report. Department of Electrical Engineering Linköpings Universitet (2013)
16. Smart Tools co.: Smart Measure Pro. GooglePlayStore, http://goo.gl/JDRu5 (2013)
17. Smith, S.W., et al.: The scientist and engineer's guide to digital signal processing (1997)
18. Sra, S.: Fast projections onto 1, q-norm balls for grouped feature selection. Machine Learning and Knowledge Discovery in Databases, pp. 305–317. Springer, Berlin (2011)
19. Tanskanen, P., Kolev, K., Meier, L., Camposeco, F., Saurer, O., Pollefeys, M.: Live metric 3d reconstruction on mobile phones (2013)
20. van den Hengel, A., Dick, A., Thormählen, T., Ward, B., Torr, P.H.: Videotrace: rapid interactive scene modelling from video. ACM Trans. Graph. (TOG) **26**, 86. ACM (2007)
21. Weiss, S., Achtelik, M.W., Lynen, S., Achtelik, M.C., Kneip, L., Chli, M., Siegwart, R.: Monocular vision for long-term micro aerial vehicle state estimation: a compendium. J. Field Robot. **30**(5), 803–831 (2013)

Printed in the United States
By Bookmasters